A GIFT OF:
FRIENDS
OF THE
SAINT PAUL
PUBLIC LIBRARY
ON THE OCCASION OF THE
SAINT PAUL PUBLIC LIBRARY'S
100TH ANNIVERSARY 1882-1982

Letters to Bab

Letters to Bab

Sherwood Anderson
to
Marietta D. Finley
1916–33

Edited by
William A. Sutton

With a Foreword by
Walter B. Rideout

University of Illinois Press
Urbana and Chicago

Manufactured in the United States of America

This book is printed on acid-free paper.

Library of Congress in Publication Data

Anderson, Sherwood, 1876–1941.
Letters to Bab.

Includes index.
1. Anderson, Sherwood, 1876–1941—Correspondence.
2. Authors, America—20th century—Correspondence.
3. Hahn, Marietta D. Finley, d. 1969. I. Hahn, Marietta D. Finley, d. 1969. II. Sutton, William Alfred, 1915– .
III. Title.
PS3601.N4Z485 1984 813'.52 [B] 83-18258
ISBN 0-252-00979-7

To Sherwood Anderson,
whose works have enriched the lives
of countless of his readers

Contents

Foreword by Walter B. Rideout
ix

Preface
xiii

Acknowledgments
xix

A Chronology of the Life of Sherwood Anderson
xxi

Letters
3

Appendix A: Sherwood Anderson's "Apology for Crudity"
333

Appendix B: The "Inaccurate" Interview
337

Index
345

Foreword

Anyone at all interested in Sherwood Anderson, from the specialized scholar to the most casual reader, owes a permanent debt to William A. Sutton. In 1941, the year Anderson died, Sutton began searching out for his doctoral dissertation facts on the early life of this storyteller whose writings helped shape modern American fiction. Without Sutton's research—made available in his dissertation (1943), a series of biographical articles, and a book, *The Road to Winesburg* (1972)—we would know far less about the true personal experience over which this highly autobiographical writer let his "fancy" play and thus produced tales the best of which rank with the best in our literature.

Although his research may be most useful to scholars and literary critics, another of Sutton's contributions is valuable for the general reader as well: the location of the large collection of Anderson's letters printed herein and the preparation of them for publication by the University of Illinois Press. In his Preface Sutton describes how he found the letters and how he quite literally brought them to safekeeping in the extensive Sherwood Anderson Collection in the Newberry Library in Chicago, and he explains who "Bab" was and something of her relationship with Anderson. What remains is to indicate why these letters should be of interest to all sorts of readers.

To use an Andersonian metaphor, all personal letters are like windows into the lives of those who write them. Even the dullest, the most contrived, the most trivial letters have about them an immediacy; and though Anderson's can on occasion be dull, contrived, or trivial, most of the time they have the extraordinary freshness of an unsystematic but perceptive mind communicating its thoughts of the moment directly to a sympathetic listener. Further, the life into which these letters allow us to look was of one who considered himself a representative American because, growing up at the end of the nineteenth century and maturing in the early twentieth, a period of massive social and economic change, he had been small-town boy, city dweller, unskilled laborer, soldier, advertising copywriter, and small business man before he resolved in a mid-thirties crisis to become a writer. The relation of himself to his time gave him, he felt, something to say to his fellow Americans. "I embrace my times," he writes in a Whitmanesque passage. "I go with my own people. If they are ugly I shall be ugly. I shall strive for the tortured and trusted beauty of my own time and place."

Very early in this sequence of letters he proposes to Bab that he write her, not "personal things, a cold in the head etc." but "observations on life and manners as they present themselves to me here and now" with the hope that when brought together they might provide "material for a book that would be of interest to others." Since Anderson frequently warmed up to his creative work in the morning by dashing off letters to Bab or to other friends, his observations are understandably closely linked to that work and to his feelings about it and himself. "I am thinking of American Art," he writes on December 21, 1916. "It must remain crude to the American. The land is not sophisticated. As a man writes or works in any field of art endeavor he is likely to become less American. His very refinement stands in his way. To be a really characteristic American he should see things only in a rather big, blustering way." Then he in effect reverses himself by saying, "There is no reason at all why Americanism should not be seen with the same intensity of feeling so characteristic of Russian Artists when they write of Russian life. Our life is so provincial. It is as full of strange and illuminating side lights. Because we have not written intensely is no reason why we should not begin." We may or may not agree with such assertions, but we will find it hard to be neutral about them. Anderson was not a philosophic thinker, but he often had acute, at the least provocative, insights into the America of his time.

Equally interesting are the connections between the letters and the creation of some of his tales. So, for example, he writes Bab from a train on October 24, 1916, imagining a scene occurring outside his window.

> Here before me is a long stretch of fields and in the distance a town. I put down my pencil and immediately a scene is enacted. Across the fields tramps a man in boots that are heavy with mud. He has a beard and wears an overcoat that is torn at the pockets. He is going to town to buy meat and has $3. Suddenly an impulse comes to him. He begins to run. Tears come into his eyes and he runs harder and harder. He is fifty years old and has been married thirty years. He is a farm hand. He had made up his mind to desert his wife and family and run away. He runs so hard across the field because he wants to get into town and board the train before his courage fails.

If we know the story "The Untold Lie" from Anderson's best known book, *Winesburg, Ohio*, we are startled here to see the story begin to form before our own eyes. Or again, writing in May 1926, he has at last after several failed attempts got his great tale "Death in the Woods" told right, and we realize how much his intense feeling for nature went into his work and still speaks to us from it.

> You become absorbed in the things of nature—the grass growing, trees in bud, then putting forth the first little hard nipples that are to become rounded fruit.
>
> The insects that destroy, wild flowers, weeds. Trees become individuals.
>
> How all important whether or not it rains.
>
> I have written a short story of an old woman's death alone in the woods.
>
> How hard and close to the ground the lives of people. One trying a little to see into lives.

Then there are the letters thatr are reminiscences or little stories in themselves: for example, the description of his nostalgic visit on December 6, 1916, to his hometown, Clyde, Ohio, the original for Winesburg, or the letters that are impressions of New York in the fall of 1918 or of Fairhope, Alabama, in the spring of 1920 or of Reno, Nevada, in 1923, vivid pictures of an earlier America. There is also the story running throughout the correspondence, now subterranean, as it were, now flashing into view, of the relation between the writer and the receiver of the letters. It is not always a pretty story, one must admit. Sherwood carefully distances himself from Bab, who clearly loves him, while at the same time he needs and uses her as a means toward self-expression. Yet she did have the letters, as we do now at last with all their fluctuating moods, their condensed tales and rendered experience, their opinions and their comments on self and art, their flashes of insight and of wisdom. "One cannot be too humble before human lives," Anderson writes in October 1920. "They are the only things in the world worth being humble about." In such a remark and in dozens, hundreds of others scattered through these letters we find the lasting quality of Sherwood Anderson.

Walter B. Rideout
University of Wisconsin–Madison

Preface

Sherwood Anderson and Marietta D. Finley first met in the autumn of 1914, beginning a friendship and a correspondence that would last for several decades. Nearly fifty years after the event, in May 1962, Marietta Finley Hahn told me about her first encounter with Anderson: "I met him at the Fine Arts Building in Chicago at the Little Theatre. My friend from Indianapolis introduced me to him and a group of people living at 735 Cass Street [as they] walked back there from the Little Theatre after a play had been produced." Although the two began writing to each other soon thereafter, the first extant letter from Anderson is dated September 26, 1916; when I asked Mrs. Hahn about the absence of earlier correspondence, she replied, "He did write me letters before that, but he asked me to destroy them. Like a fool, I did."

The 309 Anderson letters in this volume were written between September 1916, and April 1933. During this time both correspondents' personal lives took various turns; in 1928 Marietta Finley married Dr. E. Vernon Hahn, a neurosurgeon and psychoanalyst of Indianapolis, and Anderson was twice married and twice divorced. When I first met Mrs. Hahn in 1962, she greeted me with this question: "Why did Sherwood Anderson marry Tennessee Mitchell?" Cornelia Lane Anderson had filed for divorce in 1916, and Anderson had married his second wife later that same year; apparently in 1962 Mrs. Hahn was still wondering why Tennessee Mitchell had been chosen over her. However, she never said anything more definite about her feelings for Anderson. While she did think of writing about him, she planned to emphasize his extraordinary artistic abilities rather than her personal experiences with him. As she told me after turning over the transcript of the letters, "After all, it is Anderson in whom people—readers—should be interested, isn't it?" Doubtless the merely suggested character of their relationship is just as Mrs. Hahn wished it.

Mrs. Hahn was known to all her friends, including Anderson and his four wives and his three children, as "Bab." Anderson addresses her thus in many (but not all) of his letters. When his widow, Eleanor Copenhaver

Anderson, designated the Newberry Library as the repository for the Sherwood Anderson papers, she indicated that Mrs. Hahn, who had long been a close family friend, was probably a source of some materials for the collection. Dr. Stanley Pargellis, then the director of the library, wrote to Mrs. Hahn in 1947, asking her to donate her letters to the collection. (In addition to the carefully saved letters, Mrs. Hahn possessed the manuscripts of *Marching Men* and of "Seeds," two of Anderson's paintings, and autographed copies of all but one of his books.) She replied that, in view of her considerable financial help to Anderson and members of his family through the years, she would find a payment of $8,000 appropriate. The library was not in a position to offer such a sum.

I became aware of the existence of Mrs. Hahn in 1962, when I was working on *The Road to Winesburg* (1972). I made the sixty-mile journey from my home in Muncie to Indianapolis, where Mrs. Hahn, by that time a widow, was living. I made no mention of the letters upon my arrival, but after some conversation Mrs. Hahn pleased me by exclaiming, "You *do* know something about Anderson!" She then casually mentioned that she owned the manuscript of *Marching Men*. At this unheralded revelation I arranged to return to examine that treasure after she had an opportunity to get it out of storage.

When I returned for my next visit, Mrs. Hahn spread a sheet on the rug of the one-room apartment she occupied, observing that the *Marching Men* manuscript "flakes so" when handled. I begged her not to handle it further, since that was the case, and did not then examine it myself, instead urging her to put the fifty-year-old manuscript in a library where it could be preserved.

Shortly thereafter, Mrs. Hahn mentioned the letters she possessed. I feigned surprise and asked how they might be examined. She said, with a certain impish pleasure, "Your copy is on the table beside you." The package, about four inches thick, contained a carbon copy of the typescript that she had made when she and her husband were contemplating writing a "psychiatric" biography of Anderson.

Later I received a letter from Mrs. Hahn, stating that she was heeding my advice about placing the materials in a library's care. She had decided to mail the letters and the *Marching Men* manuscript to the Newberry Library as soon as she could get to the post office. Much disturbed at the thought of the crumbling manuscript's possible fate in the mail, I called her and volunteered to transport the treasures to the library.

When I picked up the suitcase full of items, she stressed that she wanted some payment from the Newberry Library. She could have realized much more by auctioning the materials, and she knew it, that was not the point.

She did, however, want the library to make a contribution. She accepted my offer to act as her agent. Thus, when I arrived in Chicago, I invited an offer from the library. Soon James Wells of the library staff informed me that the library was willing to offer $1,000 and to pay for an expert appraisal for tax purposes; I thereupon delivered the precious materials to his office. The appraisal subsequently attributed to the documents the very conservative value of $4,500. (They would have brought at least $10,000 on the open market.)

Mrs. Hahn's willingness to release the letters was doubtless releated to a very serious illness she had in early 1962; during her convalescence she apparently realized that she lacked the strength to write her own book. It is a pity that she was never up to the task, for she possessed many insights into Anderson and his literary career. Consider, for instance, these recollections of the creation of *Winesburg, Ohio*, which Anderson wrote during the most intense part of their relationship:

> Winesburg was published in 1919. It was in the process of being written from about 1917 on to its publication. It was being written while he was still in advertising and at war against the modern industrialism and the dirt and smoke of Chicago. He would go back to 735 Cass Street in the evenings or sometimes he would sneak out of work for a day or so. When he got to his room with the curtains drawn and the candles lighted on his big, bare table, the business world was shut out temporarily. He was no longer at war with it. He would begin to recreate the characters he had known best in the days with his mother and brothers and sisters. He once said that in those times he could "see the glimmer of stars in the eyes of his neighbors" of those early days. That was said in one of his more romantic, sentimental moods. Realism was forgotten for a time. Winesburg was more of an "escape" for him probably than any of his other work. He loved those people and wrote of them with love and understanding. At that time he was going on business trips to Kentucky and would stop over here in Indianapolis whenever he could make it. Always he would bring one or two of his Winesburg stories and read them to me "to see how they sounded." Several times I gave him unwanted criticism which he very seldom took. Usually he would leave with me a type-written carbon copy of a story. These I kept and once, I recall, he was camping out in the Adirondacks at [Lake] Chateaugay and there was a fire in his tent. He lost some of his Winesburg stories and asked me to send him the copies that I had. That is the closest I can come to his saying they had been destroyed and a woman friend put them together again. I do not know. Anderson had many women-friends and doubtless read Winesburg stories to them as well as to me. At any rate it was when he was writing "Winesburg" that I saw him oftenest and the stories were always part of our visit together.

He often said that the stories of the people in Winesburg fairly gushed from his pen. He wrote them rapidly and after re-reading them for corrections would sometimes marvel himself at their graphicness.

Mrs. Hahn also was acquainted with all four of Anderson's wives and with his children; indeed, during the 1920s she contributed, over a number of years, $100 a month to Cornelia for support of the children. In a letter to me, she described the first Mrs. Anderson: "Cornelia Anderson [to whom Anderson was married from 1904 to 1916] I met, I believe, in 1915. She is still a friend of mine. Naturally with three children to support, since Anderson was not too responsible, she of necessity had to be money-minded. Life had not been easy for Cornelia Anderson." Though she was not as well acquainted with Tennessee Anderson (Sherwood's wife, as mentioned, from 1916 to 1924), Elizabeth Prall Anderson (1924–32), and Eleanor Copenhaver Anderson (1933 to her husband's death in 1941), Mrs. Hahn had kind words for them all.

I asked Mrs. Hahn to "calculate the impact of each of his marriages on Anderson's art." Even though the reader will see much in the letters written to Marietta D. Finley Hahn that would provide a basis for commentary on this factor, especially on the marriages to Tennessee Mitchell and Elizabeth Prall, the reply was: "Your last question I cannot answer. As the Russians say, 'The heart is a dark forest.' And I cannot from the point of view of an outsider give any valuable opinion on this subject."

The person ardently interested in Anderson and his work and information related to it may mourn the reservations that caused such restrained comment and the circumstances of life and personality that caused Mrs. Hahn not to record her observations of Anderson, but it is a matter of rejoicing that she treasured the relationship with him and saved the letters from him that are published in this book. They make an invaluable contribution to the record of his life.

Editorial Method

These letters are presented chronologically—or as nearly so as possible. Mrs. Hahn made typescripts of most of the letters (as part of the preparation for the psychoanalytic biography referred to earlier), and in doing so she edited some letters, omitted copying others, threw away all envelopes, and annotated certain letters with dates (sometimes approximate, sometimes incorrect) and places of origin. The texts of all letters were either typed or handwritten by Anderson himself, and the letters are designated either TS (typescript) or LH (longhand). There are some gaps in the letters, and it is not now possible to determine whether these are the result of letters never having been written or because letters that were written were destroyed, at the time of receipt or later, by Bab.

My goal in editing these letters has been to make the editorial apparatus as unobtrusive as possible; therefore the following simple guidelines have been observed: Anderson's notoriously poor spellings and variant punctuation have been retained, but in the interest of greater readability all sentences have been made to begin with capital letters and to end with periods. Typographical errors in the typescripts have been silently corrected, including typing strikeovers, malformed punctuation marks, insignificant spacing errors, accidental extra punctuation, and omission or transposition of letters. Unintended word repetitions and crossed-out words have been eliminated. Conjectural readings and editorial insertions are in brackets.

When she was still alive, Marietta D. Finley Hahn wanted the letters, if published, to be to an anonymous friend. Her death in 1969 at the age of seventy-nine permits the identification of the devoted friend who has made possible an exceptional contribution to the study of Sherwood Anderson.

W.A.S.
Dunedin, Florida

Acknowledgments

Readers of Sherwood Anderson's stories and novels owe Marietta D. Finley Hahn a great debt for valuing the work and friendship of Anderson to the extent that she carefully saved the great bulk of his letters to her. I join them in this debt.

I also thank Mrs. Eleanor Copenhaver Anderson for permitting the publication of these letters. Anderson's two surviving children, John S. Anderson and Marion Anderson Spear, also gave generous assistance.

Ball State University provided me with a place to work during most of the thirty-five years of my study on and interest in Anderson. The personnel of the Ball State University Library deserve special mention for their efforts on my behalf.

Librarians all across the country have given me much help. I should like to acknowledge especially the gracious services of the staff of the Newberry Library in Chicago. The late Mrs. Amy Nyholm of that library represents to me the ultimate in efficiency and sensitivity.

A Chronology of the Life of Sherwood Anderson

1876	Born, Sept. 13, in Camden, Ohio.
1884	Family settled in Clyde, Ohio.
1896–1900	Worked briefly in Chicago as an unskilled laborer; served in U.S. Army (stationed in Cuba, but the war was over before his arrival); enrolled for one year at Wittenberg Academy, Springfield, Ohio
1900	In Chicago, as an advertising copywriter for Long-Critchfield Co.
1904	Married Cornelia Lane
1906–12	Moved back to Ohio; by 1907 was head of his own mail order firm (for paint); was writing fiction on the side.
1912	Had an apparent nervous breakdown on Nov. 27 and disappeared for several days; reappeared and made a fairly rapid recovery. Left Ohio.
1913	Returned to Long-Critchfield in Chicago.
1914	Met Marietta D. Finley.
1916	Divorced Cornelia Lane Anderson (by this time they had had three children: Robert, John, and Marion) and married Tennessee Mitchell.
	Windy McPherson's Son, his first novel, published.
1917	*Marching Men* published.
1918	*Mid-American Chants* published.
1919	*Winesburg, Ohio* published.

1920	*Poor White* published.
1921	*The Triumph of the Egg* published. Won *Dial* Award.
1922	Resigned from Long-Critchfield; moved to New York.
1923	Took up residence in Nevada, preparatory to divorcing Tennessee Mitchell Anderson.
	Horses and Men and *Many Marriages* published.
1924	Married Elizabeth Prall; moved to New Orleans.
	A Story-Teller's Story published.
1925	Bought farm at Troutdale, near Marion, Virginia.
	Dark Laughter published.
1926	Built his home, called Ripshin, on farm.
	Sherwood Anderson's Notebook and *Tar: A Midwestern Childhood* published.
1927	Bought two newspapers in Marion, Virginia.
	A New Testament published.
1928	Marietta D. Finley married Dr. Vernon E. Hahn.
1929	*Hello, Towns* published.
1931	*Perhaps Women* published.
1932	Divorced Elizabeth Prall Anderson.
	Beyond Desire published.
1933	Married Eleanor Copenhaver.
	Death in the Woods and Other Short Stories published.
1934–40	Traveled about the United States, writing articles for *Today*. The following works were published: *No Swank* (1934); *Puzzled America* (1935); *Kit Brandon* (1936); *Plays: Winesburg and Others* (1937); *Home Town* (1940).
1941	Started on an unofficial goodwill tour of South America; died of peritonitis in the Panama Canal Zone on Mar. 8.
1942	*Sherwood Anderson's Memoirs*, posthumously published.
1969	Marietta D. Finley Hahn died.

Letters to Bab

1

To Bab Sept. 26, 1916 [Chicago][1]

In the terrific confusion of things with me just now it is difficult for me to go into the analysis of your note[2] and to show you how you are not really criticizing me but yourself through me. This is, however, the impression which your letter leaves.

You would be the first to applaud my declaration that the whole secret of reality in writing depended on acknowledging the necessity of failure as a writer.[3] But you can't apply the same reasoning to women.

Somewhere in Marching Men[4] or one of my other books I have talked of the intellect as a dangerous thing. There is food for thought in the idea. You have dramatized one angle of life all out of proportion to its actual worth.[5]

TS

1. On a typescript that she had made of most of the letters, Hahn indicated this letter had been written from Chicago.

2. Only two of Finley's letters to Anderson have survived. See letters 175 and 309 herein.

3. Probably a reference to *Windy McPherson's Son*, Anderson's first novel, which was published in Sept. 1916. The *Little Review*, which had published Anderson's work since its first issue in the spring of 1914, had this unsigned comment in its Sept. 1916 issue (p. 21): "We have been waiting for what we hoped would be good comment on Sherwood Anderson's first novel, *Windy McPherson's Son*. All we will say now is that it is so much worse than Sherwood should ever be."

4. Hahn could not later recall when Anderson had given her the manuscript of *Marching Men*, published in Sept. 1917. The first draft had been written in Elyria, before 1912, and the manuscript shows massive revision in several stages. The remark here indicates Anderson gave Finley the manuscript to read prior to publication.

5. A review of Anderson's thoughts concerning *Windy McPherson's Son* and American literature at the time of this letter is found in his contribution to the "People Who Write" column of the Chicago *Daily News* for Oct. 4, 1916 (col. 2, p. 1):

> Your request that I talk about my book *Windy McPherson's Son* in the columns of the *Daily News* galvanizes into a conviction a feeling I have had since the day when I decided to begin publication of my novels.

I really believe that great progress toward a vital American literature might be made by some such plan as the following.

That every new American writer be given his stint—say a half dozen books to be written during his lifetime. When the books are written and ready to be published let him be . . . sent quietly away to some desert island, where he can neither talk of his work or hear talk of it. If after ten years of banishment he continues to write books we might do something for him. We could build him an iron statue on State and Madison Streets and let him behold us in the process of living our lives.

As you know well enough no man can talk effectively of his own work. The nut of the thing lies in this—if you read my book and the characters seem real, living and vital to you, then for you it is a good book. If the people in the book do not seem real, then for you it is a bad book.

As to all this talk concerning the technique of novel writing—it is talk, you know. The people in the book are on trial. If they live then the book lives. If they are but puppets to serve the purpose of a tale then away with the whole thing.

When it comes to the matter of difficulty confronting the novelist in America, I dare say I could fill a book with talk. We in Chicago, for example, live in a terrible state of disorder. The novelist's art is a reflective art and there is no feeling for the reflective mood among us.

And then we do not want to face the truth. No cry for truth goes up from us. From our novelists we demand only a rigid and unflinching sentimentality.

But it is an old story and your readers have heard it many times. I have written a book that I have asked people to read and should not scold. I feel like one who brings a troop of friends into your houses, and I dare say I stand about just a little anxious. I want you to like my people, to be interested in them, to take them into your lives and think about them. Perhaps you can solve the problems they meet and that I have not solved.

As to what a novel should be—well, I have a notion that the novel would come pretty near writing itself. When I was a boy I continually read George Borrow and Henry Fielding. For the most part those men achieved form by disregarding what we have come to think of as the proper form of the novel. They wrote for the fun of writing and for the healthy exercise of their ability as writers. They didn't think of happy endings and the solving of problems. They thought of life and tried to put living people into their books.

And with what delight I still read these men! Year after year I read the same books over and over. To read gives me the same kind of satisfaction that I get from looking back into the intimate thing of my own life. If in their writing these men did not get to any definite place neither have I with my own life. None of us do. It is enough that we are moving and living.

As I think this matter over I reason in this way. First there came along the short story, a more or less rigid, definite art form like the sonnet. The short story was easy to understand. It started, you see, quite definitely at one place and went to another. People liked the short story. It was definite and understandable although to my mind it was always a quite secondary art form. There are no short stories in life, but then what do people know about life?

The short story won out. Because it was understandable to the general public, it conquered the novel. Today the novel is no more than the prolonged short story. The giant you see has got a job in the vegetable garden.

There is in the world a movement for the release of art forms. In writing they have not gone very far, particularly in America.

What we have got to get at and release is the novel form. As writers we have got to be bigger and better men than the publishers. If necessary we have got to face failure and get breath back into the dying novel.

Now, what does the novel attempt to do? The short story is a solo by the second cornet. The novel is a piece by the full orchestra. It attempts to carry into the mind not one impression but a mass of impressions.

As to my novel, *Windy McPherson's Son*, it isn't a job of writing that comes up to my own ideas as to what a novel should be. Perhaps I think it isn't loose and disorderly enough to reflect the modern American life. To do that it should read as the elevated trains sound as they turn out of Van Buren street into Wabash Avenue. My people are not enough alive. They are not enough American. I have written and I am writing other books. Perhaps I shall do the job yet. Who can tell?

2

To Bab — Oct. 24, 1916 [Chicago]

Why yes—that's true enough about shutting of doors but the terribly sad thing is not to shut them. As for myself I think that if there is a note of distinction in me at all it lies in a certain power I have to challenge and rechallenge myself to the door shutting.

I can't tell you how often I've been surprised by M, H. D.[1] and others. There is a necessity of doing something, leaving home, quarreling with a father or mother. A great hue and cry is made! It is the hue and cry that amazes me. I've tricked myself into doing it a few times but really I shouldn't be, not ordinarily.

I suppose there is a kind of fate that makes it necessary for you to be the one on whom the door is shut. I can't understand why. Why not be the shutter of doors?

When I was first married a girl came to visit us. It was a pretty conventional household. I made money—was a prosperous young business man in those days.[2] Well on the first evening after she came I offered her a cigarette as we sat over our coffee. She was the first woman I ever saw smoke. The talk drifted to just this idea of door-shutting and Marian[3] said,

"I am never in the company of anyone but I am glad when they go. It does not make any difference how delightful the occasion may have been. When it is over I stand like a child in a strange place fronting new and wonderfull possibilities."

I understand that. It was so keen and true that I remember to have leaned forward and said, "And death too. I would feel that way about the death of anyone I know, except a child."

I remember the incident vividly because what I said hurt C[ornelia] as I was always hurting her. She thought I wanted her to die and I dare say I did. I have always hurt people who cared for me except the born adventurers like Marian and T[ennessee].[4]

I am on the train as I write and have a cold that has settled in my eyes so I must wear smoked glasses. The country is gloriously brown and black. I shall really think about your letter and try to answer it.

Well of course you know Powys[5] is two things—a student and an actor. He appears to know more of men than he does know but of course he is an actor. I doubt whether you will ever know things in just that way.

You will have to get the trick of thinking. Everyone has it a little and it is capable of infinite development.

Here before me is a long stretch of fields and in the distance a town. I put down my pencil and immediately a scene is enacted. Across the fields tramps a man in boots that are heavy with mud. He has a beard and wears an overcoat that is torn at the pockets. He is going to town to buy meat and has $3. Suddenly an impulse comes to him. He begins to run. Tears come into his eyes and he runs harder and harder. He is fifty years old and has been married thirty years. He is a farm hand. He has made up his mind to desert his wife and family and run away. He runs so hard across the field because he wants to get into town and board the train before his courage fails.

What an intense study the mind of the man running in the field. My mind can play with it for hours. I should be able to pick a thousand varieties of scenes like that from every field.[6]

Why fear the closing of doors?

TS

1. Doubtless Harriet Dean, an Indianapolis friend of Finley's, who was a member of the staff of the *Little Review*.

2. Anderson and Cornelia had set up housekeeping at 5854 Rosalie Court in Chicago in 1904. He worked first for the Frank B. White Company and later Long-Critchfield Company, both advertising agencies.

3. Possibly Marian Bush, mentioned elsewhere and otherwise unidentified.

4. Tennessee Mitchell, born in Jackson County, Mich., Apr. 18, 1874, was Anderson's wife from 1916–24.

5. John Cowper Powys, 1872–1963, an English author who had visited the United States.

6. This scene became part of "The Untold Lie" in *Winesburg, Ohio.*

3

To Bab — October 25, 1916 [Chicago]

Some time ago the true solution of "Mary Cochran"[1] came to me. She could not of course have married Sylvester. That I think quite clear. In the new draft Mary will be left with the realization that she has done the big thing in accepting work as her way out. She might have had Sylvester, too, had she been able to realize beauty in herself.

It may seem a terrible pronouncement that woman, although she accept work and make herself a sturdy figure in the world, is yet unworthy of love if she be not physically beautiful and not have that daring fling at life that belongs to the artist but it is true.

It seems a terrible pronouncement, I say, and yet try changing the words and make the same pronouncement about me. It works either way you see.

Only I think women have not faced the fact as men have—they have not been compelled to face it. We have lied to them so much. Women really believe that they have it in them to live as a bee has it in her to gather honey. I don't believe Mary was a lover at all. She was a worker!

TS

1. "Mary Cochran" is one of a number of works, mentioned in these letters, which were either never completed or never published. The best idea of its content is in a commentary Finley did, which is published in William A. Sutton, *The Road to Winesburg* (Metuchen, N.J.: The Scarecrow Press, 1972), pp. 581–83. William S. Pfeiffer's doctoral dissertation, "An Edition of Sherwood Anderson's 'Mary Cochran'" (Kent State University, 1975), presents three different versions of this work.

4

To Bab November 23, 1916 [Chicago]

I have an idea. Suppose instead of just writing you letters which may concern themselves with personal things, a cold in the head etc., I write you instead my observations on life and manners as they present themselves to me here and now. By this plan I may write you at times daily, at times only once a week.[1]

When these things come to hand type them, putting on date and making a carbon copy. At the end of six months or a year we will see if we haven't material for a book that would be of interest to others.[2]

In arriving at this idea I have several things in mind. In the first place I think of myself. Perhaps no man writing has had to meet just the peculiar difficulties I have. With me writing has never been in any sense a science. There are days when to save my life I could not write one good sentence. I have really no knowledge of words; no mastery of the art of sentence construction.

And then a mood comes on me. The world is of a sudden all alive with meaning. Every gesture, every word of the people about carries significance. My hand, my eyes, my brain, my ears all sing a tune. If I can get to pencil and paper I write blindly, scarcely seeing the sheets before me.[3]

At such times the terrible feeling of the utter meaninglessness of life passes. I am carried along through hours and days as by a great wind. I am happy.

Now if you can understand what it means at such times to have a man come to my office door and tell me that I am to go into a room with other men and drone for hours over the question of the advisability of advertising a new kind of hose supporters you will understand what I mean by the peculiar difficulties of my position. I go because there are children to be fed, obligations that I have not the courage to face down[4] but as I go I often feel that I could take a revolver from my pocket and begin shooting the men in the room with the greatest glee. I don't want you to misunderstand me. I don't always feel this way about the hose supporter gentlemen. At times I go with delight and all their words strike on my consciousness as just a part of the inexhaustible drollery of life.

However here is my thought. I want to save what I can of the value to me of these destroyed words. Many times when they are checked they break up into little moods. As I sit with the men I scribble little notes about them. On the street cars my mind plays with little notions about things and people. To express these things in even a fragmentary way gives me satisfaction. If the act of writing in this way has no value to others it has at least some value to me.

As you well enough know I have on now a big piece of work. It can only be completed now in a twisted, distorted way. I shall just write it blindly, pouring myself and my character Tandy into it when I can. Then when I have leisure I will go back at it, eliminating, changing[,] trying to make a book of it.[5]

In a personal way I think I can promise you that these notes will have more value to you than any formal letters I might write. There is but one way by which you can get value out of your friendship with me. If the things I write extend or enlarge your own horizon they will be of value to you. You will have to be the judge of that.

"Very well" I hear you say. "We will set out on this trail." Thank you. And now let me just add that you may begin by copying this note and that this plan of mine need not interrupt your writing to me fully of whatever wants expression in you.

November 23, 1916[6]

I went home in the rain and the car was crowded. The workingmen with their sad brutal faces climbed aboard in droves. I stood among them breathing the air that reeked with the strong scent of their bodies. I thought that I had made too much money. In my pocket was a pouch filled with bills. I put down my hand past the shaking body of a fat man and felt of the pouch. I was a little ashamed. Not because I had money when others had none but because the possession of even $75 raises me a little into the lower middle-class. There is a kind of healthy desperation in the utter lack of money. Often I have tramped in utter poverty and misery through the streets and got something out of my misery. For a moment on the car I was sentimental regarding this matter and then I laughed. My mind checked back to the notion that has again and again saved me, living as I do altogether among men of business. Again I put my hand down past the fat man and touched the pouch. I patted it affectionately. As the car rattled along I had keen joy in thinking of myself as an outlaw. "I have stolen the money from a stupid world," I whispered to myself and was happy.

TS

1. Anderson also used this idea in his association with Eleanor Anderson, to whom he wrote a letter a day for a year.

2. No such book materialized.

3. This idea continued to appeal to him, although one's belief in it is inhibited by existing examples of the revision and planning of his writing.

4. Cornelia Anderson had secured a divorce on July 27, 1916, in Benton Harbor, Mich., agreeing not to claim any alimony or support for the three children. Anderson's support of the children was at best erratic.

5. Tandy is the central character of the story by that name in *Winesburg, Ohio*, and it seems that Anderson had first intended to write a novel about this character.

6. What follows is apparently the first of the notes alluded to in the letter.

5

To Bab November 24, 1916 [Chicago]

I went to lunch with Donaghay,[1] a heavily built man who walks awkwardly. He stumbles along, banging against you and while you are crossing the street with him it is necessary to be on the alert lest he knock you under a passing car.

Donaghy is an Irishman but his people have lived in America through several generations. His father was a poor farmhand working on a farm near the town of Dayton, Ohio. He was a very religious man and driven to desperation by poverty and the burning zeal within him that could not get itself expressed[;] he finally went insane and died in an asylum.

Danaghy had one brother, a slight, tubercular fellow who became a newspaper man and went to Kansas City. There he lived for several years, being unable to work most of the time. A passing indiscretion resulted in a loathsome disease and he died suddenly. During the last year of his life he was almost constantly abed and there is a very fine story concerning the loyalty and thoughtfulness of his fellow newspaper employees. These men, who are poorly paid and many of whom have wives and families came every evening to the room of the dying boy. The wives who knew the disease from which he, at the end, suffered came in their best dresses. They brought delicacies and wine. A little pale girl with red hair who had a place as stenographer in the newspaper office sang songs. One of the reporters always stayed through the night. When the boy died they made up a purse to pay the expenses of his burial.

My friend, the heavily awkward brother, has begun to rise in the world. He writes advertisements for a company manufacturing automobiles. He is a devout student of Nietsche and often stops on a busy street to break forth into a violent declaration against the influence of Christianity. "Jesus huh!" he will cry, waving his awkward hands about. "Who was this Jesus—a weeping, wailing, little intermediate! He appealed to pity. There is no such thing as pity. Man is ruled by superman. It is right that it should be so."

When Donaghy was a boy, living with his father, the farm-hand, he knew poverty of the worst sort. He talks of his youth with touching simplicity and directness. What wonderful pictures he has made for me.

There is one of a night in the farmhouse. It was late fall and the boy with his father had been digging potatoes all afternoon. It was cold and the boy's bare hands were split and cracked. The father worked in silence except that he occasionally muttered a prayer. When night came on they carried the potatoes into the barn. The boy was too tired and cold to eat and went at once to bed.

In the bed he lay with his face to the wall, all huddled into a ball, trying to get warm. His body was fevered and his brain extraordinarily alive. The bed had been made of a great bag filled with straw. It crackled when he moved. A wind arose and rattled the boards of the house. All that night his father prayed. He had gone to bed in the next room but almost immediately arose and kneeling on the floor cried out to God. "Oh Father," he cried. "Do not let me remain here in this obscure place. My soul is afire with zeal for Thy service. Make me a shepherd fit to lead Thy flocks. Put the fire of eloquence into my mouth. Give me burning words to say. Lead me to the place Thou hast assigned to me."

Toward midnight the boy arose. Creeping to the door that separated the two rooms he looked at his father. The moonlight, coming in at the window made the figure stand out clearly. He was clad in a shirt and his legs were covered with black hair. The soles of his feet were black from the dirt of the fields. My friend, Danaghy, wanted to kill his father that night. The idea got into his fevered head and he had to force himself to return to bed. A heavy yoke, such as is used when oxen are harnessed to a wagon lay on the floor by the door. He reached down and took hold of it. "I will kill him, who is God's servant and then I will be hanged for it and go to hell," he whispered to himself and the fever of his passion was so strong in him that the effect of it left him ill for several days.

Since Danaghy has grown into a man he has married and has several children. Two of his sons are in college. His wife, a tall, quiet woman with black eyes, is like his father inclined toward the religious life. Danaghy has little to do with her. He goes to his home often and mutters prayers at the table when he is there for dinner. He even subscribes to the support of the suburban church but the home and the wife have in reality nothing to do with his life.

In the city this man has made a number of strange friends and with these he laughs, talks and delivers himself of his pronouncements against religion, marriage and the other accepted institutions of our civilization. I see him often in the company of a young Hebrew musician who has a shrill voice and a French laboring man who works at the stock yards but comes often to dine with Danaghy at some cafe in the evening.

TS

1. This character, in various spellings, seems to have been suggested by George Daugherty, who worked in the advertising agency with Anderson and who was Anderson's friend for decades.

6

To Bab November 26, 1916 [Chicago]

I have been talking to a young American musician. He came over to my room[1] with me. He talked of a mutual acquaintance. On the way he kept calling him the lucky one, saying it over and over. "He is the lucky one. Well, well he is the lucky one."

In my room I demanded an explanation and he gave it rather passionately. "There is a kind of blatant cruelty about him," he said. "Sometimes I think he hasn't the right. No sir, that's it, hasn't the right."

"Go on" I said. ["]Don't bleat like a sheep. Concerning what hasn't he this right? Come to the point, man."

He got up and walked about, smoking one of my cigarettes. "I have been here a number of times but I am not coming anymore," he said. His fingers trembled. ["]You have no sympathy with me or with my kind. I was mistaken about you as I was about him."

The musician went out of my room. I did not try to stop him. In spite of the brief and desultory nature of our talk I realized that there was something really at war in our natures and so I let him go without protest.

One morning after this incident I could not sleep and so arose and went out on our new long Municipal Pier. The pier extends far out into the lake; it extends magnificently. The long rooms running away into the distance are like the cornfields of Kansas and Illinois. The whole structure is long, orderly, breath taking. It expresses some of what American lives should be, it is the kind of thing Americans can do, should do. It points a way. The Municipal Pier is calling to American artists, telling them what to be like. "It has cost men money, the taxpayers will be made to cringe," said the street car conductor. "It does not matter," I replied. "If you and I were the only two Americans who ever came out here, it would be worth while."

On the long pier, in the silence in the early morning I understood more clearly the wrath of my friend and musician. He is the man in the monor [minor] note and some weeks before I had introduced him to another friend who is not minor.

The second man is a business man. He manufactures, I believe, wire fence. The two had talked of music and had, at my suggestion, gone to hear music.

Now here is where the strange thing comes in. The music they heard was beautiful. A woman from India sang Indian folk songs. The business man told me the story. He said the songs were wierd, haunting, lovely.

You see my friend the musician was angry that the maker of wire fence loved the singing of the woman from India. And then he grew angry at me because I understood the man's caring. Here on the pier I understood all that too.

In America we have so little come to understand the term artist that we set all artists aside, grouping them blindly in one mass. The artists accept that. They think that to become an artist they have to accept a certain viewpoint of life, give up working for money, wear long hair, or if they are women, smoke cigarettes.

You see one must realize there are many kinds of artists, the small store keeping artist, the artist who keeps a little garden and produces say, imagist poems for the early spring market, the artist who is smart and sharp like, say a Chicago advertising man, and writes stories for the Saturday Evening Post or like George Ade and Ring Lardner who is professionally funny for the Chicago Tribune.

"The Municipal Pier," I say to myself,"is like Mark Twain[2] and Whitman. It has got itself built in spite of petty politics and small minded men. A wind blew up from the cornfields and a light came into the eyes of someone, somewhere. In a brain the thing was conceived and now it has become stone and brick.["]

The man can now be forgotten. It does not matter. He understands that. The brain that has conceived these long halls and board walks, high in the air that run on and on into the blackness of stormy nights on the lakes, cannot be wasted in petty hunger for the praise of contemporaries.

My friend the musician cannot understand that. His mind does not run on and on. Having produced some minor work of art he must have his praise for that.

Some day I shall write a book to prove that art in America has been choked to death by too much appreciation. No, I shall not do that. Someone might, however. Ade was an artist and now he has a farm in Indiana and, I am told, his own private golf course. He might have become another Twain. The State of Illinois, with its corn and oat fields, its long rivers and its mighty roar of trains coming and going, is represented in the arts by little groups of stuffy people who gather in rooms and talk eternally. They are too well fed. They suffer from too much appreciation. In Russia, Dostoievsky was put up against a wall to be shot and he wrote "The Idiot."

You see my point. I think we will have an American art unlike any other art in the world. When men, like my friend, who makes fence, become artists that will happen. The art they produce will be sustained, magnificent. It will be like Whitman's poem "Out of the cradle endlessly rocking." And like this great pier on which I now sit. It will be like the cornfields.

And I suppose the little professional artist will be quite furious in the face of it. It will so utterly smash all the popular notions concerning art. America will arise and stretch itself. For a long time we will think it unbelievable that human, strong, likeable fellows can be artists. We haven't awakened to that element in Twain yet.

TS

1. At 735 Cass Street, Chicago.

2. In an interview with me at his home in Westport, Conn., in Sept. 1941, Van Wyck Brooks said that Anderson loved Twain above all writers.

7

To Bab — November 27, 1916 [Chicago]

To my mind people in general and particularly women, get too close and personal a view of men at war. I talked to Tennessee[1] of it last night and tried to make clear to her what I meant.

A thousand men are in a trench. Within an hour they are to charge across an open space. To each individual crouching there something happens. In himself he has no courage for the task before him. It is too terrible and hideous. But as he waits something happens. A thrill runs through the mass of men. Each individual is [in] an odd way infected with the combined courage of all the men. This of course needs elaboration. Perhaps I cannot elaborate in a letter. You will be down upon me with the horrors of war, starving children, etc. Sometime when I see you I will talk to you of that as I did with Tennessee. In a letter I can give you one thought. In some one of my books I have worked it out. I made a picture of trains coming in at the railroad stations in Chicago, and bearing young men from the cornfields, strong bright eyed young men, thousands of them, walking over the bridges into the loop district and to spiritual death.[2] The bodies live but the thing that made them bright eyed and eager dies. I should prefer my sons to die in the war and terror of a Verdun.

But to get on with my thought. I see in fancy the men of all those old countries going home. Can you not sense such a scene, say in a Russian village and the men telling over and over their wonder stories? What a new sense of the world they have!

And imagine a boy standing in the shadows of the door of a room at evening in a German village while the fathers talk of Verdun. Do you not see that millions of such boys must get a new heritage of beauty from that? Boys, you know, are right when they are thrilled by the tales of war and are not thrilled by the tales of the stock-exchange.

My notion is, you see, that the war will soon be over and the world facing itself. Don't believe the stories of a ruin and anarchy after the war. Clerks who declare that 2 and 2 makes four have figured that out. Trust instead the lesson men have got. I tell you that youth will run all through the old places. Poets and thinkers will arise, the old world will be sweetened by the storm, the very air will be purer. It is inevitable!

* * * * * *

It is absurd to think of even trying to help me financially.[3] I am tarred by the world. Don't you see that my only chance lies in staying in my own puddle here. I have got to live as the men right here in this office live. I have got to make my living as they do.

Chicago is horrible. The living impulses that drive the men I meet day by day are materialistic. They want to preserve the respectability of their homes and keep alive the institution of prostitution. They want not beautiful clothes but clothes that represent vaguely the idea of money spent. They are weakly sentimental, occasionally coarse beyond your comprehension and for the most part there is no life in them.

At times there comes over me a terrible conviction that I am living in a city of the dead. In the office dead voices discuss dead ideas. I go into the street and long rows of dead faces march past. Once I got so excited and terrified that I began to run through the streets. I had a mad impulse to shout, to strike people with my fist. I wanted terribly to awaken them. Instead I went to my room and shut myself in. I drank whiskey. Presently I slept. When I awoke I laughed.

Long ago I realized that I must laugh or go insane. I go along seeing little things and being amused. A kind of dreadful smartness and alertness takes possession of me. I write smart advertisements. I do little tricky things to make money. I laugh and grin like a little ape.

My head is filled with fancies that cannot get expressed. A thousand beautiful children are unborn to me. Sustained flights of thoughts break up and pass away into nothingness because I am full of the spirit of my times. Sometimes I dare to think of America. I realize that only by remaining a part of the very blood and spirit of all this aimlessness can I be an American.

We must have in us a love of the land itself. We cannot love the men and what they are doing with the land. On trains one gets a sense of vastness of possibility. That's all there is for us. If we can love *that* we can love America. There is only vastness of possibility.

TS

1. Anderson married Tennessee Mitchell on July 31, 1916, in Chateaugay, N.Y.

2. This is reminiscent of scenes in *Marching Men*.

3. Finley's offers of financial help are mentioned throughout the letters, but the only known occasion she gave him money directly occurred when she paid him $200 each for two of his paintings to help with his expenses in Europe in 1921. She did give money to his children.

8

To Bab December 1, 1916 [Chicago]

The party was lovely and the most truly lovely thing of all was the great bunch of yellow flowers that came at noon. Max came with the girl he was once engaged to—Relda, isn't it?—a fine looking woman and very intelligent. Bill was there and Margy, Vaughn, Mary McKenzie and George.[1]

Mrs. X had made us a great bowl of Russian cigarettes and we had cocktails to make every one merry. George, who is big and ponderous but tremendously loveable[,] carved the goose. The fires roared, the wind blew and everybody was happy. I drank a toast to your beautiful thoughtfulness.

Have I ever told you about Vaughn? He comes from Texas, a tall rangy youth who has been studying art here for five years. He doesn't seem to get anywhere. I have wondered why. Now I think I'm beginning to understand.

Vaughn is good. The thing is like a disease in him. Can you imagine a man's attempting to get anywhere in the arts here in America without ever indulging in any of the vices by which we all, in our crude way express ourselves?

Fellows like Vaughn have been cursed by too much mothering or fathering. You get the picture. Mother's boy is going away to the city. She doesn't want him to smoke or drink or ever to have anything to do with loose women.

She is right, too, no doubt; although there is something appalling to me in the thought of living a life without ever once having a night of debauch.

Great God, if I hold myself apart thus how am I ever to know a single man about me, how am I to love or to understand?

And Vaughn wants to be an artist. He goes into the institute here and sees pictures that have been painted by heavens knows what perplexed, drinking, weeping, laughing old fellow of long ago. He wants to paint like that and he wants to save his own soul.

Do you know I suspect there is just that damning difficulty with half, perhaps all, the weak sentimental art we in America are producing.

What we need is men perfectly willing to go to hell! We want men courageous enough to start on the road to art by saying to God, "All right then send me to hell. That is your affair. It is my affair to try and find out and to express what I really feel."

And so I wanted to whisper to Vaughn as he went out at the door. "Get out under the black sky boy. The night is dark. Creep away by yourself. Sin! Throw off this cheap mantle of purity. Why should you be saved? Look at the black sky and tell God about it. Shake your fist at him. We are all damned. When you have had your hour with God come back and be one with all the rest of us here, damned souls, condemned to try and find art and beauty in the night of industrialism."

TS

1. These people cannot be identified with certainty.

9

To Bab December 2—1916 [Chicago]

To breathe, eat, wear clothes and in occasional flashes, to hold women in our arms—that is the lot of men immersed in industrial life here in America. The average man I see who has passed his fortieth year is a nervous wreck.[1] He takes some kind of indigestion medicine.

One wonders why we do not know that this is not life? Not one in a million of us has yet found the courage within himself to embrace deep emotions.

Death is a wall that cowardice builds. Here is everybody busy building the wall. Even youth has become cautious. It piles up stones for the wall. Everywhere about we men and women are building death walls. They crouch behind the walls. They are afraid of bodily injury, sexual adventures, misunderstanding. They are afraid they will go to hell!

Men's fears are stones with which they build the wall of death. They die behind the wall and we do not know they are dead. With terrible labor I arouse myself and climb over my own wall. As far as I can see are the little walls and the men and women fallen on the ground, deformed and ill. Many are dying. The air is heavy with the stench of those who have already died.

TS

1. Anderson's own nervous breakdown, an attack of amnesia, occurred in Elyria, Ohio, on Nov. 28, 1912; see Sutton, *Road to Winesburg*.

10

To Bab — Columbus, O. Dec. 4, 1916

I am in the station waiting for a train.[1] A little middle-aged woman in a brown velvet dress had the berth opposite me in the sleeper out of Chicago. I saw her in the station there as we stood waiting by the gate in the train shed. She was with a man who must be her lover. He was tall and had blue eyes. He looked like a laborer who has managed to rise out of the ranks of labor. Perhaps he is an inventor working in steel. His hands were broad and strong and about the nails I could see, in the strong light, traces of machine oil.

I stood behind the couple in the train shed. He kept patting the little woman on the arm and saying, "Never mind, I shall see you again soon." The woman wept and kissed the sleeve of his coat.

This morning at Columbus another man was waiting for the woman. He is small and nervous and has red eyes and nose. He is surely her husband. They had breakfast together at the station and I sat at the same table. He ate greedily and with his mouth full of food scolded. "What did you want to stop in Chicago for?" he asked. "Why didn't you come on home?"

The woman was pale and looked old. When she drank coffee her hand trembled. "Ah, home! Be quiet. You talk too much," she said.

— — — — — —

An old soldier who wears a long grey beard sits behind me as I write.

He is smoking a cheap cigar that does not burn evenly. It is singeing his mustache. He is angry and keeps spitting and swearing but he does not throw the cigar away.

TS

1. Anderson's duties as an advertising consultant and salesman kept him constantly traveling by trains between Ohio, Illinois, Wisconsin, and Kentucky at this time and for a decade to come.

11

To Bab December 5, 1916 [Chicago]

I know a man here who is now forty years old. For fifteen years we have been acquainted and he occasionally comes to visit me. Of recent years I have seen him but seldom and until last night he has not been in my room to sit for an hour's talk for more than six months.

My friend's name is Alfred Tiffany and he comes from Indiana. When he was a boy his father ran a sawmill and wood yard in the town where they lived. He had one brother who has now become a farmer.

When young Tiffany first came here to the city there was something very fine and delicate about his character. I knew him well then and often in the evening we walked and talked together. For a time he was a great hero to me. One spring he threw up his place as clerk in a wholesale shoe house and went west on an adventure. How well I remember that evening. I boarded a street car and went with him to Hammond, Indiana. It was a warm rainy night and we went along the tracks and crouched in the shadow of a fence. When a freight train came along he climbed aboard. I sat in the darkness and wept because I could not go also.

For a year he stayed in the west and when he came back got a place in the office of a well-known advertising man. Gradually a change took place in his nature.

It was during the year after he had come from his western adventure that I enjoyed my friend the most. I had also become an advertising writer and we met often at lunch but that didn't count. I lived then as I do now just outside the business district on the north side and he came often to dine with me. How fine and upstanding he was. We had both of us, small salaries and we cooked the dinner over a small oil stove. There would be tea and cakes and perhaps eggs or bacon; then pipes and talk.

Alfred talked fervently. He walked up and down the room with his eyes shining and his shoulders thrown back telling me of nights spent in the company of tramps at the edge of some village in the west; of long days spent in western wheat fields; of a girl in men's clothes who once rode all day with him in an empty car and a hundred other adventures.

Alfred has changed. He was here in my room last night and I could have wept when he went away. At forty life and the old love of life has almost gone out of him. In his hour of ease now he is nervous and his eyes that once sparkled with excitement roam listlessly about. He has acquired a dozen vulgar little habits. He picks at the lobe of his ear with his finger nails. When he talks he puts his hand before his mouth and laughs slyly. He dresses in expensive clothes and wears shoes made by a fashionable shoemaker but he no longer is the handsome fellow who came from the western adventure and who used to strut before me telling of the things he had done and intended to do.

Alfred is making money. That is the trouble with him. He has listened to the talk of getting on that goes on among the men here. He still believes in a childish sort of way that presently he will be rich and will go adventuring again, not realizing that the last fifteen years have made a different man of him. Now his adventures, if he adventures at all, will be the adventures of his class. He will go with an actress to dinner at the Blackstone. Some night when he has been drinking a woman of the town will give him a disease. He will begin soon to grow fat and bald. He will know the head-waitress at the most expensive eating places but he will not know how the wind scolds and talks among the dry corn blades in western fields at night or how the heart of a boy thumps as he crouches by a fence in the darkness on a rainy night, waiting to leap aboard a passing freight train and go bravely away into the unknown.

* * * * * *

It is night and raining; Tennessee has been here.[1] She has made tea for Bill, Max and me. A man had given her ten dollars for a picture Bill painted and she gave it to him. He almost fainted with joy. With the ten dollars he is planning to go home on a visit to his mother at Louisville; get his crooked teeth straightened by a dentist; pay his room rent and give a dinner party for his friends.

* * * * * *

It is ten o'clock and has begun to rain. Every one has gone away. Only one candle is burning, and the wind tosses the flame so that the grease falls on the table. I am thinking of Alfred Tiffany who was here last night. I must tell you a tale of him in his earlier days, tell it in memory of the part of him that was my friend and that has died; tell it in memory of the beautiful boy who is becoming a successful man.[2]

There was a girl came here from England who was a designer of gowns. She did not look in the least English but was small and dark. Like the emperor of Germany she had a withered arm that she kept always concealed.

This woman was in some way related to the advertising man for whom Alfred worked when he had just come home from his adventures as a tramp. They met at a dinner given for ten or twelve people in a north side restaurant.

In those days Alfred was always excited. His straight young body was a store house of energy. The people at the table were members of our American upper middle class, people who had money. They talked and drank heavily in a dull effort to be lively and engaging.

Alfred looked at the little English girl beside him and began to talk to her. He grew confidential and told her of an adventure that came to him one evening out west. Something in her sharp little face awoke a vein of sadness in him and the sadness made him talk well. He was capable of being sensitive to people then. He told her of a girl he had seen in a farmhouse in North Dakota. He had stopped there for the night, had helped do the chores about the farm for his supper and lodging and as darkness came on sat with his back against the wall of the barn looking across the fields.

A woman came to the barn to milk the cows. She was about thirty and had broad shoulders. When she saw Alfred she stopped and smiled.

The night was warm and Alfred continued to sit in the darkness by the barn. He heard the milk striking against the sides of the tin milk bucket and the voices of the woman. She passed him again, going to the house. And then all was quiet.

Hours passed and the young man did not move. He had been told he could sleep on the hay in the barn loft but he did not feel like sleep. Suddenly in the darkness he saw something white and the voice of the woman called softly, "Young man." she called. "Young man. Where are you?"

The farm woman in the white night robe sat down beside Alfred on the ground and put her hand into his. It was roughened by toil. Nothing happened. Presently she whispered and made him understand why she had come. The farm house was isolated and she was terribly lonely. In touching Alfred's hand she felt she touched the hand of the world. She had crept out of bed, where her husband slept and had risked the whole future of her life as a wife by her action.

This simple tale told by the Alfred of long ago had a strange effect upon the English girl. She fell in love with him. He did not know that at the time but he found out later.

One day Alfred got a note from the English girl inviting him to go with her for a two days vacation with some friends who had taken a house for the summer on the eastern shore of the lake. "My Aunt and her two daughters are there," the note said. "We will go on the boat Friday evening. I have been there before so I will make all arrangements. You have but to come to the dock at the foot of Dearborn Street. My brother who lives here will take me to the boat. All arrangements will be made. You have but to walk up and down on the dock until I come. Write me if you intend to go."

The details of that evening on the boat with the English woman as told by Alfred long ago have passed from my mind. I remember that he had no notion of making love to her, had not thought of such a thing but that she had so arranged as to make love-making almost inevitable. She had only engaged one state room and as soon as the brother went away she took Alfred aboard the boat and told him. He was worried and spoke of the danger to her, of his fears that she might be seen by someone who knew her, that she might become with child and so forth. She only laughed and stroked the sleeve of his coat with her well hand.

There must have been something tremendously touching and unforgettable about that love-making. I remember vividly the figure of my friend standing in my room later and talking of it and the picture he made of himself sitting on a stool beside her berth, holding her thin little hand while he looked through the port hole at the night over the sea. "She sobbed and sobbed," he said. "With her well-hand she clung to me and almost forced me to get into bed with her. When I yielded she wept with joy. Later I found out that she wanted to have a child, was ready to risk everything to bring that about. She knew I would never make love to her again and she had fallen in love with me. She wanted everything to take place that night. When she sobbed in such a broken hearted way it was partly from depth of feeling but it was mostly from fear that the terrible, beautiful, forbidden thing she wanted would not come to pass.["]

It seems to me that Alfred Tiffany has grown old, that he is dead. I do not blame him. I do not believe he has killed himself. I think modern American industrial life has done it. Perhaps his mind was not strong enough to resist the insiduous daily suggestion borne into his ears by thousands of voices around him. Perhaps the thing he had in him so long ago when the farm woman came to sit beside him and when the English girl tried at one swift sudden stroke to win a child from him had to be lost.

I know nothing of the reasons for the change in Alfred. I only know he is changed and that I hope not to see him again. Last night I asked him again of the English girl but he wanted to talk of one evening he had spent at the Bismark Gardens. "I have forgotten. Did she have the child?" I asked. "Why do you harp on that? The woman was a fool and so was I then. I almost decided to marry her. It might have turned out a regular mess. I'm glad enough to forget it. Why not let it alone?"

TS

1. This and other information suggest that Tennessee and Anderson maintained separate establishments during their marriage.

2. Though this may be a story of an actual person, however fictionalized, the essence of it fits Anderson's life. He mourned what he considered his lost youthful innocence throughout his writings, and his concern for maimed women is notable in his work.

12

To Bab — December 7, 1916 [Clyde]

How tremendously our small town American life has changed in twenty years. I went to my home town in Ohio [Clyde][1] yesterday and spent three hours there. It is a pretty town lying some ten or twelve miles back from Lake Erie. When I was a boy there the town was isolated. To go to Fremont or Bellevue, eight miles away was to make a journey. Factories had not come in and the people were engaging in farming, the selling of merchandise or of the practice of the crafts in the old sense. Two carpenters met on the street in the evening and talked for hours concerning the best way to cut out a window frame or build a door. Now doors and window frames are made in big factories and shipped in.

I came into town by electric car from the East. We stopped at a switch and two big motor trucks bearing merchandise passed us. Automobiles driven by some of the men whom I once knew went whirling past.

As soon as I arrived in town I felt sad and lonely. I stood on a corner looking about. The section of town where the car stopped used to be a desolate spot unlighted and with weeds and bushes growing in the empty lots. Now it is all built up with neat, ugly working-men's houses.

Romance dwelt about these corners then. The old town, long before my day, had consisted of a few houses scattered along the road where the electric car runs now. When I was a boy these houses and one or two decayed brick buildings that had been stores were empty and deserted. Weeds grew high in the vacant lots. To the north stretched the open farming country. At night when I carried papers I went shivering along this road.

A girl came to town from a village called Castalia half way down to the lake. I fell in love with her, an innocent boyhood love, but, although she was young and fair she had already had lovers. How vividly I remember the evening when I found this out. She let me know because she wanted me to be her lover. The little animal had got hold of a dress cut very low that showed her round breasts. She met me on Main street and we walked down into this dark place. She took off her cloak and laughed. "Kiss me," she whispered.

That was a night for me. I was full of pride and shamed too. I reme[m]ber with what a strange mixed feeling I later went home to my mother.

Well, I walked up the street, my head singing with old memories. In the old brick house across the street lived Dr. Duse[2] who made liver pills and sold them all over the country. He had a daughter who went to Boston and became a singer. She used to come home in the summer wearing such fine clothes that we all looked upon her with awe. She was lonely and would have flirted with our young fellows but they were afraid. She seemed too grand and far away for them.

Here on a corner lived big "Mac" and his grandfather. He was a tremendously tall boy and became a baker. How strong his hands were. He used to save all his money until he had achieved twenty or thirty dollars and then go to another town on a debauch. When the money was gone he came home and went quietly to work. Later he found employment on the railroad and became a steady, working fellow. He is there now I suppose.

I am sitting in the little hotel office writing.[3] I have hardly gone to see anyone and have only walked through two or three streets. Why?——— well, because what I have already seen has awakened such a flood of memories that I am overwhelmed. I realize as I sit here that I could sit thus for hours—as long as life remained in me[,] writing of my people and the strange things that have happened to them. What real and living people they are to me. Even Jerry Donlin, the baggage man who I am told dropped dead of heart failure and who has just by chance come into my mind. His life is a living thing to me. I could write long novels concerning this sweet-hearted, profane Irishman and the wonderful things my imagination helps me to believe went on in his head while he outwardly did no more than push baggage trucks up and down this station platform here.

So here I sit and my hand shakes with excitement. Names flood in upon me. Waxy Sellinger, Pete McChine, Ed Duglas, Preey Welsh, Toughy McCreary, Turkey Clapp, Ben McHugh.

Why go on? I could write three hundred of such names and each name a story, a great book filled with strange things.[4]

The girls were not so well named. I remember only a vague and meaningless jumble of Jennies and Mabels and Minnies. And oddly enough the women I see passing the hotel here do not look interesting. What dull, heavy faces. There is no beauty in them whereas the old men, tottering about are in some way almost beautiful. Things have happened to them. Adventures have come in, whereas one feels adventures have not come to these women who were once girls and my playmates. I feel that the young women growing up are better than the women who went before but I do not feel that the young men who go into the factories are the equals of their fathers who went into the fields and into the old hand crafts.

I will not go on about my town. Some day when I am in a reflective mood I will write more of my visit—the memories awakened and the thoughts I had.[5]

In as much as I have abused women I will end by telling of a woman who lived here in my time and of whom I have often thought. There is something splendid about her.

Maria Welling came here from Sandusky. If you could sit beside me now I could point out the building where she once ran a hotel here.

Maria had been keeper of a house of ill repute. She married a gambler and they both came away to this town determined to settle down and be quiet respectable people.

There was nothing of the hypocrite about Maria. If she was ashamed of her past life she kept her shame to herself. Here she came and settled and while her husband ran the bar and the office of the little hotel she did the cooking and made the beds.

Soon the place began to shine under her labors. Trade came and money was made. Girls were employed to work in the dining room of the hotel and she made money.

Now you know how it is with girls in the dining room of a country hotel—well it wasn't that way with Maria's girls. I was a newsboy then and used to bring the evening paper to her kitchen door. Often I was invited in to have a generous [piece] out of one of Maria's pies.

And there I heard her talk, plainly and frankly to her girls not once but dozens of times. She didn't scold. That wasn't Maria's way. She knew things and she told them things. No moralizing, no windiness, just plain straight talk. "I know! I've been over the road. If you could beat the game I'd say so. You can't," she told them over and over.

One evening I remember Maria talked to me, explaining what she meant by her talk with the girls. I strolled by her place homeward bound after my evening's papers were delivered. Maria's voice called. I found her sitting in the darkness at the back door of her kitchen and she made a motion for me to sit beside her.

She put her big hand on my shoulder and talked. I won't attempt to tell what she told me but it was all about the life she had been in. To me she talked as she did to the girls.

"You stay away. It's rotten," she cried. "You're a clean boy and I want you to stay away from girls. Just mind this. Don't you pay and don't you have anything to do with [them] as takes pay. It will bring you sorrow and it brings sorrow to women but don't let it be with you the sorrow of paying or to any woman you ever know the sorrow of taking pay."

Her voice broke and she drew me down until my head lay on her breast. "I'd rather been a slut on the street because I was just naturally bad and wanted loving than to have been what I was for money," she said brokenly.

TS

1. Born in Camden, Ohio, on Sept. 13, 1876, Anderson considered Clyde, in Sandusky County, northwestern Ohio, his hometown in view of the fact that residence was established there in 1884 after a series of moves. He stayed in Clyde until he went to Chicago in 1896.

2. Actually, Dr. Luse.

3. Presumably the hotel was in Clyde.

4. The reader of *Winesburg, Ohio* will recognize the names and situations mentioned in the preceding paragraphs.

5. His novel *Windy McPherson's Son* already had much about Clyde in it.

13

To Bab — December 8th [1916] [Chicago]

For nearly seven years now,[1] ever since I began writing—and I count any happiness I have had in life as beginning when I began to scribble—I have had one thought constantly in mind. The thought has left me at times but has always come back. It must come back. There is death in forgetting!

And now I come to express that vague thought it is unspeakably difficult. I want to try to remember the relation of myself to my time and place. That is it. It sounds in written words self-conscious and foolish but as my time and place is neither beautiful nor inspiring I feel myself capable of embracing the thought and I do embrace it.

It seems to me that if I lived in France now, and had been born a Frenchman I should remain silent. My own terrible ignorance, a somewhat superficial quality in men and in life about me, would keep me silent among the great voices of France or of Russia. I would be there a quiet, rather studious man perhaps given to scribbling in secret.

And here I have allowed myself to speak. Nearly all of the qualities of the Americans of my time are embodied in me. My struggle, my ignorance, my years of futile work to meaningless ends—all these are American traits. If I fail to get at anything approaching real beauty so have my times and the men of my times failed.

Yesterday I came through Elyria where I was in business as a manufacturer five years.[2] I arrived in the evening and all day as I sat in the train or talked to men in another town there was a peculiar tightening of the muscles of my body. My feet did not want to touch the soil of Elyria. The [this?] is the truth. I was too terribly unhappy there. For five years there I fought a meaningless battle for a meaningless end. I tried to make money, become rich. The experience ended in a convulsion that touched the edge of insanity.[3]

Yesterday in a book I read the writer talked of convicts in a Russian prison. He spoke of the terrible punishment of giving men meaningless work to do. "Make a man carry dirt from one place to another and then carry it back and he will inevitably become insane," the writer said.

And I did just that for five years in Elyria. Other men were doing it there, Americans are doing it everywhere. We are all insane. The men of an industrial age will always be insane.

It was evening when I got into Elyria and rather dark and cold. My train did not go further and I had to get out and wait a half hour for another train. My body was cold and I shivered. None of the people who stood about knew me and I was glad of that. I stood in the deep shadow by the station and waited. The soul within me was weary with old memories.

Just across the track from where I stood was the factory building where I employed myself striving to grow rich. For a little time I made money and then the seeds of failure that have always been in me began to take root in the industry I was trying to manage. Uh, the memory of those years! I tried hard to be cunning, to be shrewd. I must have lied and boasted and cheated prodigiously. All day and every day the thing went on like an insane nightmare. At night I tried to heal myself. Sometimes I got drunk. At other times I walked alone through endless streets of small frame houses. I crept away into the open and lay down on the ground in the fields. I wept, I swore, I worked myself into new fits of enthusiasm concerning the thing I was doing.

How many laughable sides there are to that long struggle in which I was engaged. My wife thought me insane. She had always considered me a little twisted in the head and who can blame her? It was her fate to live with me in my terrible time and to know nothing of what went on in my soul and I could not understand what went on in her either. In the house we looked at each other with unseeing eyes. Now and then tenderness swept over us and we sat in the darkness of the house late at night and wept.

In my second year here I began to write.[4] I wrote Windy and Marching Men here and the writing saved me from insanity. Night after night I crept away to my room to write. I was without education and training. The thought came to me—"I am an intensification of the spirit of my times." I whispered to myself. "As I am ignorant so are all my brothers ignorant, as I am now terribly sad, on the point of madness so will all America some day be [sad] to the edge of insanity."

There was a woman worked in my office who was the daughter of people here. At night she stayed in the office and typed what I had written. She was strong, full of virilty and honest. Sometimes when she had typed what I had written and we were trudging homeward up the dark track she would put her hand on my arm and speak in a low voice. Tears would come into her eyes, "It would be wonderful if you could get clear of all this," she said.

During the day when the others were about this woman continually bustled about. There was a good deal [of] the tom-boy about her and she was always tearing her clothing. At the noon hour she would run into the yard and begin wrestling with one of the boys from the factory. When finally the affairs of the company became desperate and I, seeing the money entrusted to me by others, slipping away, I could not sleep at night, she watched me with motherly solicitude. One morning my mind became a blank and I ran away from Elyria, scurrying across fields, sleeping in ditches, filling my pockets with corn from the fields that I nibbled like a beast. I would have been afraid even of her then. I was afraid of everything in human form.[5] When, after several days of wandering my mind came into my body and I dragged myself weary and yet glad of my final defeat into a hospital in a strange town[6] and slept, the touch of her honest, broad hand awakened me. I sat up in bed ready to cry out, eager to express to her my joy at being back among the living but only the blank white walls of a new strange place confronted me. I had begun a new life and there was something complete and final in the low voice that whispered as I turned again to sleep. "You must leave all that life and everything that has been a part of that life behind you."[7]

TS

1. This places the beginning of his writing in Elyria, Ohio, in 1910, which fits all other available information.

2. 1907–12

3. See my *Road to Winesburg*, pp. 162–208, 552–65, for a description of Anderson's breakdown/amnesia.

4. This would be 1908, a date that does not agree with other information as well as his remark earlier in this letter. He had, of course, written extensively in Chicago. See *ibid.*, pp. 101–50.

5. This state of mind is reflected in the letter Anderson wrote when he had amnesia. See *ibid.*, pp. 552–65.

6. He actually went into a drug store in Cleveland, where he had lived in 1906–7, asked for help, and was taken to a hospital by a friend, whom the clerk summoned. See *ibid.*, pp. 162–208.

7. Anderson himself created a myth of his having left business for literature. He had returned to the advertising business in Chicago early in 1913, after recovering from his amnesia, and was in advertising when he wrote this letter.

14

To Bab — December 10, 1916 [Chicago]

Tommy sent me a little poem about K. My inclination was to abuse the poem and now I wish I had done so more roundly. There is no health in saying soft words and it was very bad.

On the same evening Mrs. W.[1] came with a book of old Chinese verse translated by some college professor. Some of it has come down from a dim time ten or fifteen centuries before Jesus lived. All of it has the same quality—simple little things such as you might write about a mood of sadness that came over you as you walked home, perhaps from leaving your electric car in the garage. It rained and the wet, ill-smelling people clung to a passing street car. A dead leaf fell out of a tree and perhaps you shivered. A broad-shouldered man in a slouch hat hurried along in the rain. You thought how old the world [was] and [that] you were tired.

The Chinese poems were like that, a glimpse of gray sky seen over a field, the swish of waves along a shore beneath a cloudy sky. "My love put his hand in at the latch of the door."

The book of old verse on the table before me and the presence of Mrs. W. and Tennessee both in such different ways beautiful set me talking.

There has been a series of lectures given by poets here. Imagine a poet lecturing on poetry.

"There should be an end of poetry that pretends to be poetry," I said to the two women. Imagine calling such a man as Ficke[2] a poet and neglecting to call Dreiser one. It is all ridiculous. Put the badge of poet on a man and you crush the poetry in him.

I was warm by now and spat words about. "True poetry is accidental," I cried. "It is like a flash of lightning revealing something in the darkness; a wide stretch of cornfields or two lovers embracing beneath a tree. It should always be buried in prose. We should make an end of the term poet and recognize only writers.["]

The poetry of the Old Testament is ruined for me when a college professor had had it experimented upon and reprinted in blank verse. Do away with the term poet and we will have an end to writers building misunderstanding by lecturing of poetry in a hall. One might as well set up for a lover and deliver a series of talks on Love and Lovers.

Of course you were never a factory hand at work in a factory among mechanics. A surprising number of them have picked up a line of some old song or group of words beautifully blended that they say over and over when they are absorbed in some task. I worked once beside an old carriage painter who stripped wheels. As he bent over his task he muttered. "La de, de! The wind roughened her long bare hands!"

TS

1. It has not been possible to identify either Tommy, K., or Mrs. W.
2. Arthur Davison Ficke (1883-1945), American poet and author of, among other books, *From the Isles* (1907) and *Sonnets of a Portrait Painter* (1914).

15

To Bab December 11, 1916 [Chicago]

Six hours steady work in the office, writing in a frenzy of wash-tubs and kitchen cabinets and a remedy for curing diseases of hogs.

I ran away for an hour in the snow. The city whirled past me in motor cars. The sky was black with smoke. Heavy trucks rumbled.

Upton Sinclair has written me a letter of remonstrance because he is afraid I am not a socialist. When I reply I will send you a copy of the things I shall say to him.

That set my head whirling. From the mood of the letter of Sinclair's I began thinking of what I am doing here in this jam of work, of men killing themselves for nothing, of life here in Chicago.

I am trying with all my might to be and remain a lover. All this writing is addressed to my beloved.

I am writing these snatches of things to women, to all women, to one woman. I am telling her of my life, of a man actively engaged in the grim wrestle of modern industrial life.

The wrestler is myself. I tug and pull at my opponent, Reality. Sweat rolls from me. Occasionally I cry out with pain.

My woman is made up of all the woman of the world. She is no longer young nor is she old. She is beautiful.

You have something of that woman in you, all women have. You have a trick with your hand when you raise it to your hair. There is a sorrow in your eyes. Your face is long like the face of a horse.

What have you of the great woman? That I love. For that I could embrace you. For that I could take you into my arms and steal away into the darkness. But this is no time for that. I had forgotten. It is cold and has begun to rain. The grass in the fields would be wet. My mind has run to other things. I must take a train and go to Iowa where I will talk with a man concerning his problem of making money.

You shall not lose me. Always I shall remember just the way you said that you were tired and the muscles of your forearms ached.

It is like this you see. I am walking along the streets in the snow. In fifteen minutes I will be back at my desk in the whirl of needless things.

I swing along relaxing, relaxing. My mind plays. It touches the lives of women, a million American women.

For the moment I believe they all want lovers, the lover. They are not really concerned about their souls or their virginity or the humdrum things everyone believes. They are not so dull as that.

I would like to be a lover. Madly I would run through the world, clasping all women in my arms, whispering, pressing, urging.

I go back to my office. The grey smoke lies over my ugly city. I am myself ugly. Then [the] mud of my times has clung to me. I will not be a lover, racing through the world, pressing women in my arms. I will grow old and have a nervous disease. I will curl up and die like a little bug. When I am dead I will dry out and be a shell that crackles and crumbles when you touch it with your hand.

But meantime I will tell the woman about it, whispering to her of it, telling all the ugly things and the lovely things. Scrawling them quickly without hope of sequence. That is my way of making love to her, to the indefinable, the unknown, the woman, all women.

TS

16

To Upton Sinclair — Tuesday, December Twelve, Nineteen Sixteen [Chicago]

My dear Sinclair:—

Your letter set me thinking. It was a cold snowy afternoon in Chicago. I left my office at four and started to walk home across the city. A man with a withered hand ran down a stairway out of a tenement. He had no overcoat and his clothes were thin. The blue veins on the back of his withered hand were ghastly blue. He saw me looking and stared into my eyes. His lips mumbled words.

A middle aged policeman came along the street. A young girl came out of an office. The cold made her cheeks glow. She was alive with life and something in the stolid figure of the policeman tempted her. Their eyes met and he stopped and stared. He perhaps had a wife and family at home but he was stirred by the sight of the young girl who was not unwilling to flirt with him. His lips also mumbled words.

And so I went along seeing things and thinking. I also muttered words. I kept thinking of you and what you had said to me about socialists and my lips moved.

Man, you seem to see and feel them as things apart. You ask me to pity and understand socialists as you might ask me to understand the Arabs or the Chinese.

Truth is, Sinclair, I'm married to a socialist and when I vote I vote that ticket myself but if I thought the fact of my doing so set me apart in the way your letter suggests I'd quit in a hurry.[1]

Really I'm tempted to go at you hard in this matter. There is something terrible to me in the thought of the art of writing being bent and twisted to serve the end of propaganda. Why should we as writers be primarily socialists or conservatives, or anarchists, or anything else.

Here is all America teeming with life that we haven't begun to really cut into or understand. We aren't making our fellows understand it. It's wrong, man, terribly wrong.

Here is the man I shall go to lunch with tomorrow. He is rich, is piling up more riches daily. And he is becoming brutalized. Dimly he knows it. He wants to know about himself. God, he don't want me to preach at him.

I have a book coming next year called "Marching Men." I hope you will read it and like it. But it also finds nothing of great value to the world in the socialists. My man McGregor meets and knows socialists. At one place he cries out to his marching men, "If men preach at you from a box knock them down and keep on marching."

Sinclair, your letter was something like a cry to me. Can I not get into this letter the beginning of a cry to you?

I do so want to see writers quit drawing themselves apart, becoming socialists, or conservatives or whatnot. I want them to stay in life. I want them to be something of brother[s] to the poor brute who runs the sweatshop as well as to the equally unfortunate brutes who work for him.

Won't we serve better thus? We are so terribly young. We haven't even begun to understand our own American life. As writers can't we leave politics and economics to the more lusty throated ones and run away, one by one, into the streets, the offices and the houses—looking at things—trying to write them down.

Damn it, you have made me go on like a propagandist. You should be ashamed of yourself. Come see me won't you when a wind blows you this way.[2]

TS

1. The pacifist policies of socialism had just been rejected in Nov. 1916, in an election that saw a Socialist candidate for mayor of Chicago, something that has never happened since.

2. The relationship with Sinclair evidently did not flourish.

17

To Bab December 13, 1916 [Chicago]

I am filled with amazement at the stupidity of people who insist on being writers. Here is life, America, Chicago, a town in Alabama. Everywhere is life with its story that aches to be expressed.

I myself insist on writing. I go home to my room and sit down. I begin to make sentences. Notions concerning a vast rhythm to be achieved in prose come into my mind.

I am ashamed and pray. I kneel on the floor of my room and pray. I ask God to let me be something not quite a fool. Why do I not let life flow through me? It is too much, too big for me, too terrible and complex, not understandable.

I want to be a wide-eyed boy, running about, a stern, ready-handed man listening with quiet understanding at a street corner where two teamsters are quarreling concerning a space for their wagons by a store door. A lover feeling with delight the blood that throbs in the fingertips of the woman; a cold man full of hatred sharpening a long knife for his enemy—a living thing in the world and a part of the world. I do not want to be a dead, dry thing, a writer mumbling over little words.

TS

18

To Bab December 21, 1916 [Chicago]

There is a thing about friendship like marriage. It has a right to endure but usually does not. To me it seems that the difficulties about friendship as about marriage are that it is taken too seriously. The light touch is the thing. Once let a friendship become a necessity and you are in danger of losing it.

You see there is freedom in life. To me it is intangible, terrible, difficult but it exists. No matter what my circumstances I can in some way preserve my integrity. I can get out into an empty space. I must retain my desire to go into the emptiness if I am to be worthy to be among people.

It was cold and snowy last night and I went for a walk. I wandered into a district where I worked as a laborer nearly twenty years ago.[1] Uh. I shiver when I think of what I endured there. The foreman over me was a German. The superintendent understood I was a boy[2] and could not do any hard tasks. He gave me light tasks but when he had gone away the German gave me only heavy work.

I did not dare complain. It was a year of hard times and I knew of no other place where I could get work. The German sent me out on the lake front where the company was laying the foundation for a new warehouse. It was bitter cold and the wind blew the spray of the lake over us. With me it became a struggle of life and death. Every night I was proud to think I had not been overcome by the cold.

In the midst of it all I continued to dream. In some way I knew I would survive—say my say. How strange it is that in a life the purpose of which cannot be told there should be this idea of surviving.

I am thinking of American Art. It must remain crude to be American. The land is not sophisticated. As a man writes or works in any field of art endeavor he is likely to become less American. His very refinement stands in his way. To be a really characteristic American he should see things only in a rather big, blustering way.

This a man cannot continue to do. He becomes less self-assertive, he is more absorbed in the minute, delicate, less obvious things of life. Almost before he knows it the American Artist passes out of his purely American place. Look at Whistler and Henry James. I saw a statement the other day that these men did not dare face America.

That is not true. They simply progressed beyond American thought and American understanding. They entered into the world of Art that has no boundary lines.

I suppose Henry James took nothing of America with him. Whistler took a good deal. What lies to be done I suppose is to understand and see more and more intensely our life here.

There is no reason at all why Americanism should not be seen with the same intensity of feeling so characteristic of Russian Artists when they write of Russian life. Our life is as provincial. It is as full of strange and illuminating side lights. Because we have not written intensely is no reason why we should not begin.

Today I said something to you about friendship. It was didactic. I never write in this cock-sure didactic way but I am ashamed of it afterward.

I like the more intensive things I am trying to do now rather than attempts at long novels. They fit better into the life I am leading. They are more true to my present impulses. I am trying to make up my mind not to labor heroically but to drift with life, seeing and putting down what I can.

Out of that cry of yours in the letter regarding the two old people I have made a story that I call impotence.[3] Now that it is written I feel some delicacy about letting you see it. There is this trick of yours of taking things personally that makes me hesitate. For to take this story personally will hurt.

Without appearing to do so I have made the girl of the story the central figure. She lives in a house with her father, a tall, feeble quiet man. Back of these two figures that represent Impotence are the people who represent force. An old woman on whom they are dependent and a beggar she has picked up in the street.

Now let me explain. If you want to see the story I shall have to have an understan[d]ing with you first. There is something gone out of my Marie that has not gone out of you. You have a thousand thing[s] she has not. I could not bear to have this story taken as an interpretation of your life. That will have to be understood or I will tear it up and throw it to the winds.

I couldn't bear not to write the story. It had such tremendous possibilities.

TS

1. This coincides with other evidence that Anderson left Clyde for Chicago in 1896. Among other things, he did work on building a warehouse, a job not otherwise recorded.
2. That Anderson was twenty on Sept. 13, 1896, and had had many demanding jobs suggests an element of fiction in this account.
3. This story has not survived.

19

To Bab December 27, 1916 [Chicago]

There is something I want to talk to you about. Before bringing up the matter I have waited to be sure it was not simply a howl I send up because my toes are trod on. I refer to the inclination so universal among critics of fixing the label of one man on the back of another.

Take Dreiser and myself for example. There is a man who might have been my friend. He writes out of a desire that I understand. We might have been much to each other but now I grow weary of the name of Dreiser and I know he wearies of my name.[1]

And Dreiser and I are no more alike than I am like Lord Byron. We are both American boys. We came out of the middle west.[2] We went to live in a city. Both have felt keenly our American civilization and we both write from mood, from desire unsatisfied rather than from ambition to get our names up in the world.

The other day somewhere I heard quoted a saying of Anatol[e] France. "I do not read my contemporaries," he said. "Having lived in the same age with them I, of course, know what they think."

There is the whole story. We all, in this time, must think alike. We have come into an age of industrialism and we must try to understand the reaction of modern life to industrialism. Now why should not a critic also understand his age and keep asking the question. "How does this man fit within his age? How much does this man tell of the story that is to be told?"

As to the matter of the Russians. These men have made a fine art of prose. They have gone beyond anyone in that. Dostoievsky for example understood there was a meaning in combinations of words beyond the meaning of the words themselves. Gorky has a sense of the same thing and I have it. I have always had it. Why, when American life is written of with clearness and understanding need we always refer to the Russians?

I showed the story of "Impotence" to a critic. In a note to me he says. "A fine piece of writing but outlandish, horrible, infernally creepy and Russianly." I want to swear. Damn it! You know where I got this tale. I saw a certain old lady's eyes shine. I always wanted to write of her. Then you gave me the tale of the old man and the vermin and I invented Marie and the rest.

In regard to the matter—men and women, about which you talk. A woman came to me at a dinner party the other evening. She was hot on having me discuss this question with her.—Are women creatures of love etc. She leaned over me and talked. "My husband says women cannot be artists—["]

I didn't go far in the matter with her. In the first place her husband who talks of artists is no artist. He is a dilletante. Such men are to the arts what the glove-maker is to the prize fighter.

Now of course when we come to discuss this matter you must remember that every woman has a father and every man a mother. Is H.D.[3] a man or woman? What is M.G.[4] What the devil is a man and what is a woman.

Of course you have put on skirts or trousers. You have arranged the conventions of your life and most people live by conventions. The artist tears them away. Most assuredly women can be artists.

I shall always believe there is a test. M.G said to you, "If a woman can't have the one thing she has utterly lost out in the game." You haven't believed that or at least you have not yet surrendered to that idea. Now and then you do appeal to sympathy, demanding it because of your position in life, but for the most part you have dignity.

TS

1. One sign of Anderson's high regard for Theodore Dreiser was his dedication of *Horses and Men* (1923): "To THEODORE DREISER/ In whose presence I have sometimes had/ the same refreshed feeling as when in/ the presence of a thoroughbred horse."
2. Dreiser was from Indiana.
3. Probably Harriet Dean.
4. No further identification.

20

To Bab December 28, 1916 [Chicago]

I have had a succession of stupid days, when no thoughts came to me. Today I am a little more alive. I dined with B.H.[1] who talked at great length of words. He proclaims himself a devotee of style and wishes to make words do what they have never done before. The only trouble with B is that he does not realize that what he wishes all wish. He asks to be called a stylist and talked of dull grubbers among thoughts. As though one could not grub in as dull a way among words too. There is something beautiful about the vegetation of a tropical country. The flori, rank growing plants are magnificent. However one soon wearies of all the rank luxurious things and if B is devoted solely to words we will grow weary of him also.

T[ennessee] has brought me a book by Dostoievsky called "A Raw Youth." It is only a trifle less wonderful than his "The Idiot."[2] Get it and read it. There is one chapter where he explains the idea of becoming another Rothchild that is about the most wonderful and illuminating piece of prose writing I have ever read. It is lyrical in its terrible clearness.[3]

TS

1. Probably Ben Hecht (1893–1964), who was a part of the Chicago scene and whom Anderson knew well. See Hecht's *A Child of the Century* (New York: New American Library, 1954).

2. A translation of *The Idiot* by Constance Garnett had been published in July and Oct. 1913 and in Nov. 1915.

3. Chapter V of Part I of *A Raw Youth*, the fictionalized autobiography of a writer, deals with the narrator's idea that he will become as rich as a Rothschild and discusses the fundamental problem of maintaining discipline in devotion to a great personal aim. Predictably, this would arouse a response in a man like Anderson, who felt within himself the struggle between conventional economic endeavor and personal indulgence in artistic activity and who would find an important outlet in fictionalized autobiography (*Tar, A Story-Teller's Story,* and *Sherwood Anderson's Memoirs*). References like this one are important contributions in understanding the relationship of Anderson's work to that of Fëdor Mikhailovich Dostoevski and other Russian writers.

21

To Bab Circa January 4, 1917 [Chicago]

The attached is a fair specimen of the sort of thing a writer meets constantly. This woman gave Windy[1] a lauditory notice in a newspaper and I wrote to thank her. She came back at me with a letter about herself and her work. She had given her copy of Windy to a friend so I sent her another and a copy of Seven Arts.[2]

And now, ye gods, she wants to give me advice as to how and what to write. She lives in America in these intense times and would like to have me write like Dickens and Hardy.

Why can't people understand that to remain at all pure one has to give themselves always to the mood of himself and his time. Hardy did his work and Dickens his. It is for Sherwood Anderson to try like hell to do his own work.

I shall say so to the lady. Not that it makes any difference at all but reassertion always helps.

You said you sometimes hungered for vulgarity. Here is my "Doctor." You will find it vulgar but there is something else in it too. Do you not think so?———

Enclosure Hollywood, Cal. Jan 4, 1917

Mr. Sherwood Anderson,

Dear Mr. Anderson; Thank you heartily for the copy of "Windy McPherson's Son," which I shall bring with me to Chicago that you may sign it to make it more valuable.

"The Seven Arts Magazine" reached me duly and I read your story. As you had preceded it with the comment that is is a fair specimen of the work you are doing at present, I took it up with considerable interest, for it is not an insignificant item in the general welfare when a writer avowedly changes his point of view. I miss in "Queer" the human touch which vivified "Windy."[3] It seems to belong to the school of realism which limns with a fierce, almost resentful brush, the harsher side of living, without that shading of idealism that is the saving grace or "atmosphere" of trite experience. Your tales will be read eagerly by the young American; they rank among the sketches that have been given the title "Futurist," because they lack any romance of the past. But this one—I hope the others are less cruel—leave[s] with the reader the same distaste for life, the same bitter, despairing and half mocking regrets that are invoked by

Russian stories. Heaven preserve our precious American literature from the Slavic influence! Think, Mr. Anderson, while there is time, whether you wish, with your strong talent to join the army of cynics. Literature is not a vehicle of personal expression, to be twisted to our moods or transient needs. Literature is all of life; hope, faith, love, suffering, patience, patriotism and parenthood. Whoever puts pen to paper without being swayed, perhaps unconsciously, by the belief that what he is doing, be it the smallest infinitesmal act, will join the wave of good or the wave of ill, which moves to and fro, has not the right conception of his responsibility. You did not ask me for sermons, and I would apologize if there was the least personal element in what I say. But I am large enough, and trust you are, to talk about things and the feelings which are merely another form of things, with sincerity.

Have you read Thomas Hardy's "The Mayor of Casterbridge"? The most remarkable recital of manly suffering and displaced ambition that any modern writer has given out. Yet the story is so thrilled with sentiment, with that deep inner current of sympathy which softens realism, that one cherishes the remembrance of it as one lays in safety a beautiful flower. It was this divine sympathy that makes Dickens immortal; the genius who never learned his art, but who knew how to speak to the hearts of men.

I am sorry that you misapprehended my reference to my personal literary experiences. I have never made my living by my pen; nor done "hack work." Dying were an easy choice when the alternative is prostitution of what one loves.

I extend to you the cordial hand of fellowship in the work we are both pledged to do for the world, and add best wishes of the Season.

Yours sincerely,

/S/ Florence Winterburn[4]

Enclosure

The Doctor.[5]

He was an old man and sat on the steps of the railroad station in a small Kentucky Town. A well-dressed man, some traveler from the city approached him and stood beside him. The old man became self-conscious. His face was all sunken and wrinkled and he had a high nose. His smile was like the smile of a very young child.

"Have you any coughs, colds, consumption or bleeding piles?" he asked. In his voice there was a pleading quality.

The stranger shook his head.

The old man arose. "The piles protrude from the rectum," he said. His tongue protruded from between his teeth and he rattled it about. He put his hand on the stranger's arm and laughed. "Bully. Pretty," he exclaimed. "I cure them all, coughs, colds, consumption and the piles that protrude. I take warts off the hand. I cannot explain how I do it. It is a mystery. I change nothing. My name is Tom. Do you like me?"

The stranger was cordial. He nodded his head. The old man became reminiscent.

"My father was a hard man," he declared. "He was like me, a blacksmith by trade but he wore a plug hat. When the corn was high he said to the poor, 'Go into the fields and pick' but when the War came he made a rich man pay five dollars for a bushel of corn."

["]I married against his will. He came to me and he said. 'Tom, I do not like that girl' 'but I love her,' I said. 'I don't' he said.

"My father and I sat on a log. He was a pretty man and wore a plug hat. 'I will get the license' I said. 'I will give you no money' he said.

"The license cost me twenty-one dollars. I worked in the corn. It rained and the horses were blind. The clerk said, 'are you over twenty-one?' I said 'yea' and she said 'yes[']. We had chalked it on our shoes. My father said 'I give you your freedom.' We had no money. The license cost twenty-one dollars. She is dead."

The old man looked at the sky. It was evening and the sun had set. The sky was all mottled with grey clouds. "I paint beautiful pictures and give them away," he declared. "My brother is in the penitentiary. He killed the man who called him a son of a bitch."

He held his hands before the face of the stranger. He opened and shut them. They were black with grime. "I pick out warts," he explained plaintively. "They are as soft as your hands. I play on an accordion. You are thirty-seven. I sat beside my brother in the penitentiary. He is a pretty man with pompadour hair. 'Albert' I said, 'are you sorry you killed a man?' 'No' he said, 'I am not sorry. I would kill ten, a hundred, a thousand.' "

The old man began to weep and to wipe his eyes with a soiled handkerchief. He attempted to take a chew of tobacco and his false teeth became displaced. He covered his mouth with his hand and was ashamed. "I am old. You are thirty-seven but I am old," he whispered. "My brother is a bad man. He is full of hate. He is pretty and has pompadour hair but he would kill and kill. I hate old age. I am ashamed that I am old."

"I have a pretty new wife. I wrote her four letters and she replied. She came here and we married. I love to see her walk. Oh, I buy her pretty clothes. Her foot is not straight. It is twisted. My first wife is dead. I pick warts off the hands with my fingers and no blood comes. I cure coughs, colds, consumption and bleeding piles. People can write to me and I answer them. If they send me no money it is no matter. All is free."

Again the old man wept and the stranger tried to comfort him. "You are a happy man?" the stranger asked. "Yes" said the old man, "and a good man too. Ask everywhere about me. My name is Tom, a blacksmith. My wife walks prettily although she has a twisted foot. I have bought a long dress. She is thirty and I am seventy-five. She has many pairs of shoes. I have bought them for her but her foot is twisted. I buy straight shoes. She thinks I do not know. Everybody thinks that Tom does not know. I have bought her a long dress that comes to the ground. My name is Tom, a blacksmith. I am seventy-five and I hate old age. I take warts off the hands and no blood comes. People may write to me and I answer. All is free."

TS

1. *Windy McPherson's Son,* Anderson's first published novel. The review has not survived.

2. An eastern literary magazine that attempted to give form and direction to newly wakened creative forces. It produced twelve issues from Nov. 1916 to Oct. 1917, losing its sponsor because it opposed the participation of the United States in World War I. The relationships Anderson formed through his connection with it were most important to his artistic development. Anderson wrote in a letter of Dec. 1940 to Ilse Dusoir that he was "deeply in accord with the magazine's anti-war policy." Noting that the magazine came out in a time he considered of "general awakening," providing an inspiration toward which writers could turn, he recalled, "I still look back to the effort made and to the men who made it with the most sincere respect." This letter is at the Newberry Library.

3. "Queer" was published in *Seven Arts* for Dec. 1916.

4. So far, no further record of Florence Winterburn has been found.

5. Published under the title of "Senility" in *The Triumph of the Egg* (1921).

22

To Bab — Thursday, January 8, 1917 [Chicago]

I somehow feel these days as though I were drifting toward some new and to me, strange adventure with life. Whenever I am not actually engaged in the affair of making a living my mind goes off to country roads, to strange towns and villages. I dramatize myself as a solitary figure tramping, tramping—tramping and waiting.

In my dreams the figures of those I love recede into the distance. I am sitting on a decaying log in a forest. I am alone in a little valley where someone has been cutting trees. I am in a boat on a stream at night.

All of those I have come to love are far off. Their beauty and the beauty of the fact that they love me becomes enhanced.

— — — — — —

I sat in a hotel room yesterday trying to talk with a man who was once my friend. He wanted to talk of the relation of men and women and so I talked with him on that subject. How difficult it was. All the subtleties and shades of things were broken down. His mind, like the minds of most men had only grasped, and crudely, the conception of the possible beauty of woman as the bearer of gifts. He could not express, he could not begin to understand the possible beauty of himself.

My efforts to convey that thought to him got me muddled in words. I floundered about. I was more ashamed of my inability than I was of his stupidity.

It began to snow and my low Ohio hills are all bare. The cattle stand starkly out against the skyline. I am tired and glad I am going away. Perhaps the week of play will give me new strength.

TS

23

To Bab January 8, 1917 [Chicago]

In all the world there is nothing so sad as human relationships that have been ruined by a too quick and eager grasping at some immediate thing. Today in the bright sunshine I have been walking about thinking of two old friendships, now quite ruined. My thoughts have been so sad that I have been almost ill.

The first of these was with a woman from a country town. I won't go into details as to how I met her but we became friends. She had a husband in her own place and they were engaged in business. She came here to buy goods but she was interested also in books. After her work was done she used to meet me and we spent hours together. The little details of her business interested me. I liked her homely absorption in details and her earnestness about things I did not think mattered. I talked to her of my own affairs, of my dreams and hopes. There was, I suppose, on her part, something clandestine about all this but it was delightful.

Another woman I knew was Englsich and very small and delicate. She was in a way the most intense person I have ever known. After seven years of not seeing her how sharply she still stands forth in my mind.

And this woman also became my friend. She had a lover somewhere in

England and often talked to me of him. We used to go away to the parks together in the evening. When it rained and was dark we ran along shouting and laughing. We wrestled and threw each other down on the wet grass.

With both of these women I was finally swept into affairs more intimate. In both cases that came about swiftly, quickly, without premeditation.

And afterward when we tried to resume the old life, to be quite simple and innocently friends we could not be. I don't know why. We were not really lovers. We had betrayed each other. For a while we tried to go on in a forced, self-conscious way but it would not work.

To-day I walked and thought of them. One hates things that end so. I was sad, half-sick with sadness.

TS

24

To Bab — January 12, 1917 [Chicago]

The possibilities of my new book grow in my mind. In it I hope to strike away from the two scenes that have been characteristic in my books—the village and then this great western city. In this book I will stay in the small place. Factories come to Winesburg, Ohio.[1] Beginning in the life of John Hardy the town becomes an industrial center. It grows into a small city. Life there will be much what it is in Canton or Columbus, Ohio—in Toledo or even in Indianapolis. After the hurried transition from an agricultural to an industrial community the children of the next generation come in. They go away to school and come back. Young men grow up who have crudely the idea of a family. Something is trying to get itself established. There is a crude vague reaching out for culture.

In this period Tom Hardy son of John Hardy a banker and industrial leader spends his life. He goes away and comes back. He falls in love and is married. He is divorced and [has] adventures. And all the time he is striving, hoping, hungering, wanting.

That is the background of my new book. In it I hope to strike at the terrible immaturity and crudeness of all our lives. Back of it I hope to get a background of love. The theme is varied, it is intense and real. I appreciate it and approach it humbly and hopefully. As always when I come to a new book I am like a boy gone to live in a strange town. I walk through the streets seeing the people, wandering who will be my friends. I am shy and afraid. At night I do not want to sleep but to think. My life here can mean so much or so little. I am in love with the possibilities of my life in this new place and afraid too.[2]

— — — — — —

You perhaps know this feeling of being a guest. At times it takes a strong hold of me. I am a guest in the life of Cornelia, of Tennessee, of George,[3] you, M. Curry,[4] John,[5] a hundred people. In marriage I am a guest and in love too.

I cannot conceive of myself as permanently anything. The thought is in some way unbearable. I suppose some wandering spirit of the night touched me in the cradle.

It is inconceivable how vivid this impression is. I never go into Tennessee's house but I go a little timidly, questioning.[6] I want to know how I am to be received. If ever I find her in the faintest way not wanting me I shall surely run away. It is so when I come to see you. You think me strong and sure. Outwardly I am. Inwardly I often quake hard enough. I am afraid you won't like me. I am afraid no one will like me. I have had thoughts and feelings you know nothing about. To me they are very real and vivid. I am sure they have left marks on me.

When will I learn to take for granted the general obtuseness of the world. Sometimes I wonder I have not been one who goes about robbing and killing. Surely no one would know. I might do a thousand things quite boldly.

I shall never forget a quite childish thing in the life of C[ornelia] and myself. Just because I was married to her when I did not want to be I imagined terrible things about her. It did not seem to me possible to escape out of marriage into life. I pictured her as my jailer and terrible hate woke in me. At night I even dreamed of killing her.

And all the time I suppose I was a quite normal, quiet-appearing fellow. I used to walk out of the house into the street at night and say to myself. "Great God, she don't know."

And of course, dear patient woman, she did not know. No one can know what they have not themselves felt. Only by feeling do we come into knowledge and I suspect that it is only by feeling deeply, deeply that we shall come to culture.[6]

TS

1. He had apparently begun to use this name in 1915 for the locale of what he called "a series of intensive studies of people of my home town, Clyde, Ohio." In a letter dated Nov. 14, 1916 (to Waldo Frank of *Seven Arts*) he gives no indication that he was aware that he was borrowing the name of a town in north central

Ohio. Howard Mumford Jones and Walter B. Rideout, eds., *Letters of Sherwood Anderson* (Boston: Little, Brown and Co., 1953), pp. 4–5.

2. Anderson did not complete this book.

3. Daugherty.

4. Wife of Floyd Dell.

5. Probably John Emerson (originally Clifford or Clifton Paden of Clyde), a life-long friend.

6. Sherwood and Tennessee maintained separate residences; he had his room on Cass Street and later a small rented house at Palos Park, Ill. She had her own apartment.

7. The evidence is that Cornelia understood Sherwood's ambitions rather well. In 1946 she said, "I still think he did the right thing" to give up his family for his artistic work and life. Sutton, *Road to Winesburg*, p. 236.

25

To Bab — January, 14, 1917 [Chicago]

How old things pass. It is Sunday and I am alone in my room with the curtains drawn. Here only two winters ago I began for the first time to live among people devoted to the arts. Our lives together did not work out but for a time how broken out with life the place was. In the next room Mary lived. Down the hall-way were Herman and little Max Grove. Max Wald was in the next room. Then came the end room with Betty and two others I have forgotten. The one was the mannish creature who was fat and used to put on a man's suit and wait for Mary in the hall. She had great breasts and looked very funny in the man's clothes.[1]

Betty of course was courting Herman in those days. Max with whom he roomed went off to work in a railroad office at seven and one would hear Betty's little feet pattering down the hall. She went to lie in bed with him for an hour and sometimes the hour extended all through the morning. I took it for granted they were lovers and mentioned the matter casually in conversation with Mary.

And after all it seems they were not. Everybody was half starved and poorly fed and Herman was a mystic and no doubt in reality an intermediate. They merely wanted to lie close to each other, to be warmed a little by the faint heat of their sensuality.

I suppose poor Betty was different. She nearly died of it before they were finally married and passed on into something else.

I must find a name for the lady of the fish-hooks and the man's clothes. She was in love with Mary and suffered horribly. She used to come into my room and smoke and talk. In a way she was the most downright honest creature I ever knew. Nothing was too blunt and sharp for her to hear and if her love was an unnatural thing it was a strong positive thing too. She would have fought and died for it I am convinced.

I took her to dinner once in a fashionable restaurant. How funny she was. When I went for her I found her rigged out in a great feathered hat and she had on a terribly tight-fitting corset and high-heeled shoes. Poor child, she thought that was the way things were done. She wanted me not to be ashamed of her but she looked like the keeper of a house of ill fame. I wanted to laugh and to cry too.

And Max Wald. I wonder how well you know him. He is a study in tenseness; a violin string drawn tight so long that nothing but shrill high tones can come from him. There is nothing of my man of the corn fields about him. He also fell in love with Mary and how tragically. He used to stand for hours, tensely in the hall while she laughed or talked with me or with someone else. I think he was capable of murder then. For years he had been a musician, striving to make a name for himself as the writer of delicate, beautiful little songs. He threw it all overboard and began to write an opera—something between ragtime and Wagner. He had dreams of becoming the author of another Floradora and becoming fabulously wealthy. Mary was the beautiful lady in the castle. He would be the knight coming out of the west, astride a great horse, and followed by a long train of slaves, bearing jewels and perfumes and silks.

In the house then to dream a thing was to have it become an actuality. Every one had a dream and talked of it as though it were a fact already achieved. In the evening the house reeked of dreams. Max played over and over the songs from his opera, putting in and taking out notes. One could hear the tramp of the camels and the horses and elephants coming softly through deep sand, bringing the treasure to lay at the feet of Mary.

Little Max Grove fell in love with Betty's sister who came on a visit from a place in Indiana. She was a country school teacher. I used to see him coming up the stairs bearing a rose, held before him as a priest would hold the sacrament. He came occasionally to typewrite for me on Sunday mornings and once when I brutally, and not understanding, kept him steadily at work for two hours he fainted. He was meagerly paid and I suspect partially supported Betty and Herman. There was much pride among them. Such things were whispered but not talked about aloud. I was to them a rich, capable, masculine thing—heavy and dangerous. Poor little shadows!

Mary was the deep cause of misunderstanding between us. She was lovely then—the born courtesan in her first beauty and come out of innocent places. She understood me, the hard working, rather stupid, grinding producing artist. She understood them and their shadow world.

She had a life of her own and she could enter into the dark passions of the lady of the fishhooks.

I have put Mary out of my door now and I hope she never comes in again. She is losing understanding, demanding the price demanded by the working courtesan. Then she could come to my door[,] knock softly[,] enter, and stand poised, just for a moment, in the deep shadows at the other side of the room, the loveliest thing imaginable.

How really beautiful she was. It wasn't physical beauty. It was instead something that cannot endure, something transitory, impossible. Life had to catch and destroy her. She had to destroy herself.

And now I must stop talking of old things and go back to my grinding work. Max still clings to the place. He has become a little less tight but is becoming bald. Again he works at the beautiful, delicate songs. The place has become slipshod and it is hard to keep alive the spirit of my room. Presently I shall move away.

And I have not told you of the tall womanish man who joined the British army or of Fedja, the strange, the dead thing who came here to live and who did actually die but I must go back to my work. Good-bye for now.

TS

1. The people mentioned in this letter are not otherwise identified.

26

To Mrs. F. H. Winterburn — Monday, January Fifteen, Nineteen Seventeen [Chicago]

Your letter sent recently has puzzled me a lot. It is so characteristic of something through which I had to think my way long ago. Really to my way of thinking you have expressed—in a gentle and courteous way to be sure—the words that have been on the lips of every man who has influenced badly the growth of real art in America in our times.

Well what a horrible accusation to bring against a perfectly innocent woman. I will amplify. I am interested in the matter in a quite impersonal way.

In the earlier days of my experience as a writer I of course saw things in a broad rather optimistic way and wrote so.[1] That was natural. It expressed the youth and the hope and the belief in me.

But I couldn't write always in one vein. I am not a writer at all in the sense of wanting to do people good or teach a moral lesson, or to point the way of life. Least, oh least of all, am I a writer in the heavy terrible sense of thinking my words important or significant. If I had that vulgar conceit in me I swear by the Gods I would not live with this Sherwood Anderson but would shoot him and throw him on a convenient ash heap forthwith.

Let me explain a little why I write. God made me in my youth a terrible liar and braggard and filled me with nameless pride of little things. I fooled, cheated and lied concerning everything. Myself I cheated, and fooled most of all. All of this brought me finally to the point of insanity.[2] I distrusted myself and everyone else.

And then I began to write and found sweetness in that.[3] With pencil and paper before me I did not lie, could not lie. So I wrote then and I write now for myself alone. If the world will take what I have done and like it, if they will even give me bread and a warm place to sleep for the reading of my writing all very well. I shall be glad enough God knows.

Now let me get this clear. I have a room here in Chicago where I work. The room is like a temple into which I go to worship. I go alone. I want to be alone there. Even art may go to the devil for all I care. There is something within me I want to keep alive, something that for years was dying. Writing helps me more than anything to creep close to the thing.

And you would have me write after the manner of Hardy or Dickens. Why? I don't understand. I do not write for you or for those who like Hardy or Dickens. I write that Sherwood Anderson may live, that he may continue a little to live. Those men you mention had no doubt the same desire. I honor them but I cannot work as they worked.

It is inevitable I suppose that people who like some of my work will not like the rest. I have never written two books in the same mood. I hope never to do so.

Now I write intensively. I see life so and I express it. I have lost hope in the broad foundation of things and turn to the intensive human things.

That is natural. To my mind it is inevitable to one who opens himself to life. We are in the midst of the terrible age of industrialism. If for beauty I, who live in this ugly, ill-smelling Chicago must go into the past, if I must write of old times and places then I am not a man of my times.

I embrace my times. I go with my own people. If they are ugly I shall be ugly. I shall strive for the tortured and trusted beauty of my own time and place. And for this I am called Russian, I who came out of a even [ever] growing town in Ohio. Before I had even read a Russian book that accusation was thrown at me. As though life here and in the villages of our land could not also be intensified.

I don't protest but I wont change, dear friend. I have my own vision and I will follow it. If it brings me only to misunderstanding what odds.

Have I not still the room where I can go and be quiet? Have I not still to gain humbleness and devotion? Am I to become one who takes himself seriously and talks of his work as though it were the manna of Heaven instead of just the scribbling of one poor twisted human in the midst of a world of twisted ones.[4]

TS

1. For an account of the material Anderson wrote for the house organ of the advertising agency for which he worked in Chicago between 1900-1906, see Sutton, *Road to Winesburg*, ch. 6.
2. This sentence counterbalances Anderson's occasional claims that his amnesia attack in Ohio was feigned.
3. He had apparently been writing for about two years before having amnesia, having written drafts of *Windy McPherson's Son* and *Marching Men*.
4. The "grotesques" of *Winesburg, Ohio*.

27

To Bab January 16, 1917 [Chicago]

I went out into a madness of snow. It whirled and flew about me. I went down to the lake shore where the ice creaked and groaned. There I ran and danced till I was weary. It was black dark. The air was filled with the mad confusion of snow flakes. I took off my hat and let the snow gather on my hair. It melted and ran down my neck. The cold of it was delicious.

Out of the air my mind caught a thought. I went soberly along. The thought concerns your life and mine.

You have a balance to keep just as I have. The emphasis put on conventionality and restriction by the nature of your life has led to an over-emphasis of the beauty of indulgence. That is your danger, that you will dramatize too vividly that side of life.

With me it is quite different. Nothing has ever restricted me. I have to make my own restrictions. I have done so fiercely and determinedly. The result has been perhaps an over-emphasis and over-dramatization of the beauties of restriction.

What is aimed at is purity. Lust may be pure and the life of a monk on the hillside may be pure. To gain and hold purity in the midst of modern life is terribly hard.

One only succeeds occasionally, at odd moments, when one writes fervently, when [one] runs in the snow, when pure physical love finds natural expression, when one maintains friends in the midst of difficulty and misunderstanding.

This is the sort of thing I felt as I tramped heavily along in the snow. "I have a rendezvous with purity," I said to myself as I went along through the darkness.

TS

28

To Bab January 17, 1917 [Chicago]

I think what your mind had stuck upon was the relation between religion and art. There is something horrible about the producing artist. He wants to produce too much. All of his fine emotions run out into stories or poems or love affairs with ladies. He cannot respect a fine emotion for its own worth. Presently he loses the power to embrace a fine emotion, struggle with it in the night. He cannot weep and pray and walk alone. To his room he must run and to his everlasting pencil and paper and tell of his emotions or he must go to his lady and talk of them.

What horrible poverty. What cowardice that in the arts we have not the courage to wait and sing in low, silent places, to submerge ourselves and die unheard.

There is something terrible in this madness for the created thing, so universal here in America. I am sick at heart when I realize what a grip it has on me too.

I imagine your own mind has been grappling with this thought and that it turned for relief to the figure of Jesus walking alone by the shores of the sea. How strong and true and virile that figure. He only, of all men deserves our complete love. He only dared to let his soul grow, asking no reward, seeking none of our silly modern goals, money, comfort, fame, an established place in a distorted world.

I understand, dear woman, our love for the figure of Jesus. He alone is the master artist.

And we have to learn here in America that art is the great, the true religion. It alone satisfies. Humbleness must in some way come to us. I am ashamed that I babble. I am ashamed that I do not slip away alone into the unknown; that I do not let more fine emotions pass through me and expire unexpressed.

TS

29

To Bab January 19, 1917 [Chicago]

I have to stop reading your letter to write down this comment. You say, "You have never known what it is to give things up, have you? ["]

What a strange question. Don't you know that is is you [who] do not give things up[?] You let them be taken from you. Cry back to the Bently physical attitude. "Let Go."[1] Sometime I shall become a God, a new John the Baptist crying in the wilderness and the burden of my cry shall be, "Let go. For God's sake, let go!"

And now I have read your whole letter and that cry still rings in my head. "Let go. Let go."

It is always in such letters that you are smallest. Reading one of them is like turning a telescope around. You run far away into the distance and become small, small.

You pervert and distort words. Friendship, you say, as though I want the word for some cold formal thing. It can contain and embrace everything. I would not live with any woman who was not first my friend. Anything else would be unbearable.

My head rings with words. "Love god. Be Humble. Stand at Attention."

Man is made in the image of God and should have dignity. It is not true—the horrible picture you draw of me. A God to whom gifts are brought.

Do you not know, will you not see that every word I have ever written that has any semblance of truth and beauty has been wrung from me. I have walked weeping through the streets, been cold and hungry and alone. If I did not feel in myself the ability to do that again, tomorrow then I should know my race was run and I would never again write a worthy word.

I am impatient with this endless reiteration of an old illusion of youth. You are as bad as M.G. You believe things are done by a trick—that things are given to some and taken from others. You want life cheap—at half price.

This way ladies. January sales of love and friendship and Truth. To be sold quick to make way for the new spring assortment of goods—see other page for advertisement of the new love, the new friendship, the new truth. Styles to fit the whims of all—Sold.

Cheap. Cheap. Cheap.

This morning I walked to work saying words. Like Whitman I gloried in words. Ohio, Illinois, Kalamazoo, Keoku[k], Tennessee, Missouri. I thought how beauty had lived on here in the face of industrialism and made a foundation for beauty.

Some day the strong race will come. Men will suffer and be unafraid. I went along praying. "My destiny is new," I said to myself. "I can believe in beauty in the midst of this hubbub. Down the wind comes the call of the new men. It plays in the corn, in my corn, in the long corn fields.["]

The corn fields shall be the mothers of men. They are rich with milk to suckle men. They will come sturdy and strong out of the west. You may prick them with spears. Their blood will run out on the snow but they are my men and shall survive.

I am a little child and I weep. My hands are cold. I run along and blow upon them. But in me is the blood of strong men. A little I have endured and shall endure. I am of the blood of strong men. The milk of the corn is in me too.

Sweet, sweet the thought of new men. I am cold and run through the streets. Sweet, sweet, the thought of new men.[2]

TS

1. Finley knew of the Alys Bentley eurythmics camp at Lake Chateaugay, N.Y., near where Anderson pitched his tent on summer visits and with whose personnel he was friendly. Tennessee Mitchell was also quite interested in such matters.

2. The last three paragraphs of this letter are, with very few changes, the text of the poem, "Hosanna"; see Anderson's *Mid-American Chants* (New York: John Lane Co., 1918), p. 67. He had not yet mentioned to Finley that he was writing poetry.

30

To Bab January 19, 1917 [Chicago]

Masculinity.

He lay on his back in a dentist chair. The chair was in a long hall. There were many curtains. He was young and strong and he laughed. He threw back his head and laughed.

From behind the curtains, one by one, came women. They crept along the floor, creeping slowly. Each in her turn arose and stood beside the chair. Her eyes shone and she kissed him.

He slapped each of the women with his hand, a ringing blow that echoes through the long hall. Then he laughed. Back he lay in the dentist's chair and laughed. The many curtains of the room trembled and more women, naked, with shining eyes came creeping, creeping.

He slapped them with his hand, a ringing slap. Then he lay back in the chair and laughed. "It has always been so," he said. "It will always be so."
Then again he laughed.

TS

31

To Bab January 22, 1917 [Chicago]

I have had two days of real illness. Out of it has grown an odd notion, that people I like very much are likely to overtax me. I get them so keenly that it does me up.

On Friday I went to lunch with a working woman here. She came from a little Indiana town and has been successful in the city. I know her brother well. He is one of my business associates. The woman to whom I refer is trained in meeting people. It is my fault that I cannot be with such a person and spend the time quietly, talking of minor things.

It is not so with me. Either I close the door altogether or else I open it wide, take the new person into my very inner consciousness. I come out from such a talk feeling that I know the inner soul of the person to whom I have been talking but I am tired, tired. My mind has groped and delved into their inner thing. I feel like one who has been running for a long time.

It was that way after my talk with the woman Friday and then Sunday I saw another woman at a luncheon. She was in a group of people and I only talked to her casually. But I watched her intensely. I began to imagine and feel her reactions to life. At night my mind went on and I dreamed of her. A thousand little things I found out but I am tired. My searching has made me tired. There is something distinctive in the desire I so often have to end by being half a hermit. I may do that yet.

TS

32

To Bab January 26, 1917 [Chicago]

Greyness is so normal a condition of the human soul that to be oblivious to it would be blindness. For weeks my own mood has been grey. I have been tired and my moods have not been sustained. For me not to be lifted out of myself is always to sink into a grey state in which I see and feel all of the ugliness of life. At such times I have no faith in people. Life is old and grey for me.

I cannot be blind to the ugliness of my own life and so I know that these moods have their seat in me but what am I—a son of my times, a product of the grey ugly industrialism of my times.

Last night I sat in a room in a hotel in Minneapolis with two men. The first was short and fat. He had a wart on the nose and a peculiar soft, child-like smile. The second man was lean and hard. His eyes were clear blue. He knows how to make money, is absorbed, is oblivious to everything else in life.

The two men are both employed by an industrial leader of the northwest. They came to consult me about various shrewd projects the man has on foot. These men are to handle the publicity; to state the big man's projects to the people. They came to me to be told how to do it cleverly, with apparent frankness and honesty.

We talked until my train left at ten o'clock and my soul was sick. I have no conscience in such matters. The right and wrong of the matter does not bother me at all. We are after all nothing but grey thieves, rats that live in a great barn but the deadly monotony of the thing wearies me terribly.

Now I am back in town with Tennessee here and things are better. I do not dare approach too close to her, make her too close a part of my life because I do not want to take into her life my greyness but to be where she is means everything.

And even this is misunderstood. I live away from this woman I have married. I go often to walk alone, to be alone. This also is misunderstood. Rumors run about. The woman is condemned because of the loneliness of my life. She is made to seem hard, cruel and indifferent when she is only big. No want of mine is left unsatisfied. In her love she, like others, is willing to give all. I will not take it. Often I shut the door and go away. And she is condemned for that.

These rumors float in to me. In the great barn the rats run over the floor. They squeal and cry out. I strive to separate myself—to know and not yet to be destroyed.

It does not matter—that I know. I shall go walk out of doors.

The Nation for Jan 11 had a wonderful review of my book. There was also one by Hackett in this week's New Republic.[1]

TS

1. The reviews were for *Windy McPherson's Son;* the one in the *Nation* (Jan. 11, 1917) was unsigned, the one in the *New Republic* (Jan. 20, 1917) was by Francis Hackett.

33

To Bab January 28, 1917 [Chicago]

It is hard to express what your letter meant. It did not hurt me. Shut up. Your jaw is flapping up and down. There is a cat on the chair behind you. He will scratch your back.

If you are not careful you will become a fine aristocrat and I will take off my hat when I see you on the street. I will, I swear I will. The terrible vulgarity of thinking your fate a hard one is going away from you. It is running out at your finger ends. Here take my handkerchief. Wipe your little paws.

Poof, poof, with H.D. Of course she fights. She is a Bob Fitsimmons among ladies.

"Go in, old Dean. Kick conventionality in the slats. Black its eye. Good, good. Hit it again old Top. Hurraw."

You are a woman and not a woman. It is morning. The wind blows. What do you care who walks with you? Wait. We all want to go along. I knew you were not just a woman. No woman walks off like that, ready to do it alone, rather preferring to do it alone.

Do you know what women are like? They are like authors who have had books published and had reviews written.[1] They are successful things and smell bad. They are dead things and have begun to decay. Here is my handkerchief. Wipe your hands again.

I have fallen in love with you and H.D. Only one thing. Don't get a wicked look in your eye like that old grandmother. Please don't. I'll be afraid of you.

And oh woman, I like you. You are getting to be a brick, a brick.

TS

1. H. W. Boynton wrote in the Jan. 1917 issue of *Bookman* that *Windy McPherson's Son* was one of ten novels published in 1916 that had "left the greatest impression" in his mind.

34

To Bab January, 1917[1] [Chicago before January 31, 1917]

The thing is lost and found, understood and not understood. I cannot keep it clear and I have come to think it cannot be kept clear. But the sweetness of life depends upon finding and holding it—the love without price. Mary[2] had a sense of it once but later she lost it and her beauty faded. The trouble lay in the fact that she asked others to give, got in the habit of asking others to give. When she was asked to give she could not. Whether or not I can stand the test I dont know. My time is coming some day when that will be asked of me. Then will come my test.

As for you, you have had to give and give. You begin to see point in senseless giving. You get beauty from that. I will not talk about it but it is splendid, what you are learning to do.

My new novel will really move. [Mrs. Hahn's note in left margin: Partly *Ohio Pagans*.] I have a splendid sense of grip on it. The theme is broad[,] real, sturdy. It is my kind of theme. I shall call the book immaturity. Did I tell you the story, how the boy by a peculiar combination of circumstances finds himself charged with personating American culture. The boy has money, he has imagination, he is really an artist at heart. The story will concern itself with the story of a quest. Many people will drift in and out. I shall try to express somehow the terrible immaturity of America.

I sent you a copy of Windy for the Liberal Club.[3] I dont want to thrust the book on them but if they will take it as the beginning of a library I shall be pleased.

The walk along under the trees meant much to me. I found something big in it. Also I learned much. Without realizing it you are constantly turning aside a curtain for me. I have myself been so much a child of the open that I have not realized the story of shut-in lives. You are teaching me that story. It is full of drama and interest. Bless you for that. I am hungry to learn.

LH

1. Hahn had added the date in longhand.
2. Anderson is referring to Mary Cochran, the main character in a manuscript by that title.
3. No trace of this Indianapolis club has yet been found.

35

To Bab January 1917[1] [Chicago before January 31, 1917]

Everything is a challenge. One steps on and on. At your house I was really ill and uncomfortable but I got you and your difficulties better than I ever have.

And I had the terrible feeling that I was making things more difficult for you.

Now I must hasten to write. Perhaps even these letters going to you may help to make your life now more difficult. It [word partly obscured] is wicked that is [so] but I want to help you by accepting it. Shall I quit writing to you? Tell me what to do.

And do not be afraid that you will loose my regard if this is necessary. There is a kind of blessing in being your friend. I dont do it gracefully or well but I understand your fine spirit in trying to meet and do your own job. I do accept you in that. I believe in your victory.

Oh I went away last night feeling you in the grip of a sense of defeat. It hurt me to go. If only out of my experience I can convey to you this—that defeat always comes—it is a part of the march of things. That sounds like a platitude but it is true, true, true.[2]

LH

1. Hahn's longhand note.
2. The bottom of the page on which this letter was written has been torn away, leaving only part of three upright and slightly slanted lines. They suggest a signature and are in the right location, but they do not seem to coincide with what would normally have been Anderson's signature.

36

To Bab January 31, 1917 [Chicago]

Last night I sensed something in Indianapolis. Oh, there is a smashing book to be written about your town. A stranger will come and do it. Look out for a short, plump man with a big voice. He wears square toed shoes and has an old leather cap. He walks round and round thump, thump. He is on to you, oh he is on to you. Look out for him. He has a room in an unpainted house and there is a well in the back yard. He will write a book concerning you. Look out for him.

TS

37

To Harriet Dean[1] January 31, 1917 [Chicago]

Brooks article in Seven Arts[2] may have somewhat a technical sound but he got to the point and expressed something we have very much got to learn. What he wanted to say and what I wanted to say is that one doesn't have to be a producing artist to justify himself to himself.[3]

In my own secret heart it doesn't matter half as much to me that I have produced certain stories and books as it does matter that I have occasionally faced myself and have thrown precaution to the wind in facing certain situations with which I have been confronted.

Let's take the case of your brother[4] (and I am talking now without knowing him). I imagine him to be like this. He isn't interested in industrial life. He feels he must justify his existence. He turns to writing and becomes absorbed in words, paragraphs, plots, and God knows whatever other nonsense writers continually talk about.

Do you not see and can he not see that such a road must lead to artistic death? Great God in the sky! The world is full, too full of this kind of writers, saying words, writing down words. They are like squirrels in a cage running round and round. They are not writing because of a driving impulse within themselves. Words are not fire that burn them. They are writing because they think that someone else may think they must justify their existence.

Do you remember the story of Christ and those who labored in the vineyard? Some worked laboriously all day, others for a half hour, casually. They were all by Christ's philosophy to be paid alike.

Why not? Are we beasts of burden? I may write a hundred books. You or Body may write each but three lines. If your three lines are more beautiful or pregnant than anything I have written you are the bigger men. Why haggle about it? God knows I haven't the time. Life is calling to me. I've a lot of living to do yet.

I have written a story called the "Story-writers."[5] It should be a terrible blow upon the head to all this nonsense. Oh, I wish you were here and your brother too. The lesson of life is so clear, so full of meaning.

Let us suppose your brother is to be a man who likes social life. He likes going and coming with people, the little play of the mind, whatever such a life involves. Why should he not be that unashamed? I'm not interested in that game but if I were I should play it and if any fool asked me what I was doing I should answer "I linger. I talk softly into the ears of ladies. I watch you fools sweat and work. I ornament life."

Would you, Harriet, want to live in a world made up of little piffling writers, snapping at the heels of art? Great Jehovah! Give me a world of laborers, of dandies, of the frivolous and the earnest. I want all life, colored by all things.

What matters it what others think of me? Life is short, terribly short. I have plunged into the sea. All about me are the black heads bobbing. The waves and the winds come rushing down upon us. One by one the heads go down. There must be left at the end only the terrible lonely sea. The long sea must lie under the pitiless sky.

That is coming but now I must swim. I am clever. I rest, I float on my back. I become frantic and struggle and then I swim, strongly and surely, away into nothingness.

And now, here in the sea, with all of these heads bobbing about I know something. Voices cry out to me. "Swim so and so" they cry. "Take such and such a stroke. Do not float idly on your back, work, labor terribly."

Fools. I must find my own way out into the limitless distance. Harriet, I swear by this pen that when I have written this note and if that impulse comes to me I shall throw pen, ink and all out of the window and never write again.

"You have written a good story. Write another."

"Go to hell. I want to play ball. I choose to talk with Tennessee. I am going to be a dandy and go among ladies."

Harriet, I am sure now. Do not send your brother's stories to me. I cannot help him and I may be nasty. The man who has written honestly, fully, out of his heart needs no one to tell him when he has done well. I have myself written lines that are splendid. They pass unnoticed. Poof. Bagh. The wind blows. The water in the river has turned brown. Did you see the boy—how he fell and hurt his nose?

Some day a man will arise and proclaim my lines—If not———

The chick in the shell has begun to struggle. It is eight o'clock. The snow beats on the windows. See the man who climbs a ladder. Poof. Bagh.

TS

1. An Indianapolis resident who went to Chicago and became a part of the staff of the *Little Review,* in which Anderson published. She introduced Marietta Finley to Anderson and his circle. Hahn added the longhand note, "To Harriet Dean."

2. Van Wyck Brooks, "The Splinter of Ice," *Seven Arts,* 1 (Jan. 1917), 270–80.

3. Anderson has here rendered into his own terms Brooks's idea that the artist is not generally encouraged by society; if the artist produces what society wants,

the real value of the unique artistic achievement of the artist will be palliated or destroyed: "the reality of the artist's vision is something quite different from the apparent reality of the world about him. The great artist floats that reality on the sea of his own imagination and measures it not according to its own set of values but according to the values that he has himself derived from his descent into the abysses of life." See *ibid*.

4. Randle C. Dean of Indianapolis—who did not become a writer.
5. "Story-writers" had been published in *Smart Set*, 43 (Jan. 1916), 243–48.

38

To Bab February 1, 1917 [Chicago]

The night is cold and I am sitting alone. I am wondering why I am so proud. I have wanted to save myself, to run a long ways. I sit pondering, wondering why.

On the street girls stand in doorways. One of them wears a blue hat with little flowers upon it. She stands in a stairway shivering. Her clothing is cheap. Across the street from where she stands is a church and the wind howls around it. I cover my mouth with my hand and run.

How cold the night. It is terribly cold. I have come to my room where it is warm but the girl with the blue hat stands in the stairway. Her lips are blue. I sit in my room and ponder. I wonder why I am so proud. My clock ticks loudly. Outside the wind blows. The night is cold, terribly cold.

* * * * * *

If war comes[1] it will make me more and more religious. My mind leaps back over history seeing not the Ceasars or Napoleons but Cromwell. I want a leader now for America who will have the courage to ask the people to pray and be sad.

TS

1. Anderson was anticipating the entrance of the United States into World War I on Apr. 6, 1917.

39

To Bab February 1, 1917 [Chicago]

It sometimes amazes me when I see how I am able to go on here year after year, giving so little for the money I get and every year giving less and less. Now and then I am caught. The smart exterior with which I meet the world breaks down and I stand revealed as a man more ignorant of the impulses that guide the people about me than the office boy.

The necessity of making a living—a necessity brought on by the fact of the children—keeps me going to the office day after day. I do go and sit at my desk. I write letters. Now and then I go out into another town to interview some man.

And at night I go home wondering what it is all about. I cannot remember what the men who have come to see me have talked about. Through my mind goes a confused jumble of merchandise that is to be sold by talking about it. Did the fat man with the gruff voice want to sell coffee, plows, automobiles or phonographs?

How intimately I remember him. His great rumbling voice, the way he had with his fat hands, the thickness of his lower lip.

But I am supposed to have concerned myself with what he has to sell. That was the point of his coming to see me. How puzzled I will be when he comes to see me tomorrow. Why do these men not discharge me? I don't know.

It is perhaps due to a terrible dullness that exists among them. They are creatures of habit and go on and on. Sometimes I feel like one walking forever in darkness, one condemned to go forth only at night. A wind of words blows all about me. I clutch at the hand of Tennessee, at your hand. You and a few others I have come to know are very real to me. The rest are all figures walking in darkness. I hear their words, the same words said over and over. I cry out to them but they are gone, lost in the darkness.

As they go they talk endlessly of the selling of merchandise, of the selling of soap, plows, phonographs and automobiles.

Why do these things need to be sold? What is the matter? Have these men nothing more important with which to concern themselves?

These are the questions I ask myself. It is night and I sleep. Tomorrow I shall go talk to the man with the thick lip. Perhaps I shall remember what it is he has for sale.

TS

40

To Bab February 3, 1917 [Chicago]

In the bigness of the things whirling and tumbling about our heads the little matter of whether I write or not is terribly unimportant. In some way these last few days have made me love and respect something in my countrymen. I really believe they do not want to enter this terrible war. If war comes we shall have the other thing—hatred and all truth and beauty dying amid a jumble of words. But now, while we wait, in this hour we are splendidly quiet. One must remember *that* in the days to come when we are all to be swung here and there by the wind of hideous words.

TS

41

To Bab Sunday, Feb. 4, 1917 [Chicago]

The Time of War.

All the time in my mind a picture of the sea, the long, black, dreary wintry sea. The sea that is so pitiless and now has become the hunting place of pitiless men, our men and theirs.

Now will the country wake. In the restaurants bands will play and the flag be wrapped about the shoulders of dancing girls. Drunken men will talk fiercely of fighting and young men will run away to enlist.

Once I did this and I still think it more noble to thus adventure than to lose your soul in commerce. The was has no glamour for me. I smell the stench of wounds that may not heal. I see sightless men walking about. Before my eyes, here in my room lies the figure of one who has had his belly shot away. He struggles and groans. The sacred silence of my room is broken by the sound of men screaming in anguish.

In my country something had begun to shine out. Now will come darkness. A little light had begun to show in the darkness of my time. Even I have now and then borne aloft a light. I have writ honestly and with hard sense. By a terrible effort I have isolated myself. The clamor of voices chattering of nothing has been still.

A greater and more terrible clamor will arise. A noise louder than the noises of my terrible town will assail the ears.

In my mind's eye I see a great, a beautiful army. It is not made of youth, going to die, to lie wounded and stinking in trenches. My army is made of silent, of mature men. It is the army of dreams, of times I will never know. Oh, that my own times could produce an army that could fight without shouting, valiantly, terribly.

In my mind's eye I see the long black sea. Snow, driven by the wind, cuts across the light of a ship. The sea is pitiless and is inhabited by pitiless men. They are not the silent, the mature, the kind men. The men have not come who can go softly to war, who can go softly and be kind.

The time of mature men has not come. A great noise will arise. Much will be forgotten. The little light that had been lighted will go out. It is the time of threats and war, not beautiful but the noisy, meaningless war.

TS

42

To Bab February 5, 1917 [Chicago]

Of course you must know that if war comes it will mean the practical death of all pure effort here in America just as it has meant that on the other side. Perhaps our best men here will be blighted just as their men have been. Hatred and prejudice will be in the saddle and we will have to wade through a more hopeless muddle of words and sentimentality than has been brought on by industrialism. This kind of war is, I suppose, industrialism gone mad.

I had some dreams when the war began. I saw in fancy men marching shoulder to shoulder and doing big deeds. Instead, as you know men have gone into the ground and there is only the horrible, mechanical guns and the deafness and the stench of decaying bodies.

Well, I wont go on! Thinking of it has driven me near to madness.

TS

43

To Bab February, 1917.[1] [Chicago before February 20, 1917]

Dear Friend,

Among other confused things I did in New York[2] was to loose your address. So I am sending this care of Edith Westcott[3] hoping it will reach you. You will understand how it caught me, the people to see, the places to dine, the things to be talked over with men.

My mind gropes and gropes out here and I fought the other groping minds. Then I meet people who are thinking hard along some lines alied to my own thinking. I want to find out to what length these men have gone, to feel my way a little along their road.

And then something else creeps into my consciousness. I find many new people to love and that confuses me. I rush from place to place. Behind my smiling front is an intense eagerness.

Back I come to Chicago with its dirt and the terrible little grind begins again. I have earned some courage I didn't have. I am for the moment better equipped.

And you, in New York had new courage, new strength. Miss Bentley told me you were wonderfully changed, that there were big rich new things growing in you.

I knew that but I wanted you to know.

And Miss Bentley with her problems and her talking got hold of me wonderfully and that fine, aristocratic M. Bush,[4] I hadn't seen for seven years.

Home I came confused. A world of love has come in to me to strengthen me. I cannot talk of it now. Everyone, everything—the things people think and hope of me. It is all beyond expression now. It has made me love life intensely.

Write me of your New York when you can. And love to you.

LH

1. Hahn's longhand note.

2. Between Feb. 5 and 20, Anderson was on a trip to New York. While there he met such people as Van Wyck Brooks and Waldo Frank of the *Seven Arts*, a magazine with which he had great sympathy. If he had any other missions, it is not known. He may very well have visited with his friend from Clyde days, John Emerson. Anita Loos, Emerson's widow, recalled in her autobiography, *A Girl Like I* (New York: Viking, 1966), that Emerson had reestablished contact with Anderson by writing to his publisher upon seeing a notice of his writing. Evidently the book was *Windy McPherson's Son* and the time between Sept. 1916 and Jan. 1917. (See Jones and Rideout, eds., *Letters of Sherwood Anderson*, p. 6.) This was Anderson's second trip to New York, the first being spent with Floyd Dell (1887–1969), who took the manuscript of *Windy McPherson's Son* with him, to find a publisher for it. Dell stated in a radio interview (Station WBAI, Boston, 1963) that Anderson slept on a couch in Dell's apartment "on the south side of Washington Square."

3. Not identified.

4. Presumably Marian Bush.

44

To Bab Tuesday, February 20, 1917 [Chicago]

It would be folly for me to try to express the multitude of impressions brought home from New York. First of all there was the feeling of having entered more or less into the affection of a great many new people. There was a sort of glowing feeling of kindliness abroad. It was good and wholesome and made me feel very happy.

I like the Seven Arts group very much indeed. They are generous and fine and listened to my provincial, middle western point of view with interest.

The whole thing, the rest, the being lifted out of life here; the feeling of running to meet and to know new people. It was all delightful.

Did you get to know M.B.[1] I quite fell in love with her. How fine and aristocratic she is and how keen her mind. Finding her again and renewing old things with her was delightful.

Truth is you see I was on a mountain top in a peculiarly impersonal way. I felt like one who has worked his way through the breakers and cross currents close to the shore and has got out into the open sea. I loved it all and I felt people loving me. Now I shall be able to go back to work with new courage and new understanding.

I shall probably go to New York to live one of these days. I picture myself as hidden away there in some room at the top of a tall building half downtown, half uptown—at the edge of the busy intellectual life that goes on there. I shall run away to a thousand places. I shall write madly, joyfully, opening new veins of life and expression.

I am learning what it is to love. The accumulative force of the love that has been given me makes my heart expand. I want to open my veins, to bleed, to know, to understand.

I dream of that. I come home dreaming of that. I will not be outdone. For the love that has been given me I will give and give.

TS

1. Presumably Marion Bush.

45

To Bab February 26, 1917 [Chicago]

I cannot tell you how deeply this inclination to song[1] has taken hold of me. Beside those you are seeing there are others singing in me. Perhaps this is the thing you have felt in me and that you would not tell me about.

Now that song has come I feel like one who has been climbing up a steep hill and has got out upon a broad, wind-swept place. In my prose I have been creeping toward rhythm and here is all of this realization of the terrible meaning and beauty of words that has not been realized. I will realize but a trifle of it but I will bring into song as I have into prose something American, something middle-western, something simple and, if I can keep fairly pure, something also fairly pure.

M.[2] said to me once long ago that I was to express beauty breaking through the husks of life and that is true. If I can do anything at all it is by this road, keeping close, understanding, believing.[3]

TS

1. The first reference to Finley of his writing poetry. He evidently sent her samples of this work and discussed it with her.

2. Presumably Marion Bush.

3. Anderson must have been encouraged in his writing by Edward J. O'Brien's listing of two of his stories, "Hands" and "Queer," as among the best fifty short stories of 1916 in the Feb. 1917 issue of *Bookman*. "Hands" appeared in *Masses*, 8 (Mar. 1916), 5, 7, and "Queer" in *Seven Arts*, 1 (Dec. 1916), 97–108. O'Brien wrote: "Two studies by a new and original artist of power who belongs to an important literary group in Chicago which bids fair to dominate the course of our American letters during the next ten years. Both of these stories are abnormal and most unlikely to be popular, but they are realised with a fulness of vision which is unique, and inaugurate a new craftsmanship which has much to teach American writers."

46

To Bab April 9, 1917 [Chicago]

About the songs. In them I see growing a great hungriness and through them I get for myself a sense of return to earthiness. Perhaps in my own way I will in the end populate the cornfields and the shadows by factory doors with mystery and faith so that sweaty men will look up from toil and feel on their faces shadows of my gods.[1]

And by the road of song I go to the Gods myself. It is my answer to life that is too sordid, too hard, too pitiless.

Perhaps, dear heart, I shall lead you too. I shall take you perhaps to the place beyond the thought of clinging lips to where your gods dwell. There is unbelievable stoutness in me, dear. The march is long but I am on my way.

Days of twisted people—songs, not sung, things in a terrible twisted hush.

Then other days of gladness.

The inclination to talk has a good deal gone out of me. I have been caught in a whirl of work in the office—a few songs, one strong and clear—"American Spring Song."—others not so clear.[2]

For the most part now less ease in amplifying my thoughts in letters, articles and stories. If that is permanent I don't care. It's a part of the challenge to adventure in life.

TS

1. Anderson's *Mid-American Chants* contains poems with titles such as "The Cornfields," "Song of Industrial America," "Industrialism," and "Chant to Dawn in a Factory Town." See Sutton, *Road to Winesburg*, pp. 382–425.

2. This poem and "Song of Stephen the Westerner," "A Visit," "Song of the Drunken Business Man," "Evening Song," and "Song of Industrial America" were published as a group under the heading "Mid-American Songs" in *Poetry*, 10 (Sept. 1917), 281–91.

47

To Bab April 17, 1917 [Chicago]

You are of course both right and wrong about me. This period has been on me again and again whenever the song in me did not work out.

Last night I went for a walk and during the walk I got to thinking of critics of life and what they meant. I remembered you when your essential desire was to be such a critic. Now I am glad for the growth of something else in you.

Now for example I can afford to laugh at your fears for me and call them childish because you will understand. To, in spirit, accept such condolence would mark the beginning of the decay I am not ready for. Do I not know that the weariness is but the intolerable carrying of some unexpressed thing? Do you not see that in me everything must be vitalized by inner experience before it becomes an outward actuality.

To go back to my thoughts of last night.[1] You do see that while the doing of things by rote, the mere treadmill production of work can be corrected by criticism really vital work cannot. In truth I have heard you express just that.

Well you must see also that what is true of the work of such a one must be true also of his inner struggle. It is so with me. I do not know the direction or the things toward which I am going. Let's not try to talk of it too much.

Carl Sandburg[2] came to see me and read my songs. He was lavish in his praise. The man is a somewhat heavy, cumbersome fellow with a good deal of working class prejudice and a gloomy Danish nature but very fine and sincere in his slow heavy way.

I think that deep within you there is something that is afraid for me. It is of happiness you are afraid for me. For a long time I have felt it in you. To you there seems something like danger of losing something else in the midst of happiness.

You forget this. One has to face all life and try to be unafraid. It is for children to believe too much in the efficacy of arts. To us arts should mean nothing when they are not instruments.

New days are here. The sap runs in trees. Let's be creeping. Let's be creeping away.

In the forest amid old trees and wet dead leaves a shrine. Christ coming to life and life calling. Lips to be pressed. God in the winds as well as the God that kneels and prays. Let's be creeping. Come away.[3]

TS

1. A reference to one of a series of otherwise undocumented visits to Finley in Indianapolis, presumably sandwiched into travel activities related to his work.

2. See Sutton, *Road to Winesburg*, pp. 290–94, for a discussion of Anderson's relationship with Sandburg.

3. These last two paragraphs seem to be an earlier version of the last two stanzas of "Song of the Mating Time." See *Mid-American Chants*, p. 59.

48

To Bab May 12, 1917 [Chicago]

Again as always when I read it I am aroused and stirred by the book *Marching Men*. In a way the whole big message of my life is bound into that volume.[1] As I work over it my mind jumps back to the time when I began to work with it, crudely and brokenly. It was all a great song to me then, a big terrible song. I was not strong enough to hold it. Sometimes I was not strong enough to hold it. I walked at night praying. My mind from too much weariness stopped working once and I was for a time a wreck, wandering as aimlessly as society is aimless.[2]

Now the story is beautifully simple. It will go far.[3] It will start a song in many hearts.

TS

1. Evidently Anderson had written "a series of ten or twelve papers about writing," which he mentioned in a letter of Feb. 1917 to Waldo Frank. The only one of the articles to appear was "From Chicago," *Seven Arts*, 2 (May 1917), 41–59. It is one of the better statements Anderson was to make about his art. Because of its reference to the way he dramatized a portion of himself in *Marching Men*, it is reproduced here.

> I am mature, a man child, in America, in the west, in the great valley of the Missisipppi. My head arises above the corn fields. I stand up among the new corn.
>
> I am a child, a confused child in a confused world. There are no clothes made that fit me. The minds of men cannot clothe me. Great projects arise within me. I have a brain and it is cunning and shrewd.
>
> I want leisure to become beautiful but there is no leisure. Men should bathe me with prayers and with weeping but there are no men.
>
> Now—from now—from today I shall do deeds of fiery meaning. Songs shall arise in my throat and hurt me.
>
> I am a little thing, a tiny little thing on the vast prairies. I know nothing. My mouth is dirty. I cannot tell what I want. My feet are sunk in the black swampy land but I am a lover. I love life. In the end love shall save me.
>
> The days are long. It rains. It snows. I am an old man. I am sweeping the ground where my grave shall be.
>
> Look upon me, my beloved, my lover who does not come. I am raw and bleeding, a new thing in a new world. I run swiftly over bare fields. Listen! There is the sound of the tramping of many feet. Life is dying in me. I am old and palsied. I am just at the beginning of my life.
>
> Do you not see that I am old, oh my beloved? Do you not understand that I cannot sing, that my songs choke me? Do you not see that I am so young I cannot find the word in the confusion of words? [This passage was published under the title of "Chicago" as one of the poems in *Mid-American Chants*, pp. 13–14.]

I.

> While he is still young and pregnant with life it behooves the artist who would stand unashamed among men to make his contribution to the attempt

to extend the province of his art. And as his struggle as an artist is and must be inseparably bound up with his struggle as a man, the attempt may fairly be said to fall under the head of an effort to extend the possibilities of human life.

Here is a field of thought that should make the fingers of the young artist tremble as those of a fine lover tremble at the approach of his beloved. What to the living is more sweetly vital than life? Fearing as all true artists do and must the danger of the approach of that self-satisfaction that is death, he will find upon this road difficulties that destroy self-satisfaction. Knowing that all about him in the world are men and women striving to fasten upon him their own insanity of conformity, the young and valiant soul will find here a constant demand for sustained clear thinking that will be to him a tonic against the insidious poison of association with the weak.

The driving impulse toward this attempt is, I should say, something like this—that the artist, having taught himself to look keenly and constantly at himself must realize that of all the figures in the world his is the most fortunate. Standing upon the high place and watching the struggle of his soul upon the wall of life, the artist among all men, so standing, knows that his soul has at least the chance of success in that struggle.

In a quite practical way also the artist is one upon whom riches have been bestowed. Does he arise in the morning half ill of the perplexities of his life, a half hour of fine surrender to his art impulse shall restore him. By a bridge near a river he stands and is stirred by the sight of the giant mechanism by which the bridge is raised for the passage of a ship. His quick imagination sees the workers in the great factories making the mechanism. If by good fortune he has been at some time also a laborer he hears in fancy the crashing blows of the great hammers and sees the beauty of the bodies of men absorbed in physical tasks. What to him at the moment is the fact that the laborer is cheated of the reward of his labor or that his own coat is somewhat shabby? In a flash his craft has restored to him the sweetness of a day. One of a million little beauties of every street scene or of every country roadside has revealed itself to him.

By his side stand men who are waiting for the footway over the bridge to be reestablished that they may cross the river. One of them, a plumber, has a heavy wrench in his hand. He begins talking to a second man and speaking of the ship that is passing. He uses nautical terms, throwing them about with more zeal than skill. The artist turns quickly. A light dances in his eyes. He has seen behind the plumber who is young and muscular a pretty waitress. He knows that the young male is but swaggering before the female, that he is not trying to deceive the men in the crowd by his assumed knowledge of ships but is honestly striving to awaken admiration in the mind of the woman. One of the hundred little inter-plays of human relations with which each of the artist's living hours are colored has come to take his mind off the rather second-rate breakfast he must eat.

In all of the concerns of his life, in the perplexities of love, in the muddle of affairs that compel him to spend hours, to him divinely precious, in the treadmill of making a living, the craft of the artist, if he be a true craftsman, is as a strong arm protecting him.

And so the artist having within him youth and the courage that has made him an artist, begins to aspire, humbly and for the most part in secret to make to his own craft some returns for the riches that have been given to him. If he be a novelist (and you must get me as always thinking as a novelist although I know no reason why that should influence your judgment of the justice of my observations), if he be a novelist, I say, he will be at the first appalled by the difficulties of the task to which he has set himself. Old masters, men long dead, strong true men have put in his hand a tool so fitting to the work he wants to do that it seems at times absurd that he should strive to make for himself and for all the brothers of his craft who will follow him a better tool. The names of Fielding, Balzac, Tolstoy, Defoe dance before him. To attempt what they did not do seems a kind of sacrilege. If he be of a fine quality and set upon modesty the artist may make the attempt but will make it in secret, not even speaking of the matter to his brother artists.

But the thing that I am asking for here is the attempt, the present day attempt, the American attempt, the attempt everywhere all over the world where the novelist with his ink pots and his lamps sits valiantly writing.

II.

The novelist is about to begin the writing of a novel. For a year he will be at the task and what a year he will have. He is going to write the story of Virginia Borden, daughter of Fan Borden, a Missouri river raftsman. There in his little room he sits, a small hunched up figure with a pencil in his hand. He has never learned to run a typewriter and so he will write the words slowly and painfully, one after another, on the white paper.

What a multitude of words! For hours he will sit perfectly still, writing madly and throwing the sheets about. That is the happy time. The madness has possession of him. People will come in at the door and sit about, talking and laughing. Sometimes he jumps out of his chair and walks up and down. He lights and relights his pipe. Overcome with weariness he goes forth to walk. When he walks he carries a heavy black walking-stick and goes muttering along.

The novelist tries to shake off his madness but he does not succeed. In a store he buys cheap writing tablets and, sitting on a stone near where some men are building a house, begins again to write. He talks aloud and occasionally fingers a lock of hair that falls down over his eyes. He lets his pipe go out and relights it nervously.

Days pass. It is raining and again the novelist is in his room writing. After a long evening of work he throws all he has written away.

What is the secret of the madness of the writer?

He is a small man and has a torn ear. A part of his ear has been carried away by the explosion of a gun. Above the ear there is a spot, as large as a child's hand where no hair grows.

The novelist is a clerk in a store in Wabash Avenue in Chicago. When he was quite young he began to clerk in the store and for a time promised to be successful. He sold goods and there was something in his smile that won its way into all hearts. How he liked the people who came into the store and how the people liked him!

In the store now the novelist does not promise to be successful. There is a kind of conspiracy in the store. Although he tries earnestly he continues to make mistakes, and all of his fellows conspire to forgive and conceal his mistakes. Sometimes when he has muddled things badly they are impatient and the manager of the store, a huge fat fellow with thin grey hair, takes him into a room and scolds him.

The two men sit by a window and look down into Wabash Avenue. It is snowing and people hurry along with bowed heads. So much do the novelist and the fat grey-haired man like each other that the scolding does not last. They begin to talk and the hours pass. Presently it is time to close the store for the night and the two go down a flight of stairs to the street.

On a corner stand the novelist and the store man, still talking, and presently they go together to dine. The manager of the store looks at his watch and it is eight o'clock. He remembers a dinner engagement made with his wife and hurries away. On the street car he blames himself for his carelessness. "I should not have tried to reprimand the fellow," he says, and laughs.

It is night and the novelist works in his room. The night is cold but he opens his window. There is, in his closet, a torn woollen jacket given him by a friend and he wraps the jacket about him. It has stopped snowing and the stars are in the sky.

The talk with the store manager has inflamed the mind of the novelist. Again he writes furiously. What he is now writing will not fit into the life-story of Virginia Borden, but, for the moment, he thinks that it will and he is happy. Tomorrow he will throw it all away but that will not destroy his happiness.

Who is this Virginia Borden of whom the novelist writes, and why does he write of her? He does not know that he will get money for his story and he is growing old. What a foolish affair. Presently there may be a new manager in the store and the novelist will lose his place. Once in a long while he thinks of that and then he smiles.

The novelist is not to be won from his purpose. Virginia Borden is a woman who lived in Chicago. The novelist has seen and talked with her. Like the store manager she forgot herself talking to him. She forgot the torn ear and the bare spot where no hair grew and the skin was snow-white. To talk with the novelist was like talking aloud to herself. It was delightful. For a year she knew him and then went away to live with a brother in Colorado where she was thrown from a horse and killed.

When she lived in Chicago many people knew Virginia Borden. They saw her going here and there in the streets. Once she was married to a man who was leader of an orchestra in a theater but the marriage was not a success. Nothing that Virginia Borden did in the city was successful.

The novelist is to write the life-story of Virginia Borden. As he begins the task a great humbleness creeps over him. Tears come into his eyes. He is afraid and trembles.

In the woman who walked and talked with him the novelist has seen many strange, beautiful, unexpected little turns of mind. He knows that in Virginia Borden there was a spirit that, but for the muddle of life, might have become a great flame.

It is the dream of the novelist that he will make men understand the spirit of the woman they saw in the streets. He wants to tell the store manager of her and the littly wiry man who has a desk next to his own. In the Wabash Avenue store there is a woman who sits on a high stool with her back to the novelist. He wants to tell her of Virginia Borden, to make her see the reality of the woman who failed, to make all see that such a woman once lived and went about among the women of Chicago.

As the novelist works events grow in his mind. His mind is forever active and he is continually making up stories about himself. As the Virginia Borden men saw was a caricature of the Virginia Borden who lived in the mind of the novelist, so he knows that he is himself but a shadow of something very real.

And so the novelist puts himself into the book. In the book he is a large, square-shouldered man with tiny eyes. He is one who came to Chicago from a village in Poland and was a leader in an orchestra in the theater. As the orchestra leader, the novelist married Virginia Borden and lived in a house with her.

You see the novelist wants to explain himself also. He is a lover and so vividly does he love that he has the courage to love even himself. And so it is the lover that sits writing and the madness of the writer is the madness of the lover. As he writes he is making love. Surely all can understand that.

III.

Consider the tantalizing difference in the quality of work produced by two men. In the first we get at times an almost overwhelming sense of proficiency in his craft. The writer, we feel, knows art forms, knows construction, knows words. How he slings the words about. His sentences stay in the mind. Word clings to word. Almost every one of his lines is quotable.

And this other fellow. His words do not cling, his art forms become at times shapeless, he stumbles, going crudely and awkwardly forward.

And how breathlessly we follow. What is he doing that he holds us so tightly? What is the secret of our love of him, even in the midst of his awkwardness?

He is revealing himself to us. See how shamelessly and boldly he is trying to tell us of the thing that is a never-ceasing marvel to him—the march of his own life; the complete story of his own adventure in the midst of the universal adventure.

It is Sunday evening and I am dining alone in a restaurant. The day is cold and cheerless and since morning I have been at work in my room.

I have been revising a book that is partly good, partly bad. That it is at all bad has chilled the fires in me. The thing should not have been bad. What a fine figure I was as the labor leader. How strange and wonderful my thoughts as I went through the city nights, hurrying from place to place, stirring the soul of labor. And how feebly I have expressed my thoughts. In the restaurant I jab at the table-cloth with my fork. "I should have done more with myself in so fine a role."

In the restaurant, that faces Wabash Avenue, my thoughts wander away from the book and I begin to think of an incident that happened on the evening before.

Some two weeks before that evening I had met a woman in another restaurant. She was an Englishwoman with a long thin face and when I came upon her she sat at a table with a party of friends. One of the party beckoned and I went to sit at the table. I sat by the Englishwoman.

At the table the entire party was in a playful mood. Wine went about. Someone sang a song. From all sides a great clatter of voices arose.

Between the Englishwoman and myself much laughing talk went on. Here and there we turned, laughing and shouting at the people seated at the table.

And then in a moment all was changed. A new quality came to color our brief acquaintanceship. There amid the noise and the laughter our two minds ran out to meet each other.

I cannot remember the details of that change. I had said something of England and its position in the world, something to the effect that England would always succeed, that English national stupidity insured success. "All successful things are stupid," I declared, looking at the woman.

The Englishwoman looked away. When our eyes met again her eyes were troubled. "Ah!" I thought quickly, "she has the rare gift of earnestness. There is wisdom in this woman. She knows that life is too short to be spent in half moods. A moment ago she was completely in fun, now she is as completely in earnest."

Hastily I withdrew my poorly digested comments concerning her native land and we talked. For five, perhaps for ten minutes, we got at each other. Like two wide-eyed children in a world full of unaccountable peoples and impulses, we talked of England, of America, of our own lives, of the strangeness and loveliness of our minds, meeting and embracing in that great noisy place.

"We must talk a whole evening away," I pleaded. "After these few moments we would be fools not to do that."

The hand of the woman, lying on the table, trembled. Perhaps my hand trembled also. Even now as I sit writing of the woman, my hand, that plays back and forth on the paper, shakes with the memory of her.

We walked in Jackson Park here in Chicago, going along the paths in silence. Thoughts arose. In so brief a time there had been built up in each of us a background of much thinking. Already our two lives were colored, each by the other. After a time words came. She was lonely in America and talked of her own country and of a wide moor that ran away toward the sunset beyond her own town. On Sundays she had gone upon the moor with the people with whom she lived and whom she loved. With a man she loved she had walked hand in hand and had talked as she and I had talked in the restaurant.

In the park it was cold and we met no people. Presently we got upon a wide open space. The dreary persistent wind roared in distant trees. In the night the open space was mysteriously vast.

Again we walked along in silence. I put out my hand and in it she put her own hand.

And then the old human problem presented itself to the woman and me. We had stopped beneath a small tree. Away in the distance a street car ran past the front of the park. It seemed immeasurable miles away. The cold wind beat about her slender figure.

I took the woman into my arms. In her face as it looked up into mine was all of the loveliness of woman. How men have ached and prayed and fought and whipped themselves to long lives of endeavor because of the unworldly beauty in the eyes of woman. Oh, there was unspeakable loveliness in her. How I longed for beauty within myself, beauty with which to match that beauty, that quiet, submissive, waiting loveliness in her.

With an impotent cry I turned and taking her by the hand led her back to walk again upon the gravel paths.

We talked then. How the words welled up in me. "Never," I cried, "shall I find beauty to match your beauty; your lover—he must have been very wonderful." Aimlessly I stumbled about, saying words, trying to make her understand how truly in my poor way I also loved her.

In the restaurant I pay my bill, and go out into the street. What matter if my hands tremble and I have forgotten to eat? What matter if the Englishwoman, met in that other restaurant, sailed for home two days after our meeting? What matter if, on that Saturday evening, I suffered from a headache and walked alone in the windswept park? What matter if I never in all my life knew such a woman?

Is my story for all these reasons the less true? Is the moment in which I look down into the loveliness of a woman's soul less a part of my life because it happened in fancy there in the restaurant in Wabash Avenue?

Again and again I proclaim the richness of life that men miss. Have you not also walked in the street reconstructing the conversations, the meetings, the brief awkward moments through which you have passed?

You were making literature then. In the actual moment you had been crude and awkward and so as you walked muttering you reconstructed the moment, made it more lovely, more alive with meaning.

In the street as you walked the sentences you made were filled with meaning, your desires honest, your acts noble.

What care I whether or not you get money from the stories of your true life and whether or not you gain fame? Do you not see that as you, in your turn, dine in your Wabash Avenue restaurant I would have your hours touched with the beauty that has come to me here after this dull working day?

IV.

I am walking in the street at evening of a summer day. The rush of people homeward bound has passed and something of the jaded weariness of their faces remains in my mind. I go heavily along by an iron railing that guards a network of railroad tracks. The tracks run away between rows of grey brick buildings into Chicago's West Side. Beside the tracks is the river that flows from the lake into the land and that carries away the sewage of the city. The river is like a drain that takes the fetid matter from a wound and the city is a wound upon the prairie.

As I walk my mind becomes heavy and dull. I have passed the middle age of life and I begin to measure the courage left to me as a traveler in a desert might look at the water in a water-bottle. I become afraid and tremble. Over a distant bridge that mounts high above the river and the tracks passes a long procession of wagons pulled by weary horses. From the wheels of the wagon dust arises. Behind the cloud of dust burns the sun, also flushed with weariness.

In a kind of desperation I begin letting my mind play with my own life, with what I have seen of the lives of others. Things seen, and that have been lying like spermatozoa on the sack of my mind, grow and are fertilized by the facts of my own journey through the world.

I am a boy who came to Chicago from a little place in Missouri. Like most boys raised in the hill country I was lean and strong. I was uneducated but much solitary riding of horses over lonely hills had led me into the habit of letting my mind play. It was a custom of mine to talk aloud and to sing at the top of my voice as I went along and at times it was difficult to restrain these impulses as I walked among the crowds in the city streets.

In the city I lived on the West Side with my sister who later went wrong and was lost in the maze of the life here. Our younger sister who is now married to a printer and lives in a suburb called Austin lived with us. She had blue eyes and a tiny hesitating voice and on Sunday mornings walked hand in hand with me in Washington Boulevard chattering away and asking questions that I could not answer.

What a struggle we had, the three of us, there in the city. For a long time I could not get work and we got into debt so that I had to write to my uncle for money. He sold three hogs that would have littered in the spring and sent the money to me. Sometimes I smile now as I think of that letter. How the words must have been misspelled and how amusing the arrangement of words. It might have been printed in a comic paper. Later, you see, I went to night school and rose in the world.

But I am thinking of that first winter. I worked with other men on a pile-driver that drove piles for the foundation of a warehouse. The warehouse is not finished and stands near the mouth of the river where the boats come in from the lake. All day the waves washed against the long flat boat on which stood the engine that lifted a heavy weight only to let it drop again on the head of the log we were driving into the soft river mud. At first the log sank rapidly, a foot or more with each blow, but later it went slowly inch by inch.

How cold it was on the boat. In the morning I liked it out there. The slapping of the waves against the boat, the heavy thump of the weight on the head of the log and the puffing of the engine made it possible to talk aloud.

I talked out everything that came into my mind. Close beside the engine I stood and the words rolled out of me. In the midst of the many noises there was a great silence, so I talked into that, telling of my hopes, my dreams, my strangely impossible ambitions in life.

There was a woman of thirty-five who sang in the choir in a church on our street and I talked of her. When she sang on Sunday mornings she sometimes put her hand on the little railing of the choir loft and, from the seat where I sat with my younger, blue-eyed sister, I could see her fingers peeping out. When I talked of her hands, out there in the noisy place on the boat, I sometimes took off my gloves and looked at my own hands. They were strong but the skin was very coarse and in places the skin was broken so that red angry flesh looked through. The skin at the edge of the wounds was like the white of a fish. The water did that.

I am thinking of the winter nights when I came away from the boat, going to my place on the West Side. I went along the railroad tracks just below where I am standing now. It was dark and only the lights at the switches, the red and green railroad lights, lighted the way.

On the boat at the edge of the lake I did not talk and sing after three o'clock in the afternoon. Those were the bad hours, from three until six, when we quit and went along boards to a wharf. From the wharf we stumbled up to a spur of the railroad tracks. Once I fell off the boards and had to be fished out of the water but even that did not increase my numbness.

All day the waves that beat against the boat sent a fine spray of water over us and this froze into ice. When the wind was off shore, however, it was not so bad. In the morning the heart beat stoutly but after three o'clock the feet and the hands and even the balls of the eyes became cold. I could not think of the woman who sang in the church choir after three o'clock and sometimes as I went along the tracks that ran into the West Side I could not see very well. How odd that a train did not hit me! I stepped away from trains like a horse that cannot be induced to run its head against a tree, even in the pitch darkness.

From the place by the railing at the edge of the tracks on the summer evening I return across the city to my own room. I am vividly aware of my own life that escaped the winter on the boat. How many such lives I have lived. Then I only made a dollar and a half a day and now I sometimes make more than that in a few minutes. How wonderful to be able to write words. I am enamored of myself because I can write words and can make my living by it. Now perhaps I could have the woman who sang in the choir and perhaps I would not take her if she offered.

In my room I sit thinking of courage—of the courage of men. The balls of the eyes of the boy on the track were numb and he could scarcely see. In the two rooms where he lived with his sisters there was a tiny coal stove by a window. It was put there to stop the cold from coming through the cracks in the window sill and that necessitated a long stove-pipe having many joints. The pipe was fastened with wires and often at night it fell down scattering black coal soot on the bed where the boy lay. He could not eat when he came home but lay on the bed until his heart beat strong again and warmth came back into his body. At nine o'clock he arose, washed, had his supper, and returned again to sleep beneath the long stove-pipe.

On my desk in my room there is a black leather note-book with leaves that may be taken out. When the leaves are all written full I take them out, fasten them with rubber bands, and put them away. Then I fill the book with new white leaves.

In my room when I come back from standing by the tracks I think how I was afraid because I have reached middle age. There is a cunning satisfaction in my heart because I think that when my body is weary I shall take the leaves from the rubber bands and go on writing year after year as though I were yet alive.

There is satisfaction in this thought until another thought comes. Not as I stood weary by the tracks, but now, as I think of the hoarded leaves of white paper in the rubber bands, has the coward appeared. To myself I say, "Am I to be less stout-hearted than the boy who stumbled half frozen along the tracks?"

And so, although the night is warm I have a fire in the fireplace in my room. One by one I burn the white leaves I have saved.

Are we, who write stories, who paint pictures and who act upon the stage to go on forever hoarding our minor triumphs, like frugal merchants who keep a secret bank account; are we to be less courageous than our brothers, the laborers?

Tomorrow I am afraid that my courage will have failed. And so, tonight, although it is warm here, I have a fire in the fire-place in my room.

V.

It is three o'clock of a winter's afternoon and I am lying in a nook among rocks on the side of a mountain in Missouri. I am clad in heavy boots that lace to the knees and they are covered with frozen mud. In a road far below an old Ozark mountaineer is riding a donkey to a distant town. He is a tall old man and his feet hang to the ground. I am in a sheltered place and the cold wind does not reach me, but across the prospect of barren hills it goes, shouting and roaring. Beyond the road that lies at the foot of the hill there is a river and along this there comes presently a raft upon which stands a man with a pole in his hand. He is singing a ballad of a country girl who went away to a distant city and there became the plaything of evil. There is a penetrating quality of beauty in the raftsman's voice and my mind is carried away by it.

I begin reconstructing the life of the country girl of the song. She is tall and strong and very lean like the girls I have seen at the doors of the cabins along the roads that run through the hills. There is in her a kind of wild beauty, tempered by ignorance. She stands within the door of the cabin also singing, and outside the door, clad in a worn man's overcoat, is an old woman who smokes a pipe. As she sings the mountain girl looks at the old woman, who is hideous. The hunger for beauty, that will presently destroy the girl, that echoes in the heart of the lonely raftsman on the river among the hills, comes up and possesses me. I turn about in my nook and stare long and hard at the cheerless hills. The oak trees have retained last year's leaves and these are now a dull red. I see death here as I have seen it so often in faces of men in the cities, but here the note of beauty has remained in the midst of death. The dull red leaves that rattle in the wind are the visible signs of it. It plays in the minds of the raftsman and the girl and in my own mind.

Again I begin the endless game of reconstructing my own life, jerking it out of the shell that dies, striving to breathe into it beauty and meaning. A thought comes to me.

When I was a boy I lived in a town in Ohio and often I wandered away to lie upon my back, thinking, as I am doing now. I reconstruct and begin to color and illuminate incidents of my life there. Words said, shouts of children, the barking of dogs at night, occasional flashes of beauty in the eyes of women and old men are remembered. I wonder why my life, why all lives, are not more beautiful.

Away to the city I take myself and I am sitting beside a woman in a room upstairs in a cheap apartment house. I am a grown man now, alive with vigor, and I am determined I shall make love to the woman. She has a tall boyish figure and strange grey eyes. Something in the eyes madden me. I rush to the woman, take her into my arms, and kiss her passionately. See, I have killed something that was lovely in the eyes of the woman. I have done my share toward putting that keen plaintive note into the voice of the ignorant raftsman. It was beautiful to make love to the woman but in making love I also killed beauty.

Again a turn of my mind. Back I come to these papers. I begin to see myself, to see all writers in a new aspect. My fingers tremble to begin explaining my thoughts.

When I was a boy in the Ohio town I was given a conventional American education which included not a few rather dreary hours in what is called God's House. As I grew older and pushed out into the world I no longer thought of the church and a peculiar, insistent something kept me from going there.

Since my twentieth year—and I am now, as I lie in the nook on the hillside, a man near forty—I have not been inside a house of worship. Before coming to the mountains I secured small editions of the four books by Matthew, Mark, Luke and John and these I have carried in my pocket and read as I lay on wind-swept peaks, or sat at night by a campfire near some chattering river's shore. I had been curious concerning the telling of that same old story by the four men who, like the man of whom they talked, were artists, no doubt the most worthy among the hundreds who told the story.

On the mountainside thoughts crowd in upon me. I begin to sense the inner purpose of these papers. They are a kind of challenge to myself and to all writers. Why should we not begin, many of us, to tell in our own way and out of our own lives, that same story? Why should there not come from among us, men also worthy to stand up beside the old artists, a Henry Rodgers from Wisconsin or a Seth Williams of Virginia, to stand with Matthew, Mark, Luke and John? It is not necessary that our man resort to the subterfuge of hiding behind the names of the disciples, the fishermen, and the collectors of taxes who went up and down with Him. Is there not in some one of us a testament, an inner story of struggle and failure, that, because of its truth, shall be found worthy to stand beside the story of another day, yes, even beside the masterful presentation made by John?

How afire I am, thinking of the fine courage of this thought. I want to tell my brother writers of it. My mind does not suggest that the stories as presented by our four predecessors are bare of the touch of life that is in the hand of the true artist. I am thinking only that time, the droning voices of the preachers, and the changing life of man has taken away some flavor that must once have been there. Have we not come into a new age filled with the stirrings of new life? Will we not forever be so coming? Why in our strivings should we be less bold than they? May we not, by the courage and nobility of our presentation of the inner story of our lives hope finally to outdo them; outdo them in the truth of the presentation of the artist who must fail to the minds of our age?

On the hillside I arise from my nook and the wind plays about my shoulders. The dreariness has gone out of the day. I am looking forward to the coming of the new artist who will give us what the old men did not completely give, the beautiful and stirring story of the spirit that failed, just as the artist himself shall fail and who, like Christ, on that dramatic night in the garden, must come at last to the facing of truth and know that he must always fail, that, even in keeping alive the memory of his struggle, all men shall fail.

Down the hillside to my own cabin I come, my mind saluting the four who tried so faithfully to tell the story of failure in the old past. I salute the four but, with the dream of the new men before me, I do not bow down to them. Firmly I stand upon the right of the new brood of writers to attempt all, to tell the story of struggle and failure so vividly that there shall come from among them many disciples; perhaps, in his turn, one so daring, so bold, and so faithful in his facing of failure, that he also shall be called the Christ.

2. *Marching Men* and *Windy McPherson's Son* were among the manuscripts typed by Anderson's secretary before his amnesia episode.

3. Anderson must have been encouraged to find his picture in *The Bookman*, May 1917, p. 306, identifying him as the author of *Windy McPherson's Son*. On the following page, along with a "slight autobiographical sketch," is the comment: "As one of the outstanding books of fiction of last year, *Windy McPherson's Son* has brought its author, Sherwood Anderson, into prominence." The sketch follows the usual pattern, with one exception: It contains a unique good word for

the combining of writing with the advertising business. "The advertising business is one that binds itself peculiarly to what I wanted to do in life. I do not understand why more novelists did not go into it."

49

To Bab May 25, 1917 [Chicago]

I am floating along waiting for this year of work to end. Now I have only next week to put in here. Marching Men has gone on its way and my mind reaches out into the future.

And I have no plans at all. The deep depression brought on by the war clings to all people. The whole human race is going through a dark place.

I think much and often of you down there. In my mind stays that little room, the vulgar woman with her knees on that table, the face of the newspaper man with its heavy complexity, the other man with his back ground of whiteness and half-exhaustion.

And then the disorder of the place. The minds and the lips saying half-smart little sayings.

Outside the town, the complex town with its problems and the flat plains of Indiana stretching away. And over all the war.

You will have to go a long journey into loneliness to people the world with your own people.

All that is the old weary story.

The gods are there, big and brutal, swift and young, tender and wise.

You for the gods of the grass and the cornfields and the rhythms that may lead to them.

TS

50

To Bab May 29, 1917 [Chicago]

I am in the office in the morning. The sun is shining. People are just coming for their day's work. On the streets soldiers and citizens hurry along. Yesterday a young revolutionist came to me. He was in a state of feverish excitement. He had been reading my things and thought I was an American who would be able to tell him what to do. I took him to lunch. There was in his mood half the fear of death and half the fear of dealing death to others. It was hard to get his mind to play steadily on one phase of the question of war.

At the best I always feel on such occasions a certain heavy and unpleasant righteousness. There is something basically unpleasant about giving advice.

You see how it is. One has the sacred old things—the dreams of love and orderly movement forward. To put these things in words makes them seem cumbersome and pretentious.

I said as much to the young man. Then I tried to say to him something else. It seems to me that all the big radicals of the country have fallen before the fact of this war. In times of peace they had taken a certain position, they had stood stoutly up for certain principles.

Then came the war and it seemed to them that their principles were to be put to the supreme test. They had braced themselves for a test. Oddly enough with their bracing came a tightening of the muscles of the mind. They had got hold of a truth you see and had become not thinkers but scientists. They are so very sure that two and two make four. In embracing their truth they have become grotesque.

Now I hold it to be true that no truth is the exact truth that is not also a lie. All of life lies in the gesture. Nothing must become so precious that it cannot be thrown away. To kill men's bodies seems to me the last thing. There is something physically and morally nauseating in the thought.

But here the matter lies. My brothers are in this war. It is a disease, a terrible thing. Would one refuse to go into a hospital and serve because millions of men lay in the hospital suffering from some horrible disease.

You see how it is. There is a woman who has answered the problem of the flesh and the spirit for me. Away deep within me I know that to play lightly with the fact of my love for her may cast me out into the world a mere sensualist. Well I hold myself unworthy of that love if I have not the courage to throw it away.

Well I had not the courage to advise the young man and I told him so. On my own soul however I take the killing and the brutalities of this war. My brothers are in the flood and I give my soul to them. I fling it into the black water.

That is what I told the young man. It left him confused. It leaves me confused. It is a time of confusion.

TS

51

To Bab Chateguay June 1917 The Adirondacks[1]

Frank[2] goes very far—but he misses much. I have found him a fine playmate with a streak of barely perceptible vulgarity beneath a rather generous and well meaning exterior. He thinks of himself as one of America's big men and in that I suspect his vulgarity lies. Tonight he has run away with one of the girls here and I find it nice to be alone in sight of the misty hills. Today I ran away from him for a moment and ran into the woods. I stretched myself out on the grass and sobbed like a woman for the glory and the quiet of this place. Deep in the ground my roots and my Gods lie. They are whispering to me.

Word comes from Tennessee that she will leave town at the end of the week. How glad I shall be for her quiet, dignified companionship and for the thing in her that understands these hills and these soft quiet nights better than this writer.[3]

How I hope you can come here dear if to come will only give you some of the quiet and rest you so much need. My love to you.

LH

1. Hahn's longhand note.
2. Waldo Frank (1889–1967), novelist, critic, translator, and one of the editors of *Seven Arts*, was just becoming one of Anderson's most important friends.
3. A summer visitor to Lake Chateaugay, Sue de Lorenzi of Chicago, recalled both Tennessee and Sherwood in a letter to me, dated Apr. 11, 1962. Of the former, she remembered Tennessee's poise, quietness, and self-reliance—like an "Indian princess." Though de Lorenzi had told Anderson that she had tried and failed to read one of his books—and had no intention of trying any others—her remark did not disturb him. When the weather was cold or rainy, he asked to write in her cabin, as his tent had no heat. De Lorenzi witnessed Tennessee and Sherwood's wedding at Chateaugay on July 31, 1916; the wedding took place under an apple tree in a ravine in the village of Chateaugay, about ten miles from the Bentley camp, which was the center of life for Sherwood and Tennessee at the lake.

52

To Bab July 30th, 1917 [Probably from Lake Chateaugay]

I do thank you for your fine letter and all the understanding you have helped to give me of strange and terrible things that go on in the world. I really think you very little understand how little of the personal there is in it all to me. One can't of course be impersonal in his attitude toward this pulsating, anxious thing in people that makes them pluck and cling like little tight-fisted frightened children. It is there and has its basic truth too. Perhaps I shall someday have the strength to come close and understand it. I can't in any personal way now.

You see the thing repeats and repeats like the striking of a midnight clock in a hot quiet city street. I have had the same thing from a man here. His hands have also clutched at me. He has wanted to come into my meditations, into my city where I live. There he has wanted to live, to hold to me personally, to come close and close.[1]

And in the midst of it all I chance to live. I want only—I ask only that you try a little to remember I am also a part of life. I have my city and I try to live and dream and work in it. Why invasion?

I have my own understanding with my gods. With them I have agreed to strip myself when the time comes; to throw off comrades, my lovers, my happiness. I have driven a hard bargain. I have renounced and the gods have renounced. For the little I have thrown off fear they have given me much joy and I shall know much joy and look often into the face of beautiful things.

TS

1. This description suggests his relationship with Dr. Trigant Burrow, the basis for Anderson's story "Seeds." See Sutton, *Road to Winesburg*, pp. 257–60.

53

To Bab October 30, 1917 [Chicago]

A grey cold day and I have just got back into town. On my desk I found several cheering letters from people interested in my books.[1] Your letter was also cheerful. It was cold but I buttoned up my coat and went for a walk. All afternoon I had travelled through a country of cornfields. In the background the red trees. The city was empty. Down the ugly streets the wind ran throwing dust about. I went back to my room and lighted candles. In the room behind mine a young girl lives. She is anxious to become acquainted. When I open my door hers creeps open. She stands looking at me.

My mind is tumbling about and trying to fit itself in a mood of sustained work. That will come. You must of course know that the things you want, the warm close thing, is the cry going up out of all hearts. Everyone in the world needs to love and be loved. I presume the lonely little thing in the next room—she is, I suppose a clerk, wants that.

And the thing to learn, I believe, is not to demand. That only gets one to a kind of madness.

Today is cold here. It will be a bleak cheerless winter and mankind will suffer as it has never before suffered in our times. Let's try to be just plain human beings and not let the universal hysteria take hold of us.

TS

1. Vincent Starrett of Chicago, in a letter to me dated Nov. 20, 1962, recounts the following story about Anderson tracking down his books. In 1917, just after *Marching Men* was published, Anderson went into the Economy Bookshop and asked if the secondhand store had any books by Sherwood Anderson. The clerk, Ben Abrahamson, recalled later that he advised the customer, whom he did not recognize, that *Windy McPherson's Son* and *Marching Men* had been published too recently to be available as used copies. He further told the customer that Anderson's sister, Margaret C. Anderson, was the subject of an article in the current issue of *Little Review*. Several months later, on being introduced to Anderson at the Dill Pickle Club, Abrahamson heard Anderson say that he remembered Abrahamson as the one who convinced him that Margaret Anderson was his sister. It has not been possible to verify Abrahamson's recollection about Margaret Anderson and that the story/article concerned an intense young woman who spent long hours at the piano. The Oct. and Dec. 1917 issues of *Little Review* did have piano advertisements (for the Mason and Hamlin piano), but there was no mention of a Margaret Anderson.

54

To Bab — November 6, 1917 [Probably Chicago]

How many thousands of nights like this have I spent on the strange streets of some little town. In the evening I go to my room and sit by a window. The people come from their houses after the evening meal. They go to moving pictures or just loaf before the lighted windows of stores. On a corner is a young woman. She chews gum vigorously and eyes the young men who pass. Now and then one stops to talk with her. About her whole figure there is something inexpressibly vulgar. She is a young trollop who nightly uses her body to whore men.[1]

In a cigar store across the way three old men sit together. They talk earnestly. One makes motions with his hand. They are discussing the war, or the election or the cost of living, three infallible subjects for such village meetings.

I have been for a long walk through residence streets and have come back to read and work. I have been a little sad as is my mood nowadays when I walk through streets of houses where people live. Perhaps I have thought too much about people and have wanted too much from them.

TS

1. Anderson wrote "An Apology for Crudity," published in Nov. 1917 issue of *The Dial* and the Chicago *Daily News*, Nov. 14, 1917, columns 1–4, p. 13. It deals with the observations alluded to in this paragraph. See Appendix A.

55

To Bab November 23, 1917 [Chicago?]

There are certain days when one who is in the midst of the vigor of life feels himself capable of sustaining with a flourish any human experience. One walks along the street looking at the people. He has a mad desire to take them all into his arms, to share with them the superabundance of strength he finds within himself.

At such times one returns to a sort of savagery. The nuances of life seem trifling and not worth while. He wants to move forward in a broad way like a river flowing to the sea. He wants to lose himself in things primitive and real. It is at such times that I realized that within me there is much of the primitive, the thing that could kill or save. The dreary time of the asking of questions passes and for a moment I stand forth, a naked man in a world clothed and choked by custom and habits of thought.

TS

56

To Bab November 1917. Chicago[1] [Before November 30, 1917]

Oh I am sorry to hear of your illness. I just got in from a long trip to a lot of small Kentucky towns. Been catching midnight trains and riding on puffy little river steamers. I got your last letter and for just a moment it seemed an entire reversal to a hurtful possessive attitude. Then when I had time to think a little I realized that it was only a part of the thing that is in the minds of all of us—depression and the general hopelessness of things just now.

Of course you will be well again soon now but my dear child I dont want to see you become subject to such times. I do beg of you not to be depressed about my attitude. As I told you once before I have really taken you for my friend and mean it.

Dont try to solve problems for me woman. I'm a child in many ways and in many others I'm old and wise. Then too I, like yourself and every one else, have times when I do not work well, when I am depressed and when I do not think clearly or well.

However I have recovered from the depression that came with the inevitable pawing over of M. M. [*Marching Men*] and am clear of it. My own impulses as a workman came back clear and strong. I'm all right. I'll always manage to work in some way and that's the great thing.

LH Written on the stationery of the Newcomb Loom Co., Davenport, Ia.

1. Hahn's longhand note.

57

November, 1917[1] [Chicago before November 30, 1917]

Thursday

Dont you see how and why your letter today had power and meaning. Up to page 23 half way down the page.[2] All through the other 22½ pages you write with power and directness. Why. Because you talked of other people in terms you know and understand. Only when you spoke of yourself were you at all bad. You are not ready to talk of yourself. Some time you will be ready and then if you want to you will write a powerful book. Now when you speak of yourself you always miss the point. There is a reason but it is somewhat complex. It doesn't need to be solved now.

The point is that here was a sustained flight of some hundreds of words, run off clearly, without flourish or nonsense. It may seem a small achievement to you but when I tell you few people in the world can do it, that even most writers fail to get periods of as clear writing in a whole book it will indicate what I think of it.

I'm going to tear up your letter because it didn't come clear through. Anyway it isn't that writing matters. It is but an aid in really doing what you say you have succeeded in doing but haven't yet. I mean staying both in and out.

The letter shows you are on the way. It is the surest expression I have had from you. Bless you for it.

Rainy day with storm on the lake. Lunch with John Emerson[3] who is passing through town. In the air white flakes against a windy dirty sky. I have written until my hands tremble and I can hardly hold a pen.

LH

1. Hahn's longhand note.
2. Only two of Finley's letters to Anderson have survived; see letters 175 and 309 herein.
3. John Emerson, then known as Clifton Paden, had been Anderson's friend during his youth in Clyde. Anderson had lived in the home of members of the Paden family in Chicago in the period before the Spanish-American War. Paden, changing his name to Emerson, had become a success on the New York stage, had gone to Hollywood, and returned to New York as a movie producer "while World War I was in full swing," according to Anita Loos, Emerson's widow. Emerson saw reviews of either *Windy McPherson's Son* or, more likely, *Marching Men* and reopened the friendship by writing to Anderson in care of his publisher. Doubtless the meeting referred to here was one of the results. Another was an invitation to Anderson to work for Emerson in New York. See letter 66 herein.

58

To Bab November 30, 1917 [Chicago]

The adventure of the war has pretty deeply upset many artists. While it is important, this surging of new impulses, it is not so terrible a thing as we all, in a more or less sentimental way, suppose. Death and horror stalk constantly in the midst of our civilization. Ones only chance is in building close about themselves and into their own relationships some elements of beauty. With war and government the artist has simply nothing to do. One has his task and it is big enough.

Why all this excitement? Has not mankind always been at war with the artist. Why should we draw back from some new manifestation of an old thing. The artist who does so is as bad as the propagandist.

TS

59

To Bab December 1917[1] [Chicago]

For some reason I still carry about me—unread—your last two letters. I have a notion that they confuse more than ever what is already confusing enough. Am I accusing you falsely. It seems to me that you more than almost anyone I know lack faith.

What I have always tried to convey to you is I admit rather confusing. It is vague and subtile. I think that anything active and beautiful, any impulse that has back of it a real wealth of reality, has of course to be self created.

Thats the reason you are wrong in centering anything upon me. I am a leaf blown by the wind. I am a steaming manure pile. It doesn't make any difference what I am.

The point I want to make is that in you yourself lies all possibilities. You are strong enough and brave enough to get what you want.

Only dont reach this way, outside of yourself and above all dont reach to me.

I am a poor confused thing, busy with many impulses and desires but at the worst and in the midst of any confusion that may come I can always so easily defeat you in your program.

Without a program and being as you truly are just a tired confused thing you acquire the same strength I have and do not need me.

Isn't that all quite clear. It seems as real and distinct as a voice in the silence of the dawn to me.

LH Written on the stationery of the Auditorium Hotel, Chicago.

1. Hahn's longhand note.

60

To Bab Christmas Morning—1917 [Chicago]

Today I choose to be a king and emperor. I have gone into my room and lighted a candle. Out of the Christmas I have gleaned two new splashing bits of color. I have put them on as a king puts on his purple. No one else in the land of the king dare wear purple and who but me dare wear a splashing feather in his hat and sox all splashed with purple and yellow.

TS

61

To Bab December 26, 1917[1] [Chicago]

I got a very tight little impression of you and your strength. It made me feel more healthy.

I've been very stupid—rather paternal. Now in the face of your determination I feel small. Thats good for me.

I hope I shall not be so stupid as to advise you in any thing again. Suddenly, imperceptible you will slip over an indefinable line into new use of your moods. Universality will come to you as your mind and your moods mature.

Dont listen to anyones advise—not mine or any other wise man. Whip yourself and suffer if you must.

I slept 15 hours.

Did I intend to write Christmas letters—give gifts.

I forgot or was too confused.[2] I appreciate your gift to me. It is strangely like a coffin. I shall fill it with cigarettes and laugh at you. You are foolish to be kind to me.

The very thought of Christmas fills me with pompous phrases. Dont you suppose that Christ on his cross laughed at the follies of men.

Never was I so much for you. Never were you so far from loosing my respect and comradship.

LH

1. Hahn's longhand note.
2. This seems to have been his normal reaction to Christmas.

62

To Bab Chicago, December 26, 1917[1]

I get much clearer. It is my own fault. I have no right to let the complications due to your situation confuse me. If I have sometimes let that happen forgive me.

You are a very brave and very vital person. I have no fear at all of your ultimate working out of your life.

In a way I hope you will not wholly escape from a kind of innocence that is now a part of you.

Greetings to you.

LH Written on the stationery of the Galt House, Sterling, Ill.

1. Hahn's longhand note.

63

To Bab April, 1918[1] [Chicago]

You have been staying in the corner of my mind for the last two or three days and I hope it is not because your illness has taken a bad turn. Now that the spring days have come you must get well and go out of doors.

I have, for the first time been reading some of the tales of Poushkin. In this connection I am wondering why you try at all to fit yourself to be a critic of writing. Something—perhaps your word[s] about May Sinclair's book[2] made me realize how profoundly unhealthy most talk of writing has become. I catch you talking like a combination of Floyd Dell, Hackett and Ben Hecht.

It is all great folly. Surely you will have, ultimately, enough money to live on. Why not write instead of talking of writing. I warn you that you will never escape the terrible mark of the parrot if you keep at the other thing.

Why all this out of Poushkin. Because he told tales well and didn't pretend and strut. Thats what criticism always does.

Of course you may never be able to write anything that is worth a whoop. But then I may not. No one can tell whether he will or not.[3]

I am leaving town to be gone for 10 days. Do get well. When you are well and strong I will come some day to see you. I will never come to see a sick person.

LH

1. Dateline is Hahn's longhand note. There is no explanation for the hiatus of several months between letters. Certain letters could have been discarded, but Hahn mentioned burning only the 1914–16 letters.

2. Anderson is probably referring to Sinclair's *Belfry* (English title, *Tasker Jevons*), published in 1916; the book recounts the author's wartime experiences in Belgium.

3. In an article entitled "Chicago Culture," Anderson wrote, "This thing is certain—that the best way to kill the growth of a distinctive middle western literature is to talk about it. . . . What I am pleading for is that our expression in Chicago shall not become too self-conscious." Chicago *Daily News*, Feb. 20, 1918.

64

To Bab April, 1918 Chicago[1]

An opportunity has come up for me to go live for two or three years in a little interior Kentucky town.[2] I may decide to do it.

Tennessee went with me on a trip south. We went to Louisville and saw the fleet beautiful thoroughbreds run the Kentucky Derby.[3] Then we went to an estate, owned by a friend of mine in the Kentucky blue grass section.

The slow life of the hill town, the drawling negroes and whites, the long quiet hours appeal to me.

I am thinking of what you say of critics and living. It is an immediate thing and has nothing to do with artistry that one should now write of the war and its effect on people. I think honestly that your mind is confused by the reaction of the war on you. A woman tells things of conditions and people in a time of stress and has strength of purpose enough to be fairly honest. You are somewhat confused by that. It may be good journalism and that is so rare that you a little fly off your head and confuse terms.

Surely if you can criticize you will need to have in you the seeds of production. You are quite wrong in thinking assimilation will solve the problem. It does need transference.

I am surely not one to say that personal transference would be the answer. That you must decide.

If however, as you lie on the banks of streams and have thoughts, you try to push your thoughts out beyond the immediate things, if you will make yourself little like a bug that looks up at towering grass stalks you will begin to understand something you havn't yet understood.

When I think back I can never remember your having given anything but lip service to the true impulses out of which art comes. That is why so many common, so called intelligent women have been and are better and more beautiful in their inner life than you.

When one really thinks of it they must know that every complaint is a cry out of a vain soul.

And you are most terrible and in a quite unforgiveable way vain. I sense the thing so keenly because it has been my own struggle. I have so often seen the worse, the most childish side of me in you.

If you will reread sometime my story "mother"[4] you will see how really and truly I love the big thing in women. You must train your eyes to that. The problem is to be, not to be loved.

I go on in this way because you speak of being a critic or producing as though it were a thing to be accomplished by the setting of jaws. Do not believe to wholly in the greyness of the life about you. Please do not pity yourself so consistently.

It seems to me that is the road to understanding of life and in that is also understanding of artistry.

I am glad you are better. Your letters are more human.

LH

1. Hahn's longhand note of the date and city may be in error here. The content of the letter makes clear that Anderson and Tennessee saw the Kentucky Derby, which was run on May 11 in 1918.

2. Possibly Owensboro.

3. Anderson's interest in racehorses was intense and, beginning in Clyde, continuous. Note, for example, *Horses and Men*, published in 1923.

4. This story appeared in *Seven Arts* in Mar. 1917 and was the fourth segment in *Winesburg, Ohio*. In the story Anderson has Elizabeth Willard say of her son George: "He is groping about, trying to find himself. . . . He is not a dull clod, all words and smartness. Within him there is a secret something that is striving to grow. It is the thing I let be killed in myself."

65

To Bab — May, 1918[1] [Chicago]

Get May 23 Dial and read Stearn's article "La Peur de la Vie." It sets forth an attitude toward the war that is much healthier than most things I have heard you say of it.[2]

The review of my chants [*Mid-American Chants*] in the same issue is smug, slippery and dishonest.[3]

My favorite critic is a woman named Ethel Colson who is literary editor of the Herald-Examiner here. She has a middle-class mind and is convinced I am dirty minded. Whenever I print a book she says that of me. I know where she stands. She is at least honest.

I commend to you the reading of Van Wyck Brooks. He has got this whole subject of American writing clearly out in front of him.[4]

In your own writing keep trying to make it serve your own purposes. If you will do that, in case of necessity whipping yourself a little into the realization that it is to be primarily an instrument for curing yourself, much will be gained.

My sister, when she was alive had a mania for what she called "doing something for the world." It destroyed her. She got into a queer fantastic notion that she was a kind of representative of Christ on earth.[5]

I've got to keep constantly whipping myself into a healthy attitude in this matter. There is the always present temtation to break over into quests.

I dont know why I should recommend writing for any other purpose than this help to self facing. When it comes to real things the autobiograpic note isn't the true note by any means. Its up and along but that doesn't need to concern you now. If the time comes for clearer sight the road will open itself to you. It and you will not need any guidance.

There is a dull drab thing in your house, your town, your street. It is not peculiar to that environment. It gets however into your blood and obscures your outlook as the drabness about us obscures view.

You've got to fight against it.

I do—for some odd secondary reason—commend to you the reading of history now. It lifts you into other fields and places. I do it and I am sure my instincts are correct in this direction anyway.

LH

1. Hahn's longhand note.

2. Anderson refers to Harold Stearns's review of Sigmund Freud's *Reflections on War and Death*, translated by Brill and Kuftner. Stearns wrote that "modern wars are the atonement we make for our lack of appreciating the human evils of a pallid, 'safe' industrialism. Anderson, who felt he was bravely assaulting the evils of industrialization, could read with approval lines like "Whatever civilization emerges from the present clash of arms, it can have no stability and no creative joy unless our former timidities are exorcised." *The Dial*, May 23, 1918, pp. 482–83.

3. Doubtless Anderson was annoyed that reviewer Louis Untermeyer was not convinced that oppressive conditions make poetry impossible and that he concluded his review by asserting: "Even if *Mid-American Chants* is composed of the stuff of poetry rather than poetry itself, we cannot withhold our admiration from one whose utterance is so vibrant. From such passion, from such rude earnestness may rise the clearer voice that is implicit in Mr. Anderson's prophetic promise." *Ibid.*, p. 485.

4. Anderson had become aware of Brooks through his relationship to *Seven Arts* and considered him a major voice of the arts as Anderson understood them.

5. Stella Anderson Hill had died suddenly during an operation earlier that month. The oblique reference suggests that the basic message concerning her death was delivered conversationally.

66

To Bab August, 1918[1] 427 West 22nd St. [New York City]

I am up in the country, sitting under an oak tree and looking down Long Island Sound. Steamers go up and down. A fresh cool wind blows.

In town I have found me a delightful place in which to live.[2] The address is 427 West 22nd. There is a large room with a fireplace and high ceiling. The house is neatly kept by an ancient maiden Irish woman of 60. Her name is Rose McCurran. At daylight she arises and goes to early mass. She is back at 7:30 and brings me up coffee toast and fruit. I am in an old dressing gown and can sit writing until noon. Nothing disturbs me. The room is at the back of the old house and the roar of the city is far away. I arise from sleep and step in[to] a created world. If letters arrive they are not opened until at noon when I shave dress and go out on the streets of the town. To one who has had to fight to maintain a mood, this is paradise. No more of the necessity of breaking in and out of the affairs of the office.

As for my making a living—that is simplified too. I do little personal news stories for the newspapers concerning John and Anita Loos. One can be done in ten minutes. There is no office to go to, no quibbling. It is amazingly simple.

Tennessee will be with me in New York in September and later I shall come west for a month or two.

Already the easement in my mind is making itself felt. A sense of struggle has gone away. A certain long swing of things is going away.

It is good too to have access to men and women of my own world—a thing sadly lacking in Chicago. I begin to sense the fact that I may never really live there again.[3]

Of course everyone will preach at me about the danger of the New York point of view etc. Some one always has been preaching at me about something. They will be afraid of my becoming a New Yorker. As though my forty years and my struggle to maintain myself and my flare at life all this time had resulted in nothing.

There is a certain definate sharpness and shallowness about the people here that I like just as I have always know[n] I would like Paris and as I love aristocrats and ladies in delicate beautiful clothes. I love them perhaps most because they are so little a part of myself.

As for my place of living it is not Greenwich nor the east side nor Fifth Ave. nor uptown. Old Chelsea is an overlooked place. Only the New Republic is down here. It is odd apart—a place from which to emerge and look and to which to retire and ponder.

As for my work—well I am engaged in new ventures. I shall not tell you about these. Some mood in you sometime ago took from you the right to know of what I am doing while I am doing it. That will come back if you want it after a while.

LH

1. Hahn's longhand note.
2. Anderson was in New York because John Emerson had offered him a movie sinecure. On June 25, 1918, Anderson had written Van Wyck Brooks that he was "looking forward with joy to the notion of wiping this dust of business off my feet for at least a time." He mentioned plans to stay in New York in the coming fall for "two or three months. . . . I want to wander about, readjust myself, get the weariness out of me and see if I can face life anew." He thought Brooks would be amused at his letter of resignation and sent him a copy; it is reprinted here. Note that his boss at Taylor-Critchfield Advertising Co. was Bayard Barton.

> Dear Barton:
>
> You have a man in your employ that I have thought for a long time should be fired. I refer to Sherwood Anderson. He is a fellow of a good deal of ability but for a long time I have been convinced that his heart is not in his work. There is no question but that this man Anderson has in some ways been an ornament to our organization. His hair, for one thing, being long and mussy gives an artistic carelessness to his personal appearance that somewhat impresses such men as Frank Lloyd Wright and Mr. Curtiniez of Kalamazoo when they come into the office. But Anderson is not really productive, as I have said, his heart is not in his work. I think he should be fired, and if you will not do the job, I should like permission to fire him myself. I, therefore, suggest that Anderson be asked to sever his connections with the company on August 1. He is a nice fellow. We will let him down easy, but let's can him.
>
> Respectfully submitted,
>
> Sherwood Anderson

3. By the end of the year Anderson was back in Chicago and wrote to Brooks: "The moving picture dependence became impossible. That isn't my way out." Anderson's life was characterized by a never-ending search for a "way out."

67

To Bab New York, Aug, 1918[1]

Your letter was very nice—like a visit from a fine friend. You did state some things that didn't exactly need stating but they were good things. It was a little stuffy of me saying that about letting you in on what I am doing. Sometime ago you grew proprietary about what I was trying to do and I always resent that. I don't know just why. The next time you write tell me more details of your life as it runs along. I always want to know about that.

I suspect you will finally be in New York. When quiet comes to you, as it will, you will be here doing some kind of work.

Right now I think you have enough to do to get bravely through your days. I sense things, the hot weary drag of days you have been through.

My life in the new place is very pleasant. Just now I am half ill, a cold from staying a long time in the sea. It was so easy and delightful to swim that I went on at it for hours. Later, it turned cold and I got chilled.

That is a passing thing.

About my days. I arise at seven and my landlady, an ancient virgin named Rose—who has already been out to early mass brings my breakfast. I eat, smoke, make sacrifice to the gods and go to work. Many new impulses flow in in [*sic*] me.

At noon I shave, bath dress and go into the town. I go to the moving picture studio, with the stuff there by which I live, get me about with friends or go by myself into some little restaurant to look at the people.

My relations with John are very delightful. He poor chap is driven like a slave. We have little half hour talks and occasionally dine together. On Sundays we perhaps go with Miss Loos for a day in the country.[2]

It is all very splendid, the complete release from business. I am happy but I work hard. I want, now that the opportunity has come to establish myself as a man of letters so that I may live by that. I shall fight for it but will not make the hurtful kind of concessions.

If you come very late this fall I shall have many new people, crept out from under my pen to tell you about. Love and courage to you.

LH

1. Hahn's longhand note.

2. Anita Loos, in a letter to me dated Oct. 28, 1974, wrote, "I can tell you that Sherwood Anderson and my late husband John Emerson were very, very close friends indeed, so close that I cannot remember a time when he was out of our minds or our consideration."

68

To Bab September 1918[1] [New York City]

I got your telegram and will get off a reply today. I am writing swiftly and constantly so if you do not hear often from me for a time you may know that it is because of my preoccupation in that.

Beside my novel I am developing three or four story themes. They are delicate things. I want to write them as one would sit down to play on a piano or violin in the evening.

Your developement of your day was almost good and true. The idea of quiet and sureness was a little underdeveloped but it was better than most writing you have done that I have seen.

People I suppose grow into expression in that way. They dramatize themselves in a certain position, as meeting it in a definate way. They write that out and the theme developes. It becomes a theme, a dramatization and grows a little out of porportion. As in your little outside things—the pregnant cat—becomes too important. It over shadows the thing in the two women that cannot yet be quite understood and handled.

The writing that has reached this stage is caracteristically American. It is good enough to be better than most magazine writing. It lacks only a kind of maturity, a cultural background created out of itself. When you have grasped these things, looking still at your own life but in some way getting it more fully and truly into its background, perceiving and approaching more nearly its truth you will have begun to achieve real writing.

I cannot now give you my impression of New York. I am gathering and assorting the impulses that flow into me but they do not fit into the brevity of such letters as I may find time to write.

You give me the impression of going bravely through your days. Nothing more could be asked. You do with courage and fortitude a difficult thing. That is achievment.

LH

1. Hahn's longhand note.

69

To Bab New York City 1918[1] [September]

The letter from the odd looking thick lipped man who has been to Russian frontiers doesn't tell much. It is like so many things that now come out of that country. I take it from what he says that he feels he has something to say but must first devote himself to the telling of what he thinks people want to hear. You say he is looking for an American artist. I wonder why he does not look within himself. That it seems to me is what one of the Russian artists would do. It seems almost a lost impulse here. There are always papa's and others to be thought of.

I work steadily along on the new book [Hahn's marginal note: *Poor White*] which seems to me to have something of the sweep of Marching Men without the tendency of that book to subvert the human element. I wont discuss the impulse of the new book, in fact I have worked on it rapidly and in silence. It will lead me I hope into deep structural impulses in our civilization and cut deeper than anything I have ever tried to do before.

As for the war it grinds along and means both more and less than its surface indicates. It is rather taken as a thing in itself whereas it is a result.

I have written two new short stories which are to go now to the typist. They are outside of the present strong drift of my impulses just as the city is and most [of] the people just now.

When I am not at work Tennessee and I go on the ferries or into the country. We went for the weekend to Jerry Blum[2] on his farm. I think him the best American painter I have found, his spirit is braver, his impulse more direct and real. I sometimes think that he is to painting here what I may some day be considered to be writing.

I shall be glad to see you when you can come here. Surely you will succeed in getting something out of your visit to the town.

LH

1. Hahn's longhand note.
2. Chicago-born painter (b. 1874), who became a close friend and correspondent.

70

To Bab September 1918.[1]

The days go marching past. Fall has come to the city and the air is like wine. I am in a detached impersonal mood and work steadily at my new book. The city with its people and its perplexities lies outside me. Everything does a little now. Mr. Brooks has published a new book and I have written an article for the Chicago Tribune about it. It is called Letters and Leadership, Hibsch [Huebsch]. Mr. Van Wyck Brooks. Get it and read it. His is to me the most sustained and thoughtful mind concerned with American criticism.[2]

I have seen almost no one. The girl Mary knew at college—called Hub I see at a luncheon place where I go often. Tennessee is here and we go often in the afternoon on sight seeing trips. I plan to write long weekly letters to the children about the city and get notes during these trips. I am also at work on a book of notes covering the impressions of a western man in this town.[3]

You will see that I am absorbed. The spirit of something keep me rather up to the mark here. I presume there is here an atmosphere I want. It comes out of the air and springs from the fact that a great many real men of vast significants in America have walked and thought thoughts in these streets.

LH

1. Hahn's longhand note.
2. The review was entitled "Our Rebirth," and appeared in the Chicago *Daily Tribune* for Saturday, Sept. 14, 1918, in columns 5–7, p. 10.
3. If written, these have not survived.

71

To Bab New York—The Hotel Brevoort/October-1918[1]

I am indeed sorry to have you in the city and ill. Do stay in bed for a day or two and get in shape to enjoy your stay here. May I be allowed to suggest. Do not go too often to the bad little resturants in Greenwich Villiage. You must while you are here get strength for the future.

One of the places I have found a God sent is Central Park. You can take the bus up there and sit for hours watching life flow past. I go there often to work. Have you things with you to read. I havn't many books but will be glad to let you have what I can find on my shelf.

Do not think too much of the difficulty we spoke of. I took a walk and talked to myself about it last evening. We are all so apparently caught in a trap. It is only a lot more evident in your case.

I should say the test of a man and woman lay in that—how can they face maturity.

And what is maturity beyond a realization that life is a trap into which we are thrown and no one knows the way out. I am sorry that I do not know much about the plays in town. One called "Lightning" at the Gaity is worth while. I do not know about the others.

If there are any publishers or others here in town I know you would like to meet I'll be glad to give you a note to them. It is a barren dessert however as far as I have traveled in it.

I hope you will wake up every morning glad for your vacation and will get all you can out of it. Dont be sick.

If you like I will come to lunch with you on Sunday.

LH

1. Hahn's longhand note.

72

To Bab December-1918 N.Y. City[1]

My Dear Bab—

I have been for an evening with Paul Rosenfeld[2] the musical critic who has just got out of the army. He had Waldo Frank's new novel that is ready to go to the publishers. I wish I could make the man see how badly it is done but he is a good deal infatuated and my saying anything would do no good.[3] The man has a genius for people and manages always to get just the right people together. Since I have come down here I have realized that this one man was responsible for the distinctive note of Seven Arts Magazine. As a writer he is impossible![4]

I shall no doubt go to Chicago for Christmas and shall then try to get a job out there and go to work again. The new novel[5] will by that time be near completion and I shall feel that I have at least gained that by my experiment. It goes steadily along now and seem to me to have power and meaning. I have become friends with Copeau[6] of the French theatre here and he is arranging for the translation of both Marching Men and Winesburg when it is published. He is very enthusiastic about Marching Men and feels that it has given him more of a feeling of the country than anything else he has read coming out of America in this generation.

I am sure the Flu[7] has all gone out of me and I know that I am no longer depressed. It was inevitable that a period of depression [should] follow the war and the worst part of that has not come yet. People still feel that something has been gained to pay for the years of killing and ugliness and for a time words can still be manufactured to keep up the illusion. It will however pass and the sickening realization will come home to the man in the street. How he will stand it I dont know.

I am glad to hear that you are on the road to health again. Do be careful and dont drive your strength too far. You will some day be free to live where you will and as you will and you must have strength left to live when that time comes.

TS

1. Hahn's longhand note.
2. Paul Rosenfeld (1890–1946), an intimate friend of Anderson's. He revised and published Anderson's *Memoirs* and was one of his literary executors.
3. The novel in question was *The Art of the Vieux Colombier*, published in 1918. In a Dec. 1918 letter to Van Wyck Brooks Anderson indicates that Rosenfeld showed Anderson the book secretly. Jones and Rideout, eds., *Letters of Sherwood Anderson*, p. 43.
4. In the letter referred to in n. 3, Anderson also wrote that he "blurted out" his feeling that Frank's writing was wordy and insincere. The friendship survived the resultant breach.
5. *Poor White*, published in 1920. Anderson was also expecting proof for *Winesburg, Ohio*.
6. Jacques Copeau (1878–1949), French critic, actor, manager, and producer, had been sent with his Vieux Colombier theatrical group as part of a cultural exchange program after World War I.
7. This letter was written during the worst influenza epidemic in American history.

73

To Bab January 1919[1] Sunday Afternoon [Chicago]

You are really quite wrong in your hunch this time. I was very greatly depressed when I first came home and had to get back into business but have quite recovered. For one thing the later part of the novel[2] has been going well and it is nearing the end. I find that I got really rested in New York. The physical ugliness of Chicago looses it's ability to hurt me when I am really at work. Beside all this I am really well.

I am sorry that your own problem remains unchanged. There is this to be said about it. When you finally get out of Indianapolis you will surely find that all places are much the same and in learning to live there you will learn to live anyplace.

Tennessee and I went last Sunday for the day with the children.[3] Robert had made me a puppet theater that was really wonderful. In the late afternoon when the light began to fail they gave a show. John lay on his belly on the floor and Robert operated the puppets.[4] It was a strikingly nice thing they had done. All the family seemed happy. Mimi has begun to pass out of infancy and become a little girl. It seems to me that Cornelia is happier and is learning better how to handle her life.

I leave town again this week but do not know when I shall get around your way. It is a matter that is on the knees of the gods.

In writing the new book I have let myself go regardless and so there will be I fancy a good deal of cutting to do. I hope to finish writing it before proof comes in from Winesburg.[5] I will let it lie for a month or two and then go in and cut as generously as I wrote. It will I am sure be much the most finished of my novels.

Do get out of doors whenever you can and try to hold yourself above the sickness in your household.

A Happy New Year To You

TS

1. Hahn's longhand note.
2. *Poor White.*
3. Doubtless at Michigan City, Ind., where Cornelia taught and reared her and Anderson's children. She stayed there until 1943, where she moved to Marion, Va., to be near her son, Robert, who was publishing the newspapers that Anderson had bought in 1927. In the summer Tennessee would visit Cornelia and the children and spend Sundays at the beach with them. Anderson loved his children but did not spend much time with them after the divorce from Cornelia.
4. During an interview in Feb. 1974 John (b. Dec. 31, 1908) said he did not remember this event.
5. *Winesburg, Ohio* was published shortly before May 27, 1919.

74

To Bab — Chicago-1919[1] [circa March]

I am doing a new series of prose experiment—an adventure in prose by way of design in words and feeling.[2]

For a long time I have had this notion that something might be done to awaken the poetry in others. I grow pretty weary of our poets, their setting up to be poets, talking of the matter etc.

Sometimes it seems to me that I get the truest poetry from people like you and a dozen others I know. When you try to express something you right away get drunk with words. Most of your letters are that way. They say nothing at all.

But sometimes when you are unconcious or weary a flash comes. It is so with tired business men, women bound, all kinds of people.

I have the most determined belief in what happens in the way that water runs out of a broken jar. It should be the matter of the most utter indifference to me whether I am a poet or not. It is a matter of importance that all people find their way to poetry.

The thing to be aimed at is the opening of doors. My new experiment is in that direction.

When you are entirely well and have some leisure you might copy these things. Make two copies of each and keep the origional.[3] I will send you more when you want them.

LH

1. Hahn's longhand note.
2. Anderson had now started to write pieces that were to be published, beginning in 1919, mainly in the *Little Review* and the *Double Dealer*. They appeared in book form when *A New Testament* was published in 1927.
3. No manuscript fragments survived with this letter.

75

To Bab — Chicago, May 1919[1]

After all I will not be able to stop at Indianapolis this trip. I will be busy here until Friday evening and Jacques Copeau is to be in Chicago Saturday. As he is in a way my guest I must be there.

I saw the Kentucky Derby and had good luck as I lost no money. It was a joy to see the thoroughbreds run. For nearly a week now I have been sitting in a room upstairs in a factory here in Owensboro. Across the street in a school yard a drill sargeant drills the school boys. Militarism has evidently come to America. When I think of the stark horror of the terms imposed on Germany and the dreadful spectacle of hitting a fallen foe going on and on I am sick of civilization and wish I never had to go back to it. What has become of the old Anglo Saxon belief that it is cowardly to hit a man when he is down.

A week in one of these small towns always brings a reaction into laziness in me. The good effects, both mental and physical only show when I get back to town.

I am trying to make a business arraingment by which I will sever my connection with a company and work indipendently. If it works out as I hope, I will have more leisure and will still make a living.[2]

You may depend on it I will come to see you at the first opportunity.

With Love

LH

1. Hahn's longhand note.

2. See reference to what was probably the same hoped-for arrangement mentioned in letter 64 herein. Another possibility was working for the D. T. Bohon Company, a manufacturer of buggies, located in Harrodsburg, Ky.; the company sold buggies and other items by mail. The owner's son, David T. Bohon, offered the following comments in a letter to me (now in the Sutton Papers, University of Illinois Library, Champaign-Urbana).

> So far as I know, Mr. Anderson was never active in preparing any advertising material for the company. However, during his visits there he and my father did become good friends and he used to visit us and spend the night at our home, which he did several times. As I recall, this was in the year of 1919. Mr. Anderson was always very much interested in the advertising being used by the Bohon company, which was entirely to the rural population and was somewhat amusing to the more sophisticated city dwellers. Mr. Anderson prepared a brochure, which was a satire on these advertising methods and which was very interesting. The little brochure was prepared entirely by Mr. Anderson, it had a picture of my father on it and was intended to be amusing and was certainly that. I had a number of these little brochures. However, over the years, they seem to have gotten away.
>
> At one time, we also had autographed copies I believe of every book that Mr. Anderson ever published. Over the years these seem to have disappeared also. It is certainly a shame that the souvenirs and mementoes of Mr. Anderson that we at one time had, have escaped from us in some way or other.
>
> I remember Mr. Anderson as being a rather flamboyant personality. As I recall, he usually dressed in very outstanding clothes which at that time were considered to be "loud." It seems to me that I remember a very brilliant checked coat which attracted attention wherever he went in our small town of Harrodsburg. On some of his trips he came by train and on others he drove a car. As I remember this was a sports car, although I do not remember the name or make. It was a roadster and Mr. Anderson was in the habit of driving it with the top down and he made a very sporty picture with this car and his colorful attire.

Whenever he visited us, Mr. Anderson and my father usually talked all night long. What they talked about I do not know but usually they were still talking when daylight arrived.

76

To Bab Chicago May 1919[1] [After May 21]

Poor Little Sick Woman—

It is too bad. Ill luck attends me. My friends become ill. Jacques Copeau came out to spend several days with me. A thief crawled through a window and stole his clothes. I have had a cold. It is dark and gloomy here.

The spring does not develope. No bright clear days come.

The change I am planning to make is not radical. I shall rent a small, quiet office of my own. Then I shall have two or three clients who will pay me a fee. I shall have some commission from the house here.

The hope is that I may escape a little from the distraction of the office which is huge and noisy. Also I shall perhaps get many quiet hours in which to work.

Have been to Detroit and just got back. Copeau went with me to lecture at the University of Mich.[2] He is the most charming man I have met and is I am convinced a very great artist.

Some of these days when you are well and able to walk out of doors I shall come to Indianapolis and see you. The new book is out and I will send you a copy tomorrow.[3]

LH

1. Hahn's longhand note.

2. Articles in the *Michigan Daily* of May 14, 20, 23, 1919, indicate that Copeau spoke on the drama and France, and particularly his own realistic theater group, under the auspices of the department of French at the University of Michigan, Ann Arbor, on May 21. None of the coverage mentions Anderson.

3. The new book was *Winesburg, Ohio;* Anderson had shown various stories to Finley in manuscript on his visits to Indianapolis, and Finley had supplied carbon copies of stories destroyed when Anderson's tent burned down at Lake Chateaugay, N.Y. See Sutton, *Road to Winesburg,* for details of serial publications of the Winesburg stories and reprinting of Chicago reviews of the collection when it was published. Hahn's effects at the time of her death included an autographed first edition of *Winesburg, Ohio.*

77

To Bab July 1919[1] [Chicago]

Dear Woman—

For some reason the last few weeks have impressed upon my mind more than ever before the reality of pain. I saw it in the fishes taken from the sea, in the writhing of the worms by which the fishes were caught, in the eyes of cattle in the field, tortured by flies. It is in your letter in a half dozen other letters that come to me here on my return from the country.[2] Today as I walk in the hot city, as I sense in the air the dull dreary hatred in men's hearts that has been at the basis of the race riots here and that was back of the equally dull, hateful war in which we have been engaged[,] I understand you, all suffering people more clearly. You have lived in the house of Pain. Too often I have walked past and looked in at the window not really understanding.

Do not think of helping me. If it ever turns out that can be done splendidly and beautifully [,] very well.[3]

In the meantime do trust to the fight in me to at least attempt to hold you in the right place as in many ways my dearest friend.

LH

1. Hahn's longhand note.
2. Probably from Ephraim, Wis.
3. An early indication of Finley's desire to help Anderson financially, which she did over a period of years.

78

To Bab August 1919/Ephraim, Wis.[1]

Naturally it seemed to me absurd that anything could have the finality of your pronouncement that evening in the car. Nothing is like that except a play or a magazine short story. We both know that well enough.

I am in the country for a few weeks but will be back in Chicago—Aug. 1st. This afternoon I have climbed the side of a high cliff and have found a ledge covered with moss where I can look down at the sea. These days out of doors, walking much alone, under trees and swimming in the sea renew me. Deep within me I am at peace. O [Oh scratched out] that I could stay here alone for months. There is a town 17 miles away over the reaches of Green Bay. On clear days and when I have climbed the cliffs that shore comes up out of the sea. Faintly the smoke of the factories discolors the sky.

I was thinking of you when your letter came. Why cannot you be patient. Some day you will be free and will be able to live comfortable. You can reach out to people. What I really thought was something like this—"We are all destroyed but some there are who do not meet a cheap defeat."

Surely life is bound to temper itself to you if you can meet it square. Perhaps what you want most may be given you. A surrender can never lead to anything at all.

This year I would like to do things more subtile and difficult than anything I have ever done and I will need strength.[2] Would that I could give up the superficial battle for a living. Once I needed that. Now I do not believe I need it any more.

In our conversation that evening there was one false note struck. I found you had been thinking of me as one capable of becoming the property of another person. I acquiessed becuse your desire for a way straight out seemed so real. It is all false. While I am the man I want to be I shall never belong to any one. I shall try to belong to the moment and the new day.

If our relationship really means to you what you say it does I have faith you will someway, somehow find a way to make it work.

About the check—Thank you. It has developed that I can accept things from you as I once couldn't.

LH

1. Probably late July; Hahn had added the Aug. date and place in longhand.

2. Anderson may have been referring to the stories that became parts of *A New Testament*. He had started them in the spring of 1919, and they appeared in the *Little Review* between Oct. 1919 and Apr. 1920. On the back cover of the June 1919 issue had appeared this notice: "In an early number we will publish an extraordinary personal document by Sherwood Anderson, called *A New Testament*. An autobiography not of the conscious but of the fanciful life of the individual." The issues of July and Aug. also mention the anticipated publication.

79

To Bab — August 1919—Chicago, Ill.[1]

It is good to think of you up in that northern country and out of doors. I was in Montreal once and remember very vividly the charm of the place.

Coming back from the country had, for a few days, a very bad effect on me. I became ill with an odd kind of psycic illness. Every face I saw on the street was old and weary. The children were no better. Even the lines of the building had been drawn by men too tired to try to draw lovely lines.

The thing got into me and made me rather ill. Any sort of doing anything for pay seemed a disease to me.

Now I seem to have gulped the mess again and am quite cheerful. My new office—being small and with no one in it but me and later a secretary will help. I moved in a week ago and go there each morning to work several hours before I look in at the Critchfield place.

Have a plan for the next 30 years of my life that may interest you. Will tell you of it when I see you again.

LH

1. Hahn's longhand note.

80

To Bab Cincinnati, Ohio September 1919[1]
Friday

Have been in Kentucky for a week and am on my way home. Every year at this time, when I have been for a season out of doors, I am made ill by the necessity of returning to the life of affairs. After a while I shall wear my harness again and do it more cheerfully.

I've a notion the whole world is somewhat ill. The reports I get from men who have recently been in England & France is that there is a hopeless illness of spirit there. One can imagain what it is in Germany. In Russia no doubt there is some hope as an experiment is at least being tried there.

One gets cured from such illness by nature as in no other way but one pays a price. After the trees men and their affairs seem such silly trifling things and one's participation in the effort to make money brings on illness.

Some time I shall talk to you about the matter you speak of in your letter but not now. It will be better when I see you again. Perhaps I shall be in a healthier state of mind then.

With love and hoping you are getting something real out of your period of release.

LH Written on stationery of the Grand Hotel, Cincinnati.

1. Hahn's longhand note.

81

To Bab September 1919[1] [Chicago]
Thursday

I am on the train going down to Anderson [Indiana] and as it has been raining hard all day nothing would have been gained had I been able to come to Indianapolis. I shall be taking the sleeper back to Chicago to-night.

The truth is that I am no fit company for anyone these days. I hunger for the out of doors and for wandering alone and am held tight to my desk. My hand writes advertisements with reluctance and I spend all my strength driving it to the bread & butter task.

Sometimes I think all mankind must be living through a period of dis-ease and ineffectualness and that I am but one of all the rest of these affected madmen. Perhaps it is all a residue of the war and the awakening from that debauch.

Nothing seems healthy but the out of doors, the corn growing in fields and the silent strips of woodland.

I do not dream any more of making my way by writing. I dream of being a wandering pedlar, a man who lives in a tiny frame house at the edge of a small town.

I dream of quiet to work and dream and live.

And as the days and months go I stand perplexed in the roaring city, hear the screams of politicians and reformers and wait—I know not for what.

I am sorry it did not turn out you could be free but you see the rain would have made the evening dismal.

LH

1. Hahn's longhand note.

82

To Bab Chicago November 1919[1]

I am mighty sorry to hear of your illness. Have been in a rather exalted state for ten days, writing furiously whenever I could get a moment away from the grind. Now I seem to have got into a dead water.

I do hope you will finally succeed in getting away from the dreadful periods of illness and you may be sure I will come to see you when I am down that way.

Just when I will come that way I dont know. They crowd great oceans of work on my desk. I try not to be caught up by it and have all my other side drowned. I succeed for a while then have to swim with the stream and rest. At such a time I am mostly dull and tired.

Still I am very well and it hurts me to think of you always passing in and out of these times. How difficult it must be for you to keep your vision clear.

I have lunched with Miss Bowlin several times as the office where she works is near my office. I suppose now that her man has come to town I shall not see so much of her. She is an interesting woman, apparently much absorbed in the revolutionist movement. Have not seen her husband. Is she a native Indianapolisian?

Your illness puzzles me. Is it physical or is it the result of too great an emotional life lived under trying circumstances.

The black ugly building[s] at which I stare every day are hidden behind a veil of snow. The night will be lovely.

Get well soon.

LH

1. Hahn's longhand note.

83

To Bab November, 1919 [Chicago]

I have been a good deal tired. All of this discussion of my soul in the public prints.[1] My temporary surrender to the odd sort of half-mood there on the stone in the darkness. Your own certainty that you completely understand my psychology.

To the country where I went in a car with five young men to see hogs caught in a new kind of trap that is to be advertised for sale. Long stretches of fat cornfields. Cold rain whipping up the dust in the road—a bleak and cheerless little hotel.

Went to walk in the deserted, rain-washed streets. In a little cigar store got in talk with an old Belgian. Red faced farmers about, all getting rich on the high price of corn. Am stealing today and spending it in my room. Something, the dull grey clouds and the cold wind had driven the gods out of the corn and here in my room there are no gods.

Perhaps you do not understand at all. The inner thing in me is a clean boy running over the hills. I turn to women because men are too concerned with making money and overfeeding their lusts. I am stupid. I forget that women are as much involved in the tangle as men. So much of the time I do not want hands on me but want to run clean and alone. I can't have that I know but like a silly fellow I keep asking it.

TS Prepared from Hahn's typescript.

1. This remark refers to reviews of *Winesburg, Ohio.*

84

To Bab Chicago December 1919[1]

Dear Woman—

Whatever you do you must not let your mind dwell on the possibilities of doing things you cant do. Remember you have enough to face. There may be years of living in the presence of illness. You yourself have not been well. To think too much would lead to a kind of madness and it will be hard enough for you always to keep a clear head and keep yourself well enough to stand up against the dullness of everyday existence.

While I realize that I cannot go on indefinately making the compromise I have made there are ways out for me. It may be that my present notion of a summer camp for grown ups and children on one of the northern lakes will succeed.[2] By some hook or crook I shall manage to creep thru the wall of life that often confronts me.

It confronts every one. That I know. It is only because I have seen another road that I am often accutely unhappy.

And the same is true of you. There is a hard fast fact. You are a squirrel in a cage.

That I know and I do not want you to fly off into dreams that will only bring rude awakenings.

Your town with its long dreary streets is a fact. Your life there is a fact. Now that you are away for a breathing time try to breath deeply and prepare for your own struggle. Do not let my heart light on your narrow shoulders.

Go to the harbor and look at the ships. Take an excursion boat thru the river around New York. Spend every possible hour out in the open air.

I shall be going to Kentucky at the end of this week and will be gone for ten day[s] or two weeks. You may address me after Saturday, c/o General Delivery, Harrodsburg, Ky. Will let you know when I get back here again.

LH

1. Hahn's longhand note.

2. Anderson had many plans to escape conventional means of providing for himself. See, for instance, letter 86 herein. It is probable that Anderson was thinking of locating such a camp in the Door County area of Wisconsin, where Ephraim is located.

85

To Bab — Dec? 1919[1] [Chicago]

It is a dark day here with clouds of smoke filling the street. I am sure the Testament will come to mean more than anything I have done, to many people. It seems to me to achieve a fine impersonality and to be more ascetic than anything else of mine. In a way that is the object.

As to E.L.M.'s things I have not read them. I have no doubt of the value and integrity of the Anthology[2] but it is aside from my own impulse in life. I read part of it when it was newly published but turned from it because I felt its essential tiredness and protest.[3]

It is a tired time filled with tired people—Everyone has a son, a mother, a brother, a wife, someone dragging them back and back.

Human relationships in such a time become instinctively clutching. One cannot feel the breath of a wind on the cheek without the need of another to feel it.

I am myself touched with all this and know that I come to a time of new cleansing. That absorbes me now.

If I have been ill it is the illness of waiting for someone else to release me & my spirit, to make a path for me.

I feel like one strengthening himself to grasp an axe and cut his own way.

But I do not wish to talk of it. Just now I can do nothing for anyone but wish them a good voyage.

LH

1. Hahn's longhand note.

2. Edgar Lee Masters, *The Spoon River Anthology*.

3. See Sutton, *Road to Winesburg*, pp. 430–31, for additional comments on the relationship between *Winesburg, Ohio* and *The Spoon River Anthology*.

86

To Bab Chicago—December 21st, 1919[1]

In an odd way money is a sweet thing to me. Sometimes it is like a breath of air to a drowning man. In spite of that dear woman you mustn't send me money. Something might happen one of these days that would make every penny important to you too.

To me of course money always means fewer hours and days devoted to business. I have come to realize that the rythm of this industrial city is gradually getting in on me. My power to recuperate becomes less every year. It takes me longer to gather strength.

This would be unimportant if it were not for the fact that the years of my best effort lie ahead of me. I want strength for those years.

This winter I shall have to give serious thought to breaking the hold of business finally and for good.

Many plans go thru my head. The most practical I think would be a summer community somewhere in the wood[s] north of Chicago. As the thing forms in my mind I would like to make it a place where grown people go to spend the summer working with children and where children go to spend the summer working with grown people.

It seems to me that I have enough power with people to give the right spiritual swing to such a project. If I decide to do it I shall go at it to raise $25,000 to be used in buying forest land by the lake and to put up the first and most necessary buildings.

Then I would go there and work out of doors six months of each year, would carry on gardening operations, raise poultry, build small houses for the people who come etc. Things like music, rythms etc. could be introduced. Men women and children would all work under the guidance of actual workmen, builders, machinists etc.

The corporation would be non profit making. It would pay back the origional money put in and all the rest would go into the community coffers to make living cost less, etc, etc.

As head of the institution I would draw a small salary at first. Would live there six months a year and have my children there three months a year. In the winter I would go to Chicago or New York and write.

Does the place not seem reasonable to you. Seems to me I could in some way raise the necessary funds to get it under way and shake the shackles of business off me for good.

Love and a good voyage to you. Write me when you can at Room 1203—Provident Bldg. 226 So. LaSalle St. Chicago.

LH

1. Hahn's longhand note.

87

To Bab Chicago—1919[1] [December?]

It is snowing heavily this morning and the dead habitual grey of our sky becomes pale. I shall be glad indeed to see Oliver Sayler[2] and hope he will call me when he comes here.

I have not been ill. Business is more like a prison to me than ever and I have, each time I come back to it, to develope a new technique. I spring up and beat against the bars until I am sometimes tired and ill. Then a half Rabelasian, half cynical sense of humor comes to my rescue. I become profane. Finally if I am fortunate I begin to write and loose myself in that.

In the midst of all this people slip away from me. It is in my nature to forget that I owe a letter to this one or that I have not had a letter from another.

People are you see going up and down doing things. Saylor lecturing to a Dramatic League, you sitting in a room watching an old woman playing with a board, some tall dark woman being buffeted by winds as she walks in Michigan Boulevard, a bewhiskered man dodging past the nose of an automobile on State Street.

For long periods everything and everybody becomes impersonal. I am compelled to float, to sink myself in the sea.

Then again someday when I am less tired you begin to emerge before my eyes as individuals. My eyes are rested and I see.

It is all right. I expect someday to sink into the sea of personalities and never to emerge. It depends upon my ability to resist weariness, not to struggle, to float on the surface of the sea when I am too tired to swim.

I talk in figures too much. The point is to convey to you my quality of being impersonal without meaning. It will account often for your hearing nothing of me.

There are points I have to think about, new adjustments I have to make now that I am back in business again. The personalities about me change. I am at once more powerful and weaker. I have to fit myself into the scheme of things anew—today—every day.

I cant write today you see. I can only look at the snow drifting over the city. I'll try some other day.

LH

1. Hahn's longhand note.
2. Oliver Martin Sayler, drama critic for the Indianapolis *News*.

88

To Bab Chicago—1919[1]

You must read a book called the Moon and Sixpense by Somerset Maugham. A striking story that will I am sure make you understand a great deal in myself. It is a story I have often thought of writing and will yet. When I do write it [I] will lay it down without explananation or all the talk Maugham indulges in.[2]

Am often startled in the presence of a woman on a fine evening to see how the mystery of trees, silence, colors, and life goes over her head.

It is because what is so vital and necessary to her is necessarily a passing thing to the man.

I am writing again and when I do much goes over my head. Suddenly things thus begin to coordinate for me. All staleness in life floats away. I find myself vitally interested in everything. I live and am strong.

That I allow the affairs of life to in any way interfere with me at such times is because I am a coward. It must be so. Why should I care if I starve.

I dont as a matter of fact. I only realize I am not as strong as I should be and so go on taking what I can get.

I am talking in riddles. It is because my mind is on the figure of a man walking on the streets of a town on a Summer Sunday evening. I am about to run away to create the story of what happened to the man.

In passing I but wave my hand to you and the rest of the world.[3]

LH

1. Hahn's longhand note.
2. W. Somerset Maugham's *The Moon and Sixpence* was published in Apr. 1919. A considerable distortion of the life of French artist Paul Gauguin, it yet presents the essential struggle, which Anderson knew intimately, of art taking precedence over other commitments, especially those relating to family. When Anderson reviewed Beril Becker's *Paul Gauguin, the Calm Madman*, in 1931, he wrote: "It is good to get the book about Gauguin. It wipes out all of that 'Moon

and Sixpence' cheapness. The man wanted everything." Thinking of how Gauguin's situation paralleled his own, he wrote: "It is good to get all this clear truth about Gauguin walking out on his wife, being cheap and heroic, straightened out" (unpublished letter, written in 1931, to Aaron B. Bernd, literary editor of the Macon, Ga., *Telegraph*).

3. Finley ends her letter of Nov. 1924 with "A wave to you—."

89

To Bab

Mobile [Ala.]—January-1920[1]
Sunday

Have been in a whirl and unable to write. Had to go to Ohio then to Kentucky now am down here in the South where I hope to be able to stay and write for a couple of months. Went to a Single Taxers resort called Fairhope but could not stand it. Found it full of middle class eccentrics, the sort who give them selves to mild reforms like Single Tax in these times of revolutionary movements.

Came to Mobile and found it charming—a sleepy old place with many fine houses. Am [in] a low room with a fireplace in such an old house. There is a brick wall about the place and quaint little windows and a fireplace. I hope to be happy and work here for a time in my isolation. In the morning I make my own breakfast and am undisturbed for as long as I can work. Brought some advertising work with me but have plunged into it and got it off my hands for the presence. Am almost well again.[2] Write me the news of yourself.

LH

1. Hahn's longhand note.

2. James Schevill (*Sherwood Anderson, His Life and Work* [Denver: University of Denver Press, 1951], pp. 122–23) states that a severe attack of influenza had left Anderson weak and depressed and that this condition was the impetus for his journeying to the South.

90

To Bab

Fairhope [Ala.] Jan. or February[1] [1920]

I havn't been in the mood for seeing anyone but that doesn't mean I dont want to see you. It means only that for the time I have nothing specially to give out of myself to others. When I do come to see you I'll be well.

Have found here a new impulse that interests me. Brought water colors with me and have been painting, striving to catch the color of trees and ships and seas. It opens up a vast new field for the sight of my eyes and leads me more into the outer world about me—a great relief after so much living within.[2]

Am in the humdrum labor of Poor White now, the slow laborious correction of my always sketchy manuscript. It always takes more time than I recon on and must be done. Two weeks more will clear it up I'm sure.

In the meantime Mary [Cochran] waits and in the back of my mind are other projects sleeping, waiting.

I have hours to walk and lie by the sea. When my body turns I listen and hear the sea rolling softly over in its bed. The fingers and lips of gods come down also out of trees and I laugh from my guts and am happy.

How rapidly my hair is greying and how diabolically young I am inside.

You should take up painting. Take no lessons. Do it secretly. Get water colors and papers and begin playing with colors. To me it is as though a savage were to come suddenly out of the forest into the presence of beautiful music.[3]

The thought of you ill is terrible when I feel health creeping into me. I cannot think of you so. My mind vomits the thought out.

LH

1. Hahn's longhand note.

2. Anderson's painting produced no memorable art, but did evoke many observations about art.

3. The specific occasion of Anderson's taking up painting is not known, but probably an important influence was that his brother, Karl, was an established painter. Later Karl tried writing, with as little success as Sherwood had painting. Karl wrote an unpublished novel about the Anderson family and Clyde, entitled "Knots in the Weaver's Loom," which I once borrowed from Karl's son.

91

To Bab — 1920—February[1] [Fairhope, Ala.]
Tuesday

It is a soft quiet day after 3 days of blustering cold with wind. I have moved to Fairhope Ala., a little villiage on Mobile Bay in order that I may be a great deal out of doors. Am hard at work on my novel "Poor White" which draws near completion. I shall finish it while I am here.

In my little house, which is within 30 ft. of the sea when the tide is in

I cook my own food, do my own housework and live in great quiet. The villiage is an ugly place but the land about is lovely. We shall be having summer days here soon.

I am more sorry then I can say of the circumstances that make your life so constantly an attendant on illness. Some day that will pass and I do hope some fullness of living will come.

In the meantime spring will soon be here and I hope there may be opportunity for you also to get out of doors.

Of the people here I know little. There is a painter with a beautiful wife[2] with whom I am to dine later in the week and there was another painter, very interesting woman who has now gone away. For the moment I care little for people. It is enough to look out at the sea, to be alive, to feel myself growing well and to work uninterrupted. When I feel hungry for other things I'll head back north.

With love

LH

1. Hahn's longhand note.
2. Mr. and Mrs. Wharton Esherick. The "very interesting woman" in the next line has not been identified.

92

To Bab Fairhope/February/1920

Dear Woman—

Im in a rush of work. Am trying to temporarily forget the things that make life dull and ill and see if blindness will cure me. In the meantime I do not write.

One thing is certain. The world is ill and our illness is a part of something universal.

One wants religion but not the religion of priests. There is a something that broods over our Mid American landscapes that can save us all if we will but give our selves.

The thing now is to survive. You have been in the presence of illness for years. All the world no[w] is ill. The thing I think you hunger for is belief in the mystery and wonder of existence. Dont loose that. Will write more when I am not so rushed. Do not apologize to me.

LH

1. Hahn's longhand note.

93

To Bab

Fairhope—1920[1] [February]

I'm sitting by my state room door on a river boat on the Tombigbee River.[2] It is evening, and lovely, unspeakable quiet and lovely. All day I've been painting. As I have seriously found something in paints I cant express any other way I'll keep painting until I know how to say what I have to say. If the gods are good, it wont be long as I'll go softlly and prayerfully, though boldly to this new door of the house of the spirit. But I hadn't told you of my painting had I.

I live in a profound crush of events and matters these days and sometimes my body is racked and shaken. I plung[e] along so many new roads.

I've told you nothing of the niggers. No one has ever told anything about them. They are the sweetest souled people in America and no one knows it. Dont tell or some fool will write a book and say so.

I am writing in the dark. The niggers are singing. The white male swears but they sing on and on. They havn't stopped singing and dancing for days although they've moved unbelievable quantities of freight and have worked day and night. They make me feel small.[3]

LH

1. Hahn's longhand note.
2. Originating in northwest Georgia, the Tombigbee River enters the state of Alabama approximately 200 miles north of Mobile and flows southward, emptying into Mobile Bay.
3. See *Dark Laughter*, published in 1925.

94

To Bab

Fairhope—1920 Alabama[1]

Have just come down from a marvelous adventurous time in the fishing villiages along the lower bay. During the trip I passed over to the Gulf of Mexico shore and had a swim on a long silent milk white beach in a sea of strange purple. Such blinding light and no man within many miles of me. One night I slept on the sand and the sand fleas bit me unmercifully but I didn't mind much.

Up a little cove I found a tall gaunt woman much like my own mother with three wild sons and a husband gone off to the snapper beds. I slept there and had a long talk with the woman. When my adventure was over I sailed up the bay in a fishing smack and the wonder of it all was that the whole trip cost me practically nothing.

Will probable leave here for Kentucky in about 3 weeks and get to Chicago around June 1st. Today have done another painting with which I am pleased. Now have four that stand up and remain beautiful. Others are coming. My painting will have to make its way again[st] all the prejudice of that craft I suspect but I am really painting and know now that it, like poetry is something I have always wanted.[2] One feels as though the doors to the spiritual house were slowly coming open. Since I have written you I have lived so fast and felt many new things so intensely that to speak to you is like calling to some one over a great distance. Well never mind I'll be along back.

Quiet warm days with thunder clouds always lurking in the distance and a sense of bells ringing over fields and hills for the joy of life.

LH

1. Hahn's longhand note.

2. Anderson seems to have reserved his most enthusiastic comments for his painting and poetry, neither of which he is noted for.

95

To Bab — Fairhope 1920[1] [Before May 15]

Dear Woman—

My plans are unsettled—in the air. I leave here in a few days and go to New Orleans. Then to Kentucky to work for a time—how long I dont know.

Sent Poor White on to Huebsch and he passed it to Brooks to read. There is a very beautiful letter about it has just come. He pronounced it the finest and most sustained thing I've done.[2] That means much to me coming from Brook's mind.

So you have been again in the terrible house of pain. You creep in and out like a little mouse, going in to nibble at the fingers of Death—then coming out to rise up again. There is something very lovely in your courage and in the fact that you do not get tired and surrender.

On all sides I see weariness, creeping behind romance, illusion, figh[t]ing against air and sunlight. I'm glad that passion is not in you.

It is difficult to make a plan but I'll surely see you one of these days in

June sometime. Now I cant even give you an address except to say I'll go to Critchfields for mail after 2 or 3 weeks. 10th Floor Brooks Bldg. Mark any letters sent there "personal."

I have me a little horse and a half tumble-down wagon. These last days I drive bear-headed through this golden lang [lane] looking at brown, soft-eyed negroes and at the color and wonder of the country where I have been more free, more alone and at the same time closer to all people than ever before in my hurried life.

Now for new adventures and new paths. I have new strength to carry me for a time. I can ask for nothing more than that. The gods have been good. I greet the gods and you too.

LH

1. Hahn's longhand note.
2. Anderson's letter to Van Wyck Brooks, expressing his gratification at Brooks's favorable response to *Poor White* is dated May 15. See Jones and Rideout, eds., *Letters of Sherwood Anderson*, pp. 54–55.

96

To Bab Fairhope 1920[1] [Before May 15]

Have been flat on my back in exquisit misery for some days. Some unknown insect stung me during my trip over to the Gulf and my sleeping on the sand on that wonderful beach. Then I got into some kind of poison weed and had a bad case of cross infection. Now I'm O.K. again. Am having great fun with my new book—Many Marriages[2] and poor Mary C[ochran] is shoved away again.

All morning have been grinding clay in an old coffee grinder. Am preparing bags of the marvelous red clay here to take with me or rather to ship to Chi where I can have it next winter. By the clay I hope to get much of the feel of things into my finger ends. Some day I shall start a school for men and women, to teach them how to sculp, paint, see and feel things about them.[3]

The clay here is lemon yellow, soft, deep red, blue and a dozen shades of all this but already I have found the red is the purest and sets and works best.[4]

Am leaving again in a day or two for another trip up some inland waters in a little freight boat. Will then pack and go over to New Orleans[5] for a few days. Then I must go to Kentucky for some work and afterward to Chicago. If you want me to will stop for an afternoon with you on the way.

LH

1. Hahn's longhand note.

2. Published in 1923. Anderson wrote to Van Wyck Brooks on May 15, 1920, that his new book, *Many Marriages*, was "rollicking, Rabelaisian" (Jones and Rideout, eds., *Letters of Sherwood Anderson*, p. 55). Neither adjective is appropriate to the book as published. The alternatives are: an extensive revision; the supplanting of one book by another; or the book may have seemed comic to Anderson but not to the book's readers.

3. When Tennessee, whom Anderson had left in Chicago, quit her job and joined him in Alabama, she "found" clay and began her career as a sculptor. See the photographs of her figures that illustrate Anderson's *The Triumph of the Egg* (1921). After their marriage broke up, roughly in 1922, she wrote, somewhat humorously, that Sherwood had made Cornelia a teacher and herself a scupltor. The Alabama period seems to have been one of reconciliation in a marriage that had become shaky.

4. No work that Anderson did in clay remains.

5. This was Anderson's first trip to New Orleans.

97

To Bab

Chicago—June, 1920[1]
Friday

After all we might have seen each other in Chicago had you come home that way but I am glad you didn't. Chicago was unspeakable hot, crowded and dirty and I was in a distraught state. A man for whom I had done work during last winter owed me money on which I had planned to scrape thru the summer. He tried to beat me out of it and I spent most of the time persueing him. Only yesterday I got settlement.

Now I am on my way to New York, my traveling expenses being paid by a business man[2] for whom I am to do some work there.

The distraction of all these things and my inability to get any quiet sleep worried me and I had one of my damned psychic lesions. The result worked its way into my body in the shape of a terrific cold in the head.

Well enough of that. I am to be back in Chicago the later part of the month and will come down to spend a half day with you. I do hope your own trip East relieved the tenseness of the life you momentarily dropped and that now you will take up again.

In New York I will be with Paul Rosenfeld in a house he has taken at Westport Conn—an hour out of the city, where my brother Karl also lives. There is still a little revising to do in my book[3] and I will do that as soon as I get there.

My peep back under the lid at Chicago convinces me that the industrial, capitalistic age is slowly choking itself to death but its death will not be a cheerful or inspiring sight. The truth is we shall probable live out our lives in the midst of intensified politica[l] and industrial ugliness.

The more reason for an intensification of the effort for real spiritual growth now. There is promise in America and it must not go the way of trickery, Christian Science or some other second rate manifestation.

Did you know Burton Rascoe lost his place as literary editor of the Chicago Tribune for saying of some book that it was "as dull as Mary Baker Eddy's Science and Health." The paper I am told recieved literally thousands of letters of protest. And so a new giant rears itself up and ugliness and repression takes a new form.[4]

B. W. Huebsch—32 W. 58th—will hold any letters sent to me in New York.

LH

1. Hahn's longhand note.
2. Unidentified.
3. *Poor White.*
4. In the course of the review Rascoe actually said that the book sounded "like the most rhapsodical section of Science and Health"; that "Mrs. Eddy is a rather better and more original literary artist"; and that the work was similar to Mrs. Eddy's "pishposh." Burton Rascoe, *Before I Forget* (Garden City, N.Y.: Doubleday, 1937), pp. 370–72.

98

To Bab Ephraim / Aug. 6 '20[1]

A steady northwest wind is blowing and I have a fire. It runs usually for two or three days with flutters of rain. No boating and swimming rough work but fine days for working.

Your letter with suggestions of continued illness was depressing. I had hoped you were walking about by now. No word comes of my Kentucky trip. Hope nothing has happened to shake me out of that rag of an income. I dont think anything has.

I've been low in mind spirit and body for two or three days. Went into my new book—I call it Ohio Pagans[2]—head down and overworked.

Sometimes I get into caracter so deeply that in a sense I loose myself. There comes a time when I am like a rock or a tree—an impersonal thing for several days. Then a break comes and I am like a bug on its back in the bottom of a bowl.

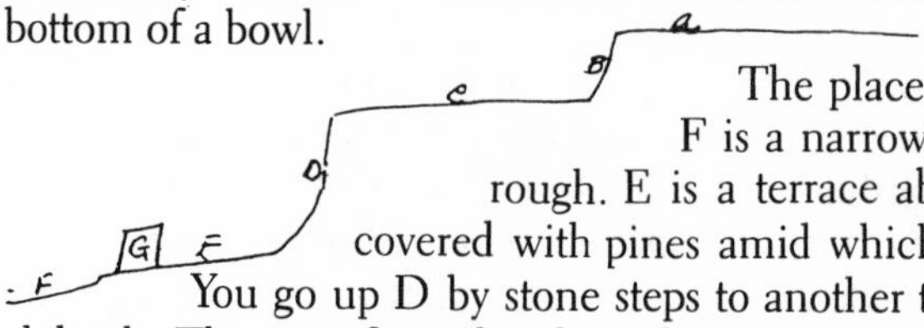

The place here is interesting. F is a narrow beach—stony and rough. E is a terrace about 100 yrds deep covered with pines amid which the house stands. You go up D by stone steps to another terrace (C) of about equal depth. This runs for miles along the coast and is cut by a path. The trees meet overhead and there is a soft cathedral light. Now and then an open place with berries (raseberries) growing in tangled masses. Back of this is a solid wall of stone (B)—75 ft. high. You go up a ladder set against rocks to the third table land (A). Here are more forest and a few upland meadows. One has a wide look of the sea down below from the cliff's edge.[3]

My new story is a highly personal tale of a girl named May Edgley of Bellevue Ohio—daughter of a teamster whose two sisters 'went on the turf' and Tom Edwards, a Welsh boy[,] grandson of Twm Ór Nant[,] a Welsh poet. It is full of working people, laborers, farmers and ice cutters and fishermen of Lake Erie—near my own home country.

For two days I have been unable to write much on it. My hand trembles and something within tells me to wait until my weariness is gone.

The gulls are fighting the wind over the sea, the sea breaths heavily and steadily, wind rocks the pines, I wish you were well.

I'll write again in a few days.

LH

1. Jones and Rideout, eds., *Letters of Sherwood Anderson*, letter 48, indicate Anderson had gone to Ephraim to join Tennessee early in July. Aug. 6 date is Hahn's longhand note.

2. This book, which was never completed, had evidently supplanted his work on *Many Marriages*.

3. The house the Andersons rented was on University Row, a series of summer places owned by professors from the University of Chicago.

99

To Bab Sunday Ephraim August 24, '20[1]

Cornelia's address is Little Point Sable Michigan and the children are with her but I am sure your letter to M.C. [Michigan City, Ind.] will reach her finally.[2] I am very well again and working steadily. I am sure you will be charmed with the little May Edgley of my new book and with Tom Edwards and his efforts to find God. The trip south is still in the air but you do not need to worry about my loosing the thing now. The adv. appropriation on which I get the commission is in for fall. Surely the call will come soon now.

In a sense, and that you understand, all my work and my relationships too are aimed at the realization of life in myself, to teach myself that in any muddle, under any circumstances life can be lived.

It is a terrific hard lesson and the harder when one has to fight illness.

To me the arts are tools, instruments to the end suggested above. One transfers from the perplexing baffling fact of life into them. Something of the kind I have always wanted to see you accomplish.

There are so many things impossible. You speak so often of the desire for a child. Is it not true that in that desire you are thinking of yourself. It is not the child's life of which you think, is it.

There is a perplexing question, the childs life, would run on and on, make its own proplem be compelled to accept it.

Perhaps we should leave child bearing to more stolid, more entirely animal-like people. As for myself I am too sensitive to children to be able to bear being with them.[3]

And there is a notion—is not the desire for children begging the question, dodging the issue? I wonder. Do not some of us fancy that a child will do for us what we do not quite dare try to do for ourself. There is enough of life. Single men and women do not control life. It runs on regardless. All a man or woman can do is to live life.

You see my thesis. On that philosophy I chose to live. My own children are here. Some chance led me to be the father of them. They are lovely bits of life but I cannot get any satisfaction at all out of the secondary fact that I bred them. I do hope I will see you soon and if anything happens I do not go to Ky in Sep I will come to see you from Chicago. I hope you will be well enough to get out often in the clear fall weather coming.

LH

1. Hahn's longhand note. Anderson's Sunday was Aug. 22; the postmark on the envelope may have been the 24th.

2. This appears to be the opening of a friendly relationship between Finley and Cornelia Anderson that lasted the rest of their lives. Later Hahn said that she gave $100 a month to Cornelia for the children for eight years. Probably the payments ended when Finley became Mrs. Hahn in Feb. 1928.

3. Anderson was not uninterested in his children, however. Though Robert

Lane Anderson seems to have resented his father, the two surviving children project an appreciation for the artistic involvement that took their father away from them in their childhood.

100

To Bab   Aug. '20—Ephraim[1]

I am shocked to hear you have been ill again. How many days and weeks you have lived in the house of pain.

A grey still day here. I got your letter yesterday and read it as I walked, in a little open space among pine trees above one-legged Harry Amonson's fish shanties. It was growing dark and I had to turn so that the last rays of daylight from the west fell on it.

What a six months this has been for me, out of doors so many hours, working so steadily. I am reading proof on the novel Poor White now and it will be gone in a day or two.[2] There is another novel—Ohio Pagans I have been steadily working on.

For ten days now I have not painted, being absorbed in these other things.

I work until I am weary then climb a hill, gather raberries, sit looking off across this sea.

I get you and others keenly. At times moments come when it seems to me I know the whole thought of the world, every emotion [and] desire. I am often shaken by these moments.

And then I am working on a book, the story of lives. I know all the story. If I had speed enough and endurance enough I could write the whole book in a day, an hour.

I think little of the future. What shall I do when I am broke. It doesn't matter now.

As to my coming dear woman that depends on events, how imperetive the call from Ken[3] is when it comes. I have to protect that, my only source of income now. In any event I'll see you going or coming and both if I can. I'll let you know at once when the call comes.

LH

1. Hahn's longhand note.
2. *Poor White* was published in Oct. 1920.
3. Kentucky.

101

To Bab

Aug. 1920[1]
Sunday—On Train

Got your letter at Ephraim last night and got at the same time a wire calling me to Kentucky. As there is a meeting I must attend in Owensboro Tuesday and as I must do several things in Chicago tomorrow I cannot stop on the way down. I will however be in Indianapolis Thursday or Friday. Will wire when I am sure. My address Owensboro will be Rudd House. Will probable get to Indianapolis at noon. If you can get me ticket & berth to Chicago will be glad—wait however until you know what day I am to come.

Your letter I think suggests the eternal struggle, never ending, that we all face. One does get after many defeats to where they can get something of interest out of the face of the wall itself, its curious working, the marks of hands, the knowledge that a great army is camped waiting under the wall. Once you said to me that by accepting certain limitations I had destroyed the limitations. It is a thought that has helped me over many rough places.

I am glad I am to see you soon.[2]

LH

1. Hahn's longhand note.
2. Such visits undoubtedly helped Finley maintain the hope that Anderson would eventually marry her.

102

To Bab

Ephraim—Sept. '20[1]

Have been in a period of absorbed work that has kept me writing until I was weak. Then I went to swim or walk, trying to come out of it and rest. For the time all people went pretty far away from me.

The visit to you was charming—the long walk, the talk, the feeling of growing comradship with you. One gets to feeling that like all real people your problem is very highly individual and will not be solved by any rule laid down.

At the same time one knows that the very persistency that has made you keep alive your faith in life in the midst of illness will count big in your own struggle. I have never heard from you that note of spiritual tiredness that expresses itself in cynisism and that is so universal in America. I hope to say something of the kind in the introduction to the book I am now writing[,] Ohio Pagans, if I can find just the words to say it in. In a way that book is closer allied to the spirit of you than any other I have written. I leave for Chicago in the morning and will get my mail at Critchfields.

LH

1. Hahn's longhand note.

103

To Bab Chicago, Sept. 20, 1920[1]

Dear Woman

I knew well enough you were ill—have been afraid of something of the kind for days. What a shame it had to come during these rare fall days. Do get well fast. How I wish you could get well fast and go away to some quiet peaceful spot where the real strain could be taken off you.

My efforts to get a place to live and work has apparently come to some end.[2] I went last week to a place called Palos Park and there got a little 3 room box of a house at the edge of a forest. I hope to move into it some time next week. It is about an hour out of Chicago—south and east.[3] Cook County has a forest reserve of some 17000 acres out that way and there is poor transportation—but a few trains a day so it is not suburban. The land rises up there out of the flat bed of what was probable once the floor of the lake and there are lovely rolling hills and fields—oak forests with now and then cultivated fields. I am very happy about it and my little place only costs me 12.50 a month and can be heated by one stove.

Now I am in Chicago, plunging into my work, striving to get clear so I can go there. I shall write and paint again.

There is to be an exhibition of my paintings at the Walden Book Store here in late October.[4] Wish you might see it.[5] I want you to have one of the things after the show here and some other shows I may make. There is an outside chance there may be a New York show.

I have been a weakling. I half promised to speak in Milwaukee[6]—half because there is a little money to be got by it—half because friends of Karl Sandburg's are back of it.

I am asking the bookstore here to send you Karl's new book, Smoke and

Steel. It should be a lovely thing to look into while you are compelled to lie in bed.

Waldo ['s][7] new Novel—The Dark Mother came and I read it. I think it a miserable thing and it hurts me to think he should have let it get printed. I'll say no more of it as you will no doubt read it.

Do get well fast—please.

LH

1. Hahn's longhand note.

2. This initial reference is to an arrangement that gave him a place away from Chicago but still allowed him to maintain contact with Tennessee and his work and life of the city.

3. Hahn, when she made a typescript of Anderson's letters, corrected this error on Anderson's part to read *west*. She also corrected Karl to Carl Sandburg in the same letter.

4. The exhibit was from Nov. 1 to Dec. 15. Anderson handed out a mimeographed statement entitled "Adventures in Form and Color." The text of the statement follows.

> There are certain images that haunt the human mind. They cannot be expressed in words, although the poet occasionally raises the power of words beyond the real possibility of words.
>
> I am not a musician, but it is not unlikely that what I have tried to do in form and color is related to the impulse of the musician.
>
> Some months ago I was in the South and in a very colorful country. Before my house lay a bay, an inlet from the Gulf of Mexico. There had been heavy rains up-country and the red soil was washed down into my little bay. The bay became red. The morning and afternoon light falling on it made a color madness that got into my brain. Although I had never before touched a brush I sent for brushes and paints.
>
> The adventures here done are done in the faith that an impulse needs but be strong enough to break through the difficulty of lack of technical training. In fact, technical training might well destroy it.
>
> These adventures are unnamed because they cannot be fixed definitely. To give them names would destroy certain values I believe they have as they stand. To you they may be ugly, meaningless or beautiful. No doubt my thoughts and impulses—like your own if they could be seen—would be, to some ugly, to others meaningless, and to still others beautiful.

5. Finley did go to the exhibition.

6. This appearance has not been documented.

7. Waldo Frank.

104

To Bab

October 1920[1]
Thursday Eve
Palos Park

This is suspicious looking stationary. I am in the country and expected today to move into my little house but the people who have been there are not out. I am therefore in a nearby farm house and found this paper in my room. It is all I have.

I shall be glad to get your reaction to Waldo's books. Have just received a long letter from Paul[2] about it. I have myself put off writing to Waldo as I cannot praise and he is very hungry for that. I dread saying what I have to say.

The country is awash with color. I have worked all day feeling like one swimming in a gorgeous sea. There was something light and at the same time sensual about the feeling I have been having.

My little house is but a box—the whole thing perhaps as large as your dining room combined with the room at the front. That is cut in[to?] a kitchen, tiny pantry a bedroom and a dining room. I shall have a kitchen range and a tiny stove. For a month I can get one meal a day with the woman at this farm house. After that I shall be my own cook.

I have walked all day, or rather floated in this sea of color. The air is warm and soft. Little flames of color dart out of the midst of the dense color of trees. The sumac is a living pulsating red.

I want health for you, steady slow growing sure health. Will it ever come. You have been so long struggling.

Before I left the city I had a piece of bad news. The slack in cotton prices in the south has ruined my clients[3] business and he may do very little advertising. That may cut my income very low.

However I shall not think of it. For the few months ahead I am all right. That is enough. Long ago I learned to trust in the gods.

Evening is coming on and as I sit on this farm porch the paper before me becomes more and more obscure. Curtain colors in the trees live on. Others sink slowly away.

How softly the night falls here. It sings softly.

The impulse of the painter comes into me often now. It rests me. One does not think of people. To the painter things live inanimately, in the flow of lines, forms, in moving color.

There are fields here that are like women but unlike women they do not confuse. They lie before you—sure, quite still. The soul is touched but not perplexed.

Women model better than they paint. It is because their hands take hold of something—they feel it.

Color & line are elusive things—hard to take hold of. The gift of doing so comes like a sweet wind—unexpectedly.

I shall come to see you, perhaps next month. Get well.

Tell me also what you feel of Carl's[4] book.

LH This letter is written on printed announcements of an exhibit by Mme. MacBride of New York, an importer of gowns, at the Hotel Sinton on Oct. 16, 17, and 18.

1. Hahn's longhand note.
2. Paul Rosenfeld.
3. An unidentified businessman, presumably from Owensboro, Ky.
4. Sandburg's *Smoke and Steel.*

105

To Bab

Palos Park—October 1920/
While I was in St. Vincent's [Hospital][1]
Tuesday.

Yesterday I started to write you a letter. I intended to tell you something about a very strange old woman here. Then the old woman became an old man and the letter became a story. When it is typed I'll send it for you to see.

The little house is really very charming and very little and it does sit on the edge of a forest. Now the forest is a flame dancing in the air. The summer is being carried away in a dancing flame.

I painted the glory of the thing that way yesterday—a great golden and brown flame swept across the sky.

How shall I tell you—you are very near and dear to me now—in this time of danger and illness. An abiding something tells me you will in the end get well and that you will have a long and very strange and interesting life. It is a prophesy from the man in the tiny house at the edge of the forest—the man who knows the language of the little folks and who loves you.

Do not try to write now. Try to lie very still and think of far away places—little house[s] in forests—the sound of bells—far off—the night call of insects.

You will be getting well. You will be getting well. The night winds here whisper it.

LH

1. Hahn's longhand note; I added [Hospital].

106

To Bab Palos Park Oct-1920[1]

I expect your reactions to Dark Mother are very like my own. It is of course all right to write a book about the mother complex and to involve it with other complexes. Life is surely so involved. The point is that Waldo should have told his story simply, straightly—as a story of life, leaving us to figure out the motives involved. There is something too paternal and involved in all this repeated emphasis. It is as tho he were afraid we would not know he knew what he was doing.

One cannot be too humble before human lives. They are the only things in the world worth being humble about and he isn't humble.

The matter of woman's breasts. There again I think the man was afraid we would not get it he was putting over the mother complex.

One knows instinctively there is a deep seated connection in both a physical and a psychic way between the male and the breasts of women. I have known many men somewhat perverted in this direction. It is all tangled up with the mother thing, with all of live.

Waldo in his book however suckles too much. One feels him being, or striving to be bold, to startle. I remember he once wrote me he was going to put into the book a line about "going in where he came out."

I laughed him out of that. "You have simple written the line to startle" I said. "Any line so written is rotten."

You will remember how he went on at a great rate and thru several pages concerning one man's taking a pipe from the lips of another man and putting it between his own lips.

It sounded like a psycho-analyst giving his class an example.[2]

Well it is too my mind a bad book and now the test comes for Waldo. He may realize it and go humble back to life and away from this silly intellectuality or he may grow angry and declare all his critics fools or think them lacking in understanding.

As for Carl. To my mind he sings very beautifully at times but he is a bit too proud of his rough-neckedness and he has never associated with enough first rate people. The man hasn't hold of his art. He is an ameutuer. One has only to revisit Whitman to find out how terrible this new singer falls short.

At that Carl does really sing. He is in earnest and is not a smart aleck. The man loves and loves deeply but I shouldn't say he loved very understandingly—should you.

I have had a period of some days of depression and lowness, nothing singing in me, nothing marching.

I've thought about your illness and your problem. The one thing that has impressed me deeply about you is—that thro all your illness you have not lost your sense of spiritual beauty. I have always felt you struggling for that toward that.

I know one wants also the wealth of physical beauty too—we all want to be gods and goddesses dancing thro life. There is a cruel—beautiful pagan world as well as the world of that drooping figure Jesus.

Something has taken the pomp and splendor of that other world away. Look at Sandburg. Look at myself. In our work it is not there.

Well perhaps it is a little there in some of my paintings. At least I know there is such a world, that kingly robes can be worn.

Perhaps we shall have to turn our backs on that. It does not cannot live in an age of factories.

The Christ is the stronger. His spirit can prevale in any age.

I have talked in rambling way. My mind is loose. It floats. I shall write again when it is more definate.

LH

1. Hahn's longhand note.
2. Anderson's doubts about psychiatrists are well recorded in "Seeds," which was included in *The Triumph of the Egg*.

107

To Bab

November—1920[1] [Palos]
Friday

I've really been involved in painting and calcimining and my little house has been in such a mess that I could not possible think or feel much of anything. Now it is clear again and I sit by my window with bright clean walls at my back and the glorious brown yellow and gold of winter oak leaves before me.

I have not lost my income from the Kentucky account but it has been so cut because of bad business conditions that there is little left. I may go to Kentucky on Monday Nov. 22 and if I do will come to see you Sunday afternoon Nov. 21. If I do come I will ask you to engage me a sleeper to Evansville. I have not seen Poor White but as soon as it comes will send you a copy.

By the way, as you know, there is great demand from all directions that authors give copies of their books. I cant afford to do it much but there are some demands hard to refuse. Jim Larkin,[2] the Irish revolutionist who went to jail for free speech in America wants Poor White sent him. I wonder if you would mind sending him a copy:

James Larkin.
Box 3. Dannemora, N.Y.

He is in Dannemora prison.

I am staying away from the place where my pictures are being shown but believe they are creating some stir. Wish you could run up to Chicago for a day to see them. It would be difficult to bring them there now that they are framed. Couldn't you come up on a morning train and go back in the evening, sometime after my trip to Kentucky.

Read Mencken on Poor White in Dec. Smart Set. I think it a well thought out, dignified article.[3]

With love

LH

1. Hahn's longhand note.
2. James Larkin (1877–1947) was known as an Irish labor champion.
3. H. L. Mencken declared, "The Anderson promise begins to be fulfilled. Here is a serious novelist who must be taken seriously." *Smart Set*, Dec. 20, 1920.

108

To Bab

November 16th, 1920
Palos Park[1]

I am sitting in my little house. The old woman next door has found in her attic an old steamer chair which she has lent me. I can sit at ease with a board on my lap and my feet up before the fire and write.

I hope you are going to like Poor White and that you will write me just your impressions of it.[2]

Also I hope you can come to Chicago. The pictures will be there until the 15th [of] December I understand. Be sure to write me a few days before if you find you can come.

The day is cold and raw and a north wind is blowing up. I was in Chicago yesterday. There it was murky and muddy.

All last night a vision kept floating before me. I must try to put it into words. A boy is given a golden goblet containing a strange liquid. The liquid is love. He runs through the world sprinkling it on people, begging them to put their lips to it.

At first the eyes of the boy are clear but they become troubled. As the lips of the people touch the magic liquid in the goblet they are transformed. Many become hidiously ugly, others remain beautiful but suffer terrible. The boy runs less and less swiftly, he looks at people doubtfully, his eyes become more and more troubled[,] and when at last the goblet is empty he finds himself suddenly become an old man and lies down to die.

About the money—what can I say. I wanted to go to New York for a time in January. Now I shall be able to do so.

Has your mother made any efforts at painting in the simply direct way of which we spoke or is such simplicity impossible to her. What about Hacketts review of Poor White.[3] It seems to me spiritually tired. Is it.

LH

1. Hahn's longhand note.
2. Anderson had sent her an autographed copy of the book.
3. In reviewing *Poor White*, Francis Hackett had made a number of negative remarks, including "Mr. Anderson's limitations make *Poor White* an incomplete, a maimed organism." See the *New Republic*, Nov. 24, 1920.

109

To Bab Palos Park/November 20th 1920[1]

The wind in the dry oak leaves made a thundering roar about my house all night. This morning there is snow and a dazzling sun. The gods have quit shouting and now go whispering and playing around the corners of my little house.

I realize that time, the intense practise of the arts and also a more fully expressed life have given me a hold of something. Also I do know why your hand trembles and slips.

As for your visit[2]—it was a warm friendly time for me too. I came home to my house here and have worked steadily since. Wrote and typed the story of the half-filled milk bottles and the advertising writer who wanted to write glowingly of his city Chicago.[3] Now I am deep in the other thing called "Out of Nothing Into Nowhere."[4] It should be a strong lovely singing story.

There is always this—once I saw you quite clearly as somewhat the person expressed in my story Impotence. Now that is all gone. You became and you are a living fact, peculiarly alive, peculiarly your own fighting self. You shall survive and blossom into your own beauty. I know that now.

I am glad you told me of C's reaction.[5] She would not have told me. I shall be curious about your reaction to Main Street. Lewis[6] has written me an enthusiastic letter. Will you return enclosed from N.Y. Eve. Post?

LH

1. Hahn's longhand note.
2. To see Anderson's pictures at the Walden Book Store. Anderson had suggested that she make the trip from Indianapolis to Chicago on a morning train and return the same evening.
3. See "Milk Bottles" in *Horses and Men*.
4. See "Out of Nowhere into Nothing" in *The Triumph of the Egg*.
5. Presumably a reference to Cornelia's willingness to accept financial aid from Finley. John Anderson did not know of this assistance until he read these letters.
6. Sinclair Lewis. This letter, not so far available, evidently praised *Poor White*.

110

To Bab — November 1920/Kentucky[1]

Your letter came at noon today. I am tired as I always am after two or three days among business men. What I suspect is that what you say of me is true of everyone.

I remember talking to a school teacher in the south. We sat on a boat and spoke of his work. He had tried to give himself to the negro race, to work for it, and had been ostracized by the whites.

Suddenly he began to speak of the arts & of literature. He had read something of mine and it had hurt him. He expressed the American philosophy, "When a thing is ugly we must close our eyes to it," he said. "You must learn to find beauty in what we are."

"You express," I suggested, "the philosophy of the romanticists."[2]

I looked at him and understood why he had failed in his work, why most Americans fail. "You're tired," I said. "Do you realized you are expressing a philosophy based upon weariness [?]"

I was hurt by the hurt look that came on his face.

Everywhere one sees it, the love that cannot love because it is tired and therefore becomes possessive.

That is something I meant when I spoke of your not having glorified illness. You see and know the temtation, to turn inward and glorify the wall one cannot break through.

I often wonder if you know how much your letters to me have changed in the last year or two. Now I receive one of them and it is a comradly message. I used to be afraid of them—they romanticized terrible, clutched. I wanted sunlight and air after reading one of them.[3]

This thing you have done for yourself—brought health in. I'm sure it is going to creep through your physical being also.

The visit was a joy to me too. I felt the new attitude of your mother and I came away—not being tired and slept peacefully. I shall enjoy coming to your house now.

Have been seeing—all day—thousands of children in schools. I wonder why I seem to understand and love the niggers most. Is it because at bottom I feel myself, like them secretly alien, an outlaw.[4]

With love,

LH

1. Hahn's longhand note.

2. An unusual use of this term, especially for its implications of Anderson's placing himself in an artistic camp. Actually, Anderson was as much a romanticist as a realist.

3. A veiled reference to the fact that Anderson, though valuing his relationship with Finley highly, was wary of a marriage.

4. Although Anderson apparently did not understand Negroes, though much more appreciative of them than most white people of his time, his reasons for special interest in them seem appropriate to his nature and experience. Certainly the blacks in *Dark Laughter* are close to the romanticized conception of them entertained by sympathetic whites.

111

To Bab December 1, 1920/Chicago[1]

Dear Woman—

Your fine feeling is often a bright streak across the often somber aspect of my life. I cannot anymore refuse what is offered in such a fine spirit although I wish it could buy you freedom instead.

I am trying to plan for three or four months next summer when I can hide myself somewhere and find courage and strength to work. There is so much I want to do. There is so little I do do.

People keep telling me I do enough as it is. They point out that this or that man with leisure has not done as much.

It does not matter. One wants to go forward to the fulfillment of his passion.

I want you to read the testament book as far as it has advanced and when I next come your way I will leave it with you for a few days so that you may read it.[2]

By it I hope to tap new scources of poetry.

On all sides of me I see men who, having faced the wall of life turn in on themselves. I want to continue to go out and out, to grow until I die.

I want to look at life, to testify to life as it is.

The newer sweeter life that is to come is for other men. I have got to fight my way up out of this life. Like you I have got to face the wall that is before me. I feel a fine dignity of living coming into you. I am glad.

LH

1. Hahn's longhand note.
2. Work on A *New Testament* continued until its eventual publication in 1927. The significance of this book to Anderson's conception of his art has been completely neglected.

112

To Bab Dec.-1920 Palos Park[1]
Tuesday[2]

I am in town today—rushing about, doing the things that must be done for the children. Have put it off so long. Now I shall have to hustle.

It is snowing hard so the city is white and very ghostly and lovely.

I am at the story—"Out of Nothing into Nowhere."[3] It is somewhat longer than I thought it would be—and very intricate and I think a delicate thing too. I'll send it along for you to see when I have finished writing it.

Will be with the children in Chicago here an[d] will be thinking of you. My plans for going to New York are still indefinate but I think I shall be there the later part of January or the first of February. I am invited into the country near New York where the man[4] is trying to make a play out of Winesburg. I am at least curious to see what he may have done.

I've an idea that in the future I shall be inclined to write more carefully and use writing more for it's own sake—that is to say for the possibilities of beauty I may be able to develope in it for myself. It is a reaction to living that grows in me.

It is strange that after one has become quite certain of things they slip away. When you were here we talked a good deal of the insignificants of place.

Then suddenly I had a great revultion to the whole middle-western country. I wanted to flee, to escape, to walk in old European and African cities, see the colorful beggars on the streets of Rome, visit all old places.

That I have always and will always live in the middle west, in a raw new civilization, that I shall perhaps die not having seen old places made me ill.

I have struggled to throw off the feeling and being again at work has helped.

It is good to think that the beginning of another year sees our friendship more firmly based, more real.

My love to you at this Christmas time.

LH

1. Hahn's longhand note.
2. Probably Dec. 24.
3. Published as "Out of Nowhere into Nothing" in the July, Aug., and Sept. 1921 issues of *Dial*.
4. Rollo Peters (1892–1967), scenic designer, actor, director, and producer. In the early 1920s Peters was a foremost figure on the New York stage.

113

To Bab Palos Park/Dec.-1920[1]

The country is white with snow. Everything is hushed and quiet in the country. I am going into town to spend Christmas with the kids.

Have two new stories in hand—one merely sketched in to fix the mood of it—the other well along in the actual writing. When I have it typed will send the copy for you to read. In a way I think it the best story I have ever written, having more beauty in it.

In regard to the matter you speak of—Doesn't the paradox [usually?] rule. "To those who have shall be given."

I can understand your mood of depression now. It has been on me too, rather deeply, Chicago, during the Christmas season is very ugly.

There is a thing appears in human nature that frightens me. It is a not uncommon thing for me, when a new book is published, to get nasty letters thru the mails. I am called a beast, a stupid egotist, a bad writer, a fool to see people as I do. The letters would not bother but for the evident deep hatred of these strangers for me. When one is depressed it is as though people came into one's work room and made made [*sic*] a mess on the floor.

In a sense all this has resulted in something and the impulse of the new story—in my mind is caught from it. I shall call it—if the gods let me write it as it lies in my mind. The Man Who Sat In His House.[2]

For both of us no doubt the Christmas will not be merry. We are scarce merry folk. I hope the day will bring some sweetness of thought to you.

I gave your name to the new editor of Bookman—and recommended you as a book reviewer. There is another effort being made to do something with it, new editors etc. They wanted me to do some reviews, but I said nix.

LH

1. Hahn's longhand note.
2. There is no evidence of the publication or survival of this story.

114

To Bab Dec.-1920 Palos[1] [Park]

It is very cold and a wind is blowing. This afternoon I went for a long walk in the deep snow then came home to sit by the fire and watch the day fade. The black tree trunks stood out for a long time aginst the white fields.

The artist who lives here is gone away and to be neighborly I keep his fires going. Late at night I go thro the wood, past a deserted house, up a hillside to his door. The trees crackly, shadows play about, my ears tingle in the cold.

I am in a somewhat depressed mood but work pretty steadily. The story on which I am at work wants beautiful telling.

Often nowdays I am overcome with a desire to get out of the middle west forever. I dream vaguely of living in some warm land where there are no factories, no ugly factory towns. I suppose it will never happen. I shall no doubt live and die here.

It seems to me people become always more and more tired. When I go into town and dine with someone I am in a strange way sucked dry. Every one seems to want to be lifted up.

The Christmas was lovely with the children. We dined in a resturant and then want to see my pictures. Later they had a mock trial and charged me with being a Bolshevik and writing literature that was against the government. Robert was the government lawyer. John wanted to defend me but it was more fun to convict. I got 20 years.

LH

1. After Christmas. Dated through Hahn's longhand note.

115

To Bab Palos 1921[1]

Some[one] lent me to read Lawrence[2]—Women in Love. It is a subscription book and sells at $15—I wish I could afford to give it to you. Buy it if you can afford to. It will not decrease in value. It was put out in this way to avoid the censorship.

Have not finished reading it but it comes very close sometimes to very great work. There is a kind of strain sometimes when I read such an effort. As an artist there is always something I want done. I'm afraid I can't do it myself. I pray that another may be permitted to do it.

For the first time for months I painted yesterday.

—an earthbound[?], bowl, filled with the warm rich colors of earth out of which come lighter more intense floating colors. It is very beautiful.

An intense day and now I am weary and have a headache and a cold. Over and over I say to myself—someday I shall leave the American west and never come back. Perhaps it is death I hunger toward—who knows.[3]

LH

1. Hahn's longhand note.
2. D. H. Lawrence. *Women in Love* was published for "subscribers only" in 1920 in New York.
3. In a letter Jones and Rideout dated as "Late December" to Paul Rosenfeld, Anderson wrote of his desire to escape from the Midwest; "I am always vaguely planning on that." Jones and Rideout, eds., *Letters of Sherwood Anderson*, p. 70.

116

To Bab

Chicago January 1921[1]
Thursday

I am in town—sitting before the fire and writing. Have painted a new thing. My paintings are gone to the Arts Club. This news I've a notion I've told you.

I shall go east about the 1st[2] but will stop at Wash[ington] & Balt[imore] on the way. There is some talk I'll go into the country near New York for a time with Rollo Peters.

I hope you'll be in New York while I am there. It would be fine to have a little playtime together. You know of course in what I'll be involved—a riot of personalities—going here and there. I'll be a hard bird to put the hand on. It is just that for me—a time of more or less giving myself to people—not trying to work—a debauch of people. I play it heartily for a time and then am thru for a long time.

We wont have much quiet time together but we could have a flight—off somewhere together for the day in a strange place.

Lawrence in his new book has tried to formulate a thing I've often spoken of—the putting of sex into its right place—not by suppression or repression but by realizing that sex is not love—any more than another hunger.

What I have thought about the sex symbolism is this. You are writing to me. When that comes in I go—I mean that I am lost in the inner contemplation of yourself and your needs. I always feel that sharply.

It is not that sex is not a part of me also. The point is that I do exist in myself—aside from my hungers.

You do too—except at these times. Wish you would read Paul Rosenfeld on Waldo Franks novels in current Dial. There is the thing set forth. It is what has destroyed so much of Franks personality and his artistry.

Reading the article will bring home to you what I mean.[3] So often in your letters I loose you—as a comrad in life altogether. I suddenly feel that you have stopped beside the pool along the road to gaze only at the reflection of yourself—all the turning life of the world is lost to you.

LH

1. Hahn's longhand note.
2. Presumably of February.
3. Rosenfeld said that he had confidence in the potential of Frank's genius but noted that "the vast talent of Frank remains, in his novels, a force still very much at war with itself" (Rosenfeld, "The Novels of Waldo Frank," *The Dial*, Jan. 1921, 104–5).

117

To Bab

Palos Jan. 23rd—1921[1]
Sunday 23rd

Well I have a bit of news for you. My New York trip is off. Last night I had a wire from Paul Rosenfeld asking me to go to Europe with him as his guest in May and I'm going to go. Because of money and because of work that must be cleared up before I leave the New York trip therefor goes by the boards.

And isn't this splendid of Paul. He will be the most delightful conceivable traveling companion, knows Europe and the languages. I'm very happy about it.

Another thing has made me happy. At the Christmas time I had a show of my pictures for the children and delivered a talk on them—as I would have talked to you or your mother. Later I sent John some paints. Now I have before me a painting of his that is one of the finest things I've seen—ever. Marins[2]—the best water color man in America would not be ashamed to sign it. The boy has that god given thing—a real color sense and to say that of a painter is to say the same thing as saying a singer has a voice. Nothing has made me so happy in months.[3]

Of course I'll say nothing of this to John and I hope nothing will make him self concious. As sure as I write he is going to be a big painter.

I'll surely be going to Kentucky some of these day and when I do I'll come to see you.

LH

1. Hahn's longhand note. Anderson's dateline was merely "Sunday 23rd."

2. John Marin (1870–1953), marine painter.

3. In a letter of Nov. 6, 1974, John wrote: "I remember just a little bit about those water color paints—that my father expressed pleasure with one of the paintings I made with them. For another painting—a sort of mountain view in which I had left the bare white paper to represent a snowfield he suggested to me that I try to devise some way to paint that white area. It was a matter of giving that area more existence in the painting."

118

To Bab — Palos Park —1921[1]

I am very much interested in what has apparently happened to Lawrence. After Sons and Lovers I thought Rainbow something of a let down. Now I have been reading a new book of his (put out by subscription to avoid the censor.) It reminds in a queer way of Franks dark mother.

The thing you spoke of in your note—the use of sex symbols. In his later manner Lawrence does that constantly. There is a kind of absorbtion, a giving way in it.

After all one should write out of a passive impulse, letting the emotion play through him and go out at his finger ends in writing or painting.

In this other thing—it is hard to define it, one often feels the hand making words out of the emotion after it has become a little perverted from its purpose.

Its true I sometimes feel it in your notes, in yourself. I felt it in Dark Mother—and now in Lawrence.

My own notion is that weariness is at the bottom of the matter. I [*sic*] false courage is churned up.

And back of this is something else. One grows weary in life thro trying to conquer life. It is swimming against the current of oneself.

The door to sex understanding that has been torn open leads into a lovely country but one must go in—devout, humble, willing to wait. Immediately one becomes arrogant the beauty is lost.

There is a kind of hypnotism. One thinks they are writing beautifully when they are not. I know what I mean but it is a very difficult, delicate thing to say. Sometimes I think women and womenish men are most like to fall into the trap. The thing is perfectly exemplified in Franks book.

I can paint a picture of a woman's womb and make it beautiful but not if the womb aroused in me (while I am making the painting) physical desire.

Do not think the moments when you write thus your most beautiful moments.

For example had I written thus of the woman in the story Lonliness[2] I should have been impelled to explain her—work her out into expressed symbols. The story would have been ruined.

Dreiser and Harris[3] are both now unimportant old men—chattering of the past. They should both be put in the soldiers home.

I am half ill of a lingering cold yet. I wait for an hour when I may work. My mind can make no plans now. I want to do the work that is here before me. I'm a little inhuman. The work time is in me and I am not well enough to work steadily. Later I shall be more friendly and human. No sane person could care to see me now.

LH

1. Hahn's longhand note.
2. "Loneliness," one of the *Winesburg, Ohio* stories.
3. Probably Frank Harris (1855–1931), American (Irish-born) writer, author of biographies, novels, short stories, and plays.

119

To Bab Palos Park 1921[1]

The impossibility of beauty in personal relations when those relations are too much talked of one sees everywhere.

Most women simple frighten me. I feel hunger within them. It is as though they wished to feed upon me.

As a matter of fact I am very strongly sexed but hard work, constant thinking, saving my strength for flights into an imagainative world. All of these things consume strength that might otherwise go into sex expression.

Sexually hungry or starved women are made angry by what therefore seems a perversion of the ends of life to them. The more noble among them do not give way to the feeling. It is however there.

More and more the critics who write of my work discuss, rather than the work, myself—what I am striving toward, what I would accomplish.

Women too feel the thing. You have a field to plow. There is iron to make the plow and a workman. Instead he begins laborious[ly] pounding out the figure of an old plowman. It is lovely but the plow is needed. There is a queer mixture of anger and admiration.

LH

1. Hahn's longhand note.

120

To Bab [n.d.]

It was a nasty scolding note I sent you and when it was mailed I was sorry. You touched me on my pride of life.

After all I think its my fault and that I do whine sometimes. Mostly though I live knowing life belongs to me to live. There are certain men who by some strange fate are lords of life and I am one of them.

At bottom no king or prince ever walked my [more?] surely. While I live [have] breath smell, taste, [I] feel I must not whine.

Who is singing.
I am singing.
Who is praying.
I am praying.
Who is walking about among people.
I am walking about among people.
Who is hearing voices.
I am hearing voices.
Who is eating ripe fruit.
I am eating ripe fruit.
Who is kissing the maiden in the shadow of the church.
I am kissing the maiden in the shadow of the church.
For whom do arms open.
The arms are opened to receive me.
Who is in the body of the man I see walking with people, embracing maidens, drinking sweet wine, breathing sweet air.
I am in the body of the man, I the singer live in his body.[1]

You see I write a song for you to make up for the bitterness of the note that came from me when you said something to humble my pride in my life.

Think not of money, prizes, solomn men giving prizes.
Please do think of me as walking, hearing, smelling, tasting.
Forgive my outbreak.

LH

1. These lines became "Answering Voice of a Second Glad Man," in *A New Testament*, pp. 105–6.

121

To Bab Palos 1921[1]

It is a curious thing in which I am engaged and you will be interested. By the recital of a few common place thoughts that have long been hidden away in a woman's mind, her mind is startled into unusual thinking. Like a flying machine her mind flits off into space, looses itself in a maze of sharp new reactions to life.

This is all in the tale "Out of Nothing Into Nowhere." It is such a delicately adjusted thing that I am uncertain whether or not I shall be able to pull it off.

There is floating in my mind also another theme. A man, past 40 enters for the first time into imagainative thinking. A new road is open to him. As the years pass he feels constantly younger. His fancy, a thing of growing delicacy[2] . . .[3]

LH

1. Hahn's longhand note.
2. Possibly related to themes expressed in *Many Marriages*, published in 1923.
3. Obviously the letter went onto a second page, but this page has not been found.

122

To Bab Palos, 1921[1]
Thursday

I know what you must be up against—and the spring days calling and the wind in trees and in the ground everything straining and pulling.

Please do not loose sight of the fact that although you take part in a struggle with death that it is life and the growing thing that is most alive in you.

What courage you have had.

Of course I knew what your reaction to my somewhat stupid letter would be. Perhaps it was only written because I felt the other thing so strongly emphasized in your letter from New York.

If you but knew how much I value in you the things that are so truly lovely.

I read Wharton's "The Age of Innocence." It struck me the woman drew men badly, unconvincingly. May the wife was so much more alive than that husband of hers and why the princess fell in love with him I couldn't make out at all.[2]

It gave me a peep into a side of your life and into other lives I'll never enter. How essentially vulgar that life really is. uh.[3]

I believe the woman doctor who is at my poor nose has discovered something that may have a good deal to do with my occasional long periods of depression. We'll see.

I'll probable go to Ken[tucky] about the middle of April and of course will stop to see you on the way back.

Keep your courage woman.

LH

1. Hahn's longhand note.

2. Anderson's reactions to May Archer, Newland Archer, and Countess Olenka in Edith Wharton's *The Age of Innocence* reveal that he did not see in the book a resemblance to his own struggle between inclination and duty.

3. Wharton's pictures of New York society in the late nineteenth century evidently made Anderson think of the life he thought Finley led.

123

To Bab March—1921—Palos Park[1]

You seem to me now like one compelled to live in the little walled city of pain. It is odd how much more now than ever you will have to keep remembering that life goes on beyond the walls, in woods, in the fields.

That doesn't at all mean you must shut yourself off from this suffering woman. You dont want to do that—couldn't do it.

I am going 3 times a week to a physician where I must stay each time some three hours. It is a bore, costs money and must be done I suppose. No doubt I have an infection. I could account for the long hours & sometimes days of depression by the intensity of my working hours but I have recently been physically affected and no doubt my body is being poisoned from some scourse.

The new book is ready to close & I have had the good fortune to sell the serial rights to Out of Nowhere to Dial.[2] It will anyway pay my doctor bill.

I am more sorry than you can know about your mother as I have come to love the soul hidden away and fighting in that little enclosed city.

LH

1. Hahn's longhand note.
2. This is the first time that he used "Nowhere" before "Nothing" in the title, in these letters, at least.

124

To Bab

April 1921[1]
Tuesday

Am going to the country today to make final clean up there. As is natural I have a thousand things to do this week. However I feel splendid.
It was a rare day—the half veil of mystery over the land, the quiet river, the sing—of the birds. It will be long before I forget it.
I can be addressed in N.Y. % B. W. Huebsch—116 W 13th St. N.Y.[2]
Sent you yesterday—The Narrow House. Just keep it until I come back.[3]
I'll write a real note when I can do more than pluck a wild moment.
Dear Friend

LH

1. Hahn's longhand note.
2. Anderson's publisher.
3. Presumably a reference to Evelyn Scott's *The Narrow House.*

125

To Bab

April
Palos Park—1921[1]

A clear frosty morning in the country. I have been for forty-eight hours depressed and miserable. It annoys me terrible that—when now that I have this good free work time I am so often unable to work.
At any rate I shall do what is necessary to be rid of this infection—tonsils, teeth—I shall loose what is necessary. "If thine eye offend thee—pluck it out."

Such a morning here. If I were well and you were here I could make you see God. But I am not well.

I shall write or wire when I know about my Kentucky trip.

Every day I think of you and your mother and what you are now going through.

Not only you but your mother, myself—all men and women pay bitterly for old sins, not our own. I realize that every time I walk in city streets. Nature pays its score so relentlessly—unfailingly.

There is however something that cant be taken.

I hope there is sun in at your window this morning and that you are not too discouraged.

The new book has gone to the publisher. I shall call it "Unlighted Lamps."[2]

LH

1. Hahn's longhand note.

2. "Unlighted Lamps" was published in *Smart Set*, July 1921, and later in *The Triumph of the Egg*. Its main character was Mary Cochran, about whom Anderson had been trying to write a novel.

126

To Bab

April 1921[1]
Saturday

I am sorry about the thoughtless brutal note written the other day. There had been a procession of clinging notes from men and women.

It was as though whenever one went to the door of his house he found someone crying on the door step.

At bottom my attitude toward you has fundamentally changed. I take you as friend—not a "case." I want you upright on the doorstep smiling at me. Im sorry.

LH

1. Hahn's longhand note.

127

To Bab

Palos Park—1921[1]
In the country

Dont take too seriously my tirades about the middle west—although I am going to get out of here. It's the climate. I work intensely and then cant relax and play in the cold. Alabama and the presence of the niggers has ruined me for the cold and the ugly neurotisism of almost everyone.

Poor dear woman—I'm so sorry for your mother. What's the sense of life when it manifests itself so. To say that I give her, by my work, any pleasure at all is about the finest and sweetest thing you could say.

Oh, Im so glad your painting. I've wondered about your color sense. This is an objective thing to give yourself too. You have sometimes seemed to me to lack true color sense. Perhaps you hadn't cared before. Watch your mother for that. I've a hunch she has it. Do try to paint without thinking too much. If you want me too I'll send you a list of colors to get for your color box. Keep well. I'm all right—working like a fool.

LH

1. Hahn's longhand note.

128

To Bab

[Chicago, 1921]

I am always doing something rather nasty and then waking up in the night and having cold shivers over it.

It is so now about the note I wrote you—yesterday or the day before.

Its like this I think—I'm essentially not a public person—do not fun[c]tion so. In such a time as this I am profoundly stirred, thrown off my center. All my effort is then centered on the task of reestablishing my own quiet so that I can begin to give out something from that.

I grow nasty when any one at such a time tries to help. Still I'm not ungrateful—a second later anyway.

What I think I want and need is negroes laughing and sleeping on a beach—and the quiet sea perhaps.

I'm very slow. It would be better—as I've always known [if] I could come at night and lay my contributions on doorsteps and then run away. Just give me quiet friendship and faith—for the time.

LH

129

To Bab — May—1921[1]
Sunday

On the train at last[2] and all the details of getting away wiped up—the last business dung ball rolled.

A grey chill day and because I was tired I took a cold last night. However I'm happy and the cold will go soon.

Am on the B & O in the Pennsylvania hills following a little river and running thru tunnels—the country I wrote about in Marching Men.

Now the new green has wiped out the blackness of coal dust and the land is wild & lovely.

Shall be with Henry Mencken[3] tonight and he will give me some drinks to take the chill away.

How often I shall think of you in the hot flat town this summer & how I shall wish you also could run away to some end of the earth.

LH

1. Hahn's longhand note.
2. Anderson was on his way to New York to start his tour of Europe.
3. Mencken lived in Baltimore.

130

To Bab — New York—May—1921[1]

What a stir of things and places. Many people to see—the few days getting quickly away.

Have been to the country with Peters[2] talking of play writing. I saw Mencken—a rather naive stupid man after all.[3] One cant take him really seriously.

You see I can give you nothing but fragments of news of my activities. I am going to Connetticut to spend the weekend with my brother[4] and later to see Waldo at a town on the Hudson.

I go swiftly from place to place, lunching, dining with people, trying to get some hurried sense of them.

I do not succeed. I only succeed in being distracted. Afterwards sharper impressions will come—perhaps on the boat in the presence of the sun.

LH

1. Hahn's longhand note.

2. Rollo Peters.

3. But Mencken had written some of the more encouraging notices about Anderson's work.

4. Karl Anderson lived in Westport.

131

To Bab

May 13, 1921[1]
Thurs. Eve

Dear Woman—

Your note came today. By the time this note reaches you we will be at sea—as we sail early Saturday. My visit here has been charming although the late evenings have tired me.[2]

Have just come from 2 days with Waldo Frank—walking in the Westchester hills, a lovely country with the Hudson below.

Saw Dell[3] up there. I predict he will become the new type of popular novelist.

Franks failure with Dark Mother has changed him. He is for the moment less the aspiring great man & more the quiet worker. I felt as I never have before that he will become a really fine writer. It was charming to be with him.

Have not seen John[4] but will lunch with him Friday. Did not feel I could go without seeing him althoug[h] I'm sure our old friendship is quite gone[.] Perhaps not.

I know what hardships the summer will bring you but I know also that you are getting ground under your feet and will stand up to life and not be embittered.

That makes me love you.

LH

1. Hahn's longhand note.

2. A note in *The Bookman* for July 1921, comments: "His friends had found him most elusive during his brief stay in New York before he left [for Europe]."

Preceding that is this note: "Sherwood Anderson and Paul Rosenfeld have sailed for Europe. At least, we think that they have sailed; for the doubt in our minds is whether Anderson finally turned up at the ship." The anonymous columnist "managed to catch" Anderson for an interview: "We had expected to see someone a little wild. But instead of that, the author of 'Marching Men' and 'Poor White' seems a very gentle middle-aged fellow, with rather piercing dark eyes. He told us of his new volume of short stories [*The Triumph of the Egg*], to be published this fall, and of his efforts at art [painting]. Distinctly a pleasant person."

3. Floyd Dell.
4. John Emerson.

132

To Bab May—1921/On board ship[1]

Being on board a boat[2]-bound for Europe is a good deal like being set down suddenly in a strange town. At first there is just a confusion of faces and personalities, then they begin to break up into groups, form and re-form. There is one woman here, a harpist. She grins continually but is I'm afraid dull. She came and introduced herself as a friend of yours.[3]

The sea has been very kind. It rolls endlessly in soft purple splendor. In the early mornings we are likely to have mist and then the sky clears and the sea becomes a splendid sparkling thing.

For the most part the passengers are poor artists or professional people going on this boat because the fare is lower or prosperous French cooks and small business men going home. The best thing on the boat is the crew, French boys in heavy wooden shoes and blouses who sing softly down below at night.

In New York I made arraingments for Huebsch to take over Windy, Marching Men & the Chants and to keep them in print. There will be a new edition of Windy later with the final chapters rewritten.

On the boat the fare is good and there is good wine at table. Before we left New York there was much talk of drinking as soon as the 3 mile limit had been passed but with the coming of the privaledge the desire passed.

I see on the boat a few men and women I know but no one very interesting or exciting. We go on and on steadily, leaving America behind, approaching the strange place. One begin[s] to realize a new adjustment. America becomes for the time at least less important. It is vast but the sea is more vast. The whole continent, towns cities, states can sink out of sight over the edge of the world.

It is going to be difficult, this summer, to think of you or others I love in America in any personal way. The sea is a barrier.

What will happen in the strange cities, among the strange people. That absorbs me. I find myself irresistable inclined to face eastward with the moving ship.

I am well, sleep soundly, am apparently a good sailor. No doubt I shall work some all summer. New York had this time little or no effect on me.

One thing I know. I want you when at last your time of freedom comes to come over the sea toward these old places also. There is something about it all I can't express, perhaps will not be able to express.

LH

1. Hahn's longhand note.
2. Anderson and his party sailed on the *Rochambeau*.
3. Probably Mildred Dilling of Indianapolis, who had a successful career (of four decades) as a harpist.

133

To Bab June—1921—Paris[1]

Here we are in a narrow little street on the left bank, but 10 minutes walk to the Louvre and the bridges. I have a comfortable room at 10 fr—or about 80 cents.[2] A tall blue eyed boy comes to the door at 8 and we wrestle about—making up a breakfast bill and then I lounge about until noon and work.

Paul is a fine companion,[3] only inclined to fight with life dreadfully. The trouble is he has never worked and has no give and take with people. He is so sensitized to passing moods in every one that being with him is often like walking a tightroap.[4] Our middle western way of blurting things out shocks him and he sees occasion for being hurt too often when I'm sure there is none.

Saw Gallimard yesterday but could have no conversation with him as he has no English. Franks book "Our America" is out here and has attracted attention, how much I dont know. Joyce is here and Pound. I haven't seen them.

Last night we walked down the left bank of the Seine and had a georgeous dinner in a little old 18th century cafe—overlooking the island, the statue of Henry IV—prancing against a wonderful evening sky and in the distance the Louvre. "Paris is worth a mass." I said it for Henry.[5]

Later we walked to Notre Dame and sat on benches for a long time looking at its dilecate and massive beauty. Little French prostitutes drifted past and there was a drunken man and his drunken misstress, both with swollen faces laughing and wrestling under the shadow of the church, the gargoyles grinning down at them. The Gothic art couldn't carry on but here it achieved something breath taking. You could never believe so huge a building could be do [so] delicately lovely or spring so lightly into the sky. I hope I shall see Chartres.

Copeau[6] is being very successful—perhaps too much so. He will no doubt be the big man in the Paris theater of the next ten years.

On the boat I grew unspeakable weary of the grinning little harpist Miss Dilly or Dillon. At the last on the train into Paris she came to ask me if I wanted to be remembered to you. What I wanted to say was "Not at your dull little hands." She plays without joy, smoothly, stupidly, I'm afraid.

It is a little strange to find a city from which you actually draw constantly. One has been so used to our cities that are a barrier, that stand between on[e] and the imagained beauty of life.

On the other hand the beauty is a constant comfort. Man kind has once and for a time turned its hands to these lovely permanent things. Here were artists who worked without signing their work. There was real purity of purpose. And its quite lovely to think that in the midst of it they insisted on those sensual, grotesques—the gargoyles of Notre Dame.

I know I am going to feel myself inadequate in the telling you of this. Its too big to tell of. What I want—when your time of freedom comes is for you to come here. I shall never be satisfied if you do not do that.

Address to July 1[7]
On envelope.

LH

1. Hahn's longhand note.

2. Though Tennessee is not mentioned in these letters, she was with him throughout. Ernestine Evans, who encountered the Rosenfeld-Anderson party on the *Rochambeau* and traveled with them, recalled in a radio interview that the Andersons' room in Paris "wasn't terribly big, but it had a rather fine bay window" and "one of those French tables with a marbled top and sometimes a little purple doily on top."

3. Evidently Ernestine Evans and Tennessee went about Paris together, and thus so did Rosenfeld and Sherwood.

4. Evans thought Rosenfeld kept remembering the difference between previous visits and his encounters with critics on behalf of his own work and that now he was the "salesman of Sherwood." It was, she thought, "sort of a bitter moment for Paul. And Tennessee and I would flee and leave them alone." She thought Sher-

wood "had great fun explaining his work" and that he was well accepted by the French.

5. Evidently Anderson's reaction was as emotional as this quoting of the supposed remark of Henry IV indicates. The *Bookman* (Oct. 1921) reported that Rosenfeld, returning ahead of Anderson, told of Anderson's first glimpse of the Place du Carrousel, near the Louvre: "He saw Anderson rubbing his eyes, and thought he must have acquired a cinder, a memory of Chicago days. Not so. Mr. Anderson was weeping, and he continued to weep through lunch, for, said he, 'It is so much more beautiful than anything I had imagined.'"

6. See Anderson to Bab, letters 72, 75, and 76 herein.

7. Probably Hotel Jacob & d'Angleterre, 44, rue Jacob, Paris.

134

To Bab Paris—June 1921[1]

Nothing in Paris has interested me more than the change I feel in Jacque[s] Copeau. When I saw him in America he was at a low ebb in his fortunes. What a charming fellow he was then.

He is charming still but a change has come over him. In Paris now he is being very successful. His therater is apparently kind of an upper middle class chapel in which Jacques is the non conformist preacher of the new art.

The result as far as art is concerned is dreadful.

I saw his company last night in 12th Night. It was really dreadful. A friend here has told me the French language is fit for nothing but declamation. It may be true and it is no doubt true Sheakspear cannot be declaimed. He has been declaimed too much. Here on the boulevards and on Broadway and Randolph Street.

No doubt there are certain plays made to fit the French temperment and what they have made of this Sheakspear comedy is something like that.

I went with Jacques and Madame Bing[2] (called by some the best actress in France. In a resturant they are charming. On the stage I have not cared for either of them.

It will be impossible for me to express what I feel of this city in letters. I am keeping a note book.[3] When I come home you may read it if you wish. I shall try to make it express as much as I can all my thoughts and feelings here.

Although there are no doubt thousands of American[s] in Paris one completely looses the sense of them by avoiding certain sections of the city. Men have the herd instinct strongly developed and all of the Americans here frequent the same places. One has only to avoid these places to avoid the Americans.

Both Ezra Pound and Joyce came to call on me. Pound is an empty man with nothing to give. Joyce has been hurt a good deal and is gloomy but thro his gloom Irish wit and humor shines. Tha man has the most delicately lovely hands I have ever seen on a human being.

I got a bad cold on the steamer crossing thro the channel and it has only now begun to go away a little. Several dark gloomy days have been followed by the most lovely day I have ever spent. Most of it has been spent alone in the garden of the Tuilleries.

LH

1. Hahn's longhand note.
2. So far unidentified.
3. This consists of fifty-six longhand pages with entries for May 28, June 2, 6, and 13. It is presently at the Newberry Library.

135

To Bab

June, 1921[1]
Friday

Your letter with the story of your hard summer came yesterday and made me realize anew what a load you continually carry. What can one say. The load can only be shifted by the hand of God—I'm afraid.

I havn't worked very much and still I do work some every morning. The proofs of the new book[2] are read and off and I have about completed the revisions of Windy.

Yesterday I went to Ameins, to the Cathrederal there and Sunday went to Chartres. Chartres is the final last word in beauty. It is almost all poetry in stone and the glass is the most lovely radient moving mass of colors and light conceivable.

Indeed I am storing up and although I sometimes scribble a little in my note book most of my impressions have to be simply stored away.

The French translation of Winesburg has turned out badly and I'm afraid will have to be done over. It's sad. The woman who has been doing it is a lovely person, the wife of a banker, very sensitive and fine. She undertook the job without pay, for pure love of the book and it will be dreadfully hard that it will not do.

However Copeau and Gallimard declare she has taken the flavor away.

By the way Winesburg is to be brought out in the Boni & Liverwright Modern Library and did I tell you had completed the arraingments for Huebsch to take over all my former books.

By the time this reaches you I will have gone on to London so do not send any more letters here. I can be reached American Express London but will only stay there for a week or two, then will go into the country.

It seems sinfull for me to be thus going about seeing beautiful places when you are bound with iron bonds but if my constant thoughts of you help at all you know you have them.

With Love

LH Written on stationery of Hotel Jacob & d'Angleterre, 44, rue Jacob, Paris.

1. Hahn's longhand note.
2. *The Triumph of the Egg.*

136

To Bab Paris—June 1921.[1]

A summer morning on my perch above the rue Rivoli facing the Place de Condardat [la Concorde]. The life of the boulevards goes on beneath me. To my left is the gardens of the Tuilleries. It is a spot I have found, very quiet like being in a shell while the wind blows outside.

I am working everyday although my work is not organized. In the afternoon I wander in Paris, seeing things, trying to get my own impressions of life here.

On Sunday I went with a French poet and with a man I know here to Provence—a town in Champaign [Champagne]. It is a little 12th Century town on a hill—narrow little streets, houses whose old beauty makes the tears come.

At night I go alone sometimes into old Paris. There are streets where one may almost touch the walls on each side. Striking figures go past. Little prostitutes shout at you. Up the narrow old stairways is the rank smell of life.

That is at night sometimes. In the daytime it is sweet to sit in the inner court of old castles, to dream of thousand year old footsteps echoing among the carved stone figures on old walls.

Wherever one finds beauty one finds the marks of the middle ages, the time of belief and faith and devotion.

Now there is more devotion here in the country, in the fields. The

French countryman is in love with the soil. He has fingered it. He has poured his life into it.

One feels the devotion of the French to the soil in the horses pulling great carts in the city.

In our country the young stallions that are to labor are castrated but here it is not so. They remain through life honorable males. What splendid fellows. If I lived in France I would choose to be a teamster driving six stallions hitched to a great cart piled high with wine barrels.

In the late morning it is fine to sit in a cafe drinking a glass of wine and watching the colorful crowds drift past on the boulevards.

How sweet the wind in the morning. There is always the faint suggestion of the sea in the morning winds of Paris.

Write me%
American Express Co.—London
After the lst
Mark—(hold)

LH

1. Hahn's longhand note.

137

To Bab France—June 1921[1]

I am in the country—at a little town on the channel where we have come to spend a few days lying in the sun and swimming in the sea before going to England. It is a little Norman town with roses growing in profusion everywhere and rather gay housed. Before we came Paul wired for rooms at a hotel but when we got to the place we found it cost nearly 300 fr a day to live there. We rode about in a carriage until we found this little hotel with a garden and good fare for about 30 fr a day.

Today, after I had been writing in the morning we climbed a hill that looks over the channel and spent a long time lying in the sun. Then a boy climbed up to us and over [offered?] to take us in a boat over an arm of the sea to where we could walk back on the hard sand—for 2 fr and we went.

Paul is becoming constantly a better companion. He is a very intense man, highly individual and suspicious and sometimes revengeful. One day last week I had to rather take things in hand and now all is clear.

The trouble was—as with so many people—that his world with its troubles, doubts, suspicions became the center of the universe. Thinking he wanted love he really wanted you to live in his world and grew angry and jealous when you became absorbed in your own thoughts or in others.

I was compelled to assert myself and even suggest I would have to go my own way before we got on a right basis. As I write now he is sitting in the garden below, occasionally looking up to grin. We have both just come from a long swim in the sea.

This is really the last of France as we shall be in England next Sunday. It has turned out well. After some doubt, on everyone's part, there seemed to be a general decision that the translations of Madame Gay were very satisfactory.

She is really a dear woman, very sensitive and fine. She had been hard at work on her english pronunciation and we were able to talk freely. Her country place is on a small lake—some 40 miles from Paris and there is a sloping garden to the water's edge. We had a delightful afternoon in the garden amid flowers.

Later—

It is Wednesday—after lunch. All morning we have been in the sea and lying on the sand. I am in my room again. Conversation comes brokenly up from the garden below. It is amazing how skillfull the French are about life. The whole life of the houses faces the rear, a garden or a small inner court. In the towns themselves there is always something gay, half joyous. The towns and the houses do not press down on you as with us.

I have been thinking of your complicated, tired life, and the twisted thing against which you are always fighting. That is a big part of life with all of us and I do not want to escape it. Your own life is America, it is a part of America and with all the real joy and the realease I have here my life is there, my love is there.

LH

1. Hahn's longhand note.

138

To Bab

Bastille day in France[1]
July 14

I'm liking London—althougth today I'm ill from too much knocking about in little public houses of the East end with English men and women—drinking with them, trying to understand their cockney.

Well its only a belly ache after all.

London has dignity. There is something solid here. At first its hard to realize you are in so vast a place and you half expect, any minute to go round a corner and come upon fields.

No such luck. The city just goes on—endlessly.

I do little sight seeing—rather I walk and walk—in smart streets, in poor streets, seeing the crowds, looking at them, thinking of them and of America too.

I'll be rather glad to go back. The trip here has taught me how much I am American, how much I want for America.

It is hot and the skies are clear. The gods never provided such processions of fine days as we have had in Europe.

I do not write much but I gather impressions—not so much concerning all these people over here as concerning the people at home, the people of my own mind.

I shall go to Oxford for a day or two and then come back here and go to the South of England somewhere until time to sail—Aug. 10.

Mail via—American Express—London. Next month at this time I'll be on the water, homeward bound.

LH Written on stationery of Cranston's Kenilworth Hotel, Great Russell Street, London WC12.

1. Hahn's longhand note.

139

To Bab

Friday—July
Oxford, England

Dear Woman,

I am sitting in the inn yard of the Golden Cross at Oxford[1] and have a typewriter here so I can work in the morning and walk over the English roads in the afternoon. Last night I dined with Edward O Brien[2]—a girlish gentle man with colorless blue eyes and something much finer about him than has ever been indicated by anything he has written.

Yesterday we walked into the country to have tea with some charming English people and tomorrow I am to play golf with the director of the Moscow Art Theater, a hindu Prince and and Englishman. So you see I am happy here and shall stay in this spot until I go down to my boat in about 2 weeks.

In London I had a really fine time and met some interesting people, among other a real novelist, John Cournos—who wrote The Mask and The Wall. Real work. Do you know his books. Read them.

Something very strange has happened in England. There is a real looking toward America. One felt it on every hand. You know, in the past, there has always been an inclination to scoff at every intellectual and artistic thing—American.

It is passing. After a week among English men of letters I've a fancy that my own work will make perhaps a deeper impression here than in America. It will be interesting to see.

In the meantime I send you greeting and soon I'll be on my way westward and will see you. If you write me after you get this address the letter to Huebsch and mark—"hold."

With Love,

LH

1. In an undated clipping Hahn had kept of a "What say!" column from the Marion, Va., papers, probably of Oct. 1928, Anderson reminisced about Oxford. A London publisher had told him he would pay his expenses at Oxford for several weeks if he would write his impressions. He referred to getting a typewriter in Oxford and taking it to "The Golden Bowl." He thought of himself writing in an upstairs room and issuing repeated calls for tankards of ale to give him more "courage." In this probably imaginative account, he referred to himself as being "as far as I knew without a drop of English blood in me" (his blood was a mixture of Italian and Norse) and to getting caught after dark in an enclosure of one of the colleges as well as punting on the Thames. He felt his straight-speaking article "stirred up a little fury."

2. Edward J. O'Brien, who had been honoring Anderson in his yearly anthologies of best short stories since 1916. Anderson wrote to O'Brien on Aug. 5, thanking him and his mother for what was evidently more than perfunctory hospitality.

140

To Bab [n.d.]

Just a little goodbye note from England. Yesterday I got your note from the garden, the night you were alone there.

Something in it makes me want specially to tell you again that my regard for you is filled with respect also. I do not feel as I once did that things you say and feel are stuffy.

In the end Paul and I worked things out to a very fine basis—all without anything really coming to the surface. Perhaps after all the great difficulty lay in my own stupidity. As you say there are no doubt old scars there.[1]

There is something of the woman in P. Things are intensified, made personal. Also he has never lived roughly with people, taking life and recieving it. We got the thing in hand after a time.

When this reaches you I will probable be at sea, nearing New York. My love to you from here and there.

LH Written on stationery of Cranston's Kenilworth Hotel, Great Russell Street, London, WC12.

1. The friendship continued until Anderson's death.

141

To Bab August 1921—Return from Europe[1]
Sunday

Everything is unsettled here as it always is when one comes home.[2] My house in the country is occupied and will be until the 1st. Then I hope to get into it and to settle down to work.

I do appreciate all the things you must be going through during this terrible summer of heat and sickness—but I do know too that one can escape nothing of life. As the cards are dealt they must be played and it is true that places make no difference.

That doesn't make me the less anxious to see you free. I want you also to go look at the lovely things men have done in that old world. It is something to carry back and remember here in this new place.

I shall be coming along later—just when will have to depend I suppose—somewhat on the whim of Mr. Steele.[3]

In the midst of everything—it is still good to be back.

LH Written on stationery of Fort Dearborn Hotel, Chicago.

1. Hahn's longhand note.
2. Anderson sailed for the United States on Aug. 10.
3. Anderson's client in Harrodsburg, Ky.

142

To Bab

Chicago—1921
The Dial Award[1]

All you say is quite true and yet there is the terrible vulgarity too. I shall cut it all as shortly as I can. Hackett sent me the other day a little drawing he had made called "Celebrity—or The Price of Fame."[2] It is illuminating and shows me with a worried look fleeing from fat men in dress suits.

One really has something to say. That is the baffling difficulty. What I really think however is that the ones who are ready to recieve what may be said already know it.

The difficulty really lies in the interruption to work. One wants to do even more difficult and delicate things. Love coming from others is healing and helpfull. The other thing is terrible. One has to begin each day by shoveling mud out of the temple.

There is however—believe me, a fine arrogance in me. I shall know how to be blunt and brutal when the time comes for that.

There is a kind of lovliness in a message said over and over in dark streets and rooms, said persistently—when it strikes something into fire in others.

Writers in New Republic, Vanity Fair—Nation—all these men have written of Triumph with fire & feeling.[3] One must be glad when the reading of these things makes others write with new freedom although one may feel they often miss the point somewhat too.

Love

LH

1. Hahn's longhand note, both lines. In the summer of 1921 *The Dial* announced that it would make an annual award of $2,000 "to a young American writer who has contributed to *The Dial*." For the first award, made as of Jan. 1, 1922, all contributors from Jan. 1920 were considered. Anderson knew by late Oct. that he was to be the first recipient.

2. This drawing has apparently not survived.

3. The following quotations suggest the character of the reviews. The episodes and stories are as "memorable as have been written by any contemporary American" (*The Nation*, 113 [Nov. 23, 1921], 602). "There is at times in his books an unbelievable and glamorous beauty . . . of things seen with delight or known in an intensity of emotion" (John Peale Bishop in *Vanity Fair*, 17 [Dec. 1921], 118). "One who reads all of the stories at a setting will scarcely miss the singleness of purpose and unity of result which give to the whole a haunting and unbelievable power" (Robert Morse Lovett in the *New Republic*, 28 [Nov. 23, 1912], 383).

143

To Bab

Palos—1921[1]
Wed.

The days go by in a procession—each a little sharper and colder. Last night there was frost and now the leave[s] of the trees will bleed.

I'm going forward with the novel—some 80,000 words written. It will be long, perhaps 125,000 words. It is a rich experience to me anyway. In feeling my way forward into these new people the actual flesh and blood people of my bodily life go far away. They are for the time like echoes, playing over these hill[s].

I am very well and for the time proud. The figures arrange themselves. There is no lonliness. My hut is filled with people, laughing perplexed, troubled.

I embrace these days. There are no plans for tomorrow and just now no yesterdays. If you get but an impersonal sense of me these days its true enough. I am like that. My love to you just the same.

LH

1. Hahn's longhand note.

144

To Bab

Palos Park—1921
November—1921[1]

There are times when, in spite of the fact that I am quite free I do not work very effectively. Today I am in the country but do not respond to it so I shall flee back to town. There is plenty of unoccupied office space at Critchfield's so I shall take one of the little offices there for the present and only come to the country when the mood comes.

For one thing the [work?] in business has quite submerged me, temporarily. One has to make a violent readjustment and that is difficult. The figures of the fancy slip away, go hide for the time. Today I am very sad and the country seems infinately sad. A sleepy whispering goes on among the dead brown leaves of the oaks. The year with its green growth and the blood running through the body of earth has died. I futilely reach, trying to remember what good work has been accomplished. "The past is a bucket of ashes" today.[2]

My visit with you seems, in the backward look now, a very human time. Some things were said that hadn't been said. There was perhaps something gained and lost.

These readjustments keep making themselves. One is continually facing little lies, told themselves and others. How many days, like this one of mine, you must have too. The cry[?] into the land seems very far away. Where is the road?

I walk about in Chicago, come into the country, see people, hear voices but the thing within myself that so often makes any and all life possible, doesn't happen. In an hour, a day, a week, the rhymic march within myself may begin again. In the meantime I sit and wait with out dreams, with all my fancies quite dead, wat[c]hing the grey sky and the slow jerking movements of leaves on the trees by my windows.

LH

1. Hahn's longhand note, both lines.
2. This quotation is from "Four Preludes on Playthings of the Wind" by Carl Sandburg.

145

To Bab

November Palos—1921
Triumph of the Egg[1]
Sunday

Indeed I have been so buried in the life of this book,[2] walking about with these people thinking their thought, feeling with them, that the actual flesh and blood people who are my own loves have for the moment grown a little vague and far off.

I also liked the peaceful quiet day with you, the mist over the river and best of all I liked the new sense of you that is growing in me.

All of the things you say I did in a way sense and understand—your delicacy in leaving me for the time with the people of my fancy and holding our time together to the quiet and lovliness of the moment itself.

What a charming march of days I have had here, the forest like a quiet strong middle aged woman at this time of year and the days going past filled with work.

As to the business, I cant tell yet whether or not I shall have any income this year but I'll get through and shall not think about it until I have too.

Think of me as thinking often of you in the hours when I am not at my desk but am walking alone in the paths in the forest trees.

LH

1. Hahn's longhand note.
2. Probably *Ohio Pagans*, not the recently published *The Triumph of the Egg*. "The Gossip Shop" of *The Bookman* (Dec. 1921) commented: "But one man, I'll venture a prognostication, who will never depart Chicago for . . . New York, is dear old Sherwood Anderson, once more established at his Palos Park estate, hard at work on a new book."

146

To Bab

November—1921[1]
Palos Park—Sunday

A day of work then later wandering about over the roads. Walked with a fat Chicago lawyer and later with a sensitive tubuculer advertising man. There was a grey curtain drawn over distances.

Whenever I am away and come back there is an accumutation of letters. It takes a half day to clear ones self. Tomorrow I shall perhaps work again.

I'm sending you copy of a part of a letter written to Paul—who is doing an article on my stuff.[2] Thought it might interest you as it covers something we've talked of. Will you return it?

Days slip away and in the distance are grew [grey] like this fall day but there is something long—that one may believe in, and work in—friendships and the arts.

I'm thinking many quiet thoughts of our talks.

LH

1. Hahn's longhand note.
2. Paul Rosenfeld's article was "Sherwood Anderson" in *The Dial* (Jan. 1922).

147

To Bab

Chicago—1921[1]

Grey and rainy days. Grey and rainy days. I keep thinking of other places and of my paint pots. I am sitting, these days, in a little office in the very heart of the city. To be sure I am only a passing thing here but it is like visiting a prison in which human souls are confined.

The reviews of Triumph are unlike anything I have had before. One feels real minds, coming as out of grey shadows, and saying "I understand.["] During these years I have been saying something over and over as into a black night. "These twisted ones have souls. Beauty lies asleep in them."

No one responded. There was the clatter, about sex obsession, about dirt and ugliness.

And now, out of their better minds, comes something like a sweet wind.

In some way the clatter and the vulgarity doesn't so much matter now. One finds new brothers to add to a few, who long ago sensed what I have been grouping for.

With Love.

LH

1. Hahn's longhand note.

148

To Bab   Palos/Dec. 1921[1]

I took 2 of the paintings to a packer to be packed for shipment to you— and to hang in the new house.[2] Unfortunately they could not tell me what the express would be and I had to send them express collect. Pardon the discourtesy of that.

I am trying to work in more or less of a jumble just now. I will tell you as a secret (the announcement will be made Dec 1st) that the Dial Prize has been awarded me. Some little fuss promises to be made—a dinner here and in New York etc.

There is an invasion. One is thrown into a difficult position. I have held away from such things but there is sincere courtesy mixed strangely with something else in these invitations.

One is constantly annoyed. I went one evening last week to meet with a group that announced itself as revolutionary painters. When I got there I found a newspaper man & a photographer. The men were themselves poor daubs trying to get thro me newspaper publicity. I swore & left.

A few nights later I went to hear Hackett address some rich intellectual jews when one of them jumped up—interrupting Hackett and in a loud voice announced my presence.

LH

1. Hahn's longhand note.

2. The two paintings that Hahn had when I knew her probably are not these. Hers had been documented as having been bought in connection with Anderson's European trip earlier in 1921. The fate of the two paintings mentioned in this letter is unknown.

149

To Bab Palos 1921—The Dial Award[1]

I am leaving here tomorrow and will stop with a friend in the country in Pennsylvania[2] before going on to New York. I've no doubt I will be there when you come. Now I want a few days in the country, in a quiet place pretty much alone before the ordeal of that.

In a sense I have to face the fact that in the future I shall not be as much a man by myself as I have been. You would understand what I mean if you could sit with me and read the morning mail that has been coming to me day after day.

It is like a lot of little streams dammed or frozen that suddenly begin to flow.

These are not people seeking a personal attachment. There is love here, healing love. It is young American men and women saying "we'll try to keep the faith and seek the truth." One knows that many of them will not do it just as one knows that tomorrow may see his own death.

But such love, coming up to one, even for a moment does something to fill empty places.

European artists do not live, isolated as we do here and some day American artists will not be so isolated.

You imagain a man walking, walking, in a silent streets.

Are the houses occupied or are they empty piles.

Suddenly doors open and faces look out, voices cry and after that you see even when one walks in streets that are grey and silent there is a new conciousness of living people there, behind the walls.[3]

Love to You

LH

1. Hahn's longhand note.

2. Presumably Rollo Peters.

3. The revulsion-attraction Anderson felt toward fame is well summed up in this letter.

150

To Bab Dec. 1921[1]

A rather mad jumble of people—faces—at dinners,[2] newspaper men with their sharp cynical eyes—many eyes—people looking curiosity, hatred, questions. I am well but tired and wanting to get clear of all people—to be alone. It will come soon.

In the midst of it all a struggle—people saying—what do you mean—explain, explain.

One cant. There is no use speaking, explaining talking.

The days bright jeweled things going bye and me in no way a part of them just now. My life taken from me—used by others for the time.

It will be sweet to escape presently and have back myself alone in the days somewhere.

LH Written on stationery of Hotel Brevoort, at 5th Avenue and 8th Street, New York City.

1. Hahn's longhand note.

2. At one of the dinners he received *The Dial* award, responding with brief, stammered thanks.

151

To Bab December 1921[1]

One might so easily get the most absurd and childish sense of power here.

One goes out to breakfast and a crowd of literary people gather about. There is a rapid fire of talk. Quick enmities and friendships are made. Vast possibilities open and close again.

People think you have something they want. You say something and it is repeated, distorted too.

Politicians and other public men must thus loose the sense of people. I cannot stand it much longer but shall run away.

The point is that you, another I know well can give me vastly more.

One has to take life more slowly, let it grow in him. There is a kind of violence in this seeing so many people.

I may be unable to stand it more than a few days more—then I will have to run. I cant help it.

LH Written on stationery of Hotel Brevoort, at 5th Avenue and 8th Street, New York City.

1. Hahn's longhand note.

152

To Bab January—1922[1]

You may be off to New York by now. I had to stay here about some advertising before going on to New Orleans. Wish I might have been in New York when you got there but I could stay no longer. At least I know that although you are terrible lonely sometimes—as God knows who isn't—you have found in some way your own footing in life and can stand on your own ground.

There was a very great deal of the other sort of thing in New York and it grew more intense the longer I stayed. But for the clean love I got from a few men and women it might have been unbearable.

Something is no doubt happening in America. The rift isn't very large but it is a rift. The immediate effect is that the old sinners are suddenly afraid, then they become frightened, next they plead. I could tell you almost unbelievable tales of men who cry and who seem to think you can give them cleanness as one might give them milk out of a bottle.

I leave here for New Orleans at 10 this morning.[2] Address me there
Hotel Lafayette
Lafayette Square.

LH Written on stationery of the Phoenix Hotel, Lexington, Ky.

1. Hahn's longhand note.
2. Tennessee returned to teaching music in Chicago; Anderson arrived in New Orleans in late January.

153

To Bab New Orleans—1922[1]

You see I think the point is this. You say "I respect the thing you give me" and yet in almost every letter you do insert an appeal for something else. May one say quite frankly that I do not think that is "respecting" the thing I do and can give.

What I have come to feel is that one has to learn to carry their own life and its impulses like a jewel in the hand.

One cannot respect another until they respect also themself. That first. Life must be carried with a certain poise as one would carry a full cup of wine in a crowd.

Back of this also is implicit a lack of faith in me, not justified by my attitude toward you. I have something I want to give.

One cannot be forced by the needs of another to crowd the growth of feeling. One is in that way choked.

Now I am writing a book called Many Marriages[2] that, if the gods are good, will make these things clearer. You see dear friend I am, more than you know at times the rather cold withdrawn workman who is trying to work something out. At such times I cannot be violated.

If there is life in the hand that hold[s] the pen there is death in it also. Do not have doubt of the quality of what I can and do give.

LH

1. Hahn's longhand note.
2. Published serially in *The Dial*, beginning Oct. 1922. It appeared as a book in 1923.

154

To Bab New Orleans—1922[1]

Dear Woman—

Such marching days of work. Do not feel forgotten if you do not hear often from me. The days are very full and there is in me a sort of temporary gesture of dismissal for all people in the flesh, a dismissal and at the same time a pulling of them closer.

There have been those here who have given me really lovely companionship these days.

There is one woman, a waitress I walk about with in the afternoons when she is off duty for two hours—one of the most beautiful women I have ever known. She gives me more richly than any one I've known, a sense of a life I'd almost forgotten.

Well she has something to teach every other woman I've ever known.

Sunshiny days are followed by cloudy days. I work and live very fully and am being very happy here.

The new book may be a year in preparation as it may go to a two or three volume affair but that gives a rich sense of plenty of work to be done. You may get some notion of what I've been up to when I tell you that I have nearly completed the whole first volume of my new work since I've been here. It may go two or even three volumes and will be called Many Marriages. It is to be told in 3 to 5 episodes. The whole thing an effort to go deeper into people and show their processes of thought and the effect of their thoughts, unexpressed on their lives—a very interesting, delicate and difficult thing to do.

I hope you are well—I am—very. I stay in my room working steadily all morning and do not try to work in the afternoons.

Well I have managed to find playmates here who will walk with me or go with me into the country. The days go bye in a kind of splendor. I dont know how long I shall stay. I will I suppose make up my mind and leave some night.

Lots of Love

LH

1. Hahn's longhand note.

155

To Bab

New Orleans—Mar 1st 22[1]

Dear Woman—

I'm O, so very sorry you have been ill again. I was afraid something of the sort was going on.

No I didn't see the Krock[?] thing but I know the man and have no respect at all for his mind. What I have come, very definately to think is that any one who can spend his live saying smart sarcastic things about politicians, must at bottom be a good deal of a child. I suppose I think that any one, having become politically minded and remaining politically minded, is also permanently immature. It sounds like a too definate pronouncement but I am quite convinced it is true.

The first episode of the long thing I am writing,[2] quite a fat volume in itself, is nearing completion and I will have to leave here at the end of this week.

By a streak of bad luck I'll not be able to stop and see you as I had planned. One of my clients in Kentucky has died and I am to meet his brother in Louisville and then he is to go on with me to Chicago—in connection with business.

So you must write me at Critchfield's, the next place I will be able to get mail.

Mardi Gras went off yesterday under a grey sky but quite happily. The town was filled with maskers and as there is little prohibition here everyone was properly gay and at least half abandoned to fun. I am writing something about New Orleans in the Double Dealer here.[3]

I went yesterday to play with the crowd and at noon met some friends. We went off to the old French Market to an Italian restaurant and ate, drank and danced all afternoon. The party went on no doubt half the night but at dusk I lit out to go into the negro section and walk there.

It is because of the negroes, the French and the Italians that there is play to be had here.

It has been a wonderful time for me—and now back I go to the industrial North. Well spring will soon come.

And I hope before long I shall be seeing you.

With Love,

LH

1. Hahn's longhand note. Anderson had an apartment at 708 Royal Street, on the corner of Royal and St. Peter streets, in the French Quarter.

2. *Many Marriages*.

3. "New Orleans, The Double Dealer and the Modern Movement in America" appeared in the Mar. 1922 issue of the *Double Dealer*. The article touches on Anderson's appreciation of New Orleans but is more dedicated to Anderson's central idea that industrialization is ruining art and the quality of life generally.

156

To Bab Palos—1922[1]

And isn't that the all of it, the beginning of the road into the city of life? First there is the realization that there is no gate, no opening into the city and then, as by a miricle the gates do swing open, a little, a crack appears.

There is no opening into the city of life, never was such an opening.

That is indeed what I think you are learning these last few years.

I think myself that all people who do not come to that knowledge are and to the end remain, children. Surely the artist who does not come to it remains a hopeless fuddler.

And there is another kind of childishness, a second stage of childishness—the kind that makes one, after the eyes have been opened a little, a hopeless cynic.

What an amazing situation. There is myself, yourself, all of us. We have been told we are all centers about which all life revolves. "Every hair of your head shall be numbered. Not a sparrow shall fall to the ground—". The old writers knew how to flatter the yokals.

It is all very childish isn't it—godhead, maidenhead, virtue its own reward, God's in his heaven all's right with the world.

In time I dare say modesty will grow among us a little.

And there is the wall before you and me. No real contacts shall be made. It is the law of life. If you have a lover better send him away. To have my lips against your lips, my brests against your breasts, my thighs against your thighs, all of the physical you pressed to the physical me, opens no doors either.

There is the wall, always confronting you and me and all of us until the breath blows out of our bodies and we are dead.

We can be glad of leaves on trees, penciling of bare lims of trees against winter skies, lips of singers singing, other lovers walking arm in arm, children playing baseball, the sun going down behind the smoke of an American city.

The wall is something. The eyes of God are not looking and you, myself, all men and women are in their places, each behind his own section of the wall. Perhaps after all God is looking. Under the wall may be the place for us.

There is always the wall however and on it are infinate tracings. How many others have stood where you are now standing. The wall is covered with tracks left by wandering minds of those others feeling their way over the face of the wall. Every artist who ever lived has worked on the face of just this wall and no place else. The marks of the old men are there, Chinese, Hindoo, Arabs, the French, the Germans, the Russians, all, all, under the wall.

America is a strange, a wonderful place, a kind of kindergarden where old things have to be taught again to new children. America the land of promise, new men making life easily wonderfull. The wall is to be torn down by a Bill Haywood[2] or a Eugene Debs.[3] As the flapper on the streets says, "where do they get that stuff?"

Land of eternal childishness where every artist whose bad artistry makes him cry out against the injustice of life. Young fellows walking in city streets and saying solomnly "I am an empty man." They have found out that being born an American does not admit them to the kingdom of heaven without a ticket and they are peved. Now they adopt cynicism. "Life is nothingness, nothingness. Life does not exist. The flesh does not exist. All I cannot understand cannot exist."

You understand all I mean, what things there are to learn. I'm really not preaching but saying over to you in my own way what you have said.

It is I think the beginning of knowledge. From there you can start being something. I can start from there. Some day I reckon all America will have to start from there.

LH

1. Hahn's longhand note.

2. William (Big Bill) Haywood, labor leader and a founder of the Industrial Workers of the World.

3. Eugene V. Debs, Socialist presidential candidate in 1900, 1904, 1908, 1912, 1920.

157

To Bab April. 1922[1]

A bad temporary jam of things. The house in which T[ennessee] has lived so long is to be torn down or rebuilt or something. Many of my possessions are there.

They must be rooted out. She must be rooted out too.

At the same time I have been driving, driving, making revisions of my new book.[2]

There is one volume done but I want to do others on this same theme.

What I have been striking for is a new, a more intensive prose. To write whole novels that will drive forward with out a break, as I have in the past written short stories.

It is a challenge to myself, more intense than any I have given myself. It seems to me now that in three four or five volumnes I can crowd the whole expression of my own impulse toward life.

I fancy you, for example have felt me, these days, somewhat more hard.

I do not believe I am really so. In a way I have stripped myself like a soldier, entering a long campaign.

There are three or four years work ahead. I go as swift[l]y as strength will let me toward that.

I find here and there, people who give me love unasking. That helps now.

I do not want to be too serious or stupid toward myself. I think of myself rather impersonally these days. I look at my body. I think of the capacity of my mind and my imagaination rather impersonally too, as one might walk in a forest, looking at threes [trees]. "This tree will have to be cut away that, that more sturdy one over there may get to the light. Here are five or six trees that must be taken away. The sunlight must come then to the grass here."

Just now Chicago gives me little. The soft skies and the lovely surroundings of my life in the south, river, niggers, ships, sunlight—made long peaceful days for the rush of work possible.

I worked sometimes there until my whole body trembled. Then the warmpth, the slow rhythm of life about me quickly restored me. On the next day I was ready to work again.

I shall go back there next winter. Perhaps if I can get together money for it I shall buy me a small house there.

I shall perhaps stay here, in the country at Palos this summer. Soon the green and warm days will come here.

I wish it were possible for me to send you Mms[3] of the new book but I cant. I have but 2 copies and they must both go different places.

Write me at Critchfields. Tell me you are well.

LH

1. Hahn's longhand note.
2. *Many Marriages.*
3. Manuscript.

158

To Bab April—1922[1]

I'm here in Chicago and very well. One comes out of the quiet of that place and the long working period to the tensity of this. There must be a new readjustment of the technique of existence.

For a few weeks I'll be here and then go to the country. Perhaps, I'll stay here this summer but if I do will run away somewhere again in the fall.

I feel a little among strangers, a little puzzled. Those times when I have to take my self as a primary person—say "Sherwood do this or that—mind your Ps & Qs now" are disconcerting.

In periods of work or when one altogether loves another for a time there is an easement. One carries the body and spirit with a certain flourish.

In New Orleans I felt that freedom. Now I do not.

However and queerly mixed up with all this is the giant army of people coming toward me—some unasking, beautifully, others badly mixed and often unintentionally nasty in their self absorbtion.

On the whole, if one can but keep all straight, the gain is greater than the loss of quiet but one must constantly readjust.

And if, dear Woman, I seem unfriendly now—it is only this temporary absorbtion in the problem.

I'm well—do you be well too.

LH

1. Hahn's longhand note.

159

To Bab May—1922[1]

I will try to write you a little more descently. Yesterday was a distracting day and this morning when I came into the city I felt empty. It was odd that it should have been so when it was at the same time the most lovely day of the year.

The thing takes a different form with her [Hahn interpolation: T (for Tennessee)], but the struggle she is having is your own too. It is the fight of the one who by the circumstances of life has become an invert. There is this terrific fight to bring the one outside ones self within the circle of the individual's life.

What I suppose is the cure is a growing reverence for the life outside and the ability to be touched, struck with wonder or amused by it.

You heard me railing against Chicago. That is absurd except as it effects the technique of life now.

As for Italy, that is a dream of next year.[2] I hope it may come true but this year and now I dream only of peace to begin the new and more complex and delicate book I have in mind.

And do I not know you are sound in your friendship with me. I am never worried or perplexed about that.

LH

1. Hahn's longhand note.
2. Anderson never visited Italy.

160

To Bab

May—1922[1]
Later

There is something. I think now it would be better if I did not any more discuss my present problem with any one.[2] It is an inevitable thing. No one, outside myself is to blame. I have perhaps now a half diseased desire to make myself as heroic as I can.

You and I have a basis of friendship and value to each other altogether aside from all this. I wish to turn back to that now. What I am or am not in a particular situation doesn't really matter. And you understand that in this I am speaking to myself rather than to you.

LH

1. Hahn's longhand note. It has not been possible to determine whether this was an addendum to another letter of May 1922 or a separate letter written shortly thereafter.
2. This seems to refer to his break with Tennessee.

161

To Bab

Kentucky June 14, 1922[1]

A very very hot two or three days in this river bottom.[2] I have been sitting at a desk with the sweat rolling off me. Last night I went with my man here down to his place on the Green River.

It is all rather absurd. I think up schemes to sell things while there is a revulsion in me. I wish everyone for whom I work would go broke I suppose.

As to my coming. Well I am in a state of mind not uncommon to me. There comes times when I cannot bear the thought of bringing any more pain to any one. That some one may be able to be self sacrificing and keep something put away for the sake of my comfort or happiness does not answer.

The truth is that I am for the time afraid of people.

It is for this reason—I think—I am happy now in the negro house in the negro section of my city. I go there in the evening and sit in my room. Well it is hot and uncomfortable but I do not mind the physical discomfort. About me are the voices of people who do not know me, whom I do not know. I do not cut down across the realities of their lives at all. The low murmur of voices arise. There is always low laughter.

I sit until darkness comes and then go into a negro restaurant to dine. I am, for the time, far awan [away] from my own people, in a strange place. Here I am nothing. I am myself as I was when I was a boy. I look out at life wonderingly.

Now I want a great deal of this sort of thing. It is a kind of pilgrimage back into the realities of life I am going to undertake now. There is something I want to accomplish. It may take me a year. It may take ten years.

You see, it may well be that I will even stop sending and receiving letters.

Well I can go too deeply into the thing. It is my own battle and it has been coming as an inevitable thing for a long time.

Some day I shall be a more social animal again.

I will be able to hold on to this slight income here for another year. That is a gain.

LH

1. Hahn's longhand note.
2. Evidently Owensboro.

162

To Bab July 6—1922[1]

I just got nit [into] C[hicago] this evening and of course just got your note. I am leaving here not later than the 20th and if you want me to come to Detroit and if I could come sometime between the 12th and 18th I could manage. I would go over and back by boat.

I shall be receiving proofs of Many Marriages here and shall want to clear them up as fast as possible as I want to have that off my hands before I settle down to a new book.

What you say about the negroes surely has in it all the blindness of the South—that one could take a negro woman for mistress but draw back from living with them is rather barbaric. The direct opposite thing is true of me. I am sure I shall never be the lover of a negro woman but I rather prefer living among them more than with any other people I have found in America. There is more laughter, more real sense of life and oddly enough more unconscious sense of beauty.

One cannot make love to them because a civilized man must love a civilized woman. Your southern man can do it because he is basically uncivilized and uncultured. That is about the truth of him.

As I did not really sleep for weeks before I left Chicago I am doing some sleeping now. The drifting through the country, the wind on the face, the monotony of it all sends me off to sleep.

Yesterday I spent with a group of my boyhood friends, now become lawyers, grocers, laborers, doctors, mechanics. We had a big feed out of doors on the shore of Sandusky bay—with wine and song. It was really charming of them. They had a notion I had done something but weren't very sure what it was so they got up this feast to celebrate anyway. One of them said, "We are proud of you. We don't know what for but we are proud of you anyway.[”]

With Love

LH

1. Hahn's longhand note.

163

To Bab Aug. '22[1]

I have about decided to chuck, once and for all, the business world. By economy I shall perhaps be able to get along and support the kids.

I may just suddenly decide to run off to Europe and stay there for two or three years.

As usually happens I spend months thinking my way through a novel or book (sometimes I write the damned thing) and then—one day, in walks the real book, I want all the time to write, takes off his hat, sits in an easy chair and say, "hello. What [have] you been fooling around about?"

I have been writing like a madman lately and the days fly. I sit in the apartment[2] in New York and work—until I am exhausted and then walk about. The days go. I am pretty happy.

LH. Written on the stationery of The Freeman, in the office of B. W. Huebsch, his publisher, at 116 West 13th Street, New York City.

1. Hahn's longhand note.
2. The apartment was courtesy of B. W. Huebsch.

164

To Bab Aug.—1922/New York[1]

It was a very lovely impulse that led you to tell me about the people in the poor stuffy street. I suppose that is about all a writer gets, the feeling that perhaps his work does make people understand each other a little better.

My mind has recently been at work on a curious thought that may interest you too. It concerns the relations of men and women, men and men, women and women.

Crudely stated it would be something like this—that in the meeting of people—the contacts, or marriages that take place, two people never really address each other directly. When two people sit in a room, lie in a bed, meet in the street, there is always a third person present.

This thing, one might call "The Third," is a composit person made up of the two presences. Toward it all things are directed. If both can give freely into the Third a contact is really made and a relationship established.

In most cases the Third becomes a half formed thing, a grotesque. It has a body but its arms are withered away. It has no breasts. Its eyes are crooked.

Do you see the curious phases that might arise from this notion. The question of lonliness is settled. It is a universal feeling. One gets a little freed from this feeling of being a unique.

I give you this thought to play with in your idle hours. It is somewhat the thought of The Man in the Brown Coat, The Dumb Man,[2] the old writer in The Book of the Grotesque.[3]

Personal beauty or lack of beauty in the other one would depends largely on what we see in the Third and what we give to the Third. The man or woman we think we speak with, dine with, make love too we never see at all, except as they are partly represented in The Third, the thing we are, at the moment also helping to make lovely or ugly.

I have taken the liberty of suggestion to my friend Geo. Daugherty of Chicago,[4] who has just written a novel that he send it to you. Perhaps it should find a publisher. He is a man, bound up in business and family life who is trying to release himself through writing.

LH

1. Hahn's longhand note.
2. Stories published in *The Triumph of the Egg.*

3. *Winesburg, Ohio.*
4. Anderson's old friend of four decades who was in the advertising business in Chicago; nothing is known of the novel.

165

To Bab August—1922 New York[1]

I have been going it like a wild man. Have written five short stories and a long poem since I got to New York about three weeks ago. As to New York. I do not see too much of it. By conceiling my address and getting my mail at Huebsch, where I only go once a week I live pretty much in the work I want to do now.

In a physical way New York like New Orleans does give back something to a tired man. In a few buildings here, a sincere expression of form that is restfull and beautiful has been achieved. Often I go to these bouildings instead of too people.

And then there is the museum nearby where I can spend afternoons in the presence of Chinese persian and Egyptian art. Is it not odd that now, after all these years we have just begun to learn again that the Greeks, held up before Western Civilization for so long were really decadent.

One wonders if all this rationalization of life, in religion, art and life itself has not about run its course. It is really amazing how sincerely the men who have devoted their lives to material progress are now apoligizing to such men as have not done so. I got a copy of Lewis's[2] new book with an apaoligy to me written on the flyleaf. How much better be at the business of squaring himself with his God and not with me.

There is a vein in me I have never worked, except quite incidentally, the vein of satire and I am beginning to work it now. Have written two new stories in the satirical vein and find myself able to handle it delicately and I think well.[3] It is a really powerful thing and nobody here uses it. I shall do a good deal in this vein.

And while I am at it I shall quite seperate from the advertising business too. The other morning I walked, thought it all out, bowed my head before the gods and took the oath that I would write no more drivel about plows or breakfast foods. Enough is enough. I am forty-six [six typed over five as correction] next week. As the matter stands I shall be very comfortable for a year and I shall work more steadily.

As for my work. The situation is this—all of the magazines are watching my work and even the Saturday Evening Post wishes to publish a story of mine. This is not because of admiration of my work but as an answer to the critisism that has been directed at them. They feel that to publish me would be an answer.

All this I have from Otto Liveright, brother of Liveright, the publisher, who is an literary agent here and who has come to me and asked me to let him handle my work. What he says is something like this. [“]Within a year some of the magazines will surrender and pay a long price to publish you. They will not dare ask you to write as they wish now. That business is settled as far as you are concerned. You have always written stories the fools could have published had they had any sense. You do not want to bother with them. Let me do it. It will be the proudest moment of my life when I make some of them pay you, as they are now paying inferior men.”

This is the situation. Take it for what it is worth. As far as I am concerned it is very nice. I write a story and send it to this man. There is no conversation with anyone about it. If he sells now and then one I dont even have to look at it in the magazine. Later at any rate I shall put anything I write that is worth it in books and that is what I am after. In the meantime the sale of two or three stories a year would solve the living problem.

All this meants also that I am through with Chicago. I may go to Europe for a year or two a little later but while I am working as I am now will stay right here. All of this—you know I am saying subsub. One of my problems here now is to stay hidden away and when the season is on that will be even harder. I have got me a small apartment which I will move into the later part of this month.

It is an amusing situation. Here is Vanity Fair begging for pages from A New Testament. I have no illusions about it. Seldes[4] says, and rightly, that it means no maore than that Ameriac cannot stand against any man who keeps going independently his own way.

Of course this doesn't mean ease but I do not want ease. It means only that I shall be a writer, nothing else and that my kids shall not starve.

TS

1. Hahn's longhand note. The letter was actually written in September; see the reference to his birthday [Sept. 13] later in the letter.

2. Sinclair Lewis's *Babbitt* was published in Aug. 1922.

3. One was probably “Ohio, I'll Say We've Done Well,” published in the *Nation*, Aug. 9, 1922.

4. Gilbert V. Seldes (1893–1970), an editor of *The Dial* from 1920–33.

166

To Bab

November—1922[1]
Friday

A wet cold rainy day in New York. Your letter that I got yesterday at Huebsch gave me real pleasure because of a new note in it regarding your own life.

I think my self that, under the circumstances it was perhaps as well we missed each other—which means no more than that I have had so little to give others—for the time.

Now I begin to feel again a new strength in myself and again to get delight from the world about me. Also—by skipping about, I have got people confused as to where I am. Perhaps I am already forgotten in New York. It is rather well if I am.

As to your own life—it gives me real joy to see you sitting down and contemplating with joy, the ring on your finger, the vase sitting on the table; the little vista through the window. That, it seems to me is the beginning of health.

Later one may perhaps go out from that a little but surely one has to begin there.

Now I am sitting in my own little room with a few pictures and a large, well-made desk. I should be able to write here as well as in another place.

That the book[2] gives you such pleasure is a real joy to me. I'll tell you a secret. It is I think even better in the book which I will be able to send you in February.[3]

And I do so thoroughly agree with you about the books, localized, recording some detail of life or lives. Surely now our writing must take wings a little, not sit forever like an old hen on her nest of China eggs.

Some of these days—when I am quite well I'll come west and stay for a visit with you.

With Love,

LH

1. Hahn's longhand note.

2. This could be a manuscript copy of *Many Marriages*, parts of which were published in the Oct., Nov., and Dec. 1922 issues of *The Dial*.

3. This could refer to the expansion of *Many Marriages*. When it appeared in book form in 1923, Anderson wrote in the introduction that "this temptation to amplify my treatment of the theme was irresistible."

167

To Bab December—1922[1]

It was thoughtful of you to send a Thanksgiving Day wire. My trip—and the escape from people—just now—seems to have set me up. I am working and only perhaps when I am working do I live at all fully.

I had to escape my own place—phones—calls—all day long. Now I have found a place—no one knows of it but me and God—where I am working.

Certain large and rather vague thoughts that have been drifting about in my head seem now to be taking form.

Physically too I am well and happy.

Good days to you too.

LH

1. Hahn's longhand note.

168

To Bab January—1923 New York City[1] Jan 2

I am O, so sorry that there are more days of illness you must endure. There are those things for which we can find no justification under the stars. The most terrible thing of all is the undeserved suffering of those one loves.

I got your very beautiful letter in regard to Many Marriages and I shall be so very glad when the book comes through and I can send it to you.[2] It is a step any way—along a road I want to go.

It has been a very strange year for me, with many hurts in it and some splendid times of work, of loving and being loved. What does the new year hold. God grant I now do in it some things I want to do.

Things seem fairly safe. It is true that my books do not sell much—the progress made in that way is very slow and hesitating.

And one gets enemies from being in a position of strength. Death is a force as well as life. It is quite dreadful to think one can be almost insanely hated by unknown peoples but then, one is loved too.

During the holidays and to avoid offending many nice people who were giving holiday parties right and left I went off into the country—to the country place of the Dudley Field Malone's, where I had a quiet house and a servant and where I worked steadily.[3]

I felt it deeply that I could not be with my children but then, they are not, I suppose making me a part of their lives.

Have plunged into a new novel[4] which was temporarily held up because I have been engaged on a short story that I had to write. It is, in some way, the best thing I've done.

Do you know dear friend I'm a terrible egotist in many ways. I laugh at myself for it. I mention the matter because when I got your letter and was walking in the street I found myself quite naively saying to myself 'she must get well as there are so many things I shall write I shall be wanting her to read.'

With Love

LH

1. Mrs. Hahn's longhand note.

2. In the copy of *Many Marriages* he gave to Finley, Anderson wrote, "One must carry one's own life and its impulses like a jewel in the hand. Life must be carried with a certain poise, as one would carry a full cup of wine in a crowd."

3. Dudley Field Malone (1882–1950), noted liberal lawyer, lived near New York City.

4. Not identified.

169

To Bab

January—1923 New York City[1]
Sunday

I do hope you have begun to get well. I have been ill for a day or two—a mild flu—on the whole a rather pleasant illness as I lay in a warm bed in a warm room dreaming dreams the whole time.

Now I am well again and am glad as I have many projects on my mind. Have just finished two rather fine stories and the new novel—a departure from anything I have done—moves along. It is rather a humorous thing—the humor of the unconscious perhaps.

Also I am thinking of undertaking—for one of the monthlies—a series of papers I would call—"The Note Book of a Modern."[2]

And so you see my life is pretty full of work and schemes.

I escape people pretty well here—have my own little place where I work and sleep sometimes.

Then there is the apartment of a friend—2 blocks away—vacant all day where I go often to work. No one knows where I am. I am hidden away like a crab in his hole at the edge of the sea.

One looks at the passing days and they seem empty and barren of accomplishment but when a year is past there is something, at least some tracings on the wall.

My old energy comes back. How did I know under what a cloud I lived. The central fact that T[ennessee] is one who of herself cannot believe in life becomes more apparent.

The dark moody terrible things always lurking there. Poor child—I know now she came toward me as toward something warm and in the end I guess tired and myself wanted warmpth outside myself.[3]

There are these things in life, one can't account for or dare not account for. Relations poison or make well.

I do grow well again now and only when one is well has he anything to give. The norm for me, I'm sure is a kind of gaiety. I come nearer that. The weariness you must have seen so much of in me is going away.

And a little, being well, I have learned how to handle my self against the background of the city. Where I go I am welcome, where I do not chose to go I do not go. It is a kind of right I have earned and I take it.

Do write and tell me you are getting well.

LH

1. Hahn's longhand note.
2. This was never published.
3. Ben Hecht, whose annotations of Anderson are notably erroneous, wrote me in Nov. 1962 that he remembered Anderson going to New York a few months ahead of Tennessee. The plan was for her to meet him at the Algonquin Hotel at Christmas. However, two days before the holiday, he told the hotel personnel and his friends that he was going to the South with someone new. He wanted everyone to know so they would tell Tennessee when she arrived, as Hecht put it, "on Christmas Eve." The previous September Anderson had written Gertrude Stein that his marriage with Tennessee had failed and that he had fallen in love and that he was trying to save money for a European trip in 1923. He had met Elizabeth Prall, a friend of Margaret Lane (sister of Cornelia Lane Anderson), in New York. Probably Hecht was dramatizing the break with Tennessee, which she was extremely reluctant to accept. It seems apparent that Anderson had turned to Elizabeth Prall by the end of 1922. Prall recalled that she met Anderson when he visited Lane, a nurse, with whom she was sharing an apartment. She notes in *Miss Elizabeth: A Memoir* (Boston: Little, Brown and Co., 1969) that Anderson told her he was determined to part from Tennessee even before he met her. Also, she found Tennessee was circulating rumors in New York that Elizabeth was the cause of Anderson's leaving her. In view of this, Prall resigned as manager of the Doubleday Doran Bookstore and went to visit her parents in California.

170

To Bab January—1923 New York City[1]

I was the more delighted to get your note of today because I had thought my last note to you somewhat rude.

One writes rudely—in a flaunting spirit and then, later, is sorry. I often wish thouse who think I write skillfully could know how much I write that must be torn up—thrown aside.

As to ones being submerged in some one other individual—there is no great danger of that. Isn't the notion rather a misunderstanding of the artists spirit. There is a certain quest to which the artist is committed. He is a man on a journey—going toward the unatainable.

Very well then—if he stops to live in a little house beside the road and to grow turnips—it does not matter too much. He is a grower of turnips rather than a pilgrim you see.

Only a pilgrim does not grow turnips.

Turginif [Turgenev]—had a story of such a fellow. He was going along a road when a fair woman came out of her house and went with him, bound his wounded feet etc.[2]

That might be a possibility. Anyway I look out of this window beside which I now sit and realize it does not belong to me. I am a guest here—looking at the street with not unfriendly eyes.

I'll tell you a great secret. The critics sometimes write of my work saying I express the soul of America. It really isn't true. America is as yet a child thinking of getting rich, owning automobiles etc. I am writing, have always written of an America not yet born.

The result is that two hundred years from now I will be understood as I am not now.

Its true and can't be helped. That is why I am not popular as a writer and yet, as a person interest people profoundly. They see in me themselves unborn.

But do not think I am too lonely or sad. I sing little songs to myself. In one of my old songs I said—"My fancy belongs to a high tossing place."[3]

Well there I am you see and its quite useless to be sad about me ever.

I am probable going away from New York before long but do not know just where I shall go.[4] I may make up my mind over night but have decided it will not be Europe. Perhaps I shall go to some part of this U.S.A. where I have not been before.

My new novel[5] will not gather itself together here—where there are too many people. I shall go where I will be quiet and isolated for a period.

Love

LH

1. Hahn's longhand note.
2. Story not yet identified.
3. This typical line is not in either *Mid-American Chants* or A *New Testament*.
4. Probably to California to join Elizabeth Prall.
5. Not identified.

171

To Bab February—1923 New York City[1]

I shall be leaving here tomorrow and will have no address for a time. Write me % Huebsch. The book[2] will be out in about 10 days and a copy is coming to you.

I have just heard from New Orleans and the letter I had was full of sunshine—wharfs, niggers etc. Half wish I was going there but I want the far west and perhaps even the deserts.[3]

Also I want to work and be by myself to gather myself together. I cannot get the technique of the hard shining surface and I suppose I dont really want it.

Lots of things are stirring in me and I want a long long time of sunshine, quiet and peace.

I shall write you more descently when I am not in the last minute rush of getting away. Love to your mother.

LH

1. Hahn's longhand note.
2. *Many Marriages*.
3. A deliberately vague reference to his visit to Berkeley, Calif., where Elizabeth Prall had joined her family. She has written that, when she arrived in Berkeley, "a sheaf of letters" from Sherwood was waiting. See *Miss Elizabeth*, p. 56.

172

To Bab February, 1923 Nevada[1] [Reno][2]
Feb. 22

I am sitting by a little clear stream—in a narrow valley with snow clad mountains all about. Down in this quiet spot the sun is warm and I could sit comfortable without my my [*sic*] coat. Near where I sit the river plunges over a falls and the water makes a gurgling talking sound. How long I shall stay in this spot I dont know. I am restless and uncertain. Just now—with the new book coming out it is good to be far far away from the voices.

As you know the last year has been a shattering one for me and I am not yet through the valley of ghosts. To one who like myself lives upon life T[ennessee] did a dreadful thing. She filled my house with the ghosts of death and it will take long in quiet places and in the sun to cure me.

As I do not know just where I will be I will give you an address out here from which mail will be forwarded to me.

℅ Max Radin
Buena Vista Way,
Berkeley Calif.[3]

For one thing my long years of living in the industrial cities of the lake region gave me, all through the fall, winter, and spring a perpetual series of nasal colds so I shall stay while I am resting and working here—a good deal in the upper mountainous country.[4]

My living is assured—for a year at least—even though Many Marriages does nothing.[5] It may be a good deal—raise a row I suppose for one thing. Anyway it is good clear artistic work—the best I have done I fancy. I think, as a piece of work, it will stand.

My task now is to go ahead and finish my "Modernist Notebook" which Harpers will publish serially—if they do not loose courage.[6] Then I shall have a new book of tales which I will call "Horses and Men."[7]

After that a novel[8] which has been written through once but which went off—because too many terrific outside things happened.

So much for myself. Give me news of yourself. Did you meet the strangely old grand thing Adalade? A curious sweet weary woman ripe with lusts of which she is afraid. However she has a mind. Most Southern women havn't. Tell me of yourself and your trip South. The new book has been ordered sent you. Perhaps you have seen it—I havn't.

Love to your mother.

LH

1. Hahn's longhand note.

2. James Schevill notes that Anderson reached Reno after a "tedious, week-long trip by train." See his *Sherwood Anderson: His Life and Work* (Denver: University of Denver Press, 1951), p. 181.

3. Max Radin was Elizabeth Prall's brother-in-law.

4. In fact, Anderson went to Reno to arrange for a divorce and to Berkeley to join Elizabeth.

5. By the end of Apr., 9,195 copies of the book had been sold; in the next six months only 1,021 copies were sold.

6. This was never published; it seems to be related to *A Story-Teller's Story*.

7. Published on Oct. 15, 1923.

8. Possibly *Straws*, published as *A Story-Teller's Story*.

173

To Bab April—1923 Nevada Reno[1]

Of course the letter disturbed me but that isn't the reason I havn't answered. I did write quite a long answer and then tore it up—thinking perhaps that was better.

You know how I feel and I can only say I am sorry for the chance remark that disturbed you so.

The truth is that I have been working very hard and when not at work have spent every possible moment out of doors. Also—for the time I have been trying to give my frayed nerves a chance to heal by keeping as far away as possible from those irational thing[s] to which I cannot answer in kind.

Here I have had for companions a railroad engineer and a young chap whose great passion in life seems to be catching trout.

The more emotional side of myself has—for the time—all gone into work—of which I have a great deal I want to do.

I'm glad you saw Robert and C. Robert is going to come out all right although he is now a problem to his mother. Sorry you did not see John & Mimi.

The days go—I work. I spend hours out of doors. I am getting well.

With Love

LH

1. Hahn's longhand note. Presumably shortly after the beginning of Mar. 1923 Sherwood and Elizabeth went to Reno to live while awaiting the divorce from Tennessee. Tennessee's objections caused delays, and the divorce was not granted until Apr. 1924. For Elizabeth's account of this period, see *Miss Elizabeth*, pp. 65–72.

174

To Bab July 6, 1923 Nevada[1]

You must get a little book of Chinese fables—called "Strange Stories from a Chinese Studio," translated by Herbert Giles—T Werner Laurie—London publisher.[2] The tale of the crab trees and the trumpet vine reminds me of these delightful tales. Both your mother and yourself would enjoy them. To make the crab tree story complete you and your mother should have watered them with your tears.

Perhaps your mother knows this country. I have got myself a small second hand car and have spent days wandering in it.[3]—A great sea of yellow sand, sun and sage brush but under the brush hugging the ground closely the most lovely brilliant little flowers. Many of the blossoms no larger than a pencil head.

There are also stra[n]ge and beautiful little lakes, far up in the mountains or across endless miles of desert.

As for my work—I have, as you know a new book of tales called Horses and Men to appear in October—a fat book of some 120000 words with many tales in it you have not seen.

The book Straws I was quite gloomy about but now it begins to form and may turn out. A great wea[l]th of material but the difficulty [is] to get them to flow along a channel. Like trying to confine flood water.

You see I quite frankly threw facts overboard when I started on the voyage. What I wanted was to give something of the spirit of the life of a modern American artist without embarrassing any who had touched that life. Out go the real person to be replaced by a troup of imagainary figures.

There are too many of them. O, how man[y] men and women have influenced my thoughts and dreams. They are like the sands of the sea.

I'm well enough now—all I can ask. My nerves have been tested long and hard but are coming through. Again I can hold the pen through several work hours a day.

There are the mountains, for one thing. All the east and the middle west are a foreign country. The mountains are a sea between. I see no newspapers—no clipping. The days come and go, the yellow stretches of sand and the blue red and gold mountains are here and I work a little again.

Have tried to paint but have only got one good thing out of many tries. The forms and colors are very very illusive. Perhaps I shall paint them when I am gone away from their presence and when they are a fixed dream in my fancy.

I want much to paint but there is a lot to write too.

Alfred Stieglitz has sent me four marvelous things to set up before myself and remind [me] of the beautiful things men have managed to do in a distraught world.

Give my love to your mother.[4] O, you will see me again. I'm on a long drift but will float back one of these days.

And in the meantime I pronounce the trumpet vine my ambassador at the court of the Finleys.

With Love

LH

1. Hahn's longhand note.
2. The publisher is Laurie and T. Werner.
3. Elizabeth wrote that Anderson bought a Dodge roadster and practiced driving it in fields; she represents him as not knowing enough to keep the tank filled with gas or to check the oil and water. See *Miss Elizabeth*.
4. Finley's mother died on Sept. 20, 1923.

175

To Sherwood Anderson[1] [Oct. or Nov., possibly Nov. 13–14, 1924]
Thursday Evening

Some lingering superstition in my nature of darky origin makes me want to begin this letter to you, at any rate, before Friday & it is now about a quarter to midnight. Your fine letter[2] was here waiting for me on my return from a shack out in the country near where I had been spending some of these glorious late fall days. It was very lively!

I was gladder to get that letter, Sherwood, than you can ever, ever know. It was so up-standing and splendid in its straightness and fineness. Once a long time ago you said that often inside yourself that you were a boy running over the hills and I got a certain litheness of spirit from you in that letter.

All that you said in your letter regarding our last conversation with each other was felt by me always. True I suppose it has been a struggle and often a cruel one for us but oh! Sherwood Anderson the struggle has brought me such an infinite sweetness and at times a white ecstacy [*sic*] of life that I feel certain you must sometimes come to know the real truth—that I have never for one instant in all these eleven years considered you brutal. Always with me you have been brave and honest—no one could have been more so—and always in me has been the question—what is there wrong in my womanhood that cannot measure up to the fineness in your manhood!

Sometimes in many ways we have both become confused but always there has been a determined effort to discover where my failure lay—not to blame you with brutality—please never say that again. There are a lot of quite lovely things too—in me that you have possibly missed. Last year when the pain of the whole readjustment I had to make blinded me I could not help wishing that you had not been so sure of your reactions to me. You had never seen me, you see, when I was free from the horrors of that pain that shadowed our existence—you did not give me a chance to become less of a burdened old woman and more of a human, laughing creature. Of course life has to be taken as it is and I will never know complete release from the memory of pain but neither, my friend, will you know release from many scars in your life.

However it does not matter—any of this. Life is as it is and I have learned that one cannot possibly comprehend the rhythm between a man & woman. All we can do is to face the beauty of it and the defeat of it without giving way to its ugliness & bitterness. I have tried to do that truly and I have succeeded. There is not one bitter thought in me regarding our relationship. And I have prayed throughout this year that I be given courage to survive because in some way I would be needed in your life. A funny thing happened about my note to you. The night I wrote you that note I was forced to write it by a consciousness I could not control. And a day or so after I wrote I found your Story Teller's Story downtown. Always as long as I have known you intimately the time of great sensitiveness concerning you has come to me when a new book came out. A queer mystic thing? Maybe—or else a response to a remark of yours sometime had impressed me greatly.

At any rate I got the book and I cannot tell you how fine and penetrating a piece of work I have found it. I and many others here in town. But I'm getting away from my idea in writing you now that you have opened the door for me to do so. There are so many, many things I want to talk to you about. My trip to New Mexico & my trip abroad this summer. It was there that I missed you so much. In my own mind & stubbornly & femininely without your sanction I had dreamed of going to Italy & having you there near me; at any rate I took a girl from New York with me & we had a wonderful trip. I'll talk to you of it sometime—but a mental break decided me to come back here & fight things out in my own way on my own ground.

Because I have so clearly realized just what my girlhood and womanhood lacked and how much I suffered from the house of pain & repression I took some money & sent my three young cousins abroad for three months. They are young and I want life to blossom a little for them if it can be done.

And that Sherwood is what I want and have always wanted for you. You must have known that surely. My physical need of you has been disciplined a great, great deal. It comes sometimes even yet in a few nights of desperate longing. But for the most part I have learned the lesson of going it alone. Only there is no getting around the fact there is no real sex- and [-] spiritual love in me that compares to my love for you. That will always remain just the same. A man as powerful as you are does not come and create a miracle for a girl as you did for me without remaining the reality for her. We must accept it.

Now I have the wherewithal to help you in times of stress and oh! I'm happy to have that chance. It is my gift, not please understand to the artist, who has created great beauty, but to the human man who has bravely looked on life and taken "the road less traveled by."

As I say this past year I used what ready money I had for myself & the others close to me. Things are tied up except for a small allowance from the estate until it is settled but after January lst I'm offering to send you a hundred dollars a month for as long as we both shall live. Oh! Sherwood it is hard to put this on paper because I know the scars of money affairs have always hurt you. But I must use my head in order to keep my "golden goose" safe to us for always. I'm planning to start an education fund for Mimi & John for Christmas, just a little to start in this year but it will grow for them after this year's tie-up is over.

Once you were horrified at such a discussion but you and the children provided for in case my adventure is not for long here. There will be no rows of relatives, you see, to hear about it—because I have so few & they are not here. And you see quite frankly you and your children are the reality & the meaning of my life. Other things may come to me—I am closing no doors—but always our friendship endures. If you want to be good to me please don't thank me in words for this. You have given me strength—this is just a slight return! I hope to hear from you and unless you want to lecture I hope you will not have to do so! After a time maybe you won't mind it but I hope you will not find it necessary. Remember that always I am here & and as I say after January I will be freer than now. I grew reckless in pain last year.

Yes, I'm staying here [Indianapolis] for a time. I love my home more dearly all the time. There is a charming group of people here now! I can leave when I want to do so & when the drive of loneliness grows too great. My mind is rousing [?] to many things. Life has meaning for me at moments. I took the liberty of giving your address to a man who is spending the winter in New Orleans, Clark Mich[?]. You met him once here & did not like him but you & he have both changed. I love you both dearly—maybe you will like each other better.—a wave to you—"Bab"

Please don't close the door on the other thing. I'm the one to decide about happiness that you can give to me & life is a long journey!

LH

1. This is the only existing letter to Anderson by Hahn while she was still Miss Finley. Internal evidence within the text of the letter was the source for the suggested dates.

2. An indication that at least one letter from this period from Anderson is missing—and there may have been others.

176

To Bab Dec. 1924[1] [New Orleans][2]

I think a woman—if she be at all delicately organized must, after having given birth to a child, have some such time of depression as I am now in. Somewhere Balzac speaks of it. He had knowledge of such things because he, like every artist, was half woman. I mean that he went through spiritual processes not unlike womans physical processes. Life [is] very wonderful profoundly wonderful and then suddenly, after the time of creation a strange deadness and lasitude.

I am writing to you by the river banks. It is cold up north—a blizzard raging but here, today a soft breeze up-river from the gulf. I am trying to stay away from my desk for some days from words and the organization of words into sentences and stories. There are many stories in me but just now I am too confused to write them.

There is a kind of confusion. Every day I get letters—three, six, from writers, painters, musicians. My book has made them feel close, so very close to me. They write, telling me of themselves, of their happiness in the book.

It is sweet to be thus something in many lives but confusing too.

I read your letter and went into a small shop to buy this tablet and paper that I might write to you as I sat on logs by the river shore. There was a very gentle woman in the store who is like Elizabeth—the same gentle aristocracy.[3]

In the store was another woman, a drunkard apparently with red disordered dress who followed me out and began to speak with me. We walked along the street together.

Suddenly she began to tell me quite simply that she had been drunk the night before and that she thought she would have to sell her furniture.

"I used to be able to get men for money but now look at me," she said and laughed.

Then I left her at the door of her house and came over here, thinking of you, your kindness and understanding—the wisdom that is growing in you.

It is the kind of aristocracy in women men like me must have. Women who havn't it, who have not suffered and got it have got nothing we want.

We are such children—so old and wise, so young and foolish.

We also have to get what we get by infinitely slow processes. That Lawrence. He is in the modern England what I am in the modern America. That I know.

It is fine of you about the money. I have no feeling but one of simple gratitude. You will allow me that. About the lecture matter. I am to be in Topeka the night of the 16 Jan. That is I think Friday. If something should be arranged in Indianapolis better have it the 19th and better wire. An eastern agent is trying to fill in dates between.

I am sure what makes you now so much to me is belonging without asking. You know of course that that makes me also belong to you.

LH

1. Hahn's longhand note.

2. Sherwood and Elizabeth lived in Berkeley for several months after their marriage in Apr. 1924. By July, traveling by way of Chicago and evidently staying there only briefly, they had gone to New Orleans to live in an apartment in the old Pontalba Building on Jackson Square. After a time they moved to a house at 540B St. Peters St.

3. Ironically, when the marriage was ending, Anderson referred to Elizabeth as "The Princess."

177

To Bab Dec. 11, 1924[1] [New Orleans]

Indeed dear friend I hope the harsh letter will not come at all. It would have been so nice of me to have miss-directed it. The whole matter of money is so difficult but I have to remember that you have not earned it by shrewdness and therefore havn't the trait that comes with gathering.

When I sit down to write you I think of a thousand things to say. Most of all I think I must try to tell you my mood about writing now.

It seems to me that I am in a state of transit. I feel about. Many stories and novels are started and few finished. Some of the driving impulses of the past are lost and others are being born.

I have an idea—havn't you dear—that one writes always his own life and the truth that is true today become false tomorrow.

You see I have to adjust to you—after these more direct experiences with the flesh of life as you do to me and as we both do to ourselves.

I think Bab that while what you say (that I have carried something rather deep into the consciousness of many people)—and have perhaps retained some freedom I have also been brutal. Perhaps I had to be to live at all.

I am trying to be less so. People like you disturb profoundly the more brutal interpretation of life. The direct contact with life becomes less absorbing and I hope sometimes there may be born a gentler, wiser man in me.

I am sure I do not hope to grow more naive. It may have been I have already gone too far that way. People are cheap, grasping slick.

But people appear. The good have their strength too it seems. One wants now a little to sit and walk often with people loved without contest.

It will be a joy to write you often now of the moods and experiences of my own life and if I can make your life richer by that it will be very, very good.

LH

1. Hahn's longhand note originally indicated 1925 and then had 1924 written over it. Internal evidence suggests nothing to contradict either date.

178

To Bab — Dec. 14, 1924[1] [New Orleans]

Just a little note on Sunday morning. I am to speak in Topeka Kans on Jan 16 and in Pittsburg the 22. If you are to be at home I could arrange my route to stop for a day on the way across.

Chicago and New York are likely to be so crowded. I shall be driven every minute and there will be so many many people I must see.

I am still in a strange state of uncertainty. As you know I am always so after I have published a book. My inner life is for the time perhaps too much invaded.

And there may be a real and basic change going on in me. Now days I dream of clothes—much o very much. I mean a kind of clothing for myself. The inner self it will perhaps be more difficult to give to others in any direct way.

Is it natural consequent of the fact that I am older? Is it a natural reserve growing up.

Or is it but the temporary thing—induced in me because I am going through the period of just having published a book.

LH

1. Hahn's longhand note.

179

To Bab Dec. 18, 1924[1] [New Orleans]

I stay rather in a stalement. It may be nothing but tired nerves. When the nerves are tired from long thinking and feeling there comes often a kind of explosion. A hundred images come—stories tales poems. None of them complete the circle. They break off—disappear.

The fingers become infected with the fever of the brain. There is chaos.

Often a single word—like the word chaos[2] written above is a stumbling block. One thinks of it, how to spell it, the exact shade of meaning, its implications.

You see what I mean—an inner confusion.

There is nothing to do but work, be with friends, watch men at physical labor. The little obscure nerves get themselves cured—or rested—after a time and then the rhythm begins again—the slower, quieter rhythm of health.

I was sent last week an article from the New York Herald in which Stewart P. Sherman has come out strong for me. It may be my book will sell so that I shall not have such constant financial worry.[3]

This is just a little note to say good morning to you from my desk.

LH

1. Hahn's longhand note.

2. Anderson had written *cho*. He drew a line through that. Then he wrote *caos*. Then he drew a line through both efforts. Finally *chaos* was written in the space above the earlier efforts.

3. From Oct. 15, 1924, to Apr. 30, 1925, *A Story-Teller's Story* sold only 6,179 copies.

180

To Bab Dec. 28, 1924[1] [New Orleans]

The Christmas time has passed. For three or four days I had as company a man from the far west going east to a meeting of philosophers.[2] It was a treat.

Until he came I did not realize how much I had been shut off. The men here are of a type. Something happens to them. Perhaps the long summers make for lazy mindedness.

The little philosopher—with his sharp face—small alert delicate body and his sophistication seemed a being from a land far away. He expects so little from life wheras I have expected so much.

Also he has lived in obscurity—expects always to live in obscurity and this has sweetened him. What I mean is that his desire is really for knowledge—not for the pretense of knowledge.

He walked about and talked, steadily, without excitement.

I thought of you. Was your Christmas lonely? Perhaps we are all of us, always destined to loneliness. Means of communication are so meager.

Actual presence—bodily expression of the desire to break down lonliness is ineffective.

Sometimes I get all things as objective—you Elizabeth—Bob—the times in the park, the church. What is beautiful seems no part of myself. I hunger toward all beautiful things and stand still.

Next week Friday I leave here as I am to lecture in Cleveland on Sunday Jan 4th. From there I will go to Chicago.

Address me Chicago

% George Daugherty.
Porter Eastman Byrne Co.
22 West Monroe St.

It is good that I am to see you soon and I hope we may have opportunity for a long talk.

With Love

LH

1. Hahn's longhand note.

2. Doubtless Elizabeth's brother, David Prall, assistant professor of philosophy at the University of California, 1921–30.

181

To Bab Jan. 8, 1925[1]

I am in Chicago and really it seems rather horrible here. I had forgotten how noisy, dirty and tense it could be. Coming up to Cleveland from New Orleans I caught a horrible cold and have been rather laid up ever since I got to town. Am lecturing here in the morning[2]—tomorrow—then go to Hammond Indiana[3]—back here for another lecture and then to Topeka[4] after that Indianapolis—the 19th.

If you need a subject for the lecture there—you can take choice of two.

1. Modern American Writing.
2. America—A Storehouse of Vitality.

I am sure Bab I shall have this horrid cold quite licked long before I get to you and I'll be so very very glad to see you.

I'm just plan dull with a stuffy head today.

LH

1. Hahn's longhand note.

2. In his lecture "America, A Storehouse of Vitality," given before the Jewish Center Forum on the morning of Sunday, Jan. 4, Anderson reportedly said: "When the American reads more of the literature of America, he will find that honest art is more interesting than any false art of the past and he will want to live in the present day."

3. At 8 P.M., on Monday, Jan. 12, Anderson gave "America, A Storehouse of Vitality" before an audience at the Beth El Social Center. Dr. and Mrs. H. A. Kuhn, with whom Anderson had "long been friends," had him as their house guest. They had a tea and a dinner for him before his appearance.

4. At 8 P.M. on Friday, Jan. 16, Anderson gave the same lecture again at the MacVicar Chapel of Washburn College in Topeka, under the auspices of the Sunday Evening Reading Club. An article in the Topeka *Daily State Journal* announced the lecture, commenting, "Two years of solicitation were necessary to persuade Anderson to accept this engagement. His only other lecture in Kansas was before the Kansas State Agricultural College two winters ago. Those who hear[d] that lecture still call it the best talk by a writing man they ever heard." The article continued, calling Anderson "the most significant voice now heard in America. . . . no one questions that he writes the most beautiful prose now being written in English." The Topeka *Daily Gazette* quoted Professor R. W. Conover of the Kansas State Agricultural College as saying, "No American writer of our time has succeeded so well as has Anderson in expressing emotions and impulses obscure in their origin and elusive in their manifestations." When Anderson

spoke, it was to an audience which included people who were forced to stand for lack of seats. A typical remark from those recorded: "As the American man becomes more and more an imaginative man he will pour his energies out more and more in channels of beauty." Evidently he was entertained by the city's wealthy book collector, who left 5,000 books on his death in 1940. Anderson autographed a second printing copy of his A *Story-Teller's Story* as follows: "To/ Chester Woodward/ During a very pleas-/ ant evening in/ his home Jan 16/ 1925/ Sherwood Anderson."

He was described by a reporter in this way: "Heavy features, black hair, just turning gray, a subdued rainbow tie draped unconventionally, and burning black eyes marked his personal appearance."

182

To Bab January 19, 1925[1]

Just a line to tell you again how much I got out of my visit with you.[2] It has given me something satisfying and very, very fine.

Another fine crowd at Pittsburg[3] and the lecture went splendidly. I am staying over here today and going to New York[4] tonight. The visit to Indianapolis and in particular the hours walking with you in that charming little town are like little rivers. They will stay in my consciousness for the rest of my life.

LH

1. Hahn's longhand note. This date, when he lectured in Indianapolis, is wrong. Anderson lectured in Pittsburgh, for which the text of the letter shows it was written, on Jan. 22. Apparently the letter is of Jan. 23. A letter of B. W. Huebsch on Jan. 14, 1925, was addressed to "Mr. Sherwood Anderson/ % Miss Finley/ 614 East 32nd. St./ Indianapolis, Ind."

2. Anderson lectured on "Modern Writing in America" at the Athenaeum in Indianapolis at 8:15 P.M. on Tuesday, Jan. 19. No account of his lecture has been found.

3. Anderson again gave his "Storehouse of Vitality" lecture at Pittsburgh on Jan. 22, before the Quill Club of the University of Pittsburgh in the Carnegie Lecture Hall. Interviewed beforehand at the William Penn Hotel, he averred: "American writing in every aspect is improving constantly for the reason that American writers are getting away from traditional English themes and are nurturing ideas distinctly their own." The most important result of the visit to Pittsburgh was Anderson's meeting of Roger Sergel, then a member of the English department at the University of Pittsburgh. As one of those anticipating the arrival

of Anderson, Sergel was quoted in *The Pitt Weekly* of Jan. 21 as saying: "Anderson is one of the outstanding figures of American literature. He ranks with the immortals. His advent was startling, and he upset many a treasured literary tradition, for until Sherwood Anderson appeared, the 'poorfolk' of American literature were merely effigies filled with sawdust. Through him, they became alive." Both Mr. and Mrs. Sergel were interested in writing, Sergel having a contribution in the *Little Review* for June 1919, for example; they later moved to Chicago and were among Anderson's closest friends the rest of his life. Upon Anderson's death in 1941, Sergel served, with Paul Rosenfeld, as an adviser to Mrs. Eleanor Copenhaver Anderson in administering her husband's literary estate.

4. Where he spoke in the Great Hall of the Cooper Union at 8 P.M. on Jan. 25, giving the "Storehouse of Vitality" lecture under the auspices of the People's Institute. No newspaper account of this appearance has yet been found.

183

To Bab January 25, 1925[1]

It has been one mad jumble—ever since I got to town. John[2] is living in a small apartment so he put me up here—at the Lambs and this will be my address until I leave—probably about Feb. 15.

Havn't got hold of John much. It['s] odd about them. They have everything apparently except nice friends. Nita runs about with actresses of a rather vulgar sort and you can always tell what they both want by what they make fun of.

There are phases they have when they would like to make fun of me but they can't quite make it.

All this mixed up with a queer sort of hunger. Poor people. They do not really know how to be nice and frank and gentle.

As to the jumble of other people. Well seeing them does not make me want to live here dear. They are too terrible.

I saw Paul[3] for a little and after the first mad rush of things has passed hope to have more quiet hours with him. He also is mixed up in some way but is at bottom sound and sweet. I love him.

At one place I saw Winter Binner[4] for a few minutes and thought of our long talk with him but had a few minutes only and that in the midst of a grand mob.

Early this week there is to be a grand luncheon[5] for me with all the town invited. Tonight I speak at Cooper Union.

Dear Lord—I think of Elizabeth—you—John—Cornelia—gentle real people—all off in corners and am so glad in some queer way you are not in this half ugly, rather exciting competitive thing.

If my letters are a jumble now they will be clearer when I am clear of it.

Lots of love

LH Written on the stationery of The Lambs, 130 West 44th Street, New York City.

1. Hahn's longhand note.
2. John Emerson.
3. Paul Rosenfeld.
4. Witter Bynner (1881–1968), American poet and president of the Poetry Society of America, 1920–22.
5. No record of this luncheon has been found.

184

To Bab Jan. 1925[1]

Still in the jam here. Will be here several days longer and then am going out to deliver three or four more lectures[2] and then back to work.

More and more my mind turns to the stage. Already scenes form in my mind. It seems to me a new, very puzzling and fastinating outlet for the fancy. Perhaps I shall be able to really do something with it.

Here of course I do not think. Things happen to fast. It is like walking in the rain and giving up all notion of being dry for the time being. On some days it seems as through half the city wanted to see and talk with me all at once. Bless God it cannot last long.

Do I think of you—do I think of people I love. Not much. I think of nothing. I walk in the rain saying let it rain.

Presently I shall be back with my own thoughts and my own fancies.

LH Written on stationery of The Lambs, 130 West 44th Street, New York City.

1. Hahn's longhand note.
2. These have not been documented.

185

To Bab January 30, 1925[1]

Dear Woman—

My New York days go past in a curious whirlwind. I see constantly people I must see but do not get them as quite human. It happens that in this strange place I am temporarily a sort of man of the hour. It means nothing much.

On the other hand I would be sorry if you were here now. Nothing could quite keep me out of the jam and, in a sense, the jam is the purpose of my being here.

The luncheon for me came off yesterday and tonight I speak. There are a thousand claimants. The city is really very tired and they go toward me—as one having some strength and freshness. I will not be long here. I think I must give to it—while I am here—all I can.

For me to a clean, clear fine memory.

I cannot write to you very clearly long.

I'll not be here—in this place very long.

LH

1. Hahn's longhand note.

186

To Bab Feb. 1925[1]

Am on the train going from Philadelphia to New York—a dull rainy morning. Spoke in Philadelphia last night—a large crowd.[2] People are very eager, very confused and rather tired. Strange how much it takes from you. It is as though every one in the crowd were hungry and asking asking—some kind of love some real evidence of sincerity.

How much can one give personally. There is so much asked.

Went for a night to the Eshericks—Wharton and Letty.[3] They are strong healthy people who live on a small farm near Philadelphia. Wharton is an artist and works now in wood and stone. He formerly painted but for him painting was always a more or less artificial process. Then he [word, meaning *started*, not decipherable] working in stone and in wood and seems to have found in this direct handling of materials a way out for himself.

With New York I will soon I hope, be through. There are still people I must see, things I must do but soon I shall be going off again to a quiet place to work and think.

There—my pen has exhausted itself. [continuing in pencil] Did I tell you that the little play made from the Eggs Story from The Triumph of the Egg is being produced by the Provincetown Players. It is very very nice. Since I have been here I have had a new desire to try to do something in the theatre. Perhaps I can. Many of my short things would so easily adapt themselves to the theatre.

A jumble of ideas—the people hungry—a rush of ideas—no time for leisure. Soon the rush will be over now.

LH Written on the stationery of The Lambs, 130 West 44th Street, New York City.

1. Hahn's longhand note.
2. Appearance undocumented.
3. Wharton Esherick (1887–1970), sculptor and woodcut designer, of Paoli, Pa.

187

To Bab

Feb. 1925[1]
Thursday Night

I have crept away from everyone tonight and am in my room—going to bed in a few minutes—very weary. It is the first time I have escaped from people for days—except to fall exhausted into bed.

And yet I have enjoyed it all. Something has happened to me since I was here before. Am I more insensible to people or am I wiser? For some reason I do not understand I have suddenly found myself able to accept the fact that people look upon me as an exceptional man. All my life I have fought the notion—now I find myself accepting it. My own notion of myself is another matter.

It is something like this. I have made a place for myself in American life. People expect me to accept the place. Very well I do.

And there is something else. Suddenly and in a way as I never have before I find myself wanting almost passionately to write for the stage. Something is happening to the stage. I feel it. I want to make my contribution. Do not be surprised if you find me going rapidly in that direction in the future.[2]

There are many things to tell you—new thoughts, new impulses crowding in on me. I can't write them now. When I am back at my desk it will be fun to write them.[3]

With love

LH Written on the stationery of The Lambs, 130 West 44th Street, New York City.

1. Hahn's longhand note.

2. All efforts by Anderson or others to bring his work to the stage have been undistinguished.

3. He never did.

188

To Bab Feb. 20, 1925[1]

Another flood of people today and then I shall be off. I make two or three more speeches on the way back south.[2] Am leaving here in the morning for a day with Henry Canby at New Haven.[3] It has all been a curious experience here in town—changes in peoples scenes [?] the spirits of people. Perhaps I do not hope for so much.

The old loves stay. For example I have seen at close hand something at Knofp and Liveright[4] and am the more pleased that I am with Huebsch. Quality counts.[5]

One night I went to a party at Liverights office. Such an affair. Some day I will tell you of it. Many of the men here—in the publishing world and in the theatre—have affairs with women and young girls as casually as rabbits. Of course they love no one. Have lost all capacity for that.

Paul[6] is in trouble and is hardly himself. It would be very very difficult to know him now. Two women love him, or think they do and he cannot decide between them. He is so terribly afraid of hurting some one that he will probably end up by hurting and perhaps loosing both.

I have seen a good deal of Steiglitz and O'Keefe. They have married at last,[7] after seven years. Steiglitz had a daughter who went into melancholia and they thought the marriage might help.

I have gone a great deal to the theatre. Not many good plays. I have really been studying acting. Believe in the end I shall write some plays.

John E.[8] has been very fine. Something has happened to him. He is more gentle and sweet.

The stain on the paper [a small spot] is from my breakfast—just brought up. Now I must rush off for another full day.

Will write you next from some more peaceful place.

With love

LH Written on the stationery of The Lambs, 130 West 44th Street, New York City.

1. Hahn's longhand note.

2. So far undocumented.

3. Henry Seidel Canby (1878–1961), editor, critic, and author.
4. Alfred Knopf (1892–1984); Horace Liveright (1886–1933).
5. Later Anderson changed his mind on this point.
6. Rosenfeld.
7. Alfred Stieglitz (1864–1946), photographer, and Georgia O'Keeffe (1887–), painter, were married on Dec. 11, 1924.
8. Emerson.

189

To Bab Feb. 26, 1925[1]

I am through with New York and all it has meant to me, just now, and am back in the South and looking forward to a long time of work. Well I am really on my way south on a slow train that has stopped at a station. It is a cool bright morning. We[2] are waiting at a junction. Negroes are walking about their warm shrill laughter making me feel jolly inside. On a truck there is a young Durham Bull in a crate being shipped away to some herd of waiting females—of the cow tribe.

I try to think of New York rationally—to see it offhand. How I was different in the face of New York than I ever had been—how it was different to me.

It was more tired than I am really, older, disillusioned in a way I seem incapable of being.

All I seemed to have gained since I was there before was a sort of a canniness. That may be a form of sophistocation. How am I to tell. I am not sophistocated, cannot be.

What I mean is only that I have less concern with peoples thoughts of me. People kept telling me that I was better, healthier, than I ever had been or that I had gone quite to pot. It seemed to depend upon my reaction to them.

A great many clutching people—as always. They came pleading for some vague thing—life perhaps—for the most part offering nothing in return. If I had learned anything it was that I had not enough to give all.

Perhaps if one loves and tries to understand a few it is enough.

Of you I have fine memories but one evening I saw something—about the corners of your mouth—weariness that passed quickly away because you are brave and do take on life like a wrestler who will not be thrown.

I got the no-longer-asking thing in you and realized more than any words of mine could say how deep down you have been.

What I want for you of course is what I get for myself at this moment—

the feeling that life is not very long and an amused appreciation of the lazy laughing negroes outside there and the lowing bull in his crate.[3]

I'll swim and so will you. I feel very close to you and full of warm friendliness that is worth more to you than I believe you quite know.

The lectures are exhausting but I can do them.

LH Written on the stationery of The Lambs, 130 West 44th Street, New York City.

1. Hahn's longhand note.
2. Elizabeth had traveled to Chicago to meet him, and they traveled to the South together, after he had lectured both in Chicago and at the University of Illinois at Urbana-Champaign. They arrived in New Orleans on Monday, Mar. 2.
3. This echoes elements he wrote into *Dark Laughter* the preceding fall.

190

To Bab March 16, 1925[1]

Monday morning. I have been for two days on Lake Ponchartrain with friends.[2] A slow rhythm of waves—slow thoughts coming & going. Your letter came about little Bob. After I had written you he and I had a long talk. What had hurt him most was his belief in smartness—a kind of slickness. We talked it over quite frankly—he cried a little, I took him into my arms and since then he has been much much sweeter. He has the stuff in him and I do think all you say is sound—that the other side of the shield is hard to look at. It takes time. Do I not know.

If the lad can be made to see and feel affection about him he will learn the most difficult lesson in life—that you can't collect.

Now, most of all, I want him to learn to feel that there is nothing in slickness—that no one ever succeeds in getting the best of anyone really.

The matter of good manners, of real gentleness is of course an inner matter.

I was so very pleased—having been taken to call on an old southern woman here when, after the visit, she said that I was gentle. It's the thing most difficult to teach the value of. John just has it.

With Bob is [it] will be a conscious process—as it must always be with me but out of the necessity of its being a conscious process may very well come the ability to get it also into work and finally—if he is lucky into relationship.

I felt your letter nothing at all shrill. You can't be shrill when you are thinking so sincerely of another—as you were of Bob—when you wrote it.

With love

LH

1. Hahn's longhand note.
2. This is possibly the occasion when Anderson, having some extra money from the sale of his forthcoming *Dark Laughter*, arranged a two-day yacht excursion on Lake Pontchartrain in honor of Anita Loos, who was to be the guest of honor. She could not come because of the deadline on *Gentlemen Prefer Blondes*. See Elizabeth Anderson's memoir, *Miss Elizabeth*, pp. 117–19.

191

To Bab March 19, 1925

note memorial here erected
to the Americans sculptor
Stanilaus Szakalski[1]

Sherwood Anderson
540 B St. Peter St.
New Orleans, La.

Postcard

1. This postcard was sent from Estes Park, Colo., and pictured the Lonesome Pine and Longs Peak from High Drive. The pine was one of the unique objects in the Rocky Mountain National Park. The postcard both gives us Anderson's New Orleans address and also testifies to his continuing interest in Stanilaus Szakalski (1896–1955), a Polish-born sculptor whom Anderson knew in Chicago.

192

To Bab March 20, 1925[1]

Dear Woman—

A cold blast from the north. I am at work on the childhood book.[2] People go huddled and hurrying across the little park in front of my window. The blast that swept through Illinois and Indiana has lashed us with cold.

In the mail a letter from Stieglitz, in bed sick, old, discouraged. A strange vain, sincere real man. Nearly all his life is devoted to others. Few have been kind to him. I hate to think of his lost years. He has wanted so much of beauty, has been such an old warrior.

I have always thought he fought too much but without the fight he has made some of our finest artists would have got just nowhere.

It is pretty hard to understand—the kind of thing that can happen to such a man. So much priggishness in the world.

One cant stop to think too much about it. Other men are blessed. Life slipping past like a procession. You and I—others looking on. We have to look on mostly.

I am trying not to feel hurried and yet to spend every possible hour at my desk with the pen running. Here, at work, as when I walk in the streets, I am sometimes happy, often miserable.

But so are you—Stieglitz—all I suspect.

John Emerson and Anita Loos are down here. Anita gains immeasurable when you have her close. John has mellowed. In Anita a hard sharp good sense that is fine. I like her better than I ever did. One of these days you must come down. I would like you to see the old town, walk about it with you.

This is just a morning word. You are so often in my mind. I hold you there fast as long as I live—I hope.

LH

1. Hahn's longhand note.
2. *Tar.*

193

To Bab March 20, 1925[1]

I have had a strange sort of session with poor little Bob this morning. What a muddled little boy—half man. The problem with such a boy is his own smartness—shall I say slickness. I feel the whole matter deeply because, in some odd way I am responsible and do not want to shirk the responsibility.

On the one hand is a rather slick quick boyish way of being nice to people and then always it comes out that he is being nice for a purpose of his own. I have never quite seen any one with so much assurance of self—so much self assurance with nothing to stand on.

Is his whole nature starved for affection. What has driven him so deeply into himself. One know[s] instinctively that he could so easily become a hard slick rather blind man of the world.[2]

The problem for such a boy is of course double hard because on all sides he sees the hard slick men succeed.

What I am doing is to try to make him face himself in the matter, see himself. It isn't easy. There is a way in which he is, as yet, quite blind.

Dear dear friend. Do you think ever that I write to you out of any sense of duty. When I have the impulse to do that I won't do it. You may depend on that. I shall not give you that kind of a slight.

What I of course really feel is that what you can give C and the children is something out of yourself that is a thousand times more valuable than any material thing.

I am full of work and plans. Full of more love too for the few people like yourself life has sifted out as belonging to me.

LH

1. Hahn's longhand note.

2. This same problem haunted Anderson himself and was perhaps the reason the appearance of it in his son bothered him.

194

To Bab — March 25, 1925[1]

Two days of rain. John Emerson is down here with his wife Nita. Nita came first and stayed at the hotel. In our own small quarters we could never have taken care of her. So many trunks, dresses, maids, cosmetics. She is really a dear honest strange little creature terrible in love with John who is not in love with her. Always she courts him, cares really for no one else. Her one dream is that he shall not be bored. That dream seems to absorb him.

He is a strange man, very generout[s] and alert, living only in action. In every way he is practical and straight but there is a world into which he never penetrates.

It is a difficult vague world. You know it as do I. He looses much and gains something.

Does he love? Can he love?

What seems lovliest to us in the old city I am afraid only seems dirty crowded and unsanitary to him. How far apart we are.

Bob becomes every day more gentle. After all his coming here has done much. He is beginning to understand a little that if you want a house lovely you have to do something, have something in yourself to help make it so.

This is just a hurried note out of a hurried time. I think of you often.

LH

1. Hahn's longhand note.

195

To Bab April, 1925[1]

Nita was here for a week—an honest—rather harsh little thing—the true gamin who would like to be a woman. She could not stay at the house. There was no room. Well she needed a maid—several trunks. In the morning she spends hours exercising, making up. After a time you get the feel of her as a little street dog. She loves John devotedly, hungrily.

He does not love her. It is harsh to say but he has found her hard sharp little brain useful.

The old beauty of this place appealed to her. She loves to walk. We go along together—an odd pair. She is a little resentful. There are two things in her. She would like to be an artist or a woman. She doesn't quite achieve either. What she does achieve is her smart sarcastic street gamin point of view.

John constantly has other women. She knows it and tries not to know. A little she resents my position with John. We belong oddly to a class to which she cannot belong.

John liked Elizabeth—her class, her gentleness, her good head.

With John and myself there in the difficulty—growing with the years of cutting through to each other. I cannot think his thoughts. He lives in a world struggle with men—trying to put things over. I dont. He has to put off his world before we can meet. This time it only [*lasted* crossed out] happened—for about two hours before he went—the laughing boyish giving thing popping up again out of that morass.

Dear, I know. We all want to be long and greatly and patiently loved. I fancy no one wins. I have been reading Henry Adams again. Oddly enough that man is nearer me than any other American. Read the Education again. There at least is clear faithfullness of a rare sort.

On Thursday or Friday of last week I died. About 5 or 6 days of death—every sinew aching—sinking and sinking into black depression. It was partly the result of too intensive work.

I am trying to buy a little house here so that I may shut off the drain of rents. Can do it on the Homestead plan—paying for it as one pays rent. It is a lovely old tiny place with a little court—and a slave quarter that can be made into a studio. The little old patio will be brick-walled. It will be a place for the children to come to.

I am writing a book of childhood—quite a different tune from Story Teller. It centers about the relation of the child to the house. Much much I want to say in it. It is the sort of thing that might conceivably sell as a serial to a woman's magazine. I want much from it.

I count on you here one of these days and walks with you in this curious lovely place.

Now I must stop writing to you and go back to work. There is too much to say. I could write all morning but I shall put other things into other notes and send them along.

Poor Cornelia. Something of the disorderly peasant. It is hopeless to try to bring order into that life but I realize that deep down I have something to do with that disorder.[2] We hurt as much as help in all but rare relations I'm afraid dear.

LH

1. Hahn's longhand note.
2. John Anderson's comment, when he read this letter in 1974, was: "Didn't think of her as 'disorderly, slam bang.'"

196

To Bab

April 11, 1925[1]
Good Friday

The cathredral bell ringing. Carpenters at work on a nearby building. I want to write you more about Robert. The lad has done wonders down here and is getting finer daily. I am glad you say something of the disorderly, slam bang side of C.[2] It makes what the children have to overcome more understandable.

I have decided Bob ought to have college—boys of his own age. What he actually learns does not matter so much.[3]

Something has happened. Liveright, of Boni & Liveright was down here last week and made me an offer to go over to him that would make it possible for me to see Bob descently started in life and help the others in turn—about college.

It is an odd situation. Ben Huebsch[4] is really not up to it. I have dreamed of sticking to him to the end regardless but dare I go on with him when it means sacrificing the children. I do not mind the hard work poverty entails for Bob and the others but dare I risk not giving them a chance at least with gentler people while they are young.

What would be largely involved is Ben Huebsch's pride. He hasn't much of any artistic sensibilities.

Write me your own thoughts.

The Jeff Davis things are interesting. Did you intnd me to keep them. I might give them to the little museum down here.

LH

1. Hahn's longhand note.

2. In 1962 Hahn did not remember Cornelia as characterized by disorganization.

3. In view of his own lack of a college education, Anderson's attitude toward college was ambivalent.

4. Anderson's publisher until the events here narrated.

197

To Bab April—1925[1][New Orleans]

The Heubsch matter is complex. My relations with him have never been what yours are with the doctor or mine with you. He is a queer man—fine and kind but more incompetent than you have any idea. We do not love the same things. He has little or no artistic appreciation. His real friends are all single taxers[,] fellows of that sort. In New York many men, men like Paul[,] Stieglitz and others are convinced he is quite in love with failure, with unsuccess.

It is hard for me to decide between the immorality of bad hesitating slovenly methods and competent raeality.

After all I have given Ben a long long chance and dear dear friend I do not want to depend on you financially. I want you to have your money for yourself or to help others.

As for Liveright I have had his offer gone over by John Emerson, who has ability and you know how he feels about me. He and I are closer than Huebsch and I.

I have always stayed with Ben, thinking him the best of a bad lot. I am the only author who has ever stuck to him. With a tremendous press back of it he has sold less than 8000 of Story Teller. In many towns stores did not get the book until a month or six weeks after publication. Do I gain anything by putting up with sheer incompetence.

On the other hand I feel this way. If Liveright can destroy me, if I can be so easily swept off the mark as a workman it had better happen.

The whole thing has been gone over with Huebsch time and again. The arts are not his central interest. His central interests are economic reform. Time and again I have put my situation before him. If there is anything he can do it should have been done long since. The man is really incompetent in the same way Cornelia is.

As for Bob—that is a problem. He knows little of boys of his own age. When he goes to school he will have to go without much money. I have urged Tulane on him but he is in the mood to try standing on his feet awhile. Perhaps I had better let him do it. Wish you could talk to him, see what you think. If he goes north this summer and you are there I shall ask him to stop for a day with you.

A blessing on you dear Bab for your friendship and love. All my direct life centers more and more on a few. My fancy only roams.

Will write more in a day or two.

LH

1. Hahn's longhand note.

198

To Bab May, 1925[1]

I am writing to you from my little hidden hole where I go to work every day. People are so very social down here that, at any time someone may drift in to interrupt. One does not feel like protesting. Bob comes in. He is beginning now to take some pride in his person and his manners. A sweet lad without self-consciousness who asks anything.

I have definately made the change in publishers.[2] Last year I had to go heavily in debt. If you had not taken over the childrens support everything would have gone quite to pieces. I was so worried by finances that I could not work.[3]

Huebsch is a sweet incompetent man and if I could afford him or if the lecturing were not so hard and did not take so much out of me I would have stuck anyway.

I couldn't. The thing had to be done and is done. I am sorry but it was inevitable. Poor man. Joyce, Lawrence and a dozen others have quit him. I am told he is sore and hurt and I do not blame him.

The man has no particular artistic sense but he is good. Goodness is rare, God knows.

About Bob, I shall try to get over to him the thing you speak of. I am myself doubtful [actually: doubt fut] about trying to hold him against his will. He seeks adventure now, new people, new places. He will come back if he goes, of that I am quite sure.

Dear woman, there are deep sadnesses, everywhere—that I should have had to do what I did to Huebsch—that you must have long sad lonely times.

Perhaps you do not know—quite—how much I value you—how dear you are—what an extraordinary person you have made of yourself.

People think of me as successful now. I have a certain name, I live and work.

It is nothing. Often our most desolate hours are the sweetest in the end.

There is so little to say. We all want so much and get so little.

LH

1. Hahn's longhand note.
2. Anderson had changed publishers before Apr. 18.
3. *Dark Laughter*, however, was written in 1924.

199

To Bab May, 1925[1]

Men like me work by some obscure rule. There are a number of men in the history of writing I know as I know the top of my own desk.

It has something to do with rhythm. We work, live laugh, feel life warm and pulsating all about.

Then the rhythm breaks. Everything recedes. We walk—lost men in a lost world.

They eyes do not see, the ears hear, the fingers feel.

We are demanding always of course an intensity of life.

I do not love one only. If I cannot love many I cannot love at all.

I want the machinery of my body adjusted to run smoothly, rapidly. There is so much to do. When I stand in idleness I am but a blind man.

You have felt what all I love feel. Often I go far away. Nothing can bring me back.

Then suddenly there is a minute adjustment and I return.

Away off in my lost place I think of you.

LH

1. Hahn's longhand note.

200

To Bab

May, 1925[1]

I have not written for several days because I have been absorbed in a piece of writing.[2] Liveright sends estatic telegrams about the novel.[3] The man is an eager rather corrupt (Im affraid) child. Huebsch is honest, fussy an old maid.

Oh well.

The new book comes a little to life. What a strange intangible thing is childhood. For several days I have worked each day to the point of exhaustion.

I have so much less to give than you think. I see the river flowing down to the sea and want to flow like that. I am a small muddy stream instead.

Bob has gone off on one of his expeditions—this time to Spain. He hooked[?] a line [?] aboard ship—a strange lad. God bless him anyway.

When I am not giving so much to just work I shall be able to write more interestingly.

Love

LH

1. Hahn's longhand note.
2. Probably *Tar*.
3. Doubtless *Dark Laughter*.

201

To Bab

May, 1925[1]

Again I am full of work and going it at a great rate. There is much to write you about but if I tried to write one tenth of what is in my head to say I would get nowhere. I am thinking you are right about Bob. I shall not send him away to Illinois. There is so much he has not got that perhaps I can give him.

We have had days of rain. It is cooler. Now it is Sunday morning and people are going to church. Freddy O'Brien—who wrote The South Seas[2] has been here and now my old friend George Daugherty is here for a few days.

I am pushing out into new things in writing again. Whenever I have extra time I spend it on the river. The negro—the river. These are the things I want now to get into my work.

LH

1. Hahn's longhand note.
2. Frederick O'Brien (1869–1932), author of *White Shadows in the South Seas* (1919).

202

To Bab May—1925[1]

It would be all very fine for me to get up-stage and talk if I never had done hurtful things. However, when I look back, I shudder. I am constantly resolved that I will never do the same again. Almost at once I do it.

It goes on so, year after year. People some times say dreadful things about me, do dreadful things to me. It makes me ill. I usually so deserve the unpleasant things.

About yourself dear I constantly think. As you know there is a kind of unbreakable connection. It has stood hard strains and will stand more.

What we do we do over and over.

It has happened that we are both highly sinsitive people. I write. Often in my writing I loose myself and am happy—for the time—but there comes always the times between.

I've an idea that, for myself I should have had the happiest life had I been able to spend my life in some kind of rude craft. When I am not working I go walk but never walk toward the business part of the city I happen to be in. I go to where men are at work with their hands. Some old instinct is choked in me too. I see the sky, trees, the earth, rivers—always in connection with men at work.

You, being woman, must have another impulse. For some reason we have to pay, not only for ourselves but for the men before us, for the civilization in which we live.

Most people, I am sure, are not so sensitive to what they miss in life. They are not so lustful, not so eager. We have to pay for being what we are. The painter who has an eye suffers most in the presence of ugliness. All sensitive people suffer.

There have been days, as you know when I have had to walk for hours with my eyes on the sidewalk to avoid looking at people. Their faces told me too much.

Even the dullness hurts. When people are sensitive they are hurt too.

What is to be done. We go on. The days pass.

I am not so sure of children. It is an instinct. The child might only come into the world to suffer and be defeated in turn. Like Anatole France I am a pessimist trying to be cheerful in the actual presence of people.

The things that are harsh and cruel in life we come to take for granted, as existing. The thing is not to hurt more than we have too. Well, we both do it constantly. We are more alike than you think.

Half neurotic, intense children both of us. God help us.

But do not think that, when I am cruel, I am any more determined upon cruelty than you are.

And that is not all.

LH

1. Hahn's longhand note.

203

To Bab May, 1925[1]

A curious week spent in an old river packet, making its way slowly up from New Orleans to Vicksburg—taking a week for the round trip. We load grain, mules and negroes largely. The great river pretty much deserted now, silent and majestic.

The river men themselves wistful old fellows letting [telling] old tales of the past glory of the craft.

It gets to be as one goes along, one of the strangest and sadest things in nature. I have talked of it some in my new novel.[2] The great river, so majestic, so strong and idle. Like a Samson bling [blind].

Above Natches hills and a sweet green country. Below lowland stretching away.

I ride in the pilot house with an old river man who tells me tales of the grand old days—when being a river pilot was something. Now they mostly run fr[?] or tug for getting out rafts of logs.

Tomorrow I'll be back in New Orleans and to work again.
Monday [on next line, as indicating day of writing].

LH

1. Hahn's longhand note.
2. *Dark Laughter*.

204

To Bab June—1925[1]

I am short paper this morning and so you will excuse this yellow stuff. Your letter touched the edge of an unexpressed thing I feel. I think really that sex is all and nothing. I have for a long time now been trying to get up into consciousness what I feel about it.

As usual with me, to express what I feel I shall have to transpose it out of myself into another. I have in mind a hulking old man, a thinker, a book man, living an isolated life, away from people of culture.

This old man has lived in my consciousness a long time. I want some day to write a book about him.

I am trying to think what he would say in answer to your letter. He would I think be a little frightened and glad.

Frightened that you should also suffer what I fancy most people think they rather suffer alone.

One wants—what. Really gentleness. Just that. Life is on the whole so harsh that one feels like walking softly softly.

On certain days I have this disperate feeling that people want to hurt one another like malicious monkeys.

I remember a flashing moment of you—among your friends in Indianapolis. All about you the possibilities of stupidity. You being hurt, made to feel isolated from human beings.

It happens everywhere to sensitive people. Now and then we turn and strike each other.

We have lost the old virtues and the new ones we are trying to get are complex and difficult. What I try—when I am at all well—is to think of myself as a passing guest in a strange place.

You see I am saying superficial things. To love, in the modern sense, involves so much.

I have come to know that money is nothing, power is hurtful.

What is left. Real gentleness—if one can get it. I can think of nothing else.

I'll think of what you say about John.[2] It is hard to do. Perhaps I can do it skillfully.

A man has offered me a trip on a slow boat up the Mississippi River. I may leave at the end of this week. The plan for the rest of the summer remains uncertain.

Your letter made me feel very very close to you. Leave me your address. I shall be able to write and say all I feel better at another time.

LH

1. Hahn's longhand note.
2. His son, John S.

205

To Bab

June—1925[1]

I am on a barge on the Mississippi river, going from New Orleans to St. Louis & back. Got the privaledge of making the trip through a friend on the New Orleans Picayune. The boats are great powerful tug boats taking strings of barges, each holding as much as a whole freight train. The great affair; like a little town of roofs and houses grinds its way up river slowly.

I have a cot on the deck so that I sleep in the open air and eat with the captain, pilots mates and engineers.

I wanted the chance to know the river and to get acquainted with it in this slowly leisurely way.

As for mail, it is uncertain about my getting any but I think, if you write to me, % Steamer Natchez—Mississippi Marinor Service, St. Louis, I will get it there.

The proof of the novel[2] has been read and sent off. I wonder if you will like it. It is so difficult from anything else I have done.

Now, for the time being, I think only of the river, of it[s] old traditions, its power and strangeness. I want to write a riverbook. I soak myself in it. As I write the yellow water slides away, a great, everchanging thing.

It is in some way the key to something I want. Will I ever grasp it fully.

I hope the summer brings you much, Bab dear. Write to me often. I'll be back in New Orleans by the 10th or 15th—July.

LH

1. Hahn's longhand note. Written after June 20, when he wrote a letter to Alfred Stieglitz from New Orleans.
2. *Dark Laughter*.

206

To Bab Troutdale July 27, 1925[1]

I got your two notes from the camp and have not answered. For several days now I have been going off early to my cabin in the cornfield under the mountain and writing until I was exhausted. A Cuban woman—or rather girl—who is living for the summer here comes to take my necessary letters but I do not want to dictate letters to those I care for.

In the afternoon I walk or ride a staid old farm horse. The people here are all very churchly—Methodosts and Baptists—and think me a heathern because I do not go to their church but they are knidly. Often I penetrate far up into the mountains and find strange sweet people. The mountain peo[ple] are either downright bad or very sweet. Their religion they call the Primitive Baptist. Once a month they hold a service and wash each other's feet. I hope to go to such a meeting. When I say some of the mountain people are bad I only mean they are silent and sullen and have a repytation for shooting on slight provcation. Little springs leak out of the mountain everywhere and run, often, directly through the cabins. Few outside people come in here—the fare is too hard.

At last my work goes well and my poor nerves are steadier. Last evenin[g] I walked six miles in the mountains in the dusk. Met several drunken mountaineers but we got on peacefully. I read your lomger letter about the camp and your mother on the way.

It seemed to me that your fate is the common fate. I can't make up my own mind about a future life, can't really think of it intelligently. My mind refuses to work there but I ask myself why a life, so lacking in worth, should be preserved after it has run its course here. The religious side of these people with whom I stay is there worse side. One sect quarrels with another. I have had many strange talks with the woman who runs the house. She is material for a book.

I shall see you surely this fall or winter. Your whole spirit these last two years has made you near and dear to me.

TS

1. Hahn's longhand note. Schevill (*Sherwood Anderson*, p. 212) says that Anderson wanted a vacation from New Orleans, to visit an "unknown place"; he wrote several friends for advice on where to go. The Andersons took the suggestion of Julian Harris, a Ku Klux Klan fighter of Columbus, Ga., to stay with the John Greear family near Troutdale, Va. Elizabeth (*Miss Elizabeth*, p. 133) says they went to live with the Greears so that Sherwood could continue work on *Tar*.

207

To Bab August—1925 Troutdale[1]

Afternoon in the cabin. The little town here has but two or three dozen people. I live in a farm house filled with children. Chickens walk about. Their dropping are everywhere. How I detest chickens. The housekeeper is rather slovenly. She talks too much.

Her husband a gentle man, ruined by his environment. Something of the old fashioned American—Lincoln & Jefferson in him.

I spend little time about the house—eat there—sleep there. There is a desserted cabin in the midst of a corn field. My desk is by an open door. Flies, wasps, beas, humming birds visit me. Spiders build their nests.

In the field—the corn keeps up a soft whispering sound.

People puzzle me more than ever. Perhaps I shall find it better to spend more time with nature. A little farm off in these hills might be the best thing. I can spend a few months a year with people then I must have nature.

I get well however. Every day I write a little more. I loose excess weight, feel again more lean and eager.

Some day I will tell you or write something about the strange religious perversions of these hill people. They are like the Dayton Tenn.[2] people.

LH

1. Hahn's longhand note. Before Aug. 14, when Sherwood went back to New Orleans, to which Elizabeth's business had already called her.
2. The location of the Scopes evolution trial of July 1925.

208

To Bab Aug. 20, 1925[1] [New Orleans]

I am in the mood to write you a note although it is poison hot. I have come back to the city and will be here now until I go away to lecture.[2] In a year or two I will quit the city entirely—living several months a year in the country.[3]

There is something—the call the old Greeks heard—the growing corn, apple trees, birds nesting.

Country life will be better for me now. I shall have enough to do writing the unwriten stuff in me.

I begin to want a little house by a brook on a side road, the smell of grass, all the things nature means.

These things appeal to those who are no longer young and soon I shall begin to grow old.[4]

I want the later years more mellow, kindly.

Nature herself becomes more and more my goddess.

I think you will also know what I mean.

I am at work. I shall be here now for at least a month. Later I am hoping I may see and talk with you.

LH

1. Hahn's longhand note.
2. Which he had planned to start on Oct. 12.
3. The pattern of the last fourteen years of his life was beginning to take shape.
4. He was to be forty-nine in Sept.

209

To Bab August 25, 1925[1] [New Orleans]

I think the proof of the solidity of our friendship—call it what you will—is that you remain so intact. I think you may have notices, in my mood, a growing inclination to get away from people. This year's lecturing is going to be very very hard for me.

I want to make enough money this year—if I can—to make myself safe for a year or two. The world of little artists gets on my nerves more.

I know you suffer—have had bad times but you remain so alive—so yourself. That's good to think about. I am saying it only because my letters to be real have to be a part of my mood of the moment and I have been thinking of you.

Like you I think I am getting more reverance. It may in me take the form of returning more and more to trees and skies—to nature.

In some way for me the breasts of the goddess are there—hidden under the leaves perhaps.

It can't be talked about much. You will know what I mean.

LH

1. Hahn's longhand note.

210

To Bab August 29, 1925[1] [New Orleans]

I am sitting under a willow tree on the banks of the Mississippi writing to you.

I came out to a little river town on a train at noon and will go back for dinner. With me I have Lucretius.[2]

As for the country—well here everything, the grasses, weeds, wild flowers, vines, trees and bushes are strange.

Even the insects and crawling things are not the ones I knew as a boy.

That is why Virginia, with all its mountains was so attractive.

A place of Andersons Beales and Smiths too. Very likely my people came from there.[3]

The chief thing though is the feeling of old familiarity with things around.

Does not Lucretius say—"Custom renders love attractive; for that which is struck by oft-repeated blows lightly, yet after long course of time is overpowered and gives way."

I have been writing pretty steadily but there are days when the prose won't walk or run.

I will send you under another cover an advance copy of the new novel.[4] Yesterday I read it, in book form, for the first time. The book is something quite separated from the Mms. It has a life of its own.

I have read the novel—the first reading always exhausts me—and think it will do. I believe the jazz rhythm has come off. Now I am trying in the childhood book,[5] to resurect the boys soul—live in it again.

I shall have a comfortable house in the country dear.[6] Perhaps this year my lecturing and writing may pay for it.

LH

1. Hahn's longhand note.
2. Roman poet and philosopher (96?–55 B.C.).
3. An admission of Anglo-Saxon background, contrary to his Italian pose. See Sutton, *Road to Winesburg*.
4. *Dark Laughter.* Finley had an autographed copy.
5. *Tar.*
6. The house is Ripshin; it still stands near Troutdale, Va.

211

To Bab September—1925[1] [New Orleans]

Just a little hurriedly scrawled note. I am writing each day[2] until I am exhaused. The life of the children—in the Moorehead household absorbs me. It is really my own childhood dramatized and lived in the person of one Tar Moorehead.

It does not matter much who I address. Im glad I am going to see you.[3]

As Always

LH

1. Hahn's longhand note.
2. On *Tar*.
3. This is one of a number of suggestions that Finley did not save all of Anderson's letters. The implication is that he had previously indicated that his travels would allow him to visit Indianapolis.

212

To Bab October 6, 1925[1]

Will be leaving here tomorrow or next day. Have given you Leigh's[2] address. I start off rather tired after my illness[3] and with little taste for the thousands I shall have to meet.[4] I do it only because I want to make money enough for a retreat from people—a little comfortable farm in a valley in the hills.

Of course my body is strong. The spirit sometimes groes tired of the much unlovliness and vulgarity.

It will be so good to see you if only for a little. You are never vulgar Bab. If you only knew what this means.

LH

1. Hahn's longhand note.
2. Lecture agent Leigh Colson.
3. No details are available.
4. This particular tour began at the University of Georgia in Athens, where Anderson spoke on Oct. 13, 1925. J. D. Wade's article in the *Georgia Alumni Record* (Oct. 1925, pp. 29–30) gives the following account of Anderson's lecture.

> The famous novelist, Sherwood Anderson spoke before the students and faculty of the University on October thirteenth. The chapel was full—every

seat occupied, the open space at the rear jammed with standing boys. Mr. Anderson spoke forty-five minutes. He had absolute attention, and there were hardly more than two or three people to slip out the back (over protesting floorboards!) during the entire time.

Mr. Anderson's speech was an attempt to explain the so-called Modern Movement in the arts. To many of us his explanation portrayed this movement as after all in its essentials not any more modern than ancient. Everybody who heard the speech heard it enthusiastically as a sincere and fresh statement of principles that give life meaning. It was good doctrine for old and young. Here are some parts of it:

"I presume that you all know that there is in the world at this time what is broadly termed a modern movement. It has expressed itself in a great many ways. Although you may not realize it, the fact is that the neckties worn by many men in this audience and the dresses worn by the women have been influenced by this movement. It has practically revolutionized painting all over the world. It has crept into the writing of prose, into the making of songs, into sculpture, into architecture. The street scene of the American city is becoming more colorful, designs are bolder. In general it seems to me that I have noticed the effect of the movement more fully in painting and in building than in any of the other arts. Architecture, long one of the most dead and dreary of the arts as practiced in America, is becoming alive. It will become every year, I believe, more alive.

"As no man can speak of the writings of a country without saying something of the history of the intellectual life of the country, I shall have to begin by speaking of that. The intellectual life of the country was being formed and controlled by English Protestants, while the physical American was being built up of a mixture of all the bloods of the Western World and the process is still, I believe, going on. In our political thought the Adamses of New England, with their desire to establish an intellectual aristocracy, are still, I believe, more powerful than Lincoln, the artist-democrat, and, though by the world in general, Whitman is recognized as our one great American poet, I have heard of no general demand that he be introduced into our public schools to take the place of the decidedly second-rate and imitative New Englander, Longfellow."

Mr. Anderson then spoke of the great change that took place in the United States during the height of this New England influence—the change from a nation of farmers to a nation of factories, and with factories came standarization. We are told the type of car we must have, the kind of cigarette we must smoke, and the kind of literature we must read—the kind that appears daily in our magazines, which boast of tremendous circulations. The owners of these magazines, the editors, are essentially business men and good business men. Their efficiency is to be admired rather than condemned. But what arises from this efficiency? What has come to meet the demand. The popular writer has come! There are, indeed many of him.

"The popular writer," Mr. Anderson said, "is just the man of talent who is willing to sell his talent to the business man who publishes the magazine or to the book publisher after large sales, and the more talented he is the better he gets paid. There is a job to be done and he does it keeping his eye always on the main chance, that is to say on the great unthinking, buying public. His position is pretty secure. In America we are in the habit of thinking of the thing that succeeds as good and therefore the man whose books sell by the hundreds of thousands is looked up to with respect. If success is the standard of measurement how can we do anything else?

"At the country fairs back in Ohio when I was a boy there used to be a kind of a faker who went about with a machine. Into the machine he put a pound of sugar and started it going. It whirled about with great rapidity and produced a kind of cloud-like candy concoction that looked tremendously inviting. A pound of sugar would make nearly a bushel of it, but when you had bought a bag of the stuff and put a whole handful into your mouth it at once melted away to nothing.

"This is in reality the effect desired in the manufacture of any popular art. You must seem to give a lot while in reality giving nothing. No one must be made to think or feel. Keep it up and you will get rich. To actually touch peoples' lives is the unpardonable sin. Thinking and feeling are very dangerous exercises and besides, people do not like them.

"In reality I think many men of talent might be saved for the the doing of good work in the arts if the whole situation could be clearly stated. Too often the younger man or woman who has talent does not get the situation in hand until he is too old or too spiritually tired to save himself. We have all been brought up with the notion, firmly planted in us, that to succeed in a material sense is the highest end of a life. Our fathers tell us that. Often our mothers tell us so. Schools and universities often teach the same lesson. We hear it on all sides and when we are young and uncertain our very youthful humbleness often betrays us. Are we to set oursleves up against the opinions of our elders? How are we to know that truth to ourselves, to the work of our hands, to our inner impulses, is the most vital thing in life? It has become almost a truism here in America that no man does good work in the arts until he is past forty. Nearly all of the so-called Moderns, the younger men, so-called, are already gray. It takes a long time for most men to get the ground under their feet, to find out a little of their own truth in life. The effort to find out the truth is what is called the Modern Movement. It is growing. Do not have any doubt about that.

"Let me state the matter again. It cannot be stated too often. The writer, the painter, the musicians, the practitioner of any of the arts who wants to do honest work has got to put the thought of money aside. He has got to forget it. There is but one way the young man or woman of talent can defeat the corrupting influences of the present day institutions that popularize art and that is by forgetting their existence and giving all his attention to his work. And again let me say that when I speak of corrupting influences I am not speaking of the men who run these institutions as corrupt individuals. I am speaking only in the workman's sense. I am speaking only of the workman in relation to his tools and materials.

"Consider for a moment the materials of the prose writer, the teller of tales.

His materials are human lives. To him these figures of his fancy, these people who live in his fancy, should be as real as living people. He should be no more ready to sell them out than he would be to sell out his men friends or the women he loves. To take the lives of these people and bend or twist them to suit the need of some cleverly thought out plot to give your readers a false emotion, is as mean and ignoble as to sell out living men and women. For the writer there is no escape, there is no real escape for any craftsman. If you handle your materials in a cheap way you go cheap. The need of making a living may serve as an excuse, but it will not save you as a craftsman. Nothing in reality will save you if you go cheap with tools and materials. Do cheap work and you are yourself cheap. That is the truth."

213

To Bab Oct. 18, 1925[1]

Saturday Night.

I am in a little town in the heart of Tennessee—between speaking engagements at Birmingham[2] and Nashville[3]—stopped here to be a[t] peace from people, to rest and to work for a day or two.

It is tiring work. Each speech takes something out of you and then the people are very insistent and very greedy.

Well, there is another side. There is something to be said. The people have such childish notions about what artists are up to and some of them are really greedy to know something.

A funny thing is that everyone has been constantly warning me not to say anything about sex in the South. Aren't people absurd. People in the South are like they are anywhere. No better no worse.

There seems to be some sort of absurd notion that, because I write of people doing certain things I am likely to do the same thing publicly—at any moment. Nothing at all is allowed for one's sense of taste or occasion. Oh well it doesn't matter. With my audience I get on fine and people flock to hear me.[4] I'll be glad when it is all over though.

You seem very far away. Everyone I love seem very far way. There is just a procession of strange faces. It will last a long time.

My blessing on you. I hope you are well.

LH Written on the stationery of the Bethel Hotel, Columbia, Tenn.

1. Hahn's longhand note.

2. No account of the Birmingham lecture has yet been found, but the following interview, by Dolly Dalrymple of the Birmingham *News*, was published on Thursday afternoon, Oct. 15; that evening Anderson spoke before the Allied Arts Club.

The quality in Sherwood Anderson beyond all others that makes him a significant writer—a writer for our times—is his sense of an abiding peril in human relations, his perception that the defenses civilized man has erected between himself and personal tragedy are unreliable. For many years to come thousands will be living who recall walking over ground where many soldiers had been buried, hastily and none too deep, and where a disordered fancy (there was no lack of them) might have imagined that some at least were protesting against the cruel iron-shod heel that took the death of men so lately living for granted. So with Mr. Anderson. The ground over which he takes us is not hollow, but it is insecure—uncanny. Something that the consent of man had thrust underground he seems to feel, stirring and heaving as he treads, in a sort of monstrous resurrection. It is uncouth and primitive. But it is very, very tenacious of life. It is shouldering and upheaving its bulk, tired of being buried, demanding a place in the sun and air, insisting men shall recognize that the social structure reared upon its thews and sinews has just so much stability as it permits and no more.

"Dig your foundations," he seems to be crying in one disquieting novel after another: "Dig your foundations, through this dubious soil, you men of seemliness and culture and fair names for crude facts. But do not blame me if the things I point out to you as you dig visit you in uneasy dreams at night!"

It was not, however of his attitude toward life nor yet his novels, "The Triumph of an Egg," "Many Marriages," "Dark Laughter" and the rest about which we talked with Sherwood Anderson when we had the pleasure of meeting him at the Tutwiler, Thursday, prior to his lecture Thursday evening under the auspices of the Allied Arts Club, for we've never read any of his novels (which he declared, smilingly, is our loss), but which we mean to do immediately since we've met the affable gentleman and found him so delightful and charming and what we've written about him we got out of a book: so, instead of these subjects we decided to be utterly frivolous at the feet of genius and add to the gaiety of the nation by asking Mr. Anderson his views on cabbages and kings—in other words, to hear genius express itself on every day subjects.

So—"Frivolity," said to "Genius."

"What in your opinion is the greatest contribution to civilization, and why do you think so?"

"Walt Whitman and Abraham Lincoln," replied "Genius" unreservedly, "because the greatest contribution that any nation can make is great men."

"Who is the ideal living American and why do you think so?" observed "Frivolity."

"The publisher who does the most for his authors," sighed "Genius."

"If we should ever have a woman president of the United States who should that woman be?"

"The most womanly woman."

"Who is the greatest humorist today?"

"Ring Lardner."

"Frivolity" granted "Genius" breathing spell just here and then resumed the questionnaire by asking:

"Who, in your opinion, is the greatest moving picture actor and why do you think so?"

"Never go to the movies," asseverated "Genius."

"What is your ambition and why?"

"To be a farmer and raise fat cattle, because it's the nearest thing to nature's heart."

"Who is America's greatest composer and why do you think so?" inquired "Frivolity."

"Ernest Bloch: I can whistle his music."

"Who is America's greatest male singer and why do you think so?"

"I live in New Orleans and few of them come there."

"And America's greatest woman's singer—surely you must have a choice in this line?"

"Ditto," said "Genius" laconically.

"Who is the greatest American dramatist and why do you think so?"

"Eugene O'Neill because he writes the best plays and knows life."

"What is America's greatest song?"

"I don't know, because I only sing in the bathroom—'Way Down South in Dixie' being my favorite song."

"What is the best play you've seen in the last decade and why do you think so?"

"Processional, which I saw in New York last season: [John Howard] Lawson has put more life in it than any other play I've seen."

"What is the greatest book you have ever read and why do you think so?"

"The Bible, because it is the best written."

"Who do you think is the greatest comedian of the day and why?"

"I am, because I'm attempting to answer all these questions."

"Who is the greatest living poet?"

"I don't dare say, I owe some of them money."

"What is the greatest novel of 1924?"

"Modesty forbids me to say, but then *Dark Laughter* is a 1923 novel."

3. T. H. Alexander's article in the Nashville *Tennessean* (Mon., Oct. 19) opened with these sentences: "Sherwood Anderson, famous American author attracted by the lure of Maury county, Tenn., blue grass as well as impelled by the imminence of an attack of influenza, stepped off the north-bound train at Columbia to recuperate for 36 hours but arrived in Nashville in time Sunday to tell *The Tennessean* that the South in a literary way is about to come into its own." He told a "group of friends with much gusto" of his being mistaken, in Columbia through similarity of names, for an official of the Anti-Saloon League. Alexander thought it ironic this should have happened to "the greatest chaffer at what he considers irksome restraints of Puritanism in the American literary world." Noting he was very fond of the South, Anderson said, "There is a charm and atmosphere about New Orleans I find delightful." He could not resist the usual fictional touch: "He was first attracted to the South, he explained, because his mother was

a Virginian and his father a North Carolinian [both were born in Ohio], and both were lovers of the South. [There is no evidence for this—Irwin M. Anderson, who fought for the North in the Civil War, was a devoted member of the Grand Army of the Republic.] Anderson stayed at the house of Mr. and Mrs. B. Kirk Rankin, 401 Twenty-fourth Avenue; Anderson had met Rankin, owner of the *Southern Agriculturist*, through his work as an advertising copywriter."

The review of Anderson's Nashville lecture by Professor Donald Davidson, of the faculty at Vanderbilt University and author and critic of national reputation, in the Nashville *Tennessean* for Oct. 20, follows.

> Nashville gave Sherwood Anderson a crowded house for his lecture at the Centennial club Thursday afternoon. He deserved a crowded house, for he brought to Nashville the clearest and simplest interpretation of modern writing that has been made in these parts, and did it in an honest, unpretentious attractive way that made his listeners his friends.
>
> Likewise he gave the audience the thrill that it (like all audiences gathered to hear a famous and more or less revolutionary writer) expected and desired. When he shuffled on to the stage, wearing a tan suit, a blue shirt (with collar attached) and a flowing tie, the audience knew at once that here was somebody quite beyond the ordinary acquaintance one has with traveling lecturers—somebody exotic, strange, maybe even queer. He looked scared, as if he would like to hide under the grand piano from the hundreds of pairs of eyes directed curiously on him. Maybe he was scared, as in fact he declared he was, for when he began his speech he rambled nervously from one side of the stage to the other, dangled his left hand oddly from his wrist and occasionally fingered his vest.
>
> He apologized for changing the subject of his speech from 'The Younger Generation' to 'Modern Writing.' He had a speech on the first subject, he said, but he never tried it out on any audience, and he hated to begin on this one. As he went on, his nervousness passed away. He spoke in an ordinary conversational tone, making his points with such earnestness and absorption in his work that nobody could help being attracted.
>
> People who came expecting to see a wicked and rakish-looking Bohemian must have been disappointed. When he put on horn-rimmed spectacles, he instantly became grave and almost reverend. People who had read "Many Marriages" and expected him to say something shocking must have been disappointed, too, for his language was eminently proper. Indeed it was smooth, simple, direct and quite without many of the peculiarities that one finds in his book-language.
>
> He got into his subject somewhat slowly. New England, he said, had an art-impulse toward God, and seldom in other directions. The New England literature, the first American literature to be developed, was moral and intellectual. The good-and-bad formula was then and still is a sure passport to a kind of success in writing. But changes in American life, such as the change from an agricultural to an industrial age, brought equally significant and sweeping

changes in literature. In the modern world it is no longer possible to treat life so simply, and eyes can no longer be shut as the New Englanders shut them to considerable portions of life.

This much by way of preliminary. The rest of his lecture was devoted to an analysis of the effects of the industrial age on the arts, and this was the heart of his lecture. What modern writers are working for could hardly be more simply and effectively stated than in terms used by Mr. Anderson Thursday afternoon. He discussed the standardization of modern American life and showed how the great modern magazine, with its columns of advertising to which the literary columns were merely the bait, is as much a factory product as a Ford car. It must have tremendous sales; therefore, its contributors must be "artful dodgers," who tread on nobody's toes, think up charming, pretty plots and nice articles without really touching life. For such writers, he said, "actually to touch people's lives is an unforgivable crime."

But the real craftsman, a word of which Sherwood Anderson is fond, must "be honest with the materials with which he works." These materials are complex and not like the pretty patterns of the highly paid writers of the "commercialized" magazines, who, he said, "have no more to do with the art of writing than movie stars with the art of acting." The honest workman resists the tremendous pressure for standardization, which everybody feels as a vaguely depressing force that is making American life too drab and uniform. Even the Ford car finds itself sometimes suddenly transformed. Boys tear off the ugly bodies of Fords and make them into racing cars, "bugs" of unique design. And that is the sort of thing the modern writer is trying to do.

Mr. Anderson found many hopeful signs, he said, that the honest craftsman is coming into his own—writers of shoddy work offer apologies; readers increase; a public grows up for the better sort of writing; literary clubs spring up everywhere, and so on. But the writer cannot win, cannot be content even with himself if he makes money. He must put cheapness aside. And in this connection many of Mr. Anderson's sentences remain firmly fixed in memory: "If you handle your material in a cheap way, you'll grow cheap." . . . "Impotence comes when men no longer shape things with their own hands." . . . "Love of craft is to man what love of children is to women."

And all was sound and honest doctrine, the most pleasing because it got quite beyond the superficial commonplace which most lecturers use. Sherwood Anderson has something very definite and valuable to say to American people in lectures as well as in novels and stories. Thursday afternoon was the proof. It was one of the most successful lectures ever given in Nashville.

After giving his lecture, "Mr. Anderson will have Tuesday to inspect a farm he has purchased in Virginia and will then resume his lecture tour which will occupy four months." Anderson had seen the farm on which Ripshin was built before he went back to New Orleans. Feeling, after he got to New Orleans, that he could take the plunge, he and Elizabeth evidently closed the sale by mail before he left for the lecture trip.

He left this impression with the writer of the above review: "Sherwood Anderson's message was one of courage and honest analysis, and it was impressive because Sherwood Anderson is a solid person. There is no show about him. He is not flashy. He does not pretend to genius or mystical inspiration. His writing is his job and he works at it patiently and honestly."

Doubtless at the request of his host, Kirk Rankin, who introduced him as "the man who formerly got away with murder in the advertising game years ago," Anderson also spoke, informally, at a noon meeting of the Nashville Exchange Club on Oct. 20. He amused himself by advising club members to buy his books, not to read but to refer to, "this being the excuse given by George Ade for purchasing a farm."

T. H. Alexander, who had interviewed Anderson two days earlier, wrote of him in his column for Oct. 20: "He is a pleasant and charming gentleman, with more poise than Sinclair Lewis, none of the wordy vagaries of Gertrude Stein, less of the occasional dullness of the impersonal and detached James Branch Cabell and considerably more of what must perforce be described as 'patriotism' then H. L. Mencken."

4. Reports generally substantiate this view. One anticipatory article in a Nashville newspaper indicated he was an "outstanding figure in the literary world of today" and that "as a lecturer he is being greeted with enthusiam wherever he appears." Another reported him to be a "speaker of force, of unusual personal charm and magnetism." In addition, "critics say no American writer for the past eight years has excited more discussion than Anderson." Anderson would hardly have hoped for more enthusiasm than was displayed in this editorial on the morning of his Nashville lecture (Nashville *Tennessean*, Oct. 19, 1925):

> To hear Sherwood Anderson lecture is more than a literary treat. It is an adventure. Such is the word of those who have heard him.
>
> Stout hearted readers who have sailed his new seas may or may not have charted his new lands or catalogued the strange monsters cast up on his new-found shores. Neither have they felt, it may be, the fresh winds that blow across his slanting, slippery decks, nor sensed the disturbing fragrance of unnamed blossoms opening in the forest depths of realms by him alone explored.
>
> It may be that the mystery of his genius baffles them, that his frank unreserve keeps them afraid, that his spirit of revolt abashes even that small remnant of conservatism that is left to them.
>
> He is not a writer to be left unread. Of that much we may be sure. Nor a talker to be left unheard, if reports are to be taken for true.
>
> Among many things this uncompromising genius has written to tempt the interest, however doubtful the complacency, "A Story Teller's Story" invariably brings out an intimate discussion. A memorable piece of autobiography, the book is one in which "our best story teller," as has been said of it, "tells his best story." Just how much of the record's hero is Anderson himself and how much his fancy there's none of us may know. The story wholly possesses its teller.
>
> People who know him personally recognize many incidents of his real life in the record.
>
> Deed and character, its actualities are strangely big in the midst of sordid

littleness, dark, but flecked with curious illuminations. The character of Anderson himself as here depicted is more mental and psychical perhaps, than real. As a whole the book is a challenge, or of more deep concern to us who read, a challenge to American life to justify itself, or of more deep concern to us who read, a challenge to our own souls to find an answer to something, but to what we cannot fathom.

In this, as in "Dark Laughter," and all the rest, something surges up from beneath, and in all of these too, there is a sense of a sardonic mirth that makes the chorus to their tragedies, implied sometimes and sometimes the actual laughter of the dark people who haunt the newest of the tales.

Many of us, passing back and forth along these devious pathways, return to the pavements and alley ways and country roads of "Winesburg, Ohio," as the answer to these baffling things, or at most it may be, as the root of their stark questions.

Nowhere is such meagerness of effort, such sparse use of words, such economy of material and such prod and grip and provocation of result. Here are ugly things casually laid bare, middle age stripped by the impelling wrong that stole its youth away, and corrupting acts that seem but mechanical after all and of no concern to the impulse that dreamed of other things.

In the midst of so much of spirit travail it seems an incredible fancy that couples this writer with a rare and simple hearted teller of tales to children, no other, though we tremble as we say it, than Hans Christian Andersen.

Here is the same simple, unadorned habit of statement. Brief sentences, setting down plain facts. No metaphor nor simile, nor bid of any kind for further thought than the words convey.

Here is the same directness that says what it means as simply as a child would say it. And here is the fancy lurking once again behind the words, the same vague wonder and understanding that stirs as if by the magic of symbol—allegory—fable—what you will that brings far visions and memories of things we never knew. There's many a sentence Anderson writes that has an aura. He knows how to set a few words into "Open, Sesame!" and you have your cave of treasure. He lifts a sentence like a baton and a flood of music answers to his gesture.

"The thing is," as he says himself, "how to get at what the writer, or the young thing in the writer, is thinking about.

"In the beginning," says Mr. Anderson, "when the world was young there were a great many thoughts but no such thing as a truth. Man made the truths himself and each truth was a composite of a great many vague thoughts. All about in the world were the truths and they were all beautiful. . . . There was truth of virginity and the truth of passion, the truth of wealth and of poverty, of thrift and of profligacy, of carelessness and abandon. . . . Hundreds and hundreds. . . ."

The writer's words made only one a half of the tale he tells. The rest is in the understanding of the reader.

We will welcome Mr. Anderson as the exponent of enigmas past our understandings, or as a leader we may follow into new revolts and strange awakenings. There can be no lack of interest in the reception we shall give him. His lecture this afternoon on "The New Generation" promises a time of vigorous upstirrings and an aftermath of argument and discussion that will last long after he has left us for new audiences to baffle and provoke as he once did us who heard him here.

214

To Bab Nov. 1st 1925[1]

Have been in the hands of a lot of nice Dartmouth boys all afternoon. Am to speak here tonight. Spoke in Boston at Pilgrim Hall Saturday.

My last two books seem to have pretty well removed the old fear of me. It may be that just the weight of many books, many tales has removed the old fear of me. People no longer seem to think me unclean. The head of the English department of Wellsley introduced me in Boston. It is all hard work but there is something gained—a sort of feeling of many kinds of Americans in many places and under many different conditions of life. As a matter of fact am standing the grind pretty well—get a kind of strength out of the crowds.

Almost everywhere big crowds—many curious people.

Do not know when I am to be in Indianapolis but it won't be long before I see you. I only get my scedual a week at a time.

Much, much love

LH Written on the stationery of the Hanover Inn, Hanover, N.H.

1. Hahn's longhand note.

215

To Bab New Orleans—Dec 24—1925[1]

Surely this book[2]—in an odd way belongs to you. There are in it so many little notes—half addressed to you when written.

Impersonal too.

The incident with the man. All my lecture trip was like that
half functioning
A failure.

Only necessity shall drive me to it after this.

There are so many things about it difficult to explain.

You were right.
Thank God I'm not a realist.
The reality of so many people makes me ill.
There is so much and so little to say at the Christmas time.
You have found out so much about me. I know you better this year.
I only hope I have stood the test as you have.

LH

1. Hahn's longhand note.
2. Very likely *Sherwood Anderson's Notebook.*

216

To Bab

January 1926[1]
On Train Monday

I land in Los Angeles tonight and start lecturing tomorrow. Will be glad when it is all over. It is hard for me to tell you how to address me out here. My scedual is not fixed until the last moment. Often it comes by wire. Better use 825 Bourbon St. Bob will be there.

He came in at the last minute Saturday having overslept and missed seeing you off. Very swollen-eyed and sorry.

I saw you on the street when I stepped out of a shop Saturday morning but did not run after you—having not a moment to spare. A dozen special things came up at the last moment.

It seemed very rotten that you would have been in New Orleans—and that I should have got so little of you. Still there was the walk by the river. I am glad we had that without the others around.

LH

1. Hahn's longhand note.

217

To Bab

January 1926[1]

As you see I am still in the mill[2] but fortunately there is only about 10 days more of it.

I wish I knew where I stood in this matter of lecturing—I mean whether I have gained or lost.

Individuals come out of the ruck of people. I am made to feel—somewhat—my hold on the imaginations of the young.

In colleges—young artists.

It makes me want to be more than I ever will be.

So many other processes.

Are they really that?

Am I the ass, standing up there and talking?

To attempt to influence any great number of people is to influence no one.

Men who love many women never love one woman.

I am merely—just now—a puzzled disconcerted man.

I want the woods, the fields, quiet to think.

This letter will, I'm sure—although so disjointed—make you feel how disjointed I am now days.

I shall be a better friend—a better man perhaps—when it is all over and I have had more time to think of it.

LH Written on the stationery of the Maryland Hotel, San Diego.

1. Hahn's longhand note.

2. Of lecturing. A page-by-page check of two San Diego newspapers for Jan. 1926 did not yield any mention of his having lectured in that city.

218

To Bab

Jan. 1926[1]
[After Jan. 24]

I am here at the last stop[2] I shall make on this trip. Lecturing has become more and more distastful to me. As always happens with me, when I do something against my nature, I have, during these last few weeks, become ill every time I have had to speak. Very well, that I have learned. I think in general the crowds like me but there is something happens.

If one remains a public speaker it would be inevitable, after a time you would be be saying things for their effect—not for their worth.

And there is something else. I am quite sure now that the public man has no private life.

I have escaped fairly well because I have been aware I think but already I notice in myself an inclination to snatch at momentary triumps.

Well tomorrow ends that except for two or three engagements in the south in the spring—made long ago.

I have had a good many letters from Perce [?][3]: In one he will be quite in dispair—in the next more cheerful and hopeful. Poor lad. Wish he did not have in him the cheap vulgar side that is always flashing out—even in his lectures. Its a mess, isn't it.

In some way, these last months I have got your own figure more clearly as accepting your life, your surrounding—living more really.

I don't need to tell you what a nice and what an alive figure yours is in my own life.

LH Written on the stationery of The Olympic, Seattle.

1. Hahn's longhand note.

2. The *Daily* of the University of Washington reported on Jan. 24, 1926, that "Anderson arrived in town this morning and toured the city and district with Prof. Glenn Hughes, head of the dramatic department." The article stated that in the evening before his lecture on Jan. 28, he and James Stevens, author of the Paul Bunyan stories, would be guests of honor "at the Wilsonian." The *Daily* for Friday, Jan. 29, carried this account of his lecture.

> "I remain an uncertain man, groping my way about."
>
> So said Sherwood Anderson, famous novelist, in a lecture on "America—A Storehouse of Vitality," given in Meany hall last night under the auspices of Sigma Upsilon, literary fraternity, of which Anderson is a member. Glenn Hughes, assistant professor in the English department, was in charge. Between 700 and 800 persons were present.
>
> "I have always wished I were an English novelist; they seem to understand Americans so easily," Anderson asserted.
>
> There has been very little done by Americans to make America better known to Americans, he declared. No one has ever actually understood America; Americans live in an age of things, of physical facts, but even so they are not quite sold on the things for which they sell their souls; America must be caught in a state of movement, in a state of flux, according to Anderson.
>
> "When men drink they are able to feel freer; they discover connections between themselves and other men, and are not so afraid of saying what they really feel," Anderson said. "At least, when I am drunk I feel like that."
>
> "Words are to the writer as drink is to the drinker, an escape to the imaginative world. I may not be able to bring you physically into my room to study you, but I can in my fancy."
>
> The write is always quite conscious of an audience, he declared. Words have no meaning unless they are read, and he is always writing for an audience, Anderson said. He explained that he had come to think of all people as readers.
>
> "There is a new class of persons in America now," Anderson declared. "People with Sunday-afternoon-automobile faces, who have no place to go, but make the rounds anyway. It is the class that go from Iowa to Florida in Fords, and then go back to Iowa, and then start out again."

"You know," Anderson said, "both Red Grange and I are closing in Seattle this week."

"On this lecture tour I have been seeing American towns mainly from the insides of a sleeper. God helping me, I will go to no more towns."

At a dinner given in his honor at the Wilsonian yesterday before the lecture, Anderson agreed that he would allow his name to be used as a contributing editor to Columns, so long as it was understood that he would not be expected to write anything for it.

"You know," he said, "one advantage of being a contributing editor is that if you are asked to write something for the magazine you can tell the editors to go to hell."

3. Not so far identified.

219

To Bab February 1926[1] [New Orleans]

I have been turning your letter over in my mind all night. It has had an odd effect on me. I keep trying to to feel through to an understanding of my own attitude toward the children.

In truth I can't tell what is right and what is wrong. As regards yourself I am pretty clear. I have seen things happen to you through much suffering. Once I tried to tell you something but saying it sounded so brutal. I remember that I began telling you that you know so little of my life—of the many roots thrust down into the soil in so many directions.

What I tried to say sounded untrue when said. Unsaid it was all right.

I was really thinking of the past of our relations. When you came you were demanding so much, asking so much.

Later that all went out of you. I felt proud that I had always known it would. I had seen the same struggle in so many—in myself too. So often it had been lost.

Now I am trying to relate all this to the children. What you have done for them, will do—the thing you tell me in your letter.

I don't think they should know. I think, sometime, if you think it best, you might tell Cornelia.

How shall I say just what I am thinking. I do not want the children to begin thinking of you in terms of their own interest—now or later. There is too much of that in C's attitude now.

I wish it might all be eliminated. It can't. We have to fit into life as it is.

Wouldn't it be better to leave yourself free. Life may bring you things you do not know of now. You should be free to change your mind. It would never make any difference to me.

On the other hand they should learn to fit into life. They are strong enough physically.

Many many things to write—on other subjects. You know I am more grateful than I can say.[2] In a few days I'll write of other things.

LH

1. Hahn's longhand note.

2. Two points should be made regarding Finley's financial contribution for support of Anderson's children. It is certain that Finley did give money to Cornelia for the children. In question are (1) the length of time during which Finley sent the money and (2) the total amount given. Hahn had told me that she contributed $100 a month for eight years for the children's support, making a total of $9,600, and I had assumed that she meant the eight years before she was married in 1928. However, on Sept. 4, 1948, replying to a request that she donate her letters to the Anderson Collection at the Newberry Library, she wrote that when Anderson "was in financial distress and I was not I took over the education of his three children relieving him for writing," and paid $8,000 for the children's support. She added that "at that time" he gave her the manuscript of *Marching Men*, "Out of Nowhere," and "Brothers." When Hahn placed her letters in the Newberry Library in 1962, in return for $1,000 and the provision of an appraisal for tax purposes, the manuscripts included then were *Marching Men* and "Seeds." She made no mention of other manuscripts to me at that time. Probably her memory is at fault. John S. Anderson, Anderson's surviving son, stated in Feb. 1974 that he had learned of Finley's gifts only through his recent reading of these letters.

220

To Bab February, 1926[1] [New Orleans]

A terrible thing has happened and I have been in distress, having bad dreams at night, thinking of little else all day.

You will remember my having told you of my brother Earl. He is the boy who left home 20 years ago and never came back.[2] He was something of a painter but had no training—a sensitive quiet fellow we all loved.

The other day[3] he was found unconscious on the streets of Brooklyn—having had a stroke. He was taken to a hospital but the woman with whom he had roomed for five years—a working man's wife knew he had an author brother. My books were in his room and she phoned to my publisher who telegraphed me.[4]

I wired to Karl who went to see him at once. He also visited the place where he lived.[5] There were many drawings there. He had worked as a baker for five years in Brooklyn.

We have had the best doctors but they are still uncertain of his recovery. How lucky I am going to the country. I shall take him there. Sunshine and rest may cure him. He is a gentle sweet man, a confirmed solitary. Perhaps he has only been lonely and shy.

What a tradegy that I should only have been able to find him through this tradegy. I must have very stupid long ago that I let him get away.[6] I have always loved him as I have loved none of the others of my family.

LH

1. Hahn's longhand note.
2. Earl lived with Sherwood, perhaps briefly, in Elyria after the fall of 1907.
3. Feb. 16, 1926.
4. On Nov. 10, 1964, the late Karl Anderson's secretary, Mrs. Anne Poor of Westport, Conn., sent me a copy of the letter Earl had written to Sherwood in care of his publisher; the letter had been found on Earl when he was taken to Roosevelt Hospital. The parentheses are Poor's additions, but Earl drew the line through the words. She was not certain of the word "preclusion" in paragraph 6. Here is the text of the letter.

I am not going to court familiarity with the family nor ask a loan nor nothing.

I have read your latest book. As long as I got something of a panning in the book I think that (I) have a right to state my case.

You may assume that this is from that silent one of whom we were all so fond and whom we would not help in the difficult matter of living. That sentiment is pure bunk.

To digress a moment—I don't think the man feeds himself nor begets himself any more effectively that [than] lower forms of life. I conclude then that the complicated machinery of man's mind is for one purpose to feed his ego.

To digress again, I think Karl had 100% parental OK upon his birth, I think each succeeding birth received less with less favors. I myself got a parental OK upon my birth close to zero. I turned to mother for affection and got a cold shoulder. Probably she was so worn out with the effort of living that she had nothing left to give. I turned to each of the rest of the famiy in succession and got a view of their backs.

Probably there is no such thing as right or wrong—if an action seems to be to a person's benefit—if it seems to be harmful to him it is wrong. That is much like food—But there (is) a preclusion (?) in food which is based upon affections and custom rather than reality—ditto behavior.

What I mean to get at is this—I wanted affection or mental support of the family because it would have been beneficial to me. They withheld that affection and mental support because they thought I had no right that my existence was pure impudence because why go further.

I may question the wisdom of that attitude of mind but I can't condemn it. So let us say that I was born with a puny and anemic ego. The hostility of the family made that ego more helpless.

If I was silent it was because I was afraid to court hostility.

Of course you let me hover around your house & eat at your table—ditto Irwin—ditto Karl—Still considering those incidents I can see no reason to alter the above statement.

Yours
Earl

5. Poor's recollection is that "Karl went to Earl's lodgings, a miserable hole-in-the-wall, and brought home what little effects Earl had. These included some drawings Earl had done (Karl thought Earl could have been a better artist than himself had Earl had the opportunity)." See her letter of Nov. 10, 1964. In a manuscript entitled "Our Unforgettable Brother" (now at the Newberry Library), Karl relates how he had tried unsuccessfully to get Sherwood to write about Earl. Having discussed the matter with Sherwood, Karl felt he might have "spoiled the impulse." Thus Karl himself left five pages of typescript dealing with Earl's care after his mother's death; Earl's being under the wing of his sister, Stella; his traumatic embarrassment at a school recitation; and his near-success as a baseball pitcher, robbed of success by being strategically reminded of the disastrous poetry recitation (which, as presented, was an erosion of his maleness). After an account of unsuccessfully trying to make a place for Earl in his studio in New York, Karl reports being informed by Sherwood that "the kid has walked out on us." He concludes that he is still full of wonder at the strange life of his brother.

6. This episode was from the period when Earl had lived with Sherwood and Cornelia; in an undated letter (now at the Newberry Library), evidently of this period, Cornelia had written: "I hope you will let me know how Earl is soon. I wrote to him after you wrote me—Suppose his recovery will be extremely slow—I have been hearing of cases of paralysis where people seem to recover entirely and are comfortable and useful for a long time." That Sherwood wrote to Cornelia about Earl's illness is testimony of the shock he felt.

221

To Bab — March 1926[1] [New Orleans]

Grey days drifting past. My brother in the hospital in New York gets better slowly. Karl will take him to his place in Connetticut[2] in a few weeks. As soon as he can come I will take him to the farm.

For a week before, during and after the Carnival the weather here was delicious. Then came rain and the grey days.

There is an invasion of people—women and men. They come at the time—day or night. Few of them think of a man as wanting quiet for his own work. They are absorbed in themselves—demand, demand, demand.

I work as steadily as I can—not being quite sure of what I do. Then days come when the veil lifts. I throw out what seems bad, not fully funtioned.

The year has been hard on my poor body—first a rather full year of work and then the long months of meeting people—thousands. I am recovering from that slowly. When I am fully recovered and can get a look back I shall know more about it.

Just now I am a stream almost dry—a thin trickly of the water of real living and feeling running down among grey stones.

LH

1. Hahn's longhand note.

2. Westport, Conn., where Karl had established a home and studio that he lived in until his death in 1956.

222

To Bab March 1926[1] [New Orleans]

My battle with teeth still goes on. There will be some three or four more sessions. Anyway I have been working again. That is a satisfactions anyway.

Edmond Wilson[2] has been here from New York. He is a likable man, very much the intellectual. It is amazing how these men can walk about seeing little. They go instinctively to books. Everything must be got at second hand. In this man there is a kind of sweetness.

In a magazine called Success a long interview with me not one word of which is true.[3] What is one to do. It shames me to see such stuff put out as authentic. Sometimes I think I will make a rule never to see reporters, particularly the women. Why they are worse I can't say. They are.

I remain ancious about poor Earl. Not being near him I constantly imagain things. What a strange life he has had. It will be good to have him near at hand. Thank Heavens I am to have the little farm.[4] It will be a place where he can live the rest of his life if he wishes. I hate to think of you off there in a strange hotel. Do you not know some people. You will get unbearbly lonesome. Do go to some place where you have friends.

What a muddled thing life is, almost unbearable sometimes. I must be rather shallow. Give me a sunshiny day, a story to work on and I think life is fascinating. It isn't surely, not to most people.

I trust everyone too much. Think people mean what they say. They do perhaps. So often we are not thinking the same kind of thing. I am thinking of the people who invade me these days, of young girl reporters. One wants so much more sophistocation, the kind of thing I think of as having come to you.

The new novel[5] forms slowly in my mind as I work on the Childhood.

With Love.

TS

1. Hahn's longhand note.
2. Edmund Wilson (1895–1972), American critic and novelist.
3. The article was "Sherwood Anderson Tells His Life Story" (evidently part of an "Adventures in Life" series), *Success*, (Mar. 1926) 55, 109–11. See Appendix B.
4. He had written Earl on Feb. 22 of his plans to move to Virginia on May 1.
5. Probably the abortive *Another Man's House*. See letter 221 .

223

To Bab March 1926[1] [New Orleans]

Later—

A note enclose[d] written several days
ago. How broken. I have been driven—worry about poor
broken Earl—dreaming of him at night—

Trying to work—to make plans.

People invade me as never before. Silly women bring
flowers to my door—write me notes.

The phone rings constantly.

One has to be rude and I hate rudeness.

I'll be so glad for the escape to the country.

I cling to the old tried loves. Bless you

LH

1. Hahn's longhand note.

224

To Bab [New Orleans]

Just a hurried note. Yours just came. Have written you two or three letters—Indianapolis. Had just finished a note to you when your's came. Remember the wide low places in that country. You'll fit in soon—find people. I hope you may be writing a little.

So many things to tell you. When I see you I don't talk. So many thing[s] will never get told—

LH

225

To Bab March 1926[1] [New Orleans]

A bright warm morning after a week of cold biting days huddled over a fire.

Had to have a lot of dental work done. It ate up my nerves—none too good just now.

However I begin to get my nerve force back. This week I suddenly wrote three testaments in the New Testament Book.[2] This has happened before in a year or two.

The beginning of poetry in me is always also the beginning of a kind of spring—things growing again.

Have bought a few things for my cabin in the country—a swinging ship's lamp—an old corner cupboard—a chair or two.

I need the escape the country will bring me. What a price must be paid for this—so-called fame. What nonsense.

People have this strange notion—a moment of contact. Some want only to go away—talk of knowing you. You know that kind.

There are others who really think a moment, a word will set their twisted life straight.

I cannot risist seeing people answering letters. There is a kind of deadly insult to the spirit involved in not answering, not seeing. Its all a false hope but what can one do.

People want so much. They are stupid. Well, what is to be done about stupidity.

Escape to the country. I know of nothing else.

I begin to have hope that the New Testament may complete itself. I want that very much.

LH

1. Hahn's longhand note.

2. Anderson had been working on and publishing segments of *A New Testament* since 1919. This book was published in 1927.

226

To Bab [New Orleans]

For so long I had been quite separated from it and then, this year, I got back into it again.

It isn't that I want to escape. I have no desire for an Ivory Tower.

I am thinking only of how deeply imbedded in life is the thought of money—how it destroys relationships, kills beauty.

One has to keep a semblance of sense.

I have been rereading proofs of the Notebook.[1] It is not a large book. Some day I shall do a more complete one. It is fragmentary.

An odd mistake. You spoke of the story Broken. I thought it was in Horses and Men but looked and it wasn't. Then I put it in this book. Last night I discovered it. It is in Horses and Men as the second part of the story—"A Chicago Hamlet."[2]

Now that the notebook—for better or worse—is off my hands I shall go back to the Childhood.[3] It needs to be inked in a lot.

To tell the truth—after my long trip I was in no mood for new impressions. I wanted to get back to my desk—away from people—walk again on the levee—hear the niggers laugh.

One gets fame and what a pest it is. Back of all this crowding and pushing is a real desire for love—in people—I am sure of that.

But what a perverted thing. How ugly it gets.

You must know that during these last two years you—by your practical help—have saved me weeks and months of worry.[4] Why you care to do it—why anyone cares to love me I can't make out—most of the time.

A whirl at the Childhood now and then for the novel.[5] I look forward to that.

When you go to Mexico let me know the time and the route. I can't tell the mechanics of my own life definitely now—but I'll be here—I'm sure.[6]

LH

1. *Sherwood Anderson's Notebook* was published in mid-1926 and was dedicated jointly to "Two Friends/ M.D.F./ and/ John Emerson." Anderson gave Finley one of his author's copies of a special edition of 225 "numbered and signed copies." Signing his name on the leaf opposite the title page, he signed again on the page inside the cover: "To/ Marietta Finley/ with Love Sherwood Anderson." Hahn gave me this copy in 1962, inscribing on this same page that it was from the "M.D.F. to whom this book was dedicated along with John Emerson." It is now in the possession of Dr. Welford Taylor of the Sherwood Anderson Society, University of Richmond, Virginia.

2. Evidently it was at this juncture that he decided not to put the story that appears as "Part Two" of "A Chicago Hamlet" of *Horses and Men* in the *Notebook*.

3. *Tar*.

4. Additional evidence of Finley's financial assistance.

5. Probably the aborted *Another Man's House*.

6. This letter could not be dated more definitely than "early 1926."

227

To Bab March 1926[1] [New Orleans]

The clutter of dark red pepers came yesterday and are now decorating the heavy green shutter of the room where I work. The color dominates the entire court—a marvelous splash. It brings something of the clear light and sunshine of New Mexico. As soon as they came the long rain of several days broke and today all is clear and bright.

A touch of color in the air too.

Edmond Wilson has been here for three or four weeks—strange man. You have met men like him. All his reactions from life are got from books. Nothing comes to him direct. Such a man is a constant wonder to me.

Well, he wants to be taken to the river. You take him. He sees nothing, is absorbed in a discussion of Conrad[2] and the sea as it is in Conrad. Later sometime he will read something about the Mississippe and will get it in his own way, through the mind of another.

He is striving not to be so. It is his dream not to be so. We talk about it sometimes as we walk. He envies me.

It is quite true I am to be envied in this respect. As we walk the negro stevedore, the night watchman on the docks, the polot on the river boat, the street car conductor—all these smile and nod at me. They feel something of themselves in me. I feel something of my self in them.

Yesterday I got through the page proofs of the book. It seemed better than at first. Perhaps I am gradually growing less tired. I work again quite consistently. Yesterday i had ten hours at my desk. That is too much but it was a special day. Suddenly I had caught just the mood and the background I have wanted for the novel—another man's house. I wanted to get enough of it down to have it hold. Think I did.

It is good to have the splash of red. It makes me think of you in the warm sunlight—in the clear light.

Do be good to yourself. Let yourself rest thoroughly.

TS

1. Hahn's longhand note.
2. Joseph Conrad (1857-1924).

228

To Bab March 29, 1926[1] [New Orleans]

Rain drops—scattered—on the bricks in the court. My brother Irwin from Baltimore is here.[2] A large man—very silent man. He has been a factory superintendent all his life—working for a big trust. Has done his job extra-ordinarily well—a driver—no mercy on himself or others.

He hasn't made much money but has a great reputation.

Now his nerves have gone back on him and he has few resources. In no sense a reflective man he is quite helpless.

In the presence of his silent misery—the fear—I must seem to him a laughing child.

Just why he has come to me I don't know. He seems to think I can help.

First Earl and now Irve. Beside them I seem strong and always before Irve has seemed so strong.

All these people with their subtile demands and I seem helpless.

I give little enough—to you—to them—to anyone.

I have to live immediately. There is no other way.

And in the midst of it to try to work.

Well I do work some. My work loosened up—became somewhat slack. I was tired. My grip slackened.

Now it tightens again.

Dear woman—when the situation becomes too hard for you let me go. You know what I mean.

You'll always be the same to me—one who has really helped—who is fine.

LH

1. Hahn's longhand note.

2. An executive for the American Can Company in Baltimore, Irwin Anderson had only a peripheral relationship with his brother. Irwin's daughter, Dorothy H. Kinney, has written (in a letter to me, Apr. 11, 1975): "Our families were far from close—only due I am certain to the fact that we were not inclined to be letter-writers. I have no recollection of my Father visiting Sherwood in New Orleans. I know he did visit his Brother, Karl Anderson, the artist, for a couple of months during a sickness he had. I went with him on this visit, at my request. . . . My Father was a tall good looking fellow with laughing brown eyes. I would not say he was a quiet man, rather a serious man pertaining to business but a fair man with high standards and fun to be around, with many friends. He had quite a good sense of humor, but expected us to do what was right. He was foremost a family man and we all admired and adored him, and secondary a business man. . . . My Mother, who I am certain was prejudiced, also claimed that if my Father had had the opportunity to go on his own that he had more talent than either Sherwood or Karl. . . . My Father would make up funny little poems for us children. I remember mine was

> 'There was a girl named Dorothy Helen
> With a heart as big as a melon
> But lacking forsooth
> When she lost her first tooth,
> You would have thought it was a calliope yelling.'"

229

To Bab

April 5, 1926[1] [New Orleans]
Sunday Morning

A long sheaf of poetry written by a Frenchman in English—no real feeling for the language. He is living over here, wants to be one of us. Sticks packed to ship.[2] When you write again after this write to Troutadale Va. I get stadily along into the novel,[3] write at every odd moment. I write in a new mood for me. Acceptance. Something that has happened to all of us these last few years. It may be because we are older. That has its dramatic value also. Not to want escape from anything, people, flesh, our towns, streets, houses, ourselves. Sometimes I think—just to accept a little dog trotting at my heels. Accept women trees skies places. Flesh is flesh, it hungers always. To acceot the hunger also.

You see what I am doing, trying to get to you brief telegraphic bits of my days of thought feeling.

Poor Ealr is worse again has had to go back to the hospital. Bob comes with a poem, a young man lying in the sun, his hairless chest, youth. Sweetly glad of that. If he is to write he will have to escape [me; letters typed over], be something sharply different.

I really hunger now for the hills, my own cabin, a long summer of work. I am well. After a period like this I shall have p riod of depression. The pace is fast at such times. I am like a horse prepared for a race. I run the race and must rest later. Now I am in the race.

Write me briefly when you can how you are feeling, what you are thinking.

TS

1. Hahn's longhand note.
2. To Virginia.
3. Presumably *Another Man's House*.

230

To Bab April 1926[1] [New Orleans]

A new tone in my mail this year. I receive few abusive letters. Daily the letters come dropping in. Long letters come. Women are unconsciously tired of their lovers. They want to tell you but can't quite. The pages are written about little details of family life.

Often it is stilted, strange.

Young men writing, wanting always a key to life.

Women who cannot find lovers.

How lustful I must have been.

Have I approached all these people—through words, making words touch them like fingers at night?

The absolute desire—contact—love making.

That is altogether secondary.

If it were not so I would not be an artist.

These people have a desire that all emotion—feeling—be centered—if but for a moment—in themselves.

A young man offered to come here from Detroit—if I would give him a ½ hour.

Thank God I could laugh. You see why I want the country.

LH

1. Hahn's longhand note.

231

To Bab April 1926[1] [New Orleans]

Just a note—on a grey morning. I have got through the Childhood[2] and at once plunged into the novel. The theme fastinates me. I am drawing, in it, from my years as a business man, advertising writer etc. A wealth of materials I have never touched before.

I am going back to an olkder caracter—Talbot Whittingham for my man. He will be an odd mixture. It is good to feel the leisure of a long summer for him.

My brother Earl has been mover out to Karl's house; at Westport Conn. Irwin is still here—getting better. A strange man, one of the vitims of the industrail age come home to my house. The man also, inside, I'm quite sure wanted to be an artist.

I have been having a long session with my tooth but it is at an end. I am well. I write all morning and in the afternoon work on some sort of amusing foolishness. Just now I am making and decoration picture frames. The days goes like birds across the grey sky when I am working so. I get into a sort of vacuim of life. My own life doesn't exist much.

It may not last long. I am thankful while it does last.

TS

1. Hahn's longhand note.

2. The references here and in the preceding letters are to *Another Man's House*, an unsuccessful effort, the manuscript for which disappeared. See Anderson to Horace Liveright, Apr. 19, 1926, in Jones and Rideout, eds., *Letters of Sherwood Anderson*, for a discussion of Anderson's intentions regarding this novel.

232

To Bab

April, 1926[1] [New Orleans]

If I havn't written you it is because I have really been at work. How silly to call it work. I mean only that I have been writing. The caracter of the man of ANOTHER MAN'S HOUSE forming itself within. Putting words down. Tearing up. At it again.

At such times I cannot read. Well I can't sit at a typewriter all the time. Association with people isn't much good. Too many people irritate me at such times. I havn't much to give.

A woman in love with me should not be irritated that I love other women. They do not take so much of me. This is what takes me. For this i dare say I would sacrifice all woman, everyone.

Why. I don't know.

When I cannot work nothing satisfoes me but doing things with my hands. I go to a store and buy old picture frames so I may work at res[t]oring them. I dabble in paint, paint chares and picture frames. I wish I knew how to sew. I would make dresses for women suits of clothes for me.

All people have their moments of beauty. It may be that T[ennessee] was very beautiful when you saw her. Perhaps the beauty was in you. Another standing by and seeing you might have thought what you thought of her.

You see how little I have to give. Even as I write I see the other sheets lying beside my machine. Ordinarily I am a good letter writtr. Now a great pile of letters lie here beside my machine unanswered.

I comfort myself by telling myself it is all but another manifestation of love.

TS

1. Hahn's longhand note.

233

To Bab

April 1926[1] [New Orleans]

My brother Earl was getting on fine and had begun to walk about. Now he has had a second set-back and is in the hospital again. I have got into the novel.[2] There is a kind of real truth in it and a lot of rather bitter plainness. All is in the air yet.

Packing is going on for moving to the farm. Last night was our first hot night this year. I went out to walk. It is well I do not have to put in another summer here.[3]

A novel like this sometimes has to make several starts. There is the mood, the tune, the rhythm of the whole. Do the people who have walked in belong to the rhythm. Often they do not. Well, they are interesting. Are you to go on with them or the theme. A decision must be made or the book ruined. Often coming to a decision involves throwing away weeks of work. IT must be done.

My little workroom here is quite bare. However there is one waiting in the mountains.

Last week I stumbled onto a painting, all out of repair. I got it cheap. There is a clipper ship in full sail over a cold blue ocean. The ocean and ship are both marveleously painted. It is just what I want for my testament—I mean the swing and rhythm of it. I shall put it up in the cabin in the mountains.

Bob would quite win your heart. He has pitched into his work and had got two raises. His room is charming. Yesterday he brought me a poem with real feeling in it—about a young boy lying in the sun and thinking of his own body. He will be a nice man and perhaps in the end a talented one.[4]

These days I could write ten thousand words a day if my nearves stood up to it. It is like running a race. If you run too far today you cannot run at all tomorrow. We men are like race horses, have to be more or less in order, in training.

Soon spring now. In the court here the Chinaberry tree is putting out bloom. It has been a cold wet spring for New Orleans. That makes the roses bloom as I have never seen them bloom down here.

The tradegy of Earl has I think drawn me, my brother Karl and Irve at Baltimore close in a way nothing else could.

I am just now a queer impersonal thing, living in others. You, for example flit back and forth through my mind a dozen times each day. Everything is much alive.

TS

1. Hahn's longhand note.

2. *Another Man's House.*

3. This and other references to Anderson's anticipation of leaving New Orleans give the lie to an impression in the minds of his friends on the *Double Dealer* who believed that "at last, his money gone, Anderson had to go back to Chicago to earn a living." See "The French Quarter's Golden Era. Young Writers Who Worked Together for Fun in the 1920s in New Orleans Are Famous Names To-

day," *Dixie*, Feb. 15, 1959. Anderson could hardly have let people think that he was returning to Chicago when he was telling interviewers in his lecture tour about his farm in Virginia.

4. Anderson had difficulty in accepting his son Bob, and Bob's final attitude toward his father was one of unhappiness. When Eleanor Anderson introduced me to Bob in 1946 (Bob was in the office of the Anderson papers in Marion), he declared, "I have nothing whatever to say about my father." In a letter of Mar. 8, 1974, Bob's widow referred to her "own bitterness," saying she felt Anderson had been unfair to both Cornelia and Bob in the letters published in 1952. She felt perhaps the references to the children in the Hahn letters "indicate more feeling than he really had. He knew Bab loved and financed them—especially Bob—and he wrote with that in mind."

234

To Bab [After May 1, 1926 Troutdale, Va.][1]

Your letter came yesterday. I have just spread new grass seed over the bit of ground on the hill where my cabin stands and the rain that came afterward may help it get a start. Now all the work is done on the cabin and my furniture and books are here.

Such a wide spread of coutry, mountains and valleys before me. All day the shadows of clouds play over the hills. The dogwood, flowering ivy and many little woods flowers are out.

Today, Sunday afternoon, there is a roaring wind over the hill and being up here is like being in a ship in a storm. The cabin however is unmoved, being very heavily built in good cou[n]try style.

Of course I would enjoy having the skin to lie on the floor before my fire but do not send it dear. You have already done too much for me. How do you know that, a year from now, you will [not] have just the place for it yourself.

I work away at the novel.[2]

About the people here, they are much what coutry people are everywhere—a little more primitive, rude, violent. The man who prepared the ground for the grass at my cabin door has killed his man. They all go in strong for religion—of the rude emotional sort. As for their own lived, in their own houses, it is primitive in a way you would hardly believe. Among them, of course, many sweet kind gentle cretures. I shall know more about them slowly, of course.

I think much of you dear friend, of what you are doing and have done for me, of the lonliness of your life. You have done something wonderful with yourself. That is a comforting thought.

TS

1. The move from New Orleans to the farm at Troutdale seems to have taken place as scheduled.
2. *Another Man's House.*

235

To Bab May 1926[1] [Troutdale, Va.]

I think of little but writing. This will be a strange intense novel[2]—if it comes off. I am almost prayerful about it.

A cabin
C stream
B house

Back of my cabin—at (A)—forests. Great trees. From the cabin you look away over the hills "D" "E" & "F" to distant hill[s] all tree clad.[3] Everything just coming into bloom. In the cabin all my books—a view to take the breath.

Wish I could tell you more of the novel. I hardly dare speak of it. The mood may break.

The theme is so delicate—so hard to keep in hand. Putting it on paper is like trying to transplant a very delicate bush. You stand anciousaly aside. Will it live—put forth bloom.

Or—transplanted thus from the dim world of imagination to words—will it die.

I'm happy—anyway having it inside myself. I[t] can be far and away the most subtile and comprehensive thing I've ever tried to do.

If there is something in the Notebook[4]—I'm glad. It is beautifully made.

In this beautiful place I should do something worthwhile. If I don't its my own fault. You have helped more than you know to make it a possibility.

LH

1. Hahn's longhand note.
2. *Another Man's House.*
3. This is now known as Ripshin Farm.
4. *Sherwood Anderson's Notebook.*

236

To Bab May 24, 1926[1] [Troutdale, Va.]

A note—as you see—misdirected. I am writing every day until I am so exhausted my hands tremble.

Then I go sit in the woods.

It is the novel—Another Man's House.

LH

1. Hahn's longhand note.

237

To Bab May 1926[1] [Troutdale, Va.]

Such a keen satisfaction to find something really well done. My cabin—on top of a mountain, near a spring, is beautifully built. Would stand hundreds of years—I'm sure. One of the builders—a descendent of old Daniel Boone. Great square log—solid stone foundations—a great stone chimney.

A view off over stretches of mountains. Just now the world alive with new bloom. I am looking forward to a long summer of peaceful work—a new novel[2] achieved.

LH

1. Hahn's longhand note.
2. *Another Man's House.*

238

To Bab May 1926[1] [Troutdale, Va.]

Mist hanging over the mountains. I am at work. A mountain man is sowing grass seed before the door of my cabin. He killed a man five years ago—in a drunken quarrel. I find him sweet and gentle.

All the mountain men are curious. They come to visit. I like them and think they will like me.

The novel[2] is in that strange uncertain state—I am really like a woman, newly pregnant, I fancy.

I think of you often. Wonder how the days go with you.

LH

1. Hahn's longhand note.
2. *Another Man's House.*

239

To Bab May 1926[1]

You become absorbed in the things of nature—the grass growing, trees in bud, then putting forth the first little hard nipples that are to become rounded fruit.

The insects that destroy, wild flowers, weeds. Trees become individuals.

How all important whether or not it rains.

I have written a short story of an old woman's death alone in the woods.[2]

How hard and close to the ground the lives of people. One trying a little to see into lives.

The hill opposite my cabin has such sensual lines that I should think a puritan would want it clothed.

There is a period, between early spring planting and working the crops when the neighbors have little to do. Some go into the woods to get out firewood or tan bark. Others get drunk.

On cold days I have a little fire. I have many little talks with you of which you know nothing.

LH Written on the stationery of Ripshin Farm, Grant and Troutdale, Va.

1. Mrs. Hahn's longhand note.
2. The story is "Death in the Woods," which Anderson later said he had been trying to write for fifteen years.

240

To Bab June 1926[1]

The organization of a novel—all those lives—a little city of lives—is exhausting.

Yesterday I wrote until I was so exhausted I could hardly get up from my chair.

Shall I try to tell you what I wrote. To do so would be to try to do it all again. Such a simple series of events and yet the caracter of a man forming under my hand.

A roaring wind blowing. There is a field of young wheat on a nearby hillside. The wind plays in it.

I am tired like a woman in pregnacy. Tomorrow I shall be rested & write again—I hope.

LH Written on the stationery of Ripshin Farm, Grant and Troutdale, Va.

1. Hahn's longhand note.

241

To Bab June, 1926[1] [Troutdale, Va.]

You would never dream what may be done in such a country as this. It takes me back to my boyhood. Here, in these mountains labor still may be had at 12¢ to 15¢ the hour. Semi-skilled labor 20¢.

I am getting most of the stone for the walls of my house in this section. They come from the creek bed—from along the road.

Just now bright moonlit nights. Last night I went to walk through the forest. A fairyland—the narrow road through the mountain forests. The moon went behing a cloud. All was dark, It came back slowly. Light creeping along hillsides, through a rye field, into the forest. The ground in the forest paterned like a carpet.

The builders build slowly. Solidly, in the country fashion. The neighbors send little presents, wild strawberries, cherries.

It is a wonder to them to have a writer here. Men come to sit in my cabin. They are honest and simple. An old woman shook her head. "I'm

afraid you came to the wrong place to write books. You can't sell them here. We never buy books—have no money. Lots of us cannot read.["]
Love

LH

1. Hahn's longhand note.

242

To Bab June 1926[1]

Its odd how minds run—a note from Fred O'Brien—Rome—all about Ellis[2]—one from Paris—the same week—same subject—yours after a river trip—one from a man in California.

The man has something very definate and real for we moderns. For a time I thought him too much the preacher.

Have been intending to ask you for a long time your reactions to Sandburg's Lincoln.[3] The book struck me as plain dull—say after Stevenson. I couldn't wade through. Is he heavy-minded—too serious about himself. I have a kind of notion of an animal craftiness about the man—foxiness.

After all we want more delicacy—subtility.

Amy Lowell's Keats[4] on the other hand strikes me as solid and fine. Someone gave it to me.

Poor old Stieglitz in New York in a hospital. My paralysed brother no better.

A long sweet letter from Paul[5]—at last. He is touched deeply by the Notebook—apparently.

As for the river[6]—nights on it, days on it. There has been song in it for me. Living on it something got into me. I'm going back to New Orleans later—more of it.

Hemingway did a book[7] to satirizing Dark Laughter. He wrote me a long letter rather patronizing.[8] "I hate to hit you but I must." That sort of thing. As though I hadn't the power to hit if I were so minded. I'm not. Got my fill of hitting long ago. The satire—if you see it—I think you will agree didn't come off. Heavy and dull. Benchley in "Life," "December," did it brilliantly.[9]

The Childhood[10] goes off—as a book, this week. I think it has charm. I have done some short things and will do more but my steady diet the rest of the summer will be another man's house.

I am waiting to get some descent snaps of my work cabin to send you.

Sent you a copy—the delux etc.—Notebook.
You know I always love you.

LH

1. Hahn's longhand note.
2. Presumably Havelock Ellis (1859-1939), author of *The Dance of Life* (1923) and a pioneer in the factual discussion of sex.
3. Carl Sandburg's *Abraham Lincoln: The Prairie Years* was published in June 1926.
4. Amy Lowell's *John Keats* was published in 1925.
5. Paul Rosenfeld, who went to Troutdale for a week's visit in mid-July.
6. Doubtless the Mississippi.
7. Ernest Hemingway's *Torrents of Spring* was published in June 1926.
8. Anderson had helped Hemingway get published and had given him a letter of introduction to Gertrude Stein when Hemingway went to Paris. Hemingway's letter seems to indicate he had to declare his independence by attacking his benefactor, a pattern seen in Hemingway's relations with Stein and others.
9. Hemingway's *Torrents of Spring* was ineffective, but Robert Benchley's "A Ghost Story (As Sherwood Anderson Would Write It If He Weren't Prevented)," *Life*, 86 (Dec. 3, 1925), 21, 64, is hardly brilliant. Anderson realized that these—and other—parodies were signs of interest in him and his writing.
10. *Tar*.

243

To Bab July 1926[1] [Troutdale, Va.]

The robe came by mail yesterday. I have had the carpenter at work today making me a low box couch to sit by the fire. I shall spread the robe over it. For a long time I have wanted just such a place to lie down when I am weary from long seiges of writing.

But how elegant. It has just that extra look of undeserved luxury I so love.

I got me a dog—an English setter—from a negro—a handsome beast (I mean the dog) and he will I am afraid fight me for the couch. It was simply charming of you—like you too.

The novel[2] seems to flow. O, for strength to sit more hours at the desk. It is a delicate theme—so nicely balanced—if I can only handle it as it deserves.

I want to tell you all about it but am half afraid to talk of it for fear the charm breaks.

Also I have driven the pen today until my arms and shoulders ache.

Such tales here in these hills too. I am sure I shall do a book called "Mountain Men"[3]—one of these days.

Paul Rosenfeld is coming here to me Saturday—after such a long time not seeing or talking to him. The thought is exciting. It should be great fun.

Again—

But how can I ever thank you. You are always too good to me.

With Love

LH

1. Hahn's longhand note.
2. *Another Man's House.*
3. An unfulfilled project.

244

To Bab July 1926[1] [Troutdale, Va.]

A strange week. Paul[2] has been here 4 days. He has come to a kind of parting of the ways.

The man thought—hoped—he could live in other artists—something like that. It is I am sure something women can do. You do it—really—although always with a struggle.

Now Paul wants to free his own fancy—let it create in the world of men and materials.

It will go hard and slow. He writes with painful exactness—has the faculty of self-critisism developed to the point where it almost stops him dead.

He works all day on two or three paragraphs. If they do not come clear he is hopeless. Then irritated.

I have taken away a couch that did not belong in the cabin.  —This sort. Had the carpenter make a bed box —of oak—on that springs from a cot—then a mattress—then the lovely skin.

It is so placed that I can lie looking at the hills.

Paul comes up the hills. With all such men I have to be extra careful. Suppose I have written a scene—a negro woman running through low cane—a cane knife in hand—toward distant swamps.

Careful now. This nervous irritable man may have had a morning of failure.

All people in close relationships gain and loose. You might cease loving me in a week if you were near me.

We talk of Brooks, Hemingway, Joyce—others.

Brooks has been near a nervous breakdown. His philosophy has gone to pieces. He sit [set] himself to prove something—that an artist cannot live in America.

What a strange perversion. How we all twist away from self.

Live so passionately in self too.

Warm rains—the forest lush with trees and grass—the corn growing in the valleys.

I am working. Like you and all people I am full of nameless hungers. My mail—from other artists grows enormous.

LH

1. Hahn's longhand note.
2. Rosenfeld.

245

To Bab July—1926[1] [Troutdale, Va.]

It rained hard all night. I have made a small lawn before my cabin. When I sowed the grass I mixed in 2 or 3 dozen packs of flowers. They are beginning to bloom. Yellow poppies scattered everywhere about the door this morning.

The letter did not offend me dear. It hurts always than I cannot give more. I think if you knew how much I have taken you as part of my life. Still there would always be the same thing.

If you lived with me, the same.

I am committed to the world of fancy. Am gone off into it for long periods.

What is real and what unreal in thoughts, moods, people, nature, I cannot tell.

Facts elude me. Truth is lost.

It does not altogether matter. Something real remains. I am pretty sure I will go to New York in September—if you are to be gone a long time.

There is 2 months yet. Paul has been wonderful. He brought me a delicious painting.

LH

1. Hahn's longhand note.

246

To Bab July 1926[1] [Troutdale, Va.]

Just a note. Cool nights. There have been slow [?] days.

A note from my brother Karl. He has succeeded in getting Earl into a Government Hospital—(because of his having been a soldier in the World War).

All this time he has been in the hospital—Karl and I paying of course. He has had three strokes now. The doctors say he cannot get well—may go anytime.

It has all been rather on Karl's hands—the terrible physical part of it I mean.

I should have gone [to] help bear the physical immediacy of it. Every day I told myself I would—know[ing] deep down in me I wouldn't.

I have been working—the words running like little rabbits. Im out to make the little rabbit words into an army—a novel.[2]

You—all who know and care for me—have to accept something. The logical cruel cruelty of the workman.

The words, at times, command me. You are dying, there is a railroad wreck—storms.

If I come away the rabbit words will never march.

I make excuses, lie, I am myself.

I tell you because it is true.

I do not excuse myself.

Now I am too old to change.

Will anyone—not an artist—ever quite understand the perplexity of all this.

Well, why talk of it.

Your letter did not offend me. I accept you too—as I do myself. When I saw you last you had suddenly grown infinately more real—healthy.

To tell the truth I do not think marriage or lack of marriage makes the difference you women think.

Still, it may be to you what his work is to the workman.
Anyway, you're all right.

LH

1. Hahn's longhand note.
2. Another reference to *Another Man's House.*

247

To Bab July 1926[1] [Troutdale, Va.]

I get it—in fancy in the shape of a God. A twisted thing but with curious, lovely lines. [Hahn note: Re remodelling of my living-room at 614 East 32nd.]

After I read your last letter I went down to the creek. Ezra was there at work. He is a curious still, childish old young man who once killed another man.

His wife came later—a dumb sluttish kind of woman, almost blind.

Ezra with depths—stillnesses.

I watched him.

Acceptance—of the sluttish wife, his own narrow life, his hand, the water of the creek, flowers, people.

Later I went and wrote a story I called "Not Today."[2]

It was about why a particular man and woman couldn't—wanting to.

It was because something started wrong. Their association—their love for each other grew in a world of fancy.

When they tried to bring it into the world of fact something got killed.

They did and something did get killed.

I do not remember now whether I wrote it that way or the other. It does not matter. I am very tired this morning. Writing a long time. At work inside me when my arms ached, putting words down.

What I started to say was that there is unsoundness in your logic when you lift what we are to each other over into the world of fact. That—for us—was settled long ago. I don't know why.

The actual is a violation.

I don't know why that is true either.

It just is.

When you try to bring it over the line—in letters etc. I understand. That is a part of you.

It isn't the fact of you in relation to us—thats all.

Water is not air—trees, hands, people. I know because you are one related to my work. To myself you are not so related.

I mean to the world of fancy.

You can't be hands and water running.

When you—being water running become hands you are not hands—and not lovely.

Its just a fact to me.

I don't know why.

When you—being water running become in fancy hands—talk as hands you are not lovely.

I don't know why.

John is here—he's a quiet conscious one.

Robert is more like you.

Robert is related more to one side of me than John.

John to one side of me than Robert.

Robert is more difficult.

I love them both in two ways.

LH

1. Hahn's longhand note.
2. Never published.

248

To Bab July 1926[1] [Troutdale, Va.]

A grey low-hanging mist over the hills. Yesterday, at last a light rain came breaking the long hot time that reached us even into these hills.

Yellow dust—thick in the roads. A hot yellow stillness.

Many springs have gone dry.

We have had to go down at night and bathe in the creek. There is a place among the stones—a kind of natural bath tub.

The difference between John and Robert almost unbelievable. John still and quiet—wise—big of body—conscious of people.

He is uncertain what he wants to be. That is natural at his age. He lets himself live and be.

Robert—self-conscious—not really nice to anyone because, being so self-conscious he hasn't much time to think of others.

Almost every act—every speech—for effect. The effect not achieved. Baffled.

Being alone has made him worse again.

At the bottom sweetness.

My heart aches for him—to think what his life will be like if he does not get some kind of inner peace.

It is a rest to be with John—a job to be with Bob.

I drive on. Getting work done, my house built.

The hills are like little brothers. The sky is close.

I have been writing, poems, short stories, articles, a novel.

Every moment of every day crowded.

LH

1. Hahn's longhand note.

249

To Bab Aug. 1926 [1] [Troutdale, Va.]

I have written to you several times. The letters seem too dreadfully impersonal. My brothers—Karl and Irwin are here. The experience with my sick brother Earl—and John were tremendous. Love sweeping over me.

The beauty of Earl—whose life has been so terrible. My mood is close to poetry. Something these days out of earth sky and ground I can't explain.

Going to Europe is in the air. I shall have to earn the money. I have been trying to get a home and get it paid for. Then I shall be free [of] half the heavy cost of living. I think John can earn enough to have 400 to 500 of his own in the fall. I will, in some way, manage the rest.

Mixed with all the rest the feeling my brothers give me of futility. It isn't fair. Life is life. One expects too much.

Poor broken Earl—his life—outwardly—most futile is satisfying completely.

LH

1. Hahn's longhand note.

250

To Bab August 1926[1] [Troutdale, Va.]

The boys have kept me fairly jumping. John is lovely. He has a charming personality. You'll see.

I work and work. One of these days the slump will come but something will have been done.

Poor Earl—my sick brother is low. I may have to go to him next week and so may not be here until Aug. 15th. My brother Irve is half sick too. More and more their lives center about myself. I can do little to help anyone. May go Monday.

LH

1. Hahn's longhand note.

251

To Bab Aug. 16, 1926[1] [Troutdale, Va.]
Sunday Morning

I have just got back from New York—tired—in 3 days a thousand things to do—no sleep.[2]

A terrific experience. Went to Newport to my paralysed brother. He is I think the most beautiful man I ever saw. I think I loved him in that half day more than I have ever loved.

He is the truest finest poet I have ever seen. I want only the chance now to give him a few lovely moments, a few lovely things before he dies.

I can't write more. God does not exist in the physical world—He exists only in the world of the imagination—in the poets world. Its enough. Thats where he should exist. . . .[3]

LH

1. Hahn's longhand note.
2. On Sept. 6, he wrote to Burton Emmett, with whom he had been corresponding since May but whom he had yet to meet in New York: "Was in New York a day—two weeks ago—to see a sick brother. Had to come right back." Sutton Collection.
3. The last line of the page has partially disintegrated. Only "with love" remains.

252

To Bab September 1926[1] [Troutdale, Va.]

The early morning light is on the hills. It is six-thirty. Often I get up at daybreak and come up here to work. What a summer.

At least I will have achieved something in the stone house. I am building it at a surprising low cost. Most of the men are not skilled—mountainmen, small farmers, moonshiners. They get drunk, fight among themselves, work for me.

I have had to hold them all in my hand.

And the renewal of direct intimate contact with my own family.

You are right. I have been in a terrible slump. I am however emerging.

Karl is however here. For years he has wanted to do a portrait. It is just begun. He is a slow workman.[2]

Next week Charles Connick[3] is coming from Boston. That is a long story.

It seems impossible that I should come to see you before you leave.

My own European trip is largely moonshine. There won't be money enough unless something unusual happens.

Still I'll probable manage. I want to do it principally for John—whom I love. Things do come about.

And Frank Dazey[?][4] is coming from New York.

You see dear it is too great a tangle.

Of course he is doing the portrait for himself. Dazey & Connick come about their own matters.

It can't be helped I'm afraid. The devil.

I have a desire to do another book of notes.[5] I shall address them to you. So many things needing running comment.

LH

1. Hahn's longhand note.

2. This portrait of Sherwood, Irwin, and Earl Anderson is in the Yale University Art Gallery, New Haven, Conn. It features a slightly larger figure of Sherwood, seated in the center; seated also to Sherwood's right, is Irwin. Behind Sherwood and to his left, with most of his body obscured by Sherwood's and looking moody, in profile, is Earl. See Jones and Rideout, eds., *Letters of Sherwood Anderson*, opposite p. 152, for a reproduction of the portrait.

3. Charles J. Connick (1875-1945), a designer of stained and leaded glass; how the two men met is not known.

4. Not identified.

5. Another unfulfilled project.

253

To Bab September 1926[1] [Troutdale, Va.]

At any rate I am building permanently. Everything is as solid as country ingenuety can make it. The old builder, named Marion Ball is nearly sixty five. A solid old man who began life as what is known in this country as, "a Buck Mountain Moonshiner." The man is a naural builder—really an artist. You cannot get him to slight anything. Everything is heavy. Already the house looks as though it had grown out of the ground. I think every man should have this experience once. In the end I shall get a book out of it.[2] Everything excites me. I learn the nems of the parts of a house. Lovely words. A worthless man comes to work and I discharge him. He threatens me. The others stand aside to see what will happen. A new look at life—through the eyes of these simple men. I must be ready to knock a man down if that is necessary. It is not necessary. The man sees I am not afraid and that ends it. People try to cheat. The man who brings me wood for my fire tries to get the best of me. If he cannot I see the respect grow in his eyes. There is a simple code—the early American code. These men are close to the soil. Every man must look out for himself. Back of it all real friendliness. "If you can take care of yourself I respect and like you."

The women in a peculiar position. It is like the Older Testament. The man of the house is the patriark. The women are little better than servants. They work in the field, sit in silence when the men talk, are ordered about like children. They are however not weak. I see many resolute faces. That is the way of life. It is accepted.

In six weeks the house should be practically done. It should outlast the children. It will be theirs. If any of them become artists it should be [a] refuge.[3] When the house is done I shall go to work gradually to make the farm self-supporting.[4] It all brings me closer to natural things. I am already stronger than I have been for several years.

It is not unlikely I shall lecture for two or three weeks in the spring. It is rediculous but so little time may pay what I will owe here. The Connicks, from Boston, the fine glass man who is my friend, were to come two weeks ago. They are arriving tomorrow. I do not know how long they will stay. As to whether I can run away depends upon that.

I am grouping still in the life of my novel.[5] So many things to distract. Often it seems to me I do nothing. Others write telling me how much vitality I have. I often seem to myself to have none. I think of you, what you have been through, your courage. My own seems nothing.

A slow coming back to the soil out of which I came as a boy.[6] The tempo of life in some way made more solid. There is an old man dying slowly as a tree dies along the road past my house. When I stop to talk to me [him] he tests me by the coutry method. I pass the test. He likes me. There is much reserve. Everything waits.

All this I must in some way throw against my life in the modern city. After all to me everything must have the two values—the value of a life experience—the value of its relation to me as a workman.

The two fighting often enough. You get the full picture. As for ourselves, in our relation to each other we gain and loose. The cards fall so.

There will be much to talk of when I do see you. We will never get it talked of I dare say.

TS

1. Hahn's longhand note.
2. Though this thought recurred, Anderson never wrote the book.
3. None of Anderson's children ever lived at Ripshin Farm.
4. This remained only an intention.
5. Presumably *Another Man's House*.
6. Though Clyde and the other Ohio communities where he lived as a child and youth were most distinctly rural, Anderson worked only briefly as a farm hand and never lived in a farm home. See Sutton, *Road to Winesburg*, for details of Anderson's early life.

254

To Bab — September 1926[1] [Troutdale, Va.]

Karl—still at the portrait. It is to have three figures—my brother Irve—Earl and myself. He works patiently—slowly, painting out, reconstructing. In every sense a different sort of workman from myself.[2]

In New York a queer tangle. Dreiser has published a poem in Vanity Fair. It is obviously lifted bodily from Tandy—in Winesburg.[3]

The whole thing an absurd accident of some sort. The man is being accused of an awkward plagerism.

What must have happened is something like this.

He did make the poem from my tale—never intending to publish it. It may have been a practice stunt of some sort.

He put it aside and forgot the circumstances under which he wrote it.

It was published and almost immediately someone discovered it.

An awkward thing to explain. It is too bad.

My novel went wrong—had to begin again.[4] It almost always happens.

In spite of myself I made a scheme for these people. They want to be themselves. I will not let them. There is a struggle.

At last I have the sense to surrender.

I am tired, busy, often perplexed—but well and strong. Monday is my birthday. [Hahn note: Sept. 16.[5]]

LH

1. Hahn's longhand note.

2. In Jones and Rideout, eds., *Letters of Sherwood Anderson*, p. 161, in a letter undated but assumed, possibly wrongly, to be of Sept. 1926 (letter 136), Anderson commiserates with Karl on his "uncertainty" about the painting.

3. Theodore Dreiser's "The Beautiful" was published in *Vanity Fair*, Sept. 1926, p. 54. Anderson's "The South" started on that page, so Anderson probably saw it as soon as any one. The forty-two lines in four stanzas represent a dramatic monologue, probably suggested by the "Tandy" story in *Winesburg, Ohio*. The woman with the new quality, "being strong to be loved," is called Beautiful instead of Tandy. It seems Dreiser liked Anderson's idea and wrote his own rendering of it.

4. Anderson told Karl that the 100,000 words he had completed, doubtless for *Another Man's House*, would "not do." See Jones and Rideout, eds., *Letters of Sherwood Anderson*, p. 161.

5. The actual date was Sept. 13.

255

To Bab Sept. 1926[1] [Troutdale, Va.]

Your letter came yesterday. You liked the story in Mercury.[2] The man you love is hurt. Anyway it is better than Europe. To feel what you feel now—know your presence there counts. I don't need to tell you. You know.

I got pretty badly muddled up but am going a bit clearer now. An artist has to fight against so many things. Himself, his admirers, those who love him.

If people only knew what the creation of a novel meant. It isn't the writing. That's fun. Its fighting through you[r] own precon[c]eived notions, other people's notions. Letting the people of the novel live and be.

We do it all the time—all of us. When we love someone we try to manage their lives. We are worried, fussy, as to whther or not they love us. Suppose we are pureer than that. We want good things to happen to those we love—what we think are good things. Eternal managment of the lives of others.

That's what you do to people of a novel. It wont work. If they are to live they must find their own way of living. You have got to let them do that. It isn't easy.

With every new thing I tackle that same struggle. I try prayer, c[o]mmon sense, everything.

Trouble is all the time I am rotten with self. I get clear a while and back it comes. It is my struggle, every artists struggle.

I've been full of it this summer. If you have sometimes felt me as not well that is what has been the matter. Just now I am a little clear of it but how long I will be I don't know. I'm half afraid to speak of the matter.

God help us all.

And I'm glad you are there now, near that man.[3] It would have been dreadful had it happened when you were on shipboard or with the sea between you.

TS

1. Hahn's longhand note.
2. "Death in the Woods" was published in the *American Mercury*, 9 (Sept. 1926), 7–13.
3. "That man" is not identified, but could possibly have been Dr. E. Vernon Hahn, whom Finley married in 1928.

256

To Bab Sept. 1926[1] [Troutdale, Va.]

Two weeks of illness. It is my own special kind. There is such a struggle. Sometimes it seems to me that if I could isolate myself for a time all would be well. I can't. I am trying to build this house for a special reason. Here living is very cheap. I am more and more happy and peaceful inside in the pr[e]snce of nature.

But as you well know building a house is something. I never quite know that I will make my payrole. Every lityle thing has to be watched. I am building with cou[n]try labor. It practically means that I am the builder.

That is all right too. It is fun. If I could devote myself to actual people, happenings.

Other people crowding in. Young men write—young artists. I fancy I have unconsciously come to stand for something in such lives. They want to talk—of themselves—of their own hopes. "What do you think. What do you think."

Then this other world—up here on this hill—the worl[d]s of my fancy. People living in that too. The two worlds get mixed up. Nothing would prevent the thing happening. I am so often like a man trying to cross Niagra Falls on a wire with a wheelbarrow—the wheel barrow filled with squirming people.

I go off suddenly, trrribly. There is a kind of nameless sickness. At times I can scarcely lift my legs to walk. It is all inside. The sickness may last two weeks, a month, a day.

While it lasts I am sunk so low it seems I can never again lift myself. The hills no longer have form. Books are meaningless. Words squirm and writhe before my eyes.

Words are nothing. I am nothing. The desease simply must spend itself.

Suddenly I am well again. I work, laugh, love.

It may just be self—too much self.

I want to write so much. There is much to write you about. I can only tell you I have been ill of this old illness. I am better again. What of you. What of the sick man you love?

TS

1. Hahn's longhand note.

257

To Bab October 1926[1] [Troutdale, Va.]

The days are growing cold. The Connics are still here. Lyle Saxon[2] writes he will be here at the week end. Maurice Hanline also is coming to see about publishing the Testement.[3]

The chances seem slim.

In the country here sugar making and corn cutting going on. At last the novel[4] seems to be really alive. It would be wonderful to have some quiet hours and talk but it seems impossible.

LH

1. Hahn's longhand note.

2. Lyle Saxon (1891–1946) was from Louisiana; he was the author of *Father Mississippi*, published in 1927.

3. Hanline was an editor for Liveright Publishing Co.; *A New Testament* was published in 1927.

4. *Another Man's House.*

258

To Bab October 1926[1]

I have been ill and last week went to a doctor at Marion[2] for an examination. As usual, during my times of illness, he could do nothing.

It is a time of spiritual let down—of sag. Such times come.

I got your letter from New York when I was in the midst of it. I had a guest here. There is one now.

Although the illnesses I have are psycic they affect me physically. I would not want to come to see you in such condition.

At such times no one is in right relation to my life. I am like a stone beside the road. Nothing in me moves. I am hard, frozen.

Why such times come I'll never know. They have come all my life. I had them as a boy. This has been a long one but I have had longer.[3]

If you grow impatient—give me up as no good[,] I'll not blame you.

LH Written on stationery of Sherwood Anderson, Ripshin Farm, Grant and Troutdale, Va.

1. Hahn's longhand note.

2. Marion was the county seat of Smyth County, which, in turn, adjoined Wythe County where Ripshin Farm was located. It was in Marion where Anderson purchased his newspapers in 1927.

3. Pyschosomatic illness played an important role in Anderson's life. The outstanding example is undoubtedly his attack of amnesia in 1912.

259

To Bab October 1926[1] [Troutdale, Va.]

A more impatient man never lived. When it comes to my illnesses—they all come back to one thing. I am unable to work at the top of my bent.

Odd that my work itself should have given those not knowing me so often the impression of great patients.

I boil and rage inside. Given anew the key to work I become a quiet pains-taking man. In a half hour I can reconcile myself to the notion of throwing a whole summers work into the fire.[2]

What I may have accomplished in the world is of little use to me. Accomplishments do not interest me much.

What is of interest is functioning as a workman.

It is the key to Heaven—to personal dignity, good manners, everything.
Perhaps I want too much. Who then put the want in me.
I want to touch the quality of music, color, light.
A year gone perhaps. It not done at all.
I do not fear death. It does not matter. If I can get at the quality I want in prose I shall not die for a long time.
And anyway that doesn't matter.
What matters I can't quite make out.

LH

1. Hahn's longhand note.
2. Something these letters suggest he had just done, at least figuratively.

260

To Bab October 1926[1] [Troutdale, Va.]

Little helps you do not know about. Our relationship must remain baffling to you. If you could see how much I am dependent. Not on you as a fact. On you as representing a kind of faith. My sister died when I was young.[2] It may just be you have come into a place she might have occupied. There was another sister who died when she was a child. It might have been her. As a matter of fact it is you. Your wanting it or not seems to have little to do with it. Perhaps no woman wants such a position with a man.

And yet, if you knew all.

What I mean just now is that after a terrible blank time I began to try to describe a certain phase of myself to you. Just the peculiar position you occupy with me made it all quite possible. It might be a year before you can know what it is all about because, to send my present writings to you, as I write them would too much disturb the flow.

If it means anything to a human being to be able to help another human being in the thing most vital to them then you have the right to know you do that. It is all I can say yet. If the gods are good there may be something more real to lay down before you later.

I have I am afraid rather ruthlessly taken from you what I can take. I continue to do just that. I can't help it but I wish you could know how important it is to me.

TS

1. Hahn's longhand note.

2. His sister Stella, to whom he was imaginatively referring, was born in 1875 and died in 1918, when she was forty-two and Sherwood forty-one. His sister Fern lived almost two years (1890–92); she was the last of his parents' children born and the first to die.

261

To Bab November 1926[1]

I am upset about Bob. First because he may well impose himself on you and not realize he is doing it.

When he wrote me that he was about to loose the job in St. Louis I at once wired and ask him to keep me in touch with his movements.

He hasn't written me at all. I presume he is ashamed that he did not pull off the St. Louis thing. After all he was very young.

The poor lad can get on your nerves and, my dear, you must not let him.

I have written Cornelia to let him have any money he needs as he is in quicker touch with her.

I am writing this hastily. A man is here from B & L to talk to me about publishing the testament[2] in the spring. In a few days I will write again.

Do not let Bob impose on you.

LH Written on the stationery of Ripshin Farm, Troutdale, Va.

1. Hahn's longhand note.
2. A *New Testament*.

262

To Bab November 1926[1]

My dear—I really understood your saying what you did and your reaction later. I do know people a little.

The whole thing—nothing could change my attitude toward you.

Whether it was true or not has of course nothing to do with the matter.

I have to make my own judgments on you and others.

I don't like our relations to make ugly gestures.

I'm not exempt.

It came at a time when I wasn't well—upset.

Will write you later—from some place along.

No matter what happens you are Bab to me—a part of what is.
I accept that—am sound, I think, in it.
It [if] I were clearer myself I could be angry I fancy.

As Always

LH Written on the stationery of the First National Bank, Troutdale, Va.

1. Hahn's longhand note.

263

To Bab November 1926[1]

This is just to say goodbye before I go.[2] I am up here with my sick brother. Such a terrific man. Im unable to bring him down town to dine at the hotel. It seems to me, when I am with him, that I have always some to give but not enough.

I suppose that is why men got the notion of Christ—who could really give. They wanted to give but like me could not give enough.

I feel very humble & useless.

LH Written on the stationery of the Perry House, Newport, R.I.

1. Hahn's longhand note.
2. Anderson wrote to Burton Emmett in an undated letter (but designated as "fall of 1926") that "Mrs. Anderson and myself with my son John are leaving for Europe Dec. 18st on the President Roosevelt." See Emmett Collection, University of North Carolina Library, Chapel Hill.

264

To Bab 1927—France[1]

I know your kindness and you may depend on my love of the boy.

However a thing like this wordy meaningless review of Dark Dawn has to be knocked in the head.

It is faky from start to finish—just as is the book itself.

The boy has in some way to learn to think clearly and honestly and if he is to write to write that way.

Your own good feeling has betrayed you.

Read the thing again.

"Locked to the ever-demanding fields—

"Rhythm of railroad sidings.

"A Stark Vivid woman." Dear Bab—don't let your desire to be kind upset your judgment.

This is the kind of writing I hate above everything on earth.[2]

I have been ill again. Leaving for America next week.

Before six weeks have passed I hope to see you and Bob—

LH

1. Hahn's longhand note. Anderson was in England and France until Mar. 1927. He was in France after mid-January.

2. The strenuousness of this statement, although not necessarily representative of a sustained attitude toward Bob (who did subsequently take over the newspapers from his father) does seem to represent a lack of sympathy that resulted in a basic distaste on the part of the son for the father. Bob's wife wrote, "Sherwood Anderson gave me a letter of Bob's outlining his plan for financing his study. He asked *nothing* from his father. Sherwood Anderson laughed about the boyish letter. I was so mad I tore it up. I recently found an old letter of Bob's to Mimi [his sister Marion] in which he said (with a strangely adult understanding) that Sherwood Anderson saw them so seldom he then felt disappointment when he met them" (letter of Mar. 8, 1974, Sutton Collection). This suggests strongly that Robert did not feel that his father loved him; apparently the other two children were less seriously affected by such a feeling, for they do not seem to have rejected their father.

265

To Bab France—1927[1]

I feel very guilty that I have not written for so long but I have been ill ever since I left America.

First in London—of which I saw nothing.

Then in France confined to my bed with a long attack of flu.[2]

Back of it all a deep depression. I am at one of those queer turning points in my life that may lead anywhere.

In a practical way there has been nothing to write. I am weary of restating the mere fact of my own defeat.

Still, for some queer reason the restless thing in me goes on. There is no rest. When I consume myself in work it is all right. Too often I consume myself in mere futility.

Still I can state my eternal gratitude to you. If you understood the reality of my gratitude it would go deeper than you know.

In France there is apparently a sort of wave of recognition. 4 books of mine are to be done here.[3] It means singularly little to me.

What means much is to find at last—if I can the new mood in which to work.

When that comes I shall live again.

LH

1. Hahn's longhand note. Presumably in Paris and in late Jan. or Feb. 1927.

2. On Jan. 19, 1927, Anderson wrote to Burton Emmett that "in London I was stuck down by a cold which, after I got to Paris, developed into flu. . . . I have been up for some time" (Emmett Collection).

3. In the same letter to Emmett, Anderson listed the books as: "The Note-book—Winesburg—A Story Teller's Story and another book of Tales. . . . Two stories—'The Man Who Became a Woman' and 'A Man's Story' have been done here and have had a distinct literary success."

266

To Bab | Europe 1927[1]

The band is playing outside the window, the sea is as smooth as this desk (almost), tomorrow we make our first stop—Halifax, then Boston on Monday—New York on Tuesday. I do not know what my short lecture trip will be but will know as soon as we get to New York.

The ship is German—only two or three Americans (German Americans) on board. It has been until today (Saturday) a quiet uneventful voyage. For the first time in months I feel that I may write again. It may have been flu—combined with nervous weariness and the inevitable time between that is so terrible.

I had to write Bob a rather harsh letter about his review—the one you sent me. It has [was] so full of bad meaningless sentences—so unfelt.

The boy must learn to come straight with his own feelings. Out of the tangle inside such a young man something must be caught.

He has infinately more cleverness than the other two—but isn't yet as straight with himself.

John has shown some real flashes of talent. I believe he will work. He is one of the kind likely to go straight on steadily.

Mimi has been atrociously handled. With the best intentions in the world C is as muddled in her treatment of the children as with her house.[2]

It is all of a piece. Perhaps everything is all of a piece. That is one reason I want Bob to face himself now.

There are so many slick writers. I would rather see him anything else in this world.[3]

In some way he must realize the sacredness of the white sheets on which he puts down the words.

No slick words.

It is a little horrible to me that such an undeveloped boy should be passing judgment on books—a reader for a publishing house—good God.

O, I know most men know no more.

That however says nothing.

With all which I love the lad.

LH

1. Hahn's longhand note. Shipping records in the New York *Times* indicate that the Hamburg-Amerika ship that best fits Anderson's timetable was the *Cleveland*, which left Hamburg on Thursday, Mar. 3, and docked at W. 44th St. in New York early on the morning of Wednesday, Mar. 16.

2. In an interview of Feb. 21, 1974, John read this passage and stated that he did not agree with this assessment of his mother.

3. Involving as it did Anderson's long anguish over what he perceived as his own "slick" writing, the relationship between father and son seems to have been torturous for both, perhaps especially for Robert. In an interview of Feb. 21, 1974, John recalled that Robert had a feeling of bitterness toward their father, but did not know what the basis of the problem was, referring to it as a "personality thing." He thought it "might have something to do with ego." He also noted that Mary, Robert's wife, was bitter about Sherwood Anderson's treatment of Robert, too.

267

To Bab 1927[1] [March]

I am on the way to Clyde Ohio to help bring my poor brother—who died just as I was getting off the boat.[2] Karl and I are taking him back to bury him beside mother.

I leave immediately for Memphis Tenn. where I am to speak at a college.[3]

I could get to Indianapolis—from Detroit—for a visit on Sunday the 27th.

If this would be convenient to you write me at

Hotel Shawnee
Springfield Ohio

Mark the letter—"hold for arrival."

I will have a visit with Robert on my way down to Memphis.

If you think it would be nice we could have him with us on the 27th I presume but as it is so long since we have seen each other it might be nicer to have the day alone.

If it would be in any way less embarassing we could spend the day at any other nearby place you may suggest.

I must be in Chicago on Monday.

LH

1. Hahn's longhand note.

2. Earl Anderson died on Mar. 16, 1927, in the early hours of which date the *Cleveland* docked in New York. An account of the funeral in the Clyde *Enterprise* notes the presence of Karl ("of Westport") and Sherwood ("of Fayerdale, Virginia"). Other survivors were Ray Anderson of Chicago and Irwin Anderson of Baltimore. Sherwood was mentioned as having left for Memphis to give a lecture. A letter of Feb. 24, 1975, from Thaddeus B. Hurd of Clyde relates this information: "The Clyde cemetery records show Earl as buried Saturday, 19 March 1927, on the same lot as his mother. This is only a half-lot which Irwin purchased at the time of Fern's death, and I think she is buried there, too, but there is no stone or record. As you know, there is a stone for Emma, but there is none for Earl. The American Legion here tried to get a veteran's stone from the government, but no one was able to come up with proof that he was ever in service, although he died in the Marine Hospital, Newport, Rhode Island. . . . I did a lot of checking and found there was no evidence of his service, and a government stone would therefore not be furnished . . . his grave is still unmarked, though there is a bronze WWI flagholder on his grave" (Sutton Collection).

3. Anderson delivered two lectures ("America—A Storehouse of Vitality" and "The Younger Generation") at the Goodwyn Institute on Mar. 22 and 23, 1927. The Goodwyn was not affiliated with any college or university.

268

To Bab 1927[1] [ca. Mar. 29, 1927]

So much to say. Of course I am tired. But seeing you was such a rest and a real joy.

What you have done for Bob is wonderful. The change in him is an amazing thing.

I spoke to Mr. Glenn Frank[2] about John. Micklejohn[3] is doing a new thing in education here. He was away from town but Frank will speak to him—a Dr. Young here will talk with him and I will of course write him.

I am asking for a scholarship—making just as much provision for expense as can be made. I hope something will come of it. I have in mind also trying to get the offer of some thing of the sort for Bob—not here—perhaps at Cornell. If he does not want to take it that will be up to him.

You are a blessed woman for doing all you are doing for Bob—and others—not to mention all you have done and are doing for one Sherwood Anderson.

LH Written on the stationery of the Hotel Loraine, Madison, Wis.

1. Hahn's longhand note. Anderson lectured at the University of Wisconsin on Mar. 29; the *Daily Cardinal* gave this account in its Mar. 31 issue:

> "It is as true as there is a sun in the sky that man cannot live without love of craft."
>
> "The practitioner of an art who wishes to be honest must put money making aside."
>
> "Popular magazines are but factories for the standardization of minds for the benefit of the factory."
>
> "The writer is a workman whose materials are human lives."
>
> "If you have talent, do not sell out your birthright. There are worse fates than being poor."
>
> A short thick-set man with a shock of iron-grey hair, Sherwood Anderson delivered himself of these and a succession of pithy sayings last night, as he paced the platform of Music Hall and twisted his fingers in nervous absorption.
>
> Speaking in voice which oscillated between a throaty rumbling and an almost feminine shrillness, he condemned the writers of popular standardized literature and lauded the efforts of the younger generation of writers who are striving to see and express the realities of life.
>
> Mr. Anderson is contemptuous of "success."
>
> "If you are to be a 'successful' writer, you must learn the art of producing in readers sensations of delight and terror without in any way touching the realities of life. No one must be hurt, no one must be offended. Keep it up and you'll get rich.
>
> "But this has no more to do with the art of writing than movie stars have to do with the art of acting."
>
> The taste for this stereotyped popular literature Mr. Anderson sees as the result of the industrial revolution which produced a taste for standardization in material goods; there then came the popular magazines which sought, and in a large measure accomplished, the standardization of literary taste.
>
> "Yet minds cannot be completely standardized," he declared. "We are all profoundly interested in one another; little human fancies creep in, and the mind is diverted from the machine to the man."
>
> This has given rise to a new movement of protest in all fields of self-expression, painting, prose, architecture, even the creation of fashions.
>
> Self-expression, the love of craft for its own sake, is the most important thing in life, he insisted.

> If men are to survive the cheapness and shoddiness of industrialism, they must get back to a sense of the importance of the job itself. If the younger generation of writers does not get this notion, all talk of progress means nothing.

In the issue of the preceding day, the paper had heralded his coming appearance:

> Tonight, Sherwood Anderson, one of the most modern exponents of modern literature, speaks in Music hall on "The Younger Generation." Sherwood Anderson, writer of advertising copy until he was almost 40, decided to write one day, and he disclosed that facile mind that set to the paper words in such an order that even the higher critics began to take notice of this former advertising man.
>
> This man who writes of sex and complexes as everyday matters should draw a crowd tonight, for he has been scorned by many literati. His subjects are not high class;—he writes of America's great Middle Class, and of its lower classes. He goes beneath the surface. He is no idealist;—he is a realist who almost revels in his realism.
>
> Sherwood Anderson is a peculiar character, perhaps another Theodore Dreiser or Maxwell Bodenheim. Stories that are not sweet go the rounds about him, as about these other men, so he will draw a crowd tonight.
>
> He may not have produced much great literature; he may be no great man of letters, but he has known how to write for his readers; he has realized what the general public will read. Stark realism clothed in not-too-soft words has appealed.
>
> Such is the Great American Mind.

2. Glenn Frank was president of the University of Wisconsin in 1927; there are no letters to or from Anderson in Frank's papers in the university archives for that year.

3. Alexander Meiklejohn was the founder of the University of Wisconsin Experimental College and served as its chairman until 1932.

269

To Bab 1927[1] [Late March]

I will have to write with a pencil—the train[2]—rattling me off east shakes so much.

After my talk with you[3] I am sure Bob should be offered the opportunity of college—if he wants it. It may be the thing he most needs now to bring him into closer touch with people of his own age.

I have a way of getting at the people back of Cornell University—at Itica N.Y., and will feel them out. At any rate I will try to give him the chance. Making him stay put for 3 or four years might be every thing now.

The legislature was in session at Madison & Mr. Glenn Frank very busy but he came to see me at my hotel. Meicklejohn—is as you know perhaps putting on a new educational experiment up there—a sort of University within a University. Dr. Frank at once suggested the school for John. I think a scholarship may be put through. I have also access in a semi-intimate way with Miecklejohn. He was not in town but I am writing him. Will know soon.

Saw Cornelia in Chicago. Had her for dinner with George Daugherty.

Am asking Bob to think about the college matter.

Tired but almost through now. Will be back at the farm about April 6 or 7.

Bless you.

LH Written on the stationery of the New York Central Lines.

1. Hahn's longhand note.
2. The eastbound New York Central train went through Indianapolis.
3. Presumably the meeting suggested for Sunday, Mar. 27, had occurred.

270

To Bab [After Mar. 27, 1927 Troutdale, Va.]

I had a talk with Mr. Herbert Croly[1] in New York and he told me he had access to a fund from which he thought it quite possible I might get tuition and $300 to $400 a year for both Bob & John.

I think if Bob had just a couple of years with kids his own age it might be wonderful for him now. It is really Mrs. Willard Straight[2]—but that is to be kept sub rosa. I will know definately in May.

The day with you was wonderful for me. But for it I could never have got through the ghastly exhibitionism[3] of the trip. Bless you.

If you go to New York do go into Karl's show[4] and if he is there introduce yourself.

LH Written on the stationery of Ripshin Farm, Grant, Va.

1. Herbert E. Croly had given leadership to the founding of the *New Republic* in 1914 and was one of its seven editors in Mar. 1927.
2. A major financial supporter of the *New Republic*.
3. A reference to additional lectures?
4. According to the New York Times of Apr. 10, Karl Anderson's paintings would be in the Ferargil Galleries until Apr. 18.

271

To Bab [Troutdale, Va., April, 1927][1]

What an unfortunate time to try to write. Stacks of letters on my desk unanswered.

And I am usually such a prompt correspondent.

Today I have been writing until my whole body aches.

Chicago is to me what it is, a part of my life.[2]

Nowdays everyone is growing a bit sentimental about my Chicago days and my Chicago work. They are dissatisfied with what I am doing now. Already some of the critic's are mourning over my grave.

I do not remember that they were very kind to me then. I cannot be what I was then.

I am trying to live from day to day, work from day to day. I am what my experiences of life make me.

Why do I tell you all this. I do not want you my friend to mourn over my past. What is emerging out of me now in the shape of work—is myself now.

Myself discouraged often, hopeful sometimes—just as you are dear friend.

I shall try to be as philosophical as I can about the children—do for them all I can.

They in turn will have to be what they are.

What they make themselves.

More than all what fate makes them.

Do have a good trip—get all you can of sunshine. Dear Bab—do not try to carry the load for us all.

Live a little more for our Bab—

LH

1. Hahn typescript has "Marion, Ia. 1927." Anderson had not yet moved from Troutdale to Marion, Va.

2. Presumably a reference to his recent visit there.

272

To Bab 1927[1] [Troutdale, Va., Apr.]

A very great deal to write. I have not written because I have been ill. The illness was all inside but took an outer form.[2]

Now I grow a little better.

It all sprung from my financial arraingment with B & L.[3] It was not their fault. They insured me a comfortable living and I agreed to deliver certain books. When the arraingment was made I felt strong and capable.

The fault lay in the arraingment itself. They did not press me but I felt under obligations. I tried to hurry.

The sense of hurry destroyed all. You I a little blamed because I thought of you as thinking of me as content and self-satisfied when I was most torn with doubt and inner anguish.

I should not have blamed you. You are a woman and I am a man. You emphasized too much my personal relations with life.

The fight has been in my own soul. It is there yet. Nothing is settled.

I know only that, in about four weeks, I will go home and make a new arraingment.[4] I will free myself from obligations. Whatever happens I will recover my freedom.

After that I know nothing. I will have in some way to live but I am not going to let that worry me.

As for my work, it waits. Trying to hurry it has, for the moment made me ineffectual with my tools. Something is forming within me—new resolves—new phases of life to be understood.

I have to stand aside and wait. Even the realization of that, come up into my consciousness is making me more healthy again.

I have to take the diseases of my age like all men. I have to cure myself of them if I can.

With love

LH

1. Hahn's longhand note.
2. In keeping with a pattern of psychosomatic illness in Anderson.
3. Boni and Liveright, his publisher since 1925.
4. It was actually settled the next fall, coincident with Anderson's purchase of the newspapers in Marion.

273

To Bab

1927[1] [May Troutdale, Va.]
Monday Morning.

Have been up to the cornfield on the hill this morning to get Turkcap lillies that grow among the corn. They are big spotted fellows and would have got chopped off up there.

Claud and Ruby, when they were hoeing the corn left them standing so I could bring them down and set them along the creek bank.

It is interesting to see how these men gradually get a sense of decoration. At first all flowers went ruthlessly, with the other things. Now they begin to bring them in. I see a neighbor coming out of the woods with what he calls a "Ragged Robin." He marks a spot where I can get plenty of them.

I am trying to make my whole garden out of native flowers, shrubs and trees. Two wagon loads of yellow and gold azalias on one bank of the creek. It should fairly flame gold and yellow.

White purple and red rhydodemdrums, laural—pink and white.

Now the whole country is a mass of color. It has been a season of heavy rains—everything grows luxuriously, the air heavy with perfume.

Just that dense thick alive time of the year. You go about half breathless.

Prayers on the lips.

I know exactly how you felt, sitting and talking with poor Bobby. Why do I say poor Bobby?

It is that we are older—I hope wiser—disillusioned somewhat.

So much ugliness, so much lying.

I think the hunger for beauty grows more intense. We have learned not to be sure of anything.

Love, friendship. You must go about in your sad low times telling yourself you deserve no love, no friendship as I constantly do.

Prayers on the lips.

We can't give that wisdom, that terror, that lonliness to the young. If they had it nothing would be done.

They would stand still in a road, on a hill or in a city street paralysed by the fact of life as we are so often.

Stand and pray.

There is no answer to the mystery.

Bob has improved immeasurably. You offered him the use of your car. He wrote me, spoke of the insurance, wanted my advice about whether or not it would be right to accept such a generous off[er], whether it would be fair to you.

That is a thousand miles from the Bob of 2 years ago.

A boy now in whose consciousness others exist. You exist for him, have your rights.

It is a long way.

I do not believe it would be at all bad for Bob to go on in school down there for a year. He would be near you, someone to talk to occasionall.

The so-called bigger world is largely illusion. In my own life now I try and try to cut the bigger world out.

I mean only that by really knowing somewhat and loving a few you know and love all.

In as much as he has himself suggested it.

I want him most of all to feel that I love him.

My brother Karl in trouble. It is a long sad story. By trying to help you hurt. I think, at 55 he has come to a sudden and terrible realization of the futility of much of his life and his art.

He wants to begin again, be young, be more daring perhaps. He can't.

He is coming here and Paul Rosenfeld is coming.

I hoped to have a copy of the Testament to send you. It hasn't come yet. If it doesn't come until after you go west let me know your address out there.

Bales of writing. I haven't begun to try to put it into form. There are several short stories—things caught here, from these people—just in rough hurried form yet.

I keep hoping you are doing some writing all the time. It is a help.

With love

LH

1. Hahn's longhand note. The references to rescuing the lilies in the first paragraph and to anticipating the sending of *A New Testament*, published in May, form the basis for dating this and the next letter.

2. Anderson hoped Bob would go to Vincennes University at Vincennes, Ind. He did not.

274

To Bab 1927[1] [May Troutdale, Va.]

Dear Friend—

I have for you one of the limited edition copies [of] "A new Testament." Perhaps I had better hold it until you return. Or you tell me where to send it.

Quiet stately days. I write and work in my garden. So much writing, done this year I will have to throw away.

I feel toward something.

It may be a new, cooler, I hope more aristocratic tone, in what I am now trying to do.

Youth is gone. I don't care about that. I want however to have some dignity in the next ten or twenty years—what I may have left.

Perhaps that is why I am here—in these hills. The days here have dignity.

I hope you may find something in the Testament. More than one of the things are addressed to you.

LH

1. Hahn's longhand note.

275

To Bab 1927[1] [August Troutdale, Va.]

The great difficulty about Bob is that I doubt if he could enter most colleges on his high school record. He just got graduated by a fluke. If he could see his way clear to go to the small college for one year, trying to pick up all his studies a bit, incidentally making a part of his living—it would be better—I'm sure.

Then he could enter some other college, perhaps as a second year man.

I have made application for John at Madison.[2] The scholarship matter didn't turn out. We will get him in and he will have to stir around and earn part of his living after he gets there.

The Vincennes notion was Bob's own. I think it a good one. If he makes a good record one year it will be ten times as easy to get help for him another year.[3]

I have an acquaintance with one of the University regents—the state of Virginia. Perhaps another year if things go well, I can do something for him there.

Of course I'll be able to help them both some as they go along. I have at least a home now and my expense will soon be cut down. I am writing Bob today.

John's letters from Paris are very interesting. He is working hard and is I think very intelligent.

Mimi has worked hard this year and has made a good record. I think her mother will find her quite a changed girl.

I can't help being inclined to smile a little over your occasional analysis of my own symptoms. Don't be offended. It has been done to me so often all my life. There is always, at least the slight suggestion of a new discovery—and that I do no thinking for myself.

Don't be hurt. I've got to laugh a little now and then.

If you come to think of it you will realize that I have some little reputation for knowing something about human impulses. Some of the so-called great psycoligists have done me the honor of saying I know rather more on the subject than anyone else.

You don't need to worry. The soft nest into which I am in danger of sinking is your own creation—a creature of your own imagaining, not mine.

Coming when I am making the hardest efforts I have every made to find my way along more complex blind paths in thought and feeling how can I help laugh.

A little bitterly too.

It would be better to trust me as an artist, often failing but at least always trying.

As I say—don't be hurt. I'm somewhat older than you both in years and living.

The odd feeling you have. It's very general now—my mail full of it.

Discouragement about live—loss of the flare for life.

Its too bad if the arts do not make something of a path for you. Its the only path that makes life continually possible for me.

I wish I could give you some word. I tried in "A New Testament." If, as a whole it doesn't bring you any faint echo of the word, well it doesn't.

Your breaking it up into fragments with which to find out what is wrong with me was at least not the way it was intended to be taken.

You will know what I mean.

LH

1. Hahn's longhand note.
2. John attended the University of Wisconsin in the fall of 1928.
3. Though this reference carries the suggestion that Bob attended Vincennes University, the university certifies that he never did—which accords with the recollection of Bob's widow. Records of the University of Virginia, Charlottesville, indicate that he was enrolled there for the academic year beginning Sept. 15, 1927. He had given his father's occupation as "writer."

276

To Bab Marion, Va., 1927[1] [Early October Troutdale, Va.]

And so you are back in your little house.[2] Well, I have much to write to you about. How very nice you have been. For the last few weeks I have been again going through one of my processes. For one thing I have been thinking a good deal of you. For a long time I have not thought of you or anyone else. I have thought almost exclusively of myself.

O, my dear friend. When I think back upon it sometimes I think that to you at least I have been in part fair. I have at least never married you, have I. I mean only that I am thinking how horrible it is to be married to such a one.

To be an artist is I dare say the best way of life. It is without a doubt the most ghastly way of life too.

I mean that when life does not flow down through my pen I am nothing—a childish dissatisfied thing.

And now Bab let me tell you about the resolution to which I have come. For a long time I have been casting about.

However, in order to make everything clear let me review. As I think you know for a great many years I made nothing by my writing. I lived by doing other work. Then at last a little success came. I retired from affairs. I built me a house. I settled down to write. For years I had been praying for just such leisure and at last, in derision, the gods gave it to me.

My god and what a life. Here I was. The days came and went. On some days I worked a little. On other days not at all.

I became dissatisfied and ugly. Having so much leisure, being thus in a queer way seperated from the life about me I began to think more and more of self. Self became a passion with me. I felt myself going to seed, eating myself up.

And here I was a strong man. I had never been physically so strong. What was I to do.

I had about decided to give up the country and go back to the city. I decided I would go back to advertising writing. You see I had got myself on the back of my own pen. I was as[t]ride it, trying to ride it. The pen, as a result was always bearing too heavily on the paper. Grace and ease had gone out of my hand. Do you know Bab I have been, in these last two years in real danger of becoming a literary hack, hating the very paper on which I wrote.

However I have not been quite blind. My mind has been casting about. At first I thought that what I needed was release from the economic pressure. Then at last I concluded that was foolish too.

After all my dear friend most of the men of the [hole in paper] have to make a living by some means not always pleasant. By seperating myself from the labor of the world I had perhaps separated myself from the world too.

I had got too far away. I knew that.

About a month ago I decided on a change in my life. Was I to go back to the city. At least for me that would not be a new adventure. There was this danger. Of making my living I knew little except through advertising writing. It would be easy to get well paid work there. But what would happen. I would go into the employ of some advertising company. They would pay me a good salary. I might even make from twenty to thirty thousand a year.

And immediately the advertising company would begin to advertise. Have your advertising writing done by Sherwood Anderson—the great writer etc. etc.

Very well that would not do. One day I was at the county fair at Marion,[3] a town of about four thousand near here. There, all about me was the life of the small town in which I was raised, that I knew so well. I began talking to another man, a small manufacturer of the town. Out of a kind of impulse I told him of my situation. We fell into a long talk.

It was from this man I got the suggestion on which I am now about to act. I have been thinking of it for a month. There is a little weekly newspaper and printing business in the town. It is quite successful, earns about six thousand a year. The man who has been running it is almost illiterate but a very nice man. His wife is ill. He will have to sell.

Very well, I am going to try to buy the paper. It can support both me and Bob. It will be building up something for him. For the present it will fill my own life.

Does this seem an absurd idea to you? Well, I shall have to have something to do with my energy. I cannot go on writing when, as often happens I am not in the mood to write. The running of a local paper of this sort is not of course writing. It should be great fun. I should be able to do much with it. You gather local news, tell of deaths and births, social affairs etc. You have a very distinct part in a town's life.

To buy the paper I shall have to raise five thousand dollars. It will cost me to buy fifteen thousand. The rest can be managed by payments out of the profits of the business itself. It may be that presently I shall take Bob in with me, have him thus as my right hand. In the end the property can be his.

As for the raising of the five thousand, to be of course eventually paid back I am going to New York[4] on Saturday of this week to see if I cannot raise it there. I may fail. If I do I shall have to turn elsewhere.

At any rate I have got to busy myself, get back into the swing of life—I mean oth[er] people's lives.

My plan for financing the thing is something like this. I shall need eight thousand cash but can raise three thousand on my property here. The profits of the business are six thousand a year now. It can be, I fancy built up to seven or eight, I shall have three years to pay the last seven thousand, that is to say I must pay at the rate of about two thousand five hundred out of the profits. With interest that will leave me about three thousand a year with what I can make by my incidental writing to live on while the business is being paid off. It will take five years to pay it off as the origional five thousand must also be paid. I am going to try in New York to get that on a long time loan.[5] There are a few rich men, interested in my work to whom I will apply. It may not come off. However I shall try. It does seem such a healthy outlet for me and Bob too.

There is something else Bab. As I think you know Boni & Liverright have been advancing me money against my forthcoming work. To date I have kept almost even with them but from now on, if I do not produce at least a book a year I will be on the wrong side with them. There will be and already is a guilty feeling. I feel myself the employee of the publishing firm and do not feel I am being fair with them unless I am pounding stuff out. Could a man be more perfectly a literary hack than to allow himself to get into this position? I shall have to escape that.[6]

Well I wish you were at this moment in New York. I could talk to you better than to write. My only object in writing is to acquaint you with my state of mind and this resolution to which I have come. It may all go up in smoke but if it does I shall try some other way of making my daily bread, other than by doing hack work at writing.

I am resolved you see to get off my pen in order that it may play more lightly over the paper. That is my real reason for all this. I can be reached in New York at Boni & Liveright 61 West 48th. May be in the city for three or four days—it depends upon what success I have.

TS

1. Hahn's typed note in her typescript of part of this letter; she generally did not distinguish between Marion and Ripshin.

2. In Indianapolis.

3. Held during the last week in August.

4. In New York, on Saturday, Oct. 8, Anderson met for the first time Burton Emmett, a wealthy advertiser and manuscript collector, who had written Anderson about acquiring some of his manuscripts in May 1926. The correspondence and several near-misses at meeting when Anderson was in New York had developed a friendship sufficient that Anderson's request for a loan was granted.

5. On Oct. 30, Anderson wrote Emmett a letter acknowledging an obligation for "the five thousand dollars ($5,000) you have loaned me without interest and that is to be used as part payment for the newspaper property I am acquiring at Marion Virginia." He enclosed two notes for $2,500 apiece and maturing four and five years later, respectively. He agreed to send the "origional manuscripts of all my published works yet in my possession and also such unpublished manuscripts as have not yet been destroyed." In addition to waiving all rights to the

manuscripts for himself and his heirs, he promised to send the manuscripts of future works as long as both parties lived. Further, he promised to "help you in any reasonable way I can in the collection of items of interest to you from other contemporary writers." In Mar. 1932 Emmett signed at the bottom of the letter a note that, in return for manuscripts, special editions, other materials of interest, "and in friendship," the obligation was declared cancelled. Burton Emmett Papers.

6. His buying the newspapers was his escape; he immediately discontinued his relationship with Boni and Liveright.

277

To Bab

1927[1]

You are quite right. What I produce in the future is a matter for the gods to decide—my attitude toward the attempt I have to take care of myself.

As long as I write the best I can—let someone else quibble.

I can't go on the street.

What always amazed me when I come back here,[2] is to find how much everyone wants you to keep straight in your attitude toward your work and life and how amazingly little we can help each other.

And we do want to help.

Little girls in book shop[s]—other writers—people you know but casually.

You come to stand for something.

Men like Otto Kahn & Berthram Russel—so different—meaning in some odd way the same thing.

So hard to help them or be helped.

The country or the small town is better for me. Fame is a whore and must be treated so.

There is however the bare chance a man's own every day life may be kept healthy.

God knows I know that is up to me.

Your own solid friendship means a lot.

LH Written on the stationery of Maurice A. Hanline, 19 East 47th Street, New York, just before Oct. 8

1. Hahn's longhand note. Because of the use of the stationery of Hanline, who was an editor for Boni and Liveright paper, and the absence of mentioning concluding arrangements for the purchase of the newspapers, I assume this was written in New York before the successful meeting with Emmett.

2. To New York. A great scavenger of stationery, Anderson would not necessarily have used Hanline's stationery only when in his office, but very possibly the use was in New York this time.

278

To Bab September 1927[1] [On or after Oct. 8, possibly written in New York]

I have completed—without difficulty—the arraingments necessary for the financing of the paper thing and have terminated the arraingment with the publisher that gave me so much unhappiness.

My dear—all you say is so true & sure. I know that what you say about a man's absolutely having to stand and fight for his own soul's health is true.

That is what I am trying to do. What I am doing may not be too wise. But where is wisdom.

It is at least new ground on which to stand and fight.

As an alternative there is for me nothing but to go back to advertising assisting in some big city.

That has—implicite in it a kind of vulgarity—I mean the use of my name etc.

I can't do that.

I can't be a laboring man. Physically I couldn't stand it.

People would give me money. I can't take it.

I want, first of all escape from putting my lady "out" on the street. That is my first love & always will be.

I can't come out now. In the first place I can't because I have already made arraingment to be in Marion—with the publisher—of the paper on Saturday.[2]

2nd. It isn't sound. You and I can't meet at Mich. City. It would be too damned uncomfortable. Our day would be spoiled.

I'll see you somewhere, some time.

& in the meantime bless you for your straight fine letter.

It is one of the finest you ever wrote me.

I'm not banking on Bob or anyone.[3]

LH Written on the stationery of Maurice A. Hanline, 19 East 47th Street, New York

1. Hahn's longhand note. This is one of the few dates that is demonstrably inaccurate.

2. On Sunday, Oct. 16, Anderson had written Burton Emmett that he would start going over to Marion from Troutdale on the next day. Emmett Collection.

3. But it was Bob who took over the papers from his father in Dec. 1931.

279

To Bab — Marion, Va. 1927[1] [After Nov. 1]

I should have written you a long time ago but have been terrible busy. So many things to do. A whole new outlook to be faced if that is possible.

Well, I have thought often enough of you, have imagained conversations.

In the first place there was the necessity of financing the thing. Partly I put a mortgage on my farm and partly raised money in [an]other way. I paid $15,000.

The papers have been making about $6000 a year. Perhaps I can do better. Perhaps I shall not do as well. As you know I had quite made up my mind never to enter any sort of business again but there was apparently but one alternative. The only thin[g] I know, aside from writing, is advertising writing. That I could not do without too much vulgar exploitation.

What I would like best of all, for the next 4 or five years is to live in as great obscurity as possible. However the discussion about me goes on. I dare say I am doomed to be what is called, a "celebrity." With all my soul I hate the idea.

Of course Bab there is this point of view. I dare say I am an introvert. There is too much absorbtion in self. Running the weekly local papers will compell me to associate constantly with all kinds of people. I have moments of good feeling about it and other moments of terror. How it will come out I don't know. It may not matter.

Life as I dare say a matter of experiences. One gets any sort of education so slowly.

During the winter I may lecture a few times—largely to get me out into the world. If I do it will only be at colleges. I hope I may at least have two or three lectures so I may get out your way.

Address me—
Marion Va.

LH

1. Hahn's note on her typescript. Anderson moved from Troutdale to Marion on Nov. 1, when he took over the operation of the newspaper in Marion.

280

To Bab 1927[1] [November]

There wasn't anything about your letter to hurt me. We all have such times. Lonliness—often futility seems to be our lot.

I dare say women loose it when they have children growing up—artists when they are at work.

I have such a queer half-formed relationship with so many people these days. So many boys coming out of colleges. They sense the dreariness of business life. Any number of them offering to come here—to work—for anything or nothing—to be near someone in whom they believe.

I can't have them of course. In the first place I can't have people working for less than they are worth and then I want the work here myself. There isn't enough for other[s].

I think the papers will pay for themselves. If they do that I shall have a living here some day—something to leave the kids.

Its about as good an occupation as one could get into and I'm not taking it too seriously.

If you see the papers you know about Buck Fever etc.[2] Its all rather broad fun.

The best part is big old farmers coming in and telling me they like it—giggling over it.

A sort of direct personal contact with your readers. It restores something I had almost lost.

A kind of free laughing contact with my fellow men.

I've even an idea I have discovered something—I mean the human contact with people—in a way they like.

Bless you woman we get little enough. You've been robbed enough I know.

LH Written on the stationery of Sherwood Anderson, Marion, Va.

1. Hahn's longhand note.
2. The character Buck Fever had made his appearance in the newspapers by Nov. 17, 1927.

281

To Bab 1927[1] [Nov. Marion, Va.]

It is an odd situation. Wherever one turns in life certain facts confront him. I had thought for so many years that I wanted leisure. Now I know that is not true. After a year on the farm I knew that I needed constant contact with people.

You know what city life in America has become. To live at all descently one has to struggle constantly with the problem of making a living. At any rate life in a small town does not offer the same necessity to rush. My training is such that there was only one thing I could do in the city. I would have had to go back into an advertising agency.

With luck I should make this paper pay its way out in three or four years. There are problems here of course. I have to go to the little merchant and solicit his advertiging. As in all places some of them have mean spirits. That however is a part of life too.

I think you, and any one who cares for me, would rather I gave all of my energy to this than to degrade myself by becoming a hack writer. It is fairer to myself and everyone concern[ed].

Certain things may develope that will make it easier than seemed possible at first. I have been sending out little circulars. A good many outside subscribers come in. It is barely possible that my own WHAT SAY column may develope into something that other newspapers will want so that I can sell it outside.[2] I hope to do in it much of what I did in my published Notebook.

Already I am better since I came here. It is good for me to be confronted by daily tasks. I think I'll swim.[3]

Bless you for all of your kindnesses to my boys. They are good boys. Poor John will have to fight an unhappy turn toward melencolio. I know that road. For him to[o] it will perhaps be better to be definately at work.

Your goodness is a constant source of pleasure to me.

Some day you must write something for my paper[.]

TS

1. Hahn's longhand note.

2. Anderson did discuss the idea of syndication in letters to his friend, Burton Emmett. See Emmett Collection.

3. A figure often used by Anderson in connection with life struggles.

282

To Bab Xmas 1927[1]

You're letter left me ashamed, of course. The holiday season has always quite stunned me. I've never been able to pull it off.

I can't send out cards. Getting a lot of gifts—all at once. The crowded stores, all that.

I do nothing. Well, I intend to write letters.

But I am not jolly and happy at such a time.

I do nothing and am ashamed of that.[2]

I havn't even thanked you for the nice blood red peppers, with all their suggestion of the sultry south that I love.

Did I ever tell you of getting off a stalled train once in Arkansas. I got off and walked through a burned over forest.

At last I came to a yellow stagnant river. Something happened there. I shall write about it some day.

There was some queer sort of wedding between myself and the seasons. It has affected my whole life since. My bag was in the train and the train went on without me. That night I walked ten miles through the soft night to a little town and slept there.

I did get my bag back the next day—or was it two days later.

All that is too long for a letter.

My life has become a rather comatose one. Work, work. It is better than what I was doing. You know something happened to me as I know.

You think one thing because you are a woman and that's all right. Truth is no woman will ever be first with me.

I would sacrifice any woman for the line of beauty when I can find it.

But love is a line of beauty too. When you love I always love you. Many times when you have thought you loved most you did not love at all. I'm only talking now of course.

What really happened was "I'm a Fool" and other things.

You aren't right about the story. It isn't a trick. It's only immature and we at least are beyond that.

I mean they took me up for a great man, gave me a great name.

It isn't a time of great men. It is a time of publicity, grandstanding.

They did succeed in making me self-conscious. I got muddled inside.

Sitting still didn't help so much. Too much time for thoughts.

I had spoken too much of precious things too.

Lots of times I said to myself—why don't I die.

The sweetness had you see gone out of me.

There is a step beyond where I have yet been through.

Years of moony thinking, the slow grind of years.

I want a new youth deep down in me.

I mean after having measured all—my own degrasion, my own cheapness.

I wonder if this is all just words.

Perhaps you want facts of me.

I bought this little shop. Almost all the paper I write myself. Its silly, a great deal of it. I'm in debt of course.

I am check to jowl with little merchants, farmers, laborers small men.

I have to keep on working yet. If I pay out I will have a living.

I'll go on living a long time—hoping—

This hand coming up out of its legarthy. I am an unusual man in my age in this. My faith is in some way deeper, stronger—than most men's.

In what?

O, dear Bab. How can I put my hand on that.

I do keep projecting a little, hoping waiting.

Our friendship has stood a long time. It will wear through to the end. I'll never loose you and you will not loose me.

I think Bob is better. There is something loose. He isn't quite first class yet. He may though pull it off. He gets toward it, I think.

John gets too depressed. I don't know how to help.

He writes asking if filing letters for bread and butter isn't madness and of course I have to write back it is.[3]

And of course publishing a local weekly paper is madness and much else.

Whatever the central thing is it doesn't show its face often to any of us.

LH Written on stationery of the General Francis Marion Hotel, Marion, Va.

1. Hahn's longhand note.

2. Anderson's customary response to Christmas.

3. In an interview of Feb. 21, 1974, John said he thought this referred to a job he had in Chicago.

283

To Bab 1928[1]

You are a terribly funny inconsistent creature sometimes. Of course you are all right. I love you a lot and it doesn't make any difference.

You love to scold me. You scold me if I do not take the children away from C[ornelia] and if I do. You pass horrible judgments on me, warn me of rocks my ship is going on, sometimes when it is most in the open sea.

And through it all you are kind and fine.

You old dear—I am at the wheel—wherever the boat goes.

When it goes down I'll go with it—I half hope with a song on my lips.

LH Written on the stationery of the Marion Publishing Co., Marion, Va.

1. Hahn's longhand note.

284

To Bab Marion, Va., 1928[1] [Date unclear]

It is curious what happens to human beings. So many years of fighting to get leisure. After all I suppose it was the worse thing in the world for me. Now here I am, having to get out two weekly newspapers every week. I go it all the time. And i[n] the midst of it I do more of my own writing than I used to.

I am not trying to make any decided change in the tome [tone] of the papers. Change must creep in. How can that be helped. I conduct each week a column of my own.[2] It is something in the spirit of my published Notebook. I put into it many things I might write to you or some other dea[r] friend. I mean of course the things always drifting through my mind.

In the meantime I am into a novel.[3] Well, I will not talk about that. I write in the shop, in my room at night, even get up in the night to write. A horribel self-consciousness had hold of me. It is slipping away.

Yesterday I had a request to lecture at the University of Louisville. I made them an offer to come, wanting the chance to see you.[4] It may be they will take me up. I do hope so.

TS

1. Hahn's note added to her typescript of an undated original letter.

2. The column was called "What Say!" Hahn subscribed to the *Smythe County News* and had saved a number of the columns.

3. Unidentified.

4. The suggestion that Anderson would be visiting Finley carries with it the implication that this letter was probably written before her marriage to Dr. E. Vernon Hahn on Feb. 28, 1928, an event not mentioned in these letters.

285

To Bab 1928[1] [Apr. 8 Troutdale, Va.]
Easter Sunday

I am sitting writing, upstairs—my back to an open fire and before me an open window. There is a small chattering stream below the window. Well, it does not chatter really. There is a low sound like wind in a distant forest in the fall.

A long Abraham Lincoln looking man has plowed a field for me and another man will plant corn and oats for my horse.

Willy Pennet, Huck Price, Sol Toliver, Charlie Grubb, Claud Rudy, Arthur Wilson.

They all came to see me yesterday. I am accepted now as one of themselves, a man of the country side. They talk, horse, the wellfare of their wives, children and cattle. A turkey has hid her nest and a man on horseback is looking for her.

Every little event runs through the valley of Ripshin Creek and into the houses.

All these men will cheat, unmercifully in a horse trade. They would steal whiskey if you had it about.

Everything else is safe.

Not Quite.

Arthur Wilson gets roaring drunk. During the winter he got drunk and went to a lonely cabin where two women lived alone.

He tried to break in the door, shouting things the while. No doubt, in his drunken frenzy he had some notion of ravaging the two women. At home he has a wife and eight children. One of the women drove him off with a shot gun.

It is the time of birds. They sing madly in the apple trees under the window. The whippoorwill calls at night.

Do you think the rhodedemdrum would grow in your yard. I would like to send you two or three bushes. It does not grow well when there is lime in the soil. Perhaps you could get a load of dirt free from lime. The plants would be about 3 ft tall and would come by express. I have a whole hedge of them. They are evergreen and the blossoms are as large as a pineapple, white, pink and lovely.

Mary Cochran has become another woman. I don't dare speak of her much. Little thing[s] in her life are slipping out of my pen onto paper these days. It is the same Mary but with the surroundings and circumstances of her life quite different.

LH

1. Hahn's longhand note. Easter in 1928 was on Apr. 8, hence the precise dating of this letter.

286

To Bab 1928[1] [Spring, Marion, Va.]

Even when a man is working pretty steadily, as I am now, there come days when he cannot work.

It is all there, what he wants to put down but there is something missing too.

I presume it is the rhythm of things—of words I think I mean—the surface.

I am going along quite well however.

It is all a little odd. I would like to tell you how it is.

I have got, dear Bab a little fame. I have been to Paris, to New York.

A certain amount of acclaim.

Other things—the children really. Trying to feel into them a little.

The worse thing the confusion of writing—talk of writing. Those interested in my work.

All sorts of things going on—Stein, Joyce.

Others talking, talking.

Here I have cut back a little to nature.

I get off the track—want to do something new, in a new way.

A corrupt notion.

I will say I came here to the country, to nature, pretty corrupt. I am corrupt still.

What I have to say I have to say in my own way. If there is an art for me it must be my own art.

Something indefinable—lets call it "it" toward which a man goes.

Trying to go by some other man's road only leads to confusion.

I have to get people as they are in nature, trees, skies, plowed fields.

When I cannot write these days I go out doors. There is an old apple tree fallen down. I sit on it and look at a hillside.

A man has planted oats on the hillside. I try to go down into the ground, feel the harrow raking me, the rain falling on me, the spring sun creeping down to me.

If I am to grow green again and put forth fruit it must be a slow patient process.

Those who love me hurt sometimes as much as the ones who hate. We make a cult of giving, become "good."

All sorts of things happen.

I sit on the tree and say to myself "be still—be still."

Being still is everything. God knows whether or not you or anyone can know all I mean.

I mean myself, my relationship with "it."

I may be getting impregnated. Old stories are told of the gods coming down to men and women.

The old stories meant what I mean now.

On the whole I'm all right. The little note from John made tears come into my eyes. I love him.

I told the man to ship the bushes.

Feel nice about me.

I can't say about going anywhere any time now. I may just run to that place and quickly back. Nothing does for me now like utter quiet—nature I suppose.

It isn't just that. It's "it." I wish I could give "it" a more definate name.

LH

1. Hahn's longhand note.

287

To Bab June—1928[1] [Marion, Va.]

In making any such arraingment for the children of course I have consulted C[ornelia] first.

My dear it is a bit inconsistent—to blame me if I do not have the children with me—and then to blame me if I do.

And there is something else. C will have to learn to divorce herself from the children. She can't live her life in them. It is a preperation for the inevitable I should think.

And I can't you know live with C.

I am as sorry as anyone could be for any sadness that comes into C's life and do appreciate her—

But what can't be helped, can't be helped. She has seen much more of them than I have dear.

LH

1. Hahn's longhand note.

288

To Bab 1928[1] [Early summer Marion, Va.]

I think John and Miss Mimi will perhaps spend the summer down here. There is the farm with the house on it. They can run back and forth to town. It will give me some chance to see something of them.

The papers drive me but I am happy to be driven. There is a constant pressure—not as in a daily, where you must be up to the minute on news.

But the machines going on. As you see I drop all sorts of things into the paper.

Poets send me verses. Stories drift in—a great many I cannot use. It is a very curious and interesting experiment, this writing for farmers and cattlemen.

Its all writing.

The shop is charming. Just a little old workshop with four men. One old chap not unlike Sponge Martin of Dark Laughter.

Constant contact with people—housewives, preachers, school teachers, merchants, farmers.

Occasionally something done of my own.

Im working anyway—not being a professional artist. Letting the artist in me happen as it will in the midst of work.

I send much love to you.

LH

1. Hahn's longhand note.

289

To Bab Marion Va. 1928[1] [April or later]

The red peppers came from Mexico, a great box of them. They are lovely. There isn't any other red quite like that one. Many many thanks for your thoughtfulness in sending them.

Bob's visit was altogether unexpected. I think you are more or less right about the matter. Bob came quite ready to give up over there. I think it was in large part my own fault. I have had too much on my hands lately. I should have managed in some way to have written him oftener and sent him more money. However I myself have been upset—or at least had been. I am getting more fun out of life now. There is something about this present work that, while not always pleasant has this to be said for it—well I dare say I am by nature too much the introvert. This brings out the other side of me.

The little print shop is a small center of movement. In a way the life of the community constantly flows through it. I have to meet people constantly, the small merchants, women who belong to clubs and various reforms they want to put through, precahers, nice old farmers. Everyone runs to the print shop. I sit here like an old spider in its web.

By my side lies a novel. You know I always did in the old days write in the midst of a clatter. I shall here. A little less the ordinary disturbances of life do not touch me. Inside I presume is going on the attempt to become some kind of a philosopher.

Bob is a great deal like myself. That is why it is hard sometimes for me to be as fair with him as I would like. I know so often when he is talking sheer nonsense as I have myself talked the same nonsense. I want to take a great leap over it and can't always understand why he can't, that I never could myself.

I think this time everything came out very well. Of course I was up-set but I do not think he knew it. We talked.

I bought him two pair of new shoes, gave him money, made him go to bed and sleep. His having been drunk did not bother me much.[2] He isn't thank God the durnkard type. That was just desperation brought on partly by lonliness, [pa]rtly because he had not been accepting his new surroundings, had not much been trying to make himself fit in etc. I would like to have him stick it out there[3] at least this year.

I do think it a handicap to be my son. Why should anyone want to imitate my life. It is beyond understanding. However they do not see my life as I do. I understand that too.

As you know dear friend with Bob my affections are not as much involved as with John but that is changing too. We get on better.

I have nothing definate about a western trip. The University at Louisville wrote me about a lecture and I thought I could go out there in order to see you. They have not responded though. I asked them two hundred.

When expenses are paid that does not leave much, the way money evaporates these days.

TS

1. Hahn's date on her typescript.
2. In "What Say!" of Apr. 18, 1928, Anderson wrote: "Your son goes and gets drunk. He raises the very devil, perhaps smashes his automobile and is lucky if he escapes killing someone. You crowd repentence on him. Try to make him think he has disgraced you forever."
3. Possibly the University of Virginia at Charlottesville. Bob attended the school for only one year.

290

To Bab 1928[1] [Marion, Va.]

Every day—lately I have been thinking I would write you. A man to do any creative work now—in the midst of all life's confusion has to sink sometimes so low. The dross has to come out. The months of seeing people—being treated as something special—the disease and hurt of that.

Then the poor people on farms now.

The quiet stately thing in nature.

Earth, rains, the clay, fire, ashes.

A seed has to rot before it can grow.

At last word[s] beginning to have meaning a little. A little music under the pen.

What I want now is so illusive, hard to grasp.

Some days I write until my whole body thrembles. There is a little left, sometimes that will stand.

Little strength left to write letters. I say so little of what is to be said.

People, here and there, loving me. I feel that. I can give them so little.

Im as near nothing as a man can be.

LH

1. Hahn's longhand note.

291

To Bab 1928[1] [Marion, Va.]

Do not be greatly disturbed by my momentary weakness . . . about my work . . . what people think of it etc. I don't really give a damn. What I do care about is that I have been through a long dead time. All creative workmen pass through such times. We get to living so much in our work. For the workmen what else is there to live for. Such a man as myself is not on[e] man. At times I am dozens. At other times I am nothing. Out of my great em[p]tiness you hear a voice coming. It is the voice of death, of nothingness.

There is a thread that will lead me again out into life. Where is it. You see grouping in the darkness. You hear a complaining whining voice. Much of the New Testament came out of that cave.

At last one day I find again the thread that leads to the light. I emerge blinking into the sun, hear the birds sing, note all of the wonders of passing life.

I think the only way it can be explained is by the symbol of pregna[n]cy. You ought to know about that. We of the artist class are very closely allied to you women. Wanting pregna[n]cy we whimper.

But who is my lover. Turn again to the new testament. You will see proclaiming the coal passer, the old newsman, the shepard, the farmer. Sometimes I have been cured by the mere gesture of amna [a man] or womab [woman] walking alone. Thank your s[t]ars you are not married to me, that you have escaped that.[2] At times there is no more caracter or nobility to me than to a sick dog.

Some day when I am in what one of my friends called, "the times between," I shall die, but not yet. I am quite sure I shall not die noble. I shall go out whimpering I have no doubt.

But before that many long years and much work to do yet. I feel it in me now again. I am all right.

Good days to you. Bob was nice. I think he will pull something off. But poor lad, how much of the worst of me he has in him. May god be good to the lad.

TS

1. Hahn's longhand note. This letter seems to be a companion in desperation of spirit to the one immediately preceding it. The reference to Bob's visit in paragraph 8 suggests the time might have been late spring or early summer.

2. A peripheral reference to Finley's marriage?

292

To Bab 1928[1] [Possibly August Marion, Va.]

It is so long since I have written you. Life goes on. I have long times of depression and then I come to life again and work. When I publish a book of tales again I want it to be gay—a kind of gay frank acceptance of life.

I am getting more here than appears on the su[r]face. The hills are gay and grave and somber and sometimes grand. I have got must out of John and Mimi this summer. Robert and I do not touch each other much. I am afraid to be near him much. Alas, it may simple be that I do not love him much.

The town, the life of the streets, the little county court, the justice trials, in the hills all mean more and more to me. I am often full of joy that I can write so that some heavy handed farmer will come down the street to the shop and take my hand. "It's good," he says. That pleases me more than most anything I have had happen in my life. Or the coal miner, over the line in West Virginia who tells me that he and his wife read my column in the paper aloud to each other and talk about it after they go to bed.

All sorts of things happening to a man in life. My own life has been pretty rich. O dear, I talk like a man about to die. I only mean that I have a queer feeling I may be a country editor the rest of my days. It's a feeling I never had before.

Your friendship is dear and dear to me. It is one of the really solid things of my existence. My dear dear woman.

TS Written on the stationery of the Marion Publishing Co., Marion, Va.

1. Hahn's longhand note.

293

To Bab Dec. 1928[1]

It is too bad I do not write you oftener. I think of you very very often, wonder about you and your life.

As for myself I go on as always, working sometimes, puzzled often—checked—stopped.

Working emotionally, as I always do and must, I am exhausted often.

Nothing I think quite holds me. It may be I am an artist pure and simple, a man to whom all things feed into a central force.

If it is so it can't be helped. It is myself.

I think I have not asked Bob to come here from any altruistic motives.[2]

I have taken these papers up and played with them for a year. I have taken them as I might have taken a woman, have in fact taken women.

For a year I have given almost everything to them. I can't do that longer.

I think Bob may be taught to do something with them. They can provide a fine living.[3] I will stay and help him.

New loves come and old one[s] drop away. The land here is lovely. I love that.

Often I look back with a queer feeling. How much I have been loved—by you—by others. How kind everyone has been.

I give little in return. Occasionally, however, something does flow up through me. I produce stories, novels, poems that have a living strength.

I am trying always to make myself take places, people, loves, as they come to me.

I understand the difficulty about Bob and myself. I can handle it. I can do him some good now. There will be bad moment[s].

If I am working—as I hope to be—it will be all right.

I have never had Bob when I have had work for him to do. That will help. I understand his sweetness, his immaturity.

It will be, at least, a new thing to work together—on something definate.

Surely, if you go to New York I shall have more chance to see you. I will not be tied down here in the future as I have been in the past. I expect Bob to untie me soon.

I shall not lecture very much. A few engagements only.

Lots of love to you dear one.

LH Written on stationery of the Marion Publishing Co., Marion, Va.

1. Hahn's longhand note.
2. Bob took charge of the newspapers in Dec. 1931.
3. Yet Bob's widow has written, "We were quite poor until after World War II" (letter to Sutton, Mar. 8, 1974).

294

To Bab December 27, 1928[1] [Marion, Va.]

It is too bad to write you a Christmas letter on this paper, and with a pencil, but I have nothing else here—and it is two days after Christmas besides.

I have been in bed ill, evidently not the flue—as I have had no fever. I think I wrote too steadily and for too many hours a day for about three week. Then I took cold and down I went.

Bob and I are alone here, for the time. He is getting out the paper.

We get along better than formerly—very well in fact.[2]

I think he might as well learn to run the paper here. I myself will grow tired of it in the long run as I do tire of things.

To tell the truth I would like to go away from this place now—for a long time. It would perhaps even be well for my general feeling if I could have a year alone somewhere.

I would like to drift, work, then drift again.

But really dear I sat down to write you some joy at this time. It isn't such a joyful time, is it?

I am going to Chicago to speak, Jan. 8[3] and if it can be managed and you are to be at home, would like to stop and see you.[4]

As Always

Will be here, at least until the end of the month.

LH

1. Hahn's longhand note.

2. John has said that he noticed a "sense of restraint" in Robert when he talked of working with his father. Interview of Feb. 21, 1974.

3. Anderson talked on modern writing and industrialism under the auspices of the Forge in an evening lecture in Mandell Hall at the University of Chicago on Tuesday, Jan. 8.

4. According to Elizabeth Prall Anderson, Sherwood told her that they could afford a trip to California for her in Jan. 1929. Her departure for California must have been about the same time as his for Chicago. A few days after arriving in California, she received a letter from Sherwood, telling her that he would prefer she did not rejoin him. See her *Miss Elizabeth*, pp. 188–89. In a long revealing letter to Hans W. Poppe, written on Sept. 15, 1947 (now at the Newberry Library), she showed her awareness that Sherwood had spent his life escaping from matters he found unpleasant and wrote that she had become one of them. Her

summation was that she loved him but he had become tired of her. At forty-five she then ran a shop in Taxco, Mexico, and was still there when she died in January 1976.

295

To Bab January 1929[1] [Jan. 6]

Monday—at ten. I am just up, after a good sleep and am breakfasting in my room. I am thinking. Do not take too seriously what I said about your brain. Your brain is all right, dear one, but you are a woman. You are very much woman, more than you think.

Your relationship to me can never be what is is to Bob and John. They, I think, feel you as both mother and friend. It will be very difficult for us to be friends. It can be done but it will be difficult. What else there might have been may have been spoiled. I don't know.

Do you think, my dear, that there is not possessiveness in you. You are full of it—a real woman. I think, in all your thoughts of me, you do not, ever perhaps, think of me as artist—a man working in abstract things. It may be that only men can give each other that affection.

The young painter, or poet, working out there, beyond me. To care for him as for a lovely object in the room.

I could give, to such a one, an affection strong and constant. You have never given me that. I am to you—a man. That is the feminine in you. You can't down it more than another woman. Words will not down it.

I may be, for the rest of my life, a man at work. I have had three women, as wives, other for [word crossed out] more or less prolonged times.

I remember walking with you by a canal bank. I see again the sky, the green bank, the water in the canal. People walking up and down.

I see you in other remembered scenes—you walking in the rain in Chicago, your little distressed figure.

Last night I loved you sitting on the couch—the people in the room.

You have, my dear, as much right to all you feel, as woman, as I have to what I feel as artist and man.

But now I am seperated from that. I have fought to get here, in this room alone. The words on paper—moulding them—my job.

It may be I will never again let women, as women in here. They have disbarked too much, spoiled too much.[2]

There will come times when I will be wanting and I will take wanting.

My dear, it is a question of values. Our values may be quite different. I am very difficult.

I want you as friend now—friend to the struggling defeated artist in myself. As to me, as a man, it should be forgotten now. I can deal with that fellow.

If you can help me sell the house I shall be very very grateful because it will help me.

I want to hang on to what I have from you, if I can.[3] It is hard to say all [that] I mean. O, if you were a man, I could say so much I cannot now say.[4]

LH Written on the stationery of the Hotel Severin, Indianapolis, Ind.

1. Hahn's longhand note. This was evidently written on the morning after Anderson's visit with Hahn, on Saturday, Jan. 5, and before he started to Chicago for his lecture on Jan. 8.

2. This passage is significant to any analysis of Anderson's life-long effort to stand and understand women, who both attracted and distracted him and became a major concern of his writing.

3. Presumably it was in a later, undated letter that Anderson indicated he had reached some accommodation within himself about Bab's marriage. "I had engaged to go to lunch with Bab Finley—she being now Mrs. Vernon Hahn. Marriage has been good for her. She has broadened out, looks fine, loves her man." Eleanor Anderson thought this letter was written in 1930.

4. There are no letters extant addressed to a man in which Anderson revealed himself as he did in these letters to Bab, although at one time Anderson once told Tennessee that her attitude was so fine as to make her seem like a man.

296

To Bab January 1929[1]

The idea is quite all right of course—from your point of view—the Princess too. By that point of view I might as well have kept the Princess.[2]

Mor[t]gages, loans from you, or gifts.

No, my dear, I shall sell the place as soon as possible. I want $35,000. I think usual commissions to real estate people run 5%.[3]

It is beautiful—a complete thing. I have also written beautiful, complete stories and novels. I do not keep them about, mull over them.

I should raise my own tulips, plant my garden on sheets of white paper.

I am going back to my own life. What is for you is not for me. I know what I am doing. If you know any one can sell the place—there is

$1750.00 to be made selling it. You will do me the greatest favor in the world by helping it along. I shall press it home.

And my dear I do appreciate your own kindness, your goodness. You are speaking from your own point of view. The artist in me—you will forgive my saying it—is a bit outside you—or any woman I dare say.

I am at the end of *things*. You would laugh to see the office here. There are two offices at the front of the shop. One the book-keeper has and I have altogether surrendered the other to Bob.

I have a small kitchen table—3 ft by 2 feet—a kitchen chair. These I move about. At this moment I am writing along side the lin-o-type machine. I can almost put my desk in my pocket. It is enough.

Bob has your point of view. At the house I have beautiful chairs, tables, chests of drawers etc. He trembles least I sell them—I won't. He and the other children can have them.

I want the world of my own fancy—not mor[t]gages, debts etc.

The princess almost took it from me.[4] I'm clear now and I shall stay clear.[5]

With love

LH Written on the stationery of the Marion Publishing Co., Marion, Va.

1. Hahn's longhand note.
2. Anderson had visited Hahn in Indianapolis as part of his trip to Chicago. The references to "the Princess," as he now called his wife Elizabeth (his way of showing his dislike of what he now considered her aristocratic, domineering, or possibly incisively accurate attitudes?), indicate that he had discussed the break-up of his marriage. Does the first paragraph suggest that Hahn wondered whether he had made a mistake?
3. Anderson was referring to Ripshin—which was never sold.
4. This is very like a remark he made about Tennessee when they separated.
5. Anderson remarried again in 1933 and was in love considerably before that.

297

To Bab Jan. 15, 1929[1] [Marion, Va.]

I did not get any New York address with your nice letter so send this via Indianapolis. I have to write like this as my eyes are tender,—after flue—and I dare not strain them.

The Princess has made up her mind to be very nice. There will be no trouble about the property here.

From Chicago I went on for a day or two in N.Y. I am having extra photographs made of the house and will send you some. Also descriptive matter. Mr. Liveright says it is foolish to sell the house at $15,000 to $20,000. His idea is $30,000 to $35,000. He says, with what seems to me some sense, that only a rich man would buy it at all. He would respect it more for paying more. He thinks, as a matter of fact that it can be well sold—partly—how absurd this is—because it is Sherwood Anderson's house.

I will send you, with the photographs, a sort of prospectus I have had drawn up for him.

About other finances, dear friend, I would rather not have that brought up between us. It is all a matter I shall have to solve and can do it now. Bob is marvelous. He can actually run the papers so that I can go away for weeks at a time.

I have a long novel in me now but shall not attempt it until I am well again. The next year I shall spend much alone.

I want actual lonliness and work. I am like a man who has been swimming a broad cold river in winter and have at last reached the other shore.[2]

You will understand that I must be free to reject or take love and friendship from my own impulses. I think, if you knew, how really my children love you you would feel that what you have done or may do for them carries its own reward.

I may be a year straightening things out but I have the capacity to do it now. I am no longer a beaten man.

Bless you, my dear, for your offer of help but I cannot take direct personal help, least of all from any woman.

It is just so, dear friend.

LH

1. Hahn's longhand note.
2. An oft-repeated figure, much like what he reportedly said to his secretary when he walked out of his office into his amnesia episode at the end of Nov. 1912: "My feet are cold, wet and heavy from long wading in a river." His secretary heard it as: "I feel as though my feet were wet, and they keep getting wetter." See Sutton, *Road to Winesburg*, pp. 186–87.

298

To Bab Feb. 1929[1] [Before Feb. 7, Troutdale Va.]

I sent [a] letter, giving a description of the house and photographs. I certainly see no reason why it should not be sold as Sherwood Anderson's house. He practically built it with his own hands.[2]

Horace thinks that it should not sell for less than $35,000. Well, I dont know.

I have been having sleepless nights, my house full of ghosts of the departed Princess. Now nearly all of her things are packed and gone and the house becomes masculine—a workshop.

I have no feeling about selling the house. It is like a novel, finished. I want to sell it, and the quicker the better.[3] A blessing on you for your friendship dear. It would be better if nothing more were thought of, I'm pretty sure.

That is my word. That is the way it seems to me.

If it is too hard for you [to do] so, throw me off my dear.

The paper, by the way, is going very well and, with this drain off it, will go better.

LH Written on the stationery of Sherwood Anderson, Marion, Va.

1. Hahn's longhand note. The date of before Feb. 7 is ascribed to this letter in view of his writing to Cornelia on Feb. 21, "I have come from a two week trip riding around in an automobile down south. I was trying to rest up. I have gotten into a highly nervous state and naturally needed to get away from here."
2. The letters of the summer of 1925 had suggested that he supervised the work but supplied little, if any, of the labor.
3. In fact, he occupied the house part-time until his death in 1941.

299

To Bab February 20, 1929[1] [Marion, Va.]

Dear Woman—

I think this is the nicest letter I ever had from you. It touched me way down where it hurt. I am sorry I cannot give you all you want. It hurts to think I can't.

You are so lovely to take all this trouble about the house. I have ordered extra photograph[s] which will be sent soon. The insurance rate on all country property is somewhat high. I think I paid $60 for $6,000 for 3 years. Taxes are low. I paid about $24.00—I think. There are from 50 to 60 acres about the house—all of one little upland valley. There are no social advantages. It would have to be sold for a real country place. However—at Marion 20 miles away—over an excellent road will be found [a] country club, fine hotel—etc.

The floor plans and drawings will have to wait until I can get over there and have them made. It may be some weeks yet.

I would not want to show the property now—on account of winter roads. Snow and rain in the mountains etc. In late May or June would be the lovely time.

That you have been ill again hurts me. That I can give you so little hurts worse.

LH

1. Hahn's longhand note.

300

To Bab March 9, 1929[1] [Marion, Va.]

I cannot of course help the feeling of responsibility to you. The picture of you, going on to the end, not getting perhaps what you want from me, is too much. It lays a sense of guilt on me.

I am like one working my way through a fog, most of the time. I am not insensitive to the fact that I have probably done better and more lasting work than any man of my time but that does not satisfied. There is something I am always trying to penetrate. It requires cruelty in me, tenderness, above all humbleness. Often I have the temerity to think of myself as a sort of man like Cezanne—"A primitive of the way."[2] I mean that there has been little accomplished in prose in my day. Last July, in the Yale Literary Magazine, there was an article by a man who understood something.[3] He felt it necessary, being a critic and having also some notion of form in his essey I think, to preach a funeral sermon over me but that did not interfear with some clear thinking. You might read that essey sometime.

As for women, to be frank, my dear, our experience has been not unlike others I have had with other women. Much has been offered to me in the way of women, in the flesh. I have taken what I felt clear and clean in taking. When I no longer felt that I have stopped, sometimes only after much bitterness. I have gone sometimes away from women with fine bodies and fine minds and have taken gladly women to whom I had no obligation, because to do so cleansed me like writing good prose.

A part of the obligation I feel is to try a little to understand all this if I can. There is so much to try to understand.

I don't know about my book for this year—"Hello Towns." It will be rather a unique book. It might just sell.[4]

As for the papers I take nothing from them. What is earned, besides

Bob's not too generous salary, must go to pay for the papers. For my own living and to help those to whom I am responsible, I must write for Vanity Fair and other magazines. It is sometimes difficult to do this and breaks a kind of long solitude I often want in the face of nature and people.

And there are the men in th[e] shop. I might make the business pay more by being less generous with them but my relationships with them are also bound up in all the rest.

In the face of things I hardly think Europe for Cornelia and Mimi is a necessity this year.

As for Bob I can give him a business here. He has a good deal of the young American in him, is swept by ambitions, wants to make money. I think I can get across to him, am in fact getting across, at least the outlines of another conception.

When I see what is going on in my time, the loose talk of the arts, the all around missunderstanding, cheapness in attitude, a [I] feel a rather deep obligation to something that must always remain dearer to me than any woman. That I think women only understand intellectually but I do not blame them.

I think there is no doubt of the clear affection of the children for you. As for C I do not know. I have not been near her for a long time but I do feel fineness in her.

I am making every effort to seel [sell] the farm. It is very lovely but there is another kind of lovliness infinately more important to me.

I would like you to know that I feel gratitude and sincere affection for you. How it will all come out, as regards my work and what I want to do I don't know. I al [am] getting almost supersticious about speaking of it.

I am very happy that the injury was not worse.

TS

1. Hahn's longhand note.
2. Paul Cezanne (1839-1906), French painter and modernist leader.
3. The article was Dwight MacDonald's "Sherwood Anderson," *Yale Literary Magazine*, 93 (July 1928), 209–43.
4. Hahn had her customary first edition of the book, which was published in Apr. 1929.

301

To Bab April 2, 1929[1] [Troutdale, Va.]

I just came home. Was in New York several days and then went to the country. Called you on the phone 3 times, without success. No one answered the phone.

About the house. You are perhaps quite right. New York men advised me to ask $35,000. I would take $25,000, or even 20,000 or 22,000.

I only want to get clear. Don't bother about it too much. Our relations have had too much of money talk. It is my fault.

Or yours for being rich.

I shall, I am sure, get the blue print in a few days now—as soon as I get to the farm.

Had planned a week longer in New York but the wife of the old foreman in the shop here is dying. That brought me scampering home.

In New York I saw almost none of my old friends. I began to write a little—with some music in my prose again.

I want only to get clear and not be bothered with property of any kind. I never will be again.

I am damn sorry I did not see you but I dreaded conversation about my personal affairs and so saw no one. Had I been able to stay a week longer I might have got more courage.

LH Written on the stationery of the Marion Publishing Co., Marion, Va.

1. Hahn's longhand note.

302

To Bab Dec. 30, 1930[1] [Marion, Va.]

I write you, a bit late, for the hollidays.

Principally to wish you a good year ahead.

It has been a curious year for me but I have come out, I think, a little ahead.

It is a curious thing an artist in America goes through. He struggles and wants to get recognition etc. Sometimes it comes. It did to me.

The world pours in on him in a curious way. The world has pretty muddy feet Bab. It doesn't leave a man's house very nice.

I have had a curious wish to get small, not big. When Tennessee died I was down south.[2] I was on a pier going out into the Atlantic,[3] on the day after I heard of her death.

It seemed very nice, death did, very still and white. It was a way to wash life away. I had to fight, as I had never fought not to slipp off the side of the pier and swim away—to death.

It wouldn't have been Tennessee, or Elizabeth or Cornelia or any other individual woman I swam toward. I have been, I think an [an abstrat crossed out] a lover of abstract womanhood. When it has appeared I have loved it.

I havn't often stopped loving when I [seemed] to.

As regards my work I have felt these last several years a going back toward my own people, working people. I have gone a lot to factories. Working women, in factories have appealed to me tremendously. In a way life just now, particularly among working people, the life of reality is more fantastic and strange to see than the imagainative life. It may be my mother calling to me.[4]

I may, more and move give myself to that.

At any rate I shall work.

I am glad for you; you have found your way. A Happy New Year to you.

LH

1. Hahn's longhand note.

2. Tennessee Mitchell Anderson was found dead in her apartment on Dec. 26, 1929, evidently having died perhaps a week before. This letter suggests, a year later, some of the anguish he felt at her passing. When a mutual friend sent Anderson a telegram about the death and the funeral arrangements, Anderson responded in a letter dated Dec. 31, 1929 (written on the stationery of the Hotel Detroit in Tampa Bay at St. Petersburg, Fla.), and postmarked Jan. 5, 1939. In part he wrote: "After a good deal of hesitation and perplexity about the notion of coming to Chicago for Tennessee's funeral I decided not too. It seemed a bit absurd when there had been so many opportunities for kindness to Tennessee alive I had let [pass] and then I was done up."

3. The pier at St. Petersburg projects into the Gulf of Mexico.

4. He struck a similarly sentimental note in dedicating *Winesburg, Ohio* to his barely literate mother.

303

To Bab October 1931[1] [Marion, Va.]

It was good to hear from you. I only heard a few days ago that you had been ill. Bob told me and said he had just heard of your luck. It has been in my mind daily to write you.

I am in the printing office here, early on Sunday morning and Bob is still asleep upstairs, hence this paper. We live togather here. Bob has taken complete charge of the papers and, with caracteristic energy, of almost everything else in town. He is in the fire department, runs the band, the local dances and about everything else. Incidentally he referees all of the foot ball games. If anything went on in this town he was not the center of he would sicken and die.

He is very popular here. The town loves him and is much happier with him running the papers than they ever were when I did it.

John and I had on the whole a very satisfactory summer together, at least it was satisfactory to me and Mimi came for a few weeks. John is a slow carefull worker but goes steadily toward what he is after and Mimi is a little peach.

I am very sorry that you should worry about the financial status of the children. I know that everyone is hard hit this year but I think everything will be managed. The papers suffer some from the depression of the times but not as much as many other businesses.

At the end of the month we make our last outside payment and then they can be turned over to Bob.[2] In ordinary years they should pay good dividends on twenty thousand and I am to sell them to Bob for ten, the ten to go to John and Mimi. With the beginning of the new year Bob should begin to make these payments. It should put them through. God knows they should be grateful to you always, as I am, and I think they are.

My winter plans are somewhat uncertain. I am trying to sell my farm here and will let it go for whatever it will bring. It is only an expense as I do not use it much. I suspect that I shall stay here with Bob until after the beginning of the year and then will get off south, to Georgia perhaps. I am doing some things in modern industry and need to be near the mills.

I have been pretty well but in a depressed state for the last two years xxx but am emerging from that at last and working again.

It is good to hear that you are yourself again and that you have found work that absorbes you. I would like to see you and meet your husband[3] but cannot say about New York. I go there very seldom, in fact have not been there for nearly eighteen months now.

Good luck, health and a thousand thanks for your kind letter and, dear Bab, for all your kindnesses.

TS

1. Hahn's longhand note.
2. The newspapers were turned over to Bob after his marriage to Mary Chryst, a teacher at Marion College, on Dec. 18, 1931.
3. Dr. Hahn had not been mentioned in the correspondence previously.

304

To Bab December 9, 1931

Of course it was ungracious of me to dictate a letter to you,[1] which I did the last time I wrote, and which alas, I am doing again but not nearly as ungracious as your first answer, old dear.

Now you are your own charming self again and have written me this delightful letter. I dictate an answer because I am jammed with work and do not want to put off writing to you any longer.

Also, I just came home and I am going away again tomorrow. It was mighty nice of you to write me about my book[2] as you did.

My love to you and the doctor and a happy Christmas and New Year.

TS Written on the stationery of the Marion Publishing Co., Marion, Va. The letter was typed by a secretary, and Anderson signed it.

1. This is perhaps the most overt evidence that this series of letters does not contain all of the letters written to Bab.
2. *Perhaps Women* was published in 1931.

305

To Bab May—1932[1] [March, Marion, Va.]

I shall indeed try to do it. I am uncertain about just when I will start but want to be in Chicago, for a few days with Mimi before the ordeal of the lectures begins.

It was charming of you to ask me.

LH

1. Hahn's longhand note. Anderson had spoken in Detroit at the Athletic Club on Mar. 12 and was in Chicago on Mar. 14 to discuss with his daughter Mimi her forthcoming wedding.

306

To Bab May—1932[1]

A 1000 thanks for a grand time.

I have written Bob to send Lady Chatterly—by express. It might be siezed in the mail.

My first lecture is tonight.

Did I leave in your house a red & black flask. If I did will you please send it to Marion.

I like your man.

Havn't seen John yet, as he is at Point Sable but think we will go home through Ohio.

Love

LH

1. Hahn's longhand note. This letter is perhaps misdated; the period of May 1932 is covered by a diary (at the Newberry Library) that does not mention the suggested visit to Indianapolis.

307

To Bab September 16, 1932

I was distressed to hear of your bum luck but was delighted that being in the hospital stirred you up to send me a greeting. I have been terribly busy and I believe very healthy and in good spirits this year. My new novel[1] is just published and I really like it. I went suddenly off to Europe about a month ago to attend a peace conference at Amsterdam and have just come back. I rather think I will go to Russia about the middle of ne[x]t month and spend the winter there. It is possible I may be in the Middle West to make a few talks out there in late March or early April next year.

The new novel is not published yet but will be within a week. When you see it I will be delighted to have you sit down and write me your impressions. I am in grand spirits these days and working every day at the top of my speed.

Do get well fast and get out doors into this grand fall weather. Give my best to your husband.

You will forgive me for dictating this, I know, because I am just home and in a hurry to get off a greeting to you.

With love,

TS Written on the stationery of the Marion Publishing Co., Marion, Va. The letter was typed by a secretary, and Anderson signed it.

1. *Beyond Desire.*

308

To Bab April 1933[1] [Kansas City, Mo.]

Is there a public market in Indianapolis and, if there isn't one now, would there have been one 25 or 30 years ago. It seems to me that, in driving about with you, I saw such a place once. The point is that I am writing a long novel,[2] using, for the first time, the material that would come out of my years of experience as an advertising writer in Chicago.

My man—his name is Frank Blandin—came from a town—say 15 or 18 miles from Indianapolis. His father was a little nervous American who married an Italian girl, the daughter of a Italian in Indianapolis—who ran either a small vegetable & fruit store or had a booth in a public market. The boy used to drive there in the night, with his father. The father was a truck gardener and the Italian mother worked with him in the fields.

Of course Bab I have known many such public markets in American cities—they have always fastinated me but I am vague about Indianapolis.

If there is one there—or would have been—say about the time automobiles were beginning to be used—write and tell me where it is. Describe the surrounding. Are there Italians there? If a boy walked, in the early morning—in late May, or June, in the neighborhood, what would he see?

You see I am trying to confirm impressions I may have got in some other city.

Would it be far from the center of town, Monument Square etc.

Would it be in a section of the city where there might have been formerly prostitution?

Would house wives come to market in the morning etc.

How are you? Have you improved and are you at home?

I'll give you briefly the news.

Bob keeps the paper going & has got a wife & a 5 acre farm near town & John is there, works, running the lin-o-type machine in the evenings & paints during the day. As you probably know the 3 children own the 2 newspapers. Mimi is going to have her first baby soon.

I have been working hard. I am publishing this spring a book of short stories[3] and have made a play out of Winesburg that will probably be produced in the fall in N.Y.

I keep afloat by some hook or crook and still have the Ripshin house—near Marion. I'll go back there to live this summer.

Would like you, in particular, to read the story Brother Death—in the new story book. Write me about the market.

S(not Sherwood) Anderson
Hotel Puritan,
9th & Wyandotte,
Kansas City, Mo.

My best to Vernon.

LH

1. Hahn's longhand note.
2. This book evidently did not survive.
3. *Death in the Woods.*

309

To Sherwood Anderson November 7, 1933

This summer while we have been living in the country I have been hard at work upon something that I think will be a real contribution to American Contemporary literature—namely the compilation of your letters which have been written during the period of our friendship. I have selected the impersonal ones dealing with your running comment upon life and living and I am most anxious to get your permission to send the ms to a publisher.

This winter my husband is taking a time off for study and I shall be in New York for a time doing some work there. I will contact several publishers and should like to have your permission to submit the ms. Naturally I would submit you the galley should the ms be taken for your comment and revision and I feel sure the book would be of value. You have very little idea I presume of what interesting material is contained in those letters.

Life is going most interestingly for me these days. My income is reduced to nearly nothing since my holdings have been in real estate. However I am forced now to work which is what should happen. It is sad to realize that it takes necessity to bring that about but I am a very human person in that respect.

It seems long since I have had direct news of you. Rumor has come of your marriage.[1] If that is true I am wishing you a good adjustment. I have come now to know that marriage is not a goal but an adjustment both pleasant and otherwise. But worth the effort nevertheless.

I am staying here in the country with a friend of ours for a week or ten days finishing up the numerous details of business before leaving for a long period. If you will, write me soon your idea regarding the matter of the "letter ms"—I should like to have a foreword from you if you will give it—and my suggestion for a title would be—Letters to M.D.F.—since the letters are somewhat similar in tone to your Notebook which was dedicated to John Emerson and me.[2]

My best wishes to you and yours.

Always affectionately

TS

1. After a long courtship, Anderson married Eleanor Copenhaver of Marion, Va., on July 6, 1933.

2. Anderson is not known to have replied to this letter.

Appendix A

Sherwood Anderson's "Apology for Crudity"

For a long time I have believed that crudity is an inevitable quality in the production of a really significant present day American literature. How, indeed, is one to escape the obvious fact that there is as yet no native subtlety of thought or living among us? And if we are a crude and childlike people how can our literature hope to escape the influence of that fact? Why, indeed, should we want to escape?

If you are in doubt as to the crudity of thought in America, try an experiment. Come out of your offices, where you are sitting and thinking, and try living with us. Get on a train at Pittsburgh and go west to the mountains of the Colorados. Stop for a time in our towns and cities. Stay for a week in some Iowa corn shopping town, and for a week in one of Chicago's clubs. As you loiter about read our newspapers and listen to our conversations, remembering, if you will, that as you see us in the towns and cities so we are. We are not subtle enough to conceal ourselves, and he who runs with open eyes through the Mississippi valley may read the story of the Mississippi valley.

It is a marvelous story, and we have not yet begun to tell the half of it. A little, I think I know why. It is because we who write have drawn ourselves away. We have not had faith in our people and in the story of our people. If we are crude and childlike, that is our story, and our writing men must dare to come among us until they know the story. The telling of the story depends, I believe, upon their learning that lesson and accepting that burden.

To my room which [is] on a street near the loop in the city of Chicago come men who write. They talk and I talk. We are fools. We talk of writers of the old world and the beauty and the subtlety of the work they do. Below us the roaring city lies like a great animal on the prairies, but we do not run out to the prairies. We stay in our rooms and talk.

And so having listened to talk and having talked overmuch, I grow

From the Chicago *Daily News*, Nov. 14, 1917, cols. 1–4, p. 13.

weary of talk and walk in the streets. As I walk alone, an old truth comes home to me and I know we shall never have an American literature until we return to faith in ourselves and to the facing of our own limitations. We must, in some way, become in ourselves more like our fellows, more simple and real.

For surely it does not follow that because we Americans are a people without subtlety we are dull and uninteresting people. Our literature is dull, but we are not. One remembers how Dostoevsky had faith in the simplicity of the Russians and what he achieved. He lived and he expressed the life of the time and people. The thing that he did brings hope and achievement to our men.

But let us first of all accept certain truths. Why should we Americans aspire to a subtlety that belongs not to us but to old lands and places? Why talk of intellectual life when we have not accepted the life that we have? There is death on that road and following it has brought death into much of American writing. Can you doubt what I say? Consider the smooth slickness of the average magazine story.

There is a great subtlety of thought and phrase, but there is no reality. Can such work live? The answer is that the most popular magazine story or novel does not live in our minds for a month.

And what are we to do about it? To me it seems that as writers we shall have to throw ourselves with greater daring into life here. We shall have to begin to write out of the people and not for the people. We shall have to find within ourselves a little of that courage. To continue along the road we are traveling is unthinkable. To draw ourselves apart, to live in little groups and console ourselves with the thought that we are achieving something intellectually, is to get nowhere. By such a road we can only go on producing a literature that has nothing to do with life as it is lived in these United States.

To be sure, the doing of the thing I am talking about will not be easy. America is a land of objective writing and thinking. New paths will have to be made. The subjective impulse is almost unknown to us. Because it is close to life it works out into crude and broken forms. It leads along the roads that such masters of prose as James and Howells did not want to take, but if we are to get anywhere we shall have to travel that road.

The road is rough and the times are pitiless. Who, knowing our America and understanding the life in our towns and cities, can close his eyes to the fact that life here for the most part is an ugly affair? As a people we have given ourselves to industrialism and industrialism is not lovely. If anyone can find beauty in an American factory town I wish he would show me the way. For myself I cannot find it. To me, I am living in industrial life, the whole thing is as ugly as modern war. I have to accept that fact and I believe a great step forward will have been taken when it is more generally accepted.

But why, I am asked, are crudity and ugliness necessary? Why can a man like Mr. Dreiser write in the spirit of the early American? Why cannot a man see fun in life? What we want is the note of health. In the work of Mark Twain, there is something wholesome and sweet. Why cannot the modern man be also wholesome and sweet?

To this I make answer that to me a man, say like Mr. Dreiser, is wholesome. He is true to something in life about him, and truth is always wholesome. Twain and Whitman wrote out of another age, out of an age of a land of forests and rivers. The dominant note of American life in their time was the noisy, swaggering raftsman and the hairy breasted woodsman. To-day this not so. The dominant role in American life today is the factory hand. When we have digested that fact, we can begin to approach the task of the present day novelist with a new point of view.

It is, I believe, self-evident that the work of the novelist must always lie somewhat outside the field of philosophic thought. Your true novelist is a man gone a little mad with the life of his times. As he goes through life he lives, not in himself, but in many people. Through his brain march figures and groups of figures. Out of many figures, one emerges. If he is at all sensitive to life about him and that life be crude, the figure that emerges will be crude and will crudely express itself.

I do not know how far a man may go on the road of subjective writing. The matter, I admit, puzzles me. There is something approaching insanity in the very idea of sinking yourself too deeply into modern American industrial life.

But it is my contention that there is no other road. If one would avoid neat, stock writing, he must at least attempt to be brother to his brother and live as men of his time live. He must share with them the crude expression of their lives. To our grandchildren the privilege of attempting to produce a school of American writing that has delicacy and color may come as a matter of course. One hopes that will be true, but it is not true now. And that is why, with so many of the younger Americans, I put my faith in the modern literary adventurers. We shall, I am sure, have much crude, blundering American writing before the gift of beauty and subtlety in prose shall honestly belong to us.

Appendix B

The "Inaccurate" Interview

"I have spent my life traveling up and down America, observing her people—so that I might know their innermost life—what makes them laugh and what makes them cry!

"Everywhere I go I find adventure—some human soul shares with me his misery or his joy. All America is alike to me—I judge all Americans on an equal footing, whether high or low or rich or poor. Everything becomes human if you know it well enough. I never read a newspaper or a magazine. I find infinitely more inspiration, information, and amusement in life itself. But, no matter where I drift up and down America—I will always be a Middle Westerner, born and bred—a man from Ohio. It is a man's early environment, the place and people which he has unconsciously absorbed in his youth and which later becomes the background of his tales. I like New Orleans because it is a more relaxed civilization than you find elsewhere in the United States, but the greater part of my life has been spent in the Middle West—in factory towns, in mining towns, in stretches of Ohio and Illinois countryside, in smoke-hung cities.

"My childhood in Ohio was lived in many houses—some of them haunted—due to the fact that my father never spent money on rent. Whenever remuneration was demanded, we moved. His ability to ignore realities and weave romance made life exciting and interesting for his children. A boy enjoys being an outlaw, and I have looked back upon those days with a particular tenderness when my feet have slipped toward respectability.

"My father was a romantic and thrilling sleight-of-hand performer with the truth. I don't mean that he was a liar, for he always stuck to the facts, but he wove those facts into magnificent new patterns. What adventures he could tell, with himself always the hero! From him came my inclination to be a teller of tales.

"When our family disbanded, after our mother's death, I answered the

From *Success*, 10 (Mar. 1926), 55, 109–11

call of the factories which were coming to the mid-American states in great numbers. It was the beginning of the New Age, with oil and gas bursting from the ground, and prosperity was in the air. And so until I was twenty-four, I was a laboring man, but I never stayed long enough in one place to become a skilled workman."

Sherwood Anderson is talking—with his accustomed frankness. We are in a taxicab on our way from New York to the Jersey ferry. It is a dark, dismal night with beating rain and he has had no supper.

Could there be any better way to get at what a man really thinks than to ask him to talk under such conditions as these.

The taxi jerked and skidded, and in the blackness of the interior only Anderson's lighted cigarette showed that he was there.

"The Spanish war brought these early wanderings to a temporary end," he resumed. "At that time, I had often thought that being a Jesse James or a Napoleon would suit me—becoming Corporal Anderson was the next best thing.

"Eventually I found myself the owner of a factory in Ohio that manufactured house paint. In those days I was an esteemed citizen. But being a bright young captain of industry only made me feel that I was prostituting my life. My whole nature demanded that I be a teller of tales. So one day, without any notice at all, I walked out of my office, away from the factory and the town—in order that I might put words upon sheets of white paper."

"Women never do write—not really," declared Mr. Anderson when I asked him about woman's place in literature. "I mean that in as much as they are artists they aren't women. The relation of a man to tools and materials is the same as woman's relation to children."

With memories of all of the distinguished women who have left their imprint on the literature of the past, and those of the present who are acclaimed by the critics as among the distinguished, I couldn't help stuttering a feeble protest. "You don't mean that literally, Mr. Anderson?"

"There are women who write, yes, but don't you see—they (long pause) they are neither one thing nor the other. They're mules," he drawled.

I didn't like to ask Mr. Anderson what he meant when he said that the women who had evidenced genius were mules. The implication could be, if one were sensitive, quite unpleasant. If he merely meant stubbornness, that wasn't particularly uncomplimentary, but if he meant the disagreeable vocal manifestations of the ungainly offspring of a jackass and a mare—well that was another thing again.

"Yes, they're mules," he muttered as the taxi cavorted through the downpour on its way to the Fort Lee Ferry. Then he rubbed the mist off the window and began to think—something like this—

("I've got to make that lecture—I wonder if I'll get there on time—I haven't had a thing to eat, and I'm hungry—yes, they are mules, these women who write—lots of women are mules—hybrids, neither one thing nor the other—I wonder how many people there'll be over there to-night—got to get there on time—Cleopatra was no mule—neither was Nell Gwynn—Potiphar's wife—guess Joseph found out she was all woman—suffrage leaders women's rights, all got a mission—mules. Some of them help run department stores, lead parades—politics—anything but what they are best fitted for, and that's being a woman—God, what a fool to want to be anything else but a beautiful woman—If I don't get a bite to eat before that lecture I'll cut it short—funny stuff this lecturing—kind of a kick in it at that—that Creole girl—well for that matter hardly any Creole girl could be a mule . . .").

"What did you say?" I questioned, breaking a long silence.

"Oh," he said, "I just wanted to know if you had the chance of marrying the man you wanted to and having children, wouldn't you rather do that than write a great novel?"

I told him I'd rather write the novel; but I could see he thought I was an awful liar.

Sherwood Anderson has gotten his knowledge of life first hand, for he never reads a newspaper or a magazine.

"I once read a story about a man in modern life who just wandered around without ever becoming aware of such important facts as flappers and coal strikes. He reminded me of myself. I never know when there's a coal strike. I don't look at newspapers even over other people's shoulders, and I haven't bought or borrowed one in the three weeks I have been East.

"I never worked on one, so it is not a personal aversion. I simply find it more interesting to go walking around the streets—how many miles I have walked along the streets of American cities! No, all newspapers are alike, so why should I want to see them? I would rather read the Old Testament. I always carry it in my grip and have read it for twenty years because I like the beautfiul, simple prose, the poetry and rhythm of it. When I traveled around the country as an advertising man, I used to cut books out of Gideon's Bibles in the hotel rooms, and carry them in my pocket.

"In the pages of books, I have always found a refuge from the tangle of life. But most of my reading has been in hall bedrooms—I have lived in more than I care to remember—they are a blurred memory of grey holes into which I crept. It was from listening to my neighbors in other such rooms that I became impressed with the fact that American men and women seldom sing or laugh in their homes. It is only when you walk through the Negro districts of our cities that you hear laughter."

As we walked to the forward deck of the ferry, Mr. Anderson's blue-green shirt, necktie and scarf produced a pleasant thrill upon the tired New Jersey commuters. Outside was deserted, and the driving rain blurred the other shore, veiling even the electric advertising sign.

"The river out front there isn't unlike the Mississippi down at New Orleans," he observed.

"No, I'm not lecturing in order to get closer to the great American public. I guess I've seen most of it. I lecture for the money that is in it. Of course, it gives me something of a thrill. You see I'm kind of a showman, sort of an actor. When my talk goes over, I get the same satisfaction that a showman does. But I don't get so much that I'd do it except to pay the mortgage on the farm. I suppose everyone is a little ashamed of the actor in him, everybody except an actor. No reason why we should feel so. It may be nothing but shyness. I am awfully fond of loud clothes, but when I realize that I am attracting attention I am ashamed of them.

"Let's grab a bite to eat over in that corner place," he suggested, as we came out of the ferry house. The lunch room clock showed that he had time for only a plate of soup—then into the trolley where he was as uneasy as a caged animal, peering through the rain-blurred windows—restless for fear of going on beyond the hall where he was to lecture. Thanks to a consultation with two passengers and the motorman-conductor, he wasn't carried past the street.

There were young Princeton graduates and flappers from a finishing school in his audience, and the latter were torn between curiosity about the author of "Many Marriages," and what he might say. There were also stiff, dignified matrons present who sat bolt upright in a prepared and critical attitude until Sherwood Anderson made mention of his wife and son, when they deemed it safe to relax, and enjoy themselves. After all, perhaps he wasn't as dangerous as certain passages in his books might suggest. And then he was saying, "Only very vain or silly people want to shock their readers by what they write. . . . We are all tellers of tales. We all lead the imaginative life as well as the physical. . . . Prose writing, if it be an art at all, is the art that lies closest to the American man. . . . It's a good age in which we are living. In the past all the energy of America, the new country, went into building bridges and sky-scrapers.

"Now, we have about all the railroads and buildings that we need and the Harrimans, the Rockefellers—the men of action—must step aside and let the imaginative man come to the fore. That doesn't mean that the building won't be going on, but it won't exhaust the country. When we ride on our fastest train its speed no longer absorbs our attention. Our minds are filled with the more important consideration of what we are going to do when we get to our destination, and are asking, 'Where are we going?'"

A minister broached the author of *Dark Laughter* to ask if he thought it was just right to put on paper some of the thoughts that the man and woman in this book had had.

"Why not?" Sherwood Anderson asked. "I have them, you have them."

"Yes, I admit I do," the minister replied, becoming a little restive under the penetrating scrutiny of Anderson's sombre Italian eyes, "but, is it a good thing to let the younger generation read them?"

"There's more of such thoughts going on in their heads than in ours," Anderson answered, and the minister, after viewing such a possibility for a few seconds, made his uneasy retreat.

Returning on the ferry, we ate hot dogs while New York held the gaze of the writer from the West, her millions of lights penetrating the sheets of rain and mist. It is about his own craft that Sherwood Anderson talks best and with most enthusiasm. Of *Dark Laughter*, he said,

"I couldn't have written that novel if I hadn't lived in New Orleans. The plot of course, could have been used anywhere, but it is what happens to the story after you think and feel about it for a long time that is important. It is your reaction to the story that counts, not the plot. I think the form of *Dark Laughter* is complete. It functions all the way through. But an author can't go back to the book that he did last year and if he hasn't another in him he isn't any good.

"It's the mechanics of writing that a teller of tales loves—the sheets of blank white paper, the smell of ink, and the little words. Out of the love of craft culture springs. As an advertising or publicity man, you can turn words into money, but it is pleasanter to write unprofitable books. If truth and honesty must be abandoned before profitable authorship is attained, I think it not worth doing. I depict life as it is, and not as the reader would like to have it. The true history of life is but a history of movements, and it is only at rare moments that we live. I have always preferred knowing what a man was thinking rather than what he was doing.

"Yes, someone told me that Mr. Galsworthy had been quoted as saying that Sinclair Lewis and I are doing a great deal toward establishing a new school, but I don't think there is any new school. Lewis and I aren't breaking the ground. That was done for us—thanks to Theodore Dreiser. It just happens that some men have come along who have some respect for writing and they have because it is more fun to try to do it decently than to do it flashily. Just the same way that it is more fun to make a chair that is comfortable to sit in than one that is just good to look at."

At one time hair cloth furniture was considered the most elegant thing imaginable, as were the fish nets that held the family photographs and the dear old cozy corners with their dusty hangings. These were considered blessings that would abide with us. The memory of them made me wonder if it were possible for contemporaries to recognize real beauty in either furniture or literature, so I asked Mr. Anderson if, in his opinion, it were possible to recognize the writer of immortal work during the man's lifetime?

"Immortality is one of those dreadful words that doesn't mean anything," he answered. "There have been more forgotten people than we know of whom their contemporaries called by that name—and in every age there are groups hailing each other as such and advertising fellows do it for pay. Every minor poet, in certain moods, thinks his work is ageless. I don't see why anyone should care very much whether or not they are immortal. You are interested in doing the job. Of course, in secret, I think all my fellow writers are punk," he laughed, "and they think it about me. Probably none of us read each other's work. But I am interested in what is written about me—everybody is interested in reading about himself. If Walt Whitman were alive, he'd be indignant at being left out of the Hall of Fame, but he isn't alive."

When asked upon what writers based their judgments of fellow craftsmen's work, Mr. Anderson answered,

"I base my judgment of a man's work on whether or not I think he functions. It comes down to his grasp of form—does he really completely function in the materials that he is handling. A man can't write who doesn't have an essential reaction to a piece of white paper. He feels toward it something the way he might towards a beautiful woman. What counts is how life feels to your fingers. You won't have any fine art without a great deal of sensual reaction.

"An artist likes everything: the streets, women, buildings, fields, skies. He is more alive to them than the layman because he has developed his senses. That's why you don't have to pay tribute to an artist; he'll get his share out of life all right. I think the fellows who grind around an office ought to have the money—I don't believe they have any fun. People may look alike but there's a difference in their makeup—call it fibre. And that is what I like—the fibre of people. It's what we are always looking for, isn't it?"

Concerning the awarding of prizes to authors, Sherwood Anderson, who won the Dial prize in 1921, believes they should go to those writers whose talent may culminate, to someone obscure and climbing, not the man or woman who has a public.

"I don't believe the awarding of prizes has elevated writing in America or anywhere else," he said. "What makes the Dial prize unusual is the fact that it is never given to a successful, recognized writer. They give the

$2,000 to someone who they think shows a genius for writing, not for one particular piece of work. His writing as a whole must be a real contribution. The money is intended to give him some leisure, just the sort of thing I used it for—a trip abroad. But other prizes are given to the man who has raised the moral standard of America, and what has an artist to do with the moral standard?"

Back on the New York side, Mr. Anderson found he had ten minutes in which to add another mouthful or two to his fragmentary dinner. Perched on a stool in front of a lunch counter, he talked of his plans for the coming year,

"I want to write a novel and build a house. Could you have more fun than that? We have bought a farm in Virginia on which we are going to build a stone house. I have thought of ten novels, but I know I'll never get them all done. I may write other things too—plays and more short stories. The novel is more fascinating and difficult than the short story, however. You do the latter in a rush, in one sitting, but with the novel you must carry the mood five or six months through all sorts of things that interrupt that mood. That is why we respect the novelist more than we do the writer of the short story. Once a man in introducing me before a lecture spent thirty-five minutes in telling what a deep sea diver I am. Now what kind of a story teller would I be it I were like that? I would be a psycho-analyst and make some real money. My next book is going to be called A *Mid-American Childhood*. It's the story, told in the second person, of a boy from the age of consciousness until he is twelve or thirteen."

As to how much of it was biographical, he said,

"By the time your imagination has played around with an idea, you can't tell how much of it is real and how much isn't."

One more skidding, lurching taxi ride, and the Pennsylvania station was reached. As Anderson dashed for the train that was to take him West, I recalled how his first book was published by an English firm because the American publishers couldn't see it. Now he is considered by many America's most interesting writer. Certainly he looks like a genius.

Index

Abraham Lincoln: The War Years, 166
Abrahamson, Ben, 56
Adams, Henry, 216
Ade, George, 14
"Adventures in Form and Color," 131
Advertising, 8, 10, 14, 15, 19, 30, 55, 62, 82, 83, 102, 111, 112, 118, 127, 128, 138, 168, 174, 182, 186, 230, 297, 301, 302
Africa, 141
Age of Innocence, The, 150
Agricultural Advertising, 50
Alabama, 33, 118, 153
Alexander, T. H., 18, 29, 50, 81, 280, 321
Allied Arts Club, 234
"America—A Storehouse of Vitality," 204, 244, 265–66, 287
American Can Company, 255
American Mercury, The, 278
"American Spring Song," 68
Amiens, France, 160
Amnesia, 18, 29, 50, 81, 280, 321
Amonson, Harry, 128
Amsterdam, Holland, 330
Andersen, Hans Christian, 236, 240
Anderson, Cornelia, xiii, xvi, xxi, 6, 10, 45–46, 104, 124, 126–27, 138, 191, 195, 207, 215, 217, 219, 245–46, 248, 260, 282, 285–86, 290, 307, 310, 322, 324, 326
Anderson, Earl, 246–50, 254, 256–58, 266, 269, 272–74, 276, 283, 286, 289
Anderson, Eleanor, xiii, xvii, xix, xxii, 9, 260, 320, 332
Anderson, Elizabeth, xvi, xxii, 191, 193, 195, 200–201, 204, 206–8, 213–14, 216, 227–28, 231, 239, 283, 317, 319–20, 326
Anderson, Emma Smith, 286, 287, 326, 337
Anderson, Erwin, 254, 257, 259, 272, 273
Anderson, Fern, 281, 282, 287
Anderson, Indiana, 111
Anderson, Irwin M., 231, 255, 274, 287, 337
Anderson, John S., xix, xxi, 104, 128, 138, 143, 145–46, 195, 199, 207, 213, 218, 225–26, 246, 271–72, 274, 283, 285–86, 290, 296, 306–7, 317, 324, 326
Anderson, Karl, 119, 125, 154, 246–48, 255, 257, 259, 269, 272, 274, 276, 286–87, 290, 294
Anderson, Margaret C., 86
Anderson, Ray, 287
Anderson, Robert L., xxi, 104, 127, 143, 195, 204, 213–14, 216, 219–22, 242, 256, 259–60, 271–72, 274, 282–87, 289–90, 293–96, 298, 301–2, 304, 306, 312–18, 320–21, 324, 326–27, 329, 331
Anderson, Mrs. Robert L., 260, 284, 286, 296, 316, 326
Anderson, Tennessee Mitchell, xiii, xvi, xvii, 6–7, 14, 16, 19, 23, 29, 38, 45–46, 53, 55, 60, 62, 84, 96, 100–101, 104, 124, 126, 131, 158, 174, 179, 181–82, 191, 194–95
Ann Arbor, Mich., 107
Another Man's House, 250, 253, 254, 256–63, 266, 267, 276–77, 279
"Apology for Crudity," 87, 333–35

Arkansas, 305
Art, xvi, 4, 5, 7, 12, 14, 16, 17, 34, 37, 38, 46, 48, 49, 51, 57, 59, 60, 64, 69, 70–81, 89, 93, 95, 100, 107, 117, 127, 135, 137, 144, 150, 156, 158, 159, 170, 172, 178, 186, 192, 200, 204, 209, 215–16, 218, 229, 232, 234, 243, 248, 256–57, 267–69, 277–78, 288, 294, 297, 301, 303, 305, 310–11, 314, 316, 318, 319, 320, 324, 342
Art Institute (Chicago), 17, 317
Art of the Vieux Columbier, The, 103
Athens, Ga., 231

Babbitt, 187
Ball, Marion, 273
Baltimore, 144, 154, 259, 287
Balzac, Honore, 200
Barton, Bayard, 97
"Beautiful, The," 277
Before I Forget, 125
Bellevue, Ohio, 23, 126
Benchley, Robert, 265–66
Bently, Alys, 52–53, 65, 84
Benton Harbor, Mich., 10
Berkeley, Calif., 193–94, 201
Beth El Social Center, 204
Beyond Desire, xxii, 330
Bible, 236, 339
Bing, Madame, 159
Birmingham, Ala., 234
Birmingham News, 234
Bishop, John Peale, 167
Bloch, Ernest, 236
Blum, Jerry, 100
Bodenheim, Maxwell, 289
Bohon, Davis T., 106
Bonaparte, Napoleon, 61
Boni and Liveright, 292, 300, 302
Bookman, 56, 67, 81, 142, 170
"Book of the Grotesque," 185
Boone, Daniel, 262
Borrow, George, 4
Boston, Mass., 24, 65, 241, 274, 285
"Broken," 252
Brooks, Van Wyck, 14, 59–60, 65, 94–95, 97, 101, 103, 122, 268
"Brother Death," 331
"Brothers," 246
Buck Fever, 303
Burrow, Dr. Trigant, 53, 85
Burton, Emmett, Papers, 300, 304
Bush, Marian, 6, 65–67
Bynner, Witter, 207–8

Cabell, James Branch, 239
California, 242, 265
Camden, Ohio, xxi, 26
Canby, Henry Seidel, 211–12
Canton, Ohio, 44
Castalia, Ohio, 23, 44
Cezanne, Paul, 324
"Chant to Dawn in a Factory Town," 68
Chateaugay, N.Y., 16. *See also* Lake Chateaugay, N.Y.
Chicago, Ill., xv, xxi, 3–8, 10, 12, 14, 16, 18–19, 23, 26, 29, 30, 32–34, 36, 38–39, 42–44, 46, 48, 50–54, 56–64, 66–69, 82–87, 89–94, 96, 102–5, 107–9, 111–13, 115–17, 122–24, 127–28, 130–32, 136, 138, 140, 142, 144, 151, 153, 166–67, 169, 170, 174, 177, 179, 181–83, 185, 187, 189, 201–5, 207, 213–14, 246, 260, 286–87, 317–18, 320, 326, 329
Chicago, University of, 319
"Chicago Culture," 92
Chicago Daily News, 4, 87, 92, 333
"Chicago Hamlet, A," 253
Chicago Herald Examiner, 94
Chicago Tribune, 4, 101, 125
Child of the Century, A, 38
Cincinnati, Ohio, 110
Clapp, Turkey, 24
Clemens, Samuel L., 335
Cleveland, Ohio, 203, 205
Clyde, Ohio, xxi, 23, 26, 36, 45–46, 65, 89, 94, 97, 134, 276, 286
Colson, Ethel, 94
Columbia, Tenn., 234, 236
Columbus, Ga., 227
Columbus, Ohio, 18
Connick, Charles, 274
Conover, R. W., 204
Conrad, Joseph, 253–54
Copeau, Jacques, 102–3, 105, 107, 158–60
Cornell University, 288–89
Cournos, John, 165

Croly, Herbert, 290
Cromwell, Oliver, 61
Cuba, xxi
Curry, Marjorie, 45

Daily Cardinal, The, 288
Dalrymple, Dolly, 234
Dance of Life, The, 266
Dannemora Prison, 136
Dark Dawn, 283
Dark Laughter, xxii, 121, 138, 213–14, 220, 222, 224, 226, 230, 235, 240, 265, 311, 341
Dark Mother, The, 131, 134, 146, 155
Dartmouth College, 241
Daugherty, George, 12, 46
Davenport, Ia.,87
Davidson, Donald, 237
Davis, Jefferson, 219
Davis T. Bohon Co., 106
Dayton, Ohio, 10
Dayton, Tenn., 228
Dazey, Frank, 274
Dean, Harriet, 6, 37, 56, 59–60
Dean, Randle C., 39–60
"Death in the Woods," 263
Debs, Eugene, 178–79
Dell, Floyd, 46, 65, 178
de Lorenzi, Sue, 84
Detroit, Mich., 107, 183, 286, 329
Dial, The, 87, 94–95, 138, 141, 144, 150, 167, 175, 187–88, 190
Dial Award, xxii, 167, 171–73, 257, 342
Dickens, Charles, 40, 49
Dill Pickle Club, 86
Dilling, Harriet, 157–58
Dixie, 259
"Doctor," 40
Dostoievsky, Feodor, 13, 37–38, 277, 289, 335, 341
Double Dealer, The, 105, 177, 259
Dreiser, Theodore, 29, 37, 147, 276–77, 289, 335, 341
Duglas, Ed, 24
"Dumb Man, The," 185
Dusoir, Ilse, 42

Economy Book Store, 86
Eddy, Mary Baker, 125
Education of Henry Adams, The, 216
"Egg, The," 209
Ellis, Havelock, 265
Elyria, Ohio, xxi, 3, 18, 26–28, 50, 70, 247
Emerson, John, 46, 65, 88–89, 96–98, 155, 207–8, 211–12, 215–16, 218, 253
Emmett, Burton, 273, 283, 285, 299, 300, 302, 304
England, 110, 162
Ephraim, Wis., 108, 114, 125–26, 128–29
Esherick, Wharton, 209–10
Estes Park, Colo., 214
Eurythmics, 53
Europe, 113, 141, 145, 154, 166, 172, 184, 187, 191, 272, 277, 285, 324, 330
Evans, Ernestine, 158
Evansville, Ind., 136

Fairhope, Ala., 118–24
Father Mississippi, 279
Ferargil Galleries, 290
Ficke, Arthur Davison, 29, 290
Fielding, Henry, 4
Fitzsimmons, Bob, 56
Floradora, 47
"Four Preludes on Playthings of the Winds," 169
France, 110, 162, 283–84, 292
Frank B. White Co., 6
Frank, Glenn, 287, 289
Frank, Waldo, 45, 65, 70, 84, 102–3, 131–32, 134, 144, 146, 154–55, 157
Freeman, The, 184
Fremont, Ohio, 23
"French Quarter's Golden Era, The," 259
Freud, Sigmund, 95
"From Chicago," 70–81

Gallimard, 157, 161
Galsworthy, John, 341
Garnett, Constance, 38
Gauguin, Paul, 117
Gay, Madame, 163
Gentlemen Prefer Blondes, 214
Georgia, University of, 231
Georgia Alumni Record, 231
Germany, 110
"Ghost Story, A," 266
Giles, Herbert, 196
"Golden Bowl, The," 165

Goodwyn Institute, 287
Gordon, George (Lord Byron), 37
Gorky, Maxim, 37
Grand Army of the Republic, 237
Greear, John, 227
Green Bay, Wis., 108

Hackett, Francis, 55, 92, 137, 167, 171
Hahn, Dr. E. Vernon, xiii, xxii, 218, 278, 307, 328, 331
Halifax, N.S., 285
Hamburg, Germany, 286
Hamburg-American Line, 287
Hammond, Ind., 19, 204–5
"Hands," 67
Hanline, Maurice, 279, 300–301
Hanover, N.H., 241
Hardy, Thomas, 40, 49
Harper's, 194
Harris, Frank, 147
Harris, Julian, 227
Harrodsburg, Ky., 106, 114, 166
Haywood, William D., 178–79
Hecht, Ben, 38, 92, 191
Hello Towns, xxii, 323
Hemingway, Ernest, 265–66, 268
"Here's Looking at You," 97
Hill, Stella Anderson, 94–95, 281–82
Home Town, xxii
Horses and Men, xxii, 37, 94, 138, 194, 196, 252–53
"Hosanna," 53
Huebsch, B. W., 122, 125, 151, 156, 161, 165, 184, 186, 188, 193, 206, 211–12, 218, 220
Hughes, Glenn, 244
Hurd, Thaddeus B., 287

Idiot, The, 14, 38
Illinois, 12, 13, 19, 52, 214, 222, 337
Illinois, University of, 213
"I'm a Fool," 305
"Impotence," 35, 37, 138
India, 13
Indiana, 37
Indianapolis, Ind., xiii, xiv, 6, 44, 57–60, 69, 82, 94, 104–5, 107, 112–13, 123–25, 128, 136, 138–39, 150, 154, 156–58, 169–70, 197, 201–2, 205–6, 219, 225, 227, 229, 231, 246, 251, 286–87, 290, 317–20, 329–30
Industrial Workers of the World, 179
Iowa, 31
Italy, 181
Ithaca, N.Y., 289

James, Henry, 35
Jackson County, Mich., 7
Jefferson, Thomas, 228
Jesus, 11, 29, 51, 59, 69, 135, 283
Jewish Center Forum, 204
John Keats, 266
John the Baptist, 52
Jones, Howard Mumford, 46, 65, 122, 126, 144, 257, 274, 277
Joyce, James, 157, 160, 220, 268, 309
Julius Caesar, 61

Kahn, Otto, 300
Kalamazoo, Mich., 52
Kansas, 12
Kansas City, Mo., 10, 308
Kansas State Agricultural College, 204
Kentucky, xv, 19, 87, 93, 110, 118, 122, 124–25, 127–28, 133, 139, 145, 150–51, 177, 182
Kentucky Derby, 93, 105
Keokuk, Ia., 52
Kinney, Dorothy H., 255
Kit Brandon, xxii
Knopf, Alfred, 211
"Knots in the Weaver's Loom," 119
Krock, 176
Kuhn, Dr. and Mrs. H. A., 204

Lady Chatterley's Lover, 329
Lake Chateaugay, N.Y., xv, 53, 84, 107
Lake Erie, 126
Lake Michigan, 109
Lake Pontchartrain, La., 213–14
Lane, Margaret, 191
"La Peur de la Vie," 94
Lardner, Ring, 14, 235
Larkin, James, 136
Lawrence, D. H., 144, 147, 201, 220, 329
Lawson, John Howard, 236
Letters and Leadership, 101
Letters of Sherwood Anderson, 46, 65, 122, 126, 274, 277
Lewis, Sinclair, 138, 186–87, 239, 341
Lexington, Ky., 174
Liberal Club, 57

Life, 265
Lightning, 102
Lincoln, Abraham, 226, 232, 235, 265, 308
Little Point Sable, Mich., 126, 329
Little Review, The, 3, 6, 60, 86, 97, 105, 109, 207
Liveright, Otto, 187
London, 161, 163, 166, 284–85
"Loneliness," 147
Long-Critchfield Co., xxi, xxii, 6, 110, 123, 130, 168, 177, 179
Longfellow, Henry W., 232
Loos, Anita, 65, 89, 96, 98, 207, 214–16
Los Angeles, Calif., 242
Louisville, Ky., 20, 93, 177
Louisville, University of, 307, 312
Lowell, Amy, 266
Lucretius, 230
Luse, Dr., 26

McChine, Pete, 24
McCreary, Toughy, 24
McCurran, Rose, 96, 98
MacDonald, Dwight, 324
McHugh, Ben, 24
Macon (Ga.) Telegraph, 118
Madison, Wis., 287, 290, 295
Main Street, 138
Malone, Dudley, Field, 189–90
"Man in the Brown Coat, The," 185
"Man Who Became a Woman, The," 285
"Man Who Sat in His House, The," 142
"Man's Story, A," 285
Many Marriages, xxii, 123–24, 126, 149, 175–77, 180, 183, 188, 190, 193–95
Marching Men, xiv, xxi, 3, 16, 28, 33, 69–70, 82, 86, 88–89, 100, 102, 154, 156, 246
Marin, John, 145–46
Marine Hospital, 287
Marion, Va., xxii, 104, 165, 260, 286, 292, 296, 299, 301–17, 319–30
"Mary Cochran," 7, 57, 119, 123, 152, 308
Mask, The, 165
Masses, 67
Masters, Edgar Lee, 114
Maugham, W. Somerset, 117
Meiklejohn, Alexander, 287, 289–90
Memphis, Tenn., 286–87
Mencken, Henry, 136, 154–55, 239
Metamorphoses, 230
Michigan, University of, 107; and its *Daily*, 107
Michigan City, Ind., 104, 126, 301
Mid-American Chants, xxi, 53, 68–69, 92, 94–95, 156, 193
"Mid-American Songs," 68
"Milk Bottles," 138
Milwaukee, Wis., 130
Minneapolis, Minn., 55
Miss Elizabeth: A Memoir, 191, 195, 197, 206, 214, 227, 317
Mississippi River, 225–26, 230, 265
Missouri, 52
Mobile, Ala., 118
"Modern American Writing," 205–6, 232, 237
Moon and Sixpence, The, 117
Montreal, Quebec, 109
"Mother," 93
Mountain Men, 267

Narrow House, The, 151
Nashville, Tenn., 234, 237, 239
Nashville Exchange Club, 239
Nashville Tennessean, The, 236, 239
Natchez, Miss., 224, 226
Nation, The, 55, 167, 187
Nevada, xxii, 194–96
"New Generation, The," 241
New Haven, Conn., 211
New Orleans, La., xxii, 122–24, 174–77, 186, 193, 200–202, 204–6, 213–14, 216, 218, 220–22, 224–31, 236–37, 241–42, 245–46, 248–59, 261, 265, 340
New Orleans Picayune, 226
New Republic, The, 55, 137, 167, 187
New Testament, A, xxii, 106, 109, 114, 140, 187, 193, 251, 252, 259, 279, 283, 294, 296, 314
New York City, xxiii, 64–66, 89, 96–97, 99–104, 113, 115, 124, 130, 137–38, 141, 144–45, 149, 151, 154–56, 170, 172–74, 184–86, 188, 190, 192–93, 201–2, 206–12, 218, 247, 249, 268, 273–74, 276, 280, 286–87, 299–301, 309, 316, 320, 325, 328
New York Herald, 203
New York Times, 286, 290
Newberry Library, xiv, xv, xix, 248

Newcomb Loom Co., 87
Newport, R.I., 273, 283
Niagara Falls, N.Y., 279
Nietzsche, Friedrich, 10
North Carolina, 237
No Swank, xxii
"Not Today," 270
"Novels of Waldo Frank, The," 144
Nyholm, Mrs. Amy, xix

O'Brien, Edward, 67, 164–65, 222–23, 365–66
Ohio, 19, 43, 49, 52, 118, 237, 337
"Ohio, I'll Say We've Done Well," 187
Ohio Pagans, 57, 125, 128, 130
O'Keeffe, Georgia, 211–12
O'Neill, Eugene, 236
Our America, 157
"Our Unforgettable Brother," 248
"Out of Nowhere into Nothing," 138, 140–41, 149–51, 246
"Out of the Cradle Endlessly Rocking," 14
Ovid, 230
Owensboro, Ky., 94, 105–6, 128, 133, 183
Oxford, England, 164–65

Paden, Clifton, 46, 89
Painting, xiv, 16–17, 100, 119–22, 128, 130–32, 136–38, 143–46, 172, 248
Palos Park, Ill., 46, 108, 130–32, 136–37, 140–42, 144–47, 149
Panama Canal Zone, xxii
Paoli, Pa., 210
Paris, 96, 157–59, 265, 285, 295, 309
Paul Gauguin, Calm Madman, 117
Pennet, Will, 308
Pennsylvania, 154, 172
"People Who Write," 3
People's Institute, The, 207
Perhaps Women, xxii, 328
Peters, Rollo, 141, 155
Pfeiffer, William S., 7
Philadelphia, Pa., 209–10
Pitt Weekly, The, 207
Pittsburgh, Pa., 206
Plays: Winesburg and Others, xxii
Poetry, 29, 53, 67, 69, 95, 105, 122, 140, 148, 186, 251, 255, 272, 311
Poetry, 68
Poor, Mrs. Anne, 247
Poor White, xxii, 100, 103–4, 119, 122, 125, 127–28, 136–38
Poppe, Hans W., 317
Pound, Ezra, 157, 160
Powys, John Cowper, 7
Powys, John Llewellyn, 6
President Cleveland, 286–87
President Roosevelt, 283
Price, Huck, 308
Provence, 160
Provincetown Players, 209
Pushkin, Alexander, 92
Puzzled America, xxii

"Queer," 42, 67, 247

Radin, Max, 194–95
Rankin, Mr. and Mrs. B. Kirk, 251
Rascoe, Burton, 125
Raw Youth, A, 38, 308
Reflections on War and Death, 95
Reno, Nev., 195
Rideout, Walter B., 46, 65, 122, 126, 144, 257, 274, 277
Ripshin Farm, xxii, 230, 238, 249, 262–64, 276, 280, 282, 290, 319, 322
Road to Winesburg, The, xiv, 7, 29, 46, 50, 68, 81, 85, 97, 107, 114, 276, 280, 321
Rochambeau, 156–58
Rome, 141, 265
Roosevelt Hospital, 247
Rosenfeld, Paul, 103, 125, 132–33, 144–45, 157, 162, 166, 170, 207, 210–11, 218, 265–67
Rothschild, 38
Rudy, Claude, 308
Russell, Bertrand, 300
Russia, 14, 26, 100, 110, 330

St. Louis, Mo., 226, 282
St. Petersburg, Fla., 326
San Diego, Calif., 243
Sandburg, Carl, 69, 130–31, 133, 168–69, 265–66
Sandusky, Ohio, 25
Saturday Evening Post, 14, 187
Saxon, Lyle, 27
Sayler, Oliver, 116
Schevill, James, 118, 195, 227

Scott, Evelyn, 151
Science and Health, 125
Seattle, Wash., 243–44
"Seeds," xiv, 97, 135, 246
Seldes, George, 187
Sellinger, Waxy, 24
"Senility," 42, 85
Sergel, Mr. and Mrs. Roger, 206–7
Seven Arts, 39, 42, 45, 59, 60, 65–67, 70–81, 84, 94–95, 102
Shakespeare, William, 159
Sherman, Stuart P., 203
"Sherwood Anderson," 170, 324
Sherwood Anderson, His Life and Work, 118
"Sherwood Anderson Tells His Life Story," 250
Sherwood Anderson's Memoirs, xxii, 38, 103
Sherwood Anderson's Notebook, xxii, 24, 242, 252, 261–62, 265, 285, 304, 307
Sinclair, May, 92
Sinclair, Upton, 30, 32–33
Smart Set, 60, 136, 152
Smoke and Steel, 130, 132–33
Smyth County News, The, 307
"Song of Industrial America," 68
"Song of Steven the Westerner," 68
"Song of the Drunken Businessman," 68
"Song of the Mating Time," 69
Sons and Lovers, 141
"South, The," 277
Southern Agriculturist, The, 237
Spanish-American War, xxi, 63, 89, 338
"Splinter of Ice, The," 60
Spoon River Anthology, 114
Springfield, Ohio, xxi
Starrett, Vincent, 86
Stearns, Harold, 94–95
Steele, ———, 166
Stein, Gertrude, 239, 266, 309
Sterling, Ill., 91
Stevens, James, 244
Stevenson, Robert Louis, 265
Story-Teller's Story, A, xxii, 38, 195, 198, 217, 218, 236, 239, 285
"Story-writers," 59
Straight, Mrs. Willard, 290
Strange Tales from a Chinese Studio, 196
Straws, 195–96
Success, 249–50, 337
Szakalski, Stanislaus, 214
Szold, Bernadine Fritz, 266

"Tandy," 9, 276–77
Tar, xxii, 38, 217, 222, 227, 230–31, 250, 252–53, 257, 265–66, 343
Taxco, Mexico, 318
Taylor-Critchfield Advertising Co., 97
Texas, 16
Today, xxii
Toliver, Sol, 308
Tombigbee River, 121
Topeka, Kans., 201, 202, 204–5
Topeka Daily Gazette, 204
Topeka Daily State Journal, 204
Torrents of Spring, 266
Triumph of the Egg, The, xxiii, 42, 97, 124, 135, 138, 152, 160, 167, 170, 185, 209, 235
Troutdale, Va., 227–28, 255, 260–64, 266–73, 276–82, 290, 292, 294–95, 302
Turgenev, Ivan, 192
Twelfth Night, 159

"Unlighted Lamps," 151
Untermeyer, Louis, 95
"Untold Lie, The," 7
Urbana, Ill., 213

Vanderbilt University, 237
Van Gogh, Vincent, 118
Vanity Fair, 167, 187, 324
Verdun, France, 15
Vicksburg, Miss., 224
Vincennes, Ind., 294–96
Virginia, 230, 343; University of, 296, 313
"Visit, A," 68

Wade, J. D., 231
Wagner, Richard, 47
Walden Book Store, 138
Wall, The, 165
Walsh, Percy, 24
Washburn College, 204
Washington, University of, 244; and its *Daily*, 248
Washington, D.C., 144
WBAI, 65

Wellesley College, 241
Welling, Marie, 25
Wells, James, xv
Westcott, Edith, 64
Wharton, Edith, 149–50
"What Say!" 165, 307, 313
Whistler, James McNeill, 35
White Shadows in the South Seas, 222–23, 266
Whitman, Walt, 14, 52, 232, 235, 335
Whittingham, Talbot, 257
Wilson, Arthur, 308
Wilson, Edmund, 249–50, 253
Windy McPherson's Son, xxi, 3, 5, 26, 28, 39, 42, 55–57, 65, 81, 86, 89, 156, 160
Winesburg, Ohio, xv, xvi, xxi, 7, 10, 26, 44–45, 55–56, 65, 81, 86, 89, 102, 104, 107, 141, 160, 276, 331
Winterburn, Florence, 42
Wisconsin, 19, 113, 115
Wisconsin, University of, 288, 295–96
Wittenburg Academy, xxi
Women in Love, 144
World War I, 61
Writing, 3–4, 7–8, 15, 24, 26, 29–30, 33, 35, 37, 39, 49–50, 52, 58–59, 62–63, 66, 68, 83, 85, 88, 92, 94, 96, 98–100, 102, 104, 107, 109, 111, 115, 117, 126, 128–29, 134, 136, 141–43, 146, 149, 155–56, 160, 162, 168–69, 175–76, 179, 184–90, 194, 200–201, 202–3, 207, 208–9, 215, 217, 221–22, 227, 229–32, 234, 238, 241, 248, 250–51, 254–55, 258–59, 261–63, 266–67, 269, 271–73, 277, 279, 281, 284–85, 288, 291, 294, 297, 307–9, 311–13, 316–17, 325, 333–35, 343

Yale Literary Magazine, 323
Yale University Art Gallery, 274
"Younger Generation, The," 237, 287, 289

Note on the Editor

WILLIAM A. SUTTON is professor emeritus of English at Ball State University (Muncie, Indiana); he presently lives in Dunedin, Florida. A graduate of Case Western Reserve University, Mr. Sutton received his M.A. and Ph.D. degrees from Ohio State University. After teaching at Ohio State University, Muskingum College, and the University of Tennessee, Mr. Sutton went to Ball State in 1947, where he taught for thirty-three years. He is the author of *The Road to Winesburg* (1972), *Sexual Fairness in Language* (1973), *Black Like It Is/Was: Erskine Caldwell's Treatment of Racial Themes* (1974), *Newdick's Season of Frost* (1976), and *Carl Sandburg Remembered* (1978) and various periodical publications on American literary figures. He has been a student of the life of Sherwood Anderson since 1941.

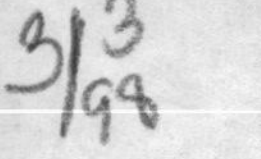